For Amy Thielen, having people over isn't reserved for special occasions. In her corner of rural Minnesota, it's a way of life. With her debut cookbook, *The New Midwestern Table*, and celebrated memoir, *Give a Girl a Knife*, Amy established herself as a champion of gastro-chic, grandma-style Midwestern home cooking. *Company* is Amy's eagerly awaited collection of trusted, unpretentious recipes that invite us directly into her laid-back, pre-dinner kitchen sanctum.

In companionable, outspoken prose, Amy shares a genuine, infectious passion for the process and rhythms of cooking. Granting us permission to find pleasure in casual meals, Amy soothes the most common party anxieties one by one. The food here is earthy but elevated, not afraid of meat (but obsessed with vegetables), healthy (but never devoutly so), and arranged into 20 composed, seasonal menus. These menus all contain recipes sure to become signatures, such as the silky make-ahead Lemon Nemesis ice cream cake, or the perfectly dialed-in holiday Pâté Grandmére, or the simple dish of Sopped Greens with Buttered Roasted Walnuts that doubles so well as a weeknight regular. Start with a Saturday night dinner for six to eight, then progress to a holiday feast for a dozen, and soon, with Amy's guidance, cooking for twenty will seem a whole lot more doable and fun.

In recipes and methods written with a focus on down-in-the-pan cooking nerdery, *Company* is a real cook's cookbook—but it's also a book for readers. Whether kept in the kitchen or at the bedside, reading the recipe methods in this book will give us the tools, and the will, to cook for others with more frequency, and less formality, than ever before.

With over 125 recipes and a feast of gorgeous photography by Kristin Teig, *Company* encourages a return to the pleasures of standing in the kitchen cooking for family and friends without thinking twice about it. Not only to impress others with our enviable culinary grace, but simply because we want company.

Company

Also by Amy Thielen

The New Midwestern Table

Give a Girl a Knife

Company

*the radically casual art
of cooking for others*

AMY THIELEN

photography by Kristin Teig

W. W. NORTON & COMPANY
Celebrating a Century of Independent Publishing

For information about permission to reproduce selections from this book, write to
Permissions, W. W. Norton & Company, Inc., 500 Fifth Avenue, New York, NY 10110

For information about special discounts for bulk purchases, please contact
W. W. Norton Special Sales at specialsales@wwnorton.com or 800-233-4830

Manufacturing by TransContinental
Book design by Studio Polka
Production manager: Julia Druskin

Library of Congress Cataloging-in-Publication Data

Names: Thielen, Amy, author.
Title: Company : the radically casual art of cooking for others / Amy Thielen.
Description: First edition. | New York, NY : W.W. Norton & Company, Inc., [2023] | Includes index.
Identifiers: LCCN 2023006227 | ISBN 9781324001508 (hardcover) | ISBN 9781324001515 (epub)
Subjects: LCSH: Entertaining. | Cooking. | Menus. | LCGFT: Cookbooks.
Classification: LCC TX731 .T454 2023 | DDC 642/.4—dc23/eng/20230222
LC record available at https://lccn.loc.gov/2023006227

W. W. Norton & Company, Inc.
500 Fifth Avenue, New York, N.Y. 10110
www.wwnorton.com

W. W. Norton & Company Ltd.
15 Carlisle Street, London W1D 3BS

1 2 3 4 5 6 7 8 9 0

*To Natty (2011–2020), our gentle golden giant,
who never knew a stranger (or a bowl
of food) he didn't love, but met all
with a slow, accepting wag.*

Contents

Introduction   9

A Few Notes Before We Begin   12

Saturday Night
PARTIES OF SIX TO EIGHT   20

Holiday
TABLES OF EIGHT TO TWELVE   112

Perennial Parties
GROUPS OF SIX TO TEN   216

Casual Walkabouts
BUFFETS FOR FIFTEEN TO TWENTY, OR MORE   282

A Note on Cleaning Up   318

A Well-Battered Batterie de Cuisine: Tools and Equipment   321

Food Bunker Basics: Ingredients   329

Individual Recipe Index   337

Acknowledgments   341

Index   342

Introduction

You could say I throw a lot of parties.

Holiday parties, birthday feasts, longest-day-of-the-year barbecues, no-occasion dinner parties. Winter feasts on -30°F nights for a dazed crew of hibernating northerners who exit five hours later into the burning-cold night with loud voices and restocked tanks. Big sprawling summer bashes, with kids jetting through the slamming screen door, more guests than I have chairs for, mismatched thrift-store plates, paper napkins, wine poured into any kind of vessel that will hold it—and, always, a bright buffet line of food snaking around my kitchen island.

In my corner of the world, in-house entertaining is more than a way of life—it's pretty much our only option. Like many of my friends here in northern Minnesota, my husband, Aaron, and I and our son, Hank, live in the woods—close to the night stars but far from any nightlife. In the dark, the howls of the resident timberwolves sound close and the bark of our nearest neighbor's dog like a distant subwoofer. Anyone who lives within a twenty-minute drive is considered a close neighbor. And when we want to get together, we don't drive twenty-five miles to meet at one of the three restaurants in town; we go visiting. Which simply means that you go to someone's house, check out their garden, their pets, and their projects, eat all of their food, drink their homemade alcohol, and toddle off into the night holding a jar of canned pickles.

Some of you will no doubt think that this never-ending dinner party habit sounds just lovely and others will think it sounds as fun as a stress test. Veteran cooks might scan these pages for standout recipes to add to their already developed repertoire. I think of this as my "so-called" entertaining book, because after living for all these years in the rural countryside, I've developed a steep aversion to the formality of the E-word. I'm not concerned about napkin rings or guest lists or wine pairings or expensive Italian charcuterie (which I couldn't buy here anyway). This book focuses on the precious pre-party hours, when we're standing in the dim late-afternoon kitchen holding a zucchini and having an internal debate: Should we poach it and sauce it with muddled mint oil, or slice it raw for carpaccio? Or should we make something saucier instead, like creamed corn? I wrote these recipes, menus, and tangential thoughts for a circle of exactly three: you, me, and our cooking practice. But our conversation will come to an end when the people arrive. I'm sure you can take it from there.

Halfway through writing this, I realized why menu cookbooks are so rare, and why they're generally more formal than casual. A casual home-cooked meal is sprawling, unkempt, and hard to capture in a single frame. Only one attention-seeking vegetable dish can fit on a dinner plate at a time. Individual recipes are modern; menus are hopelessly analog. They're an album full of easy-to-love hits and simple, buttery vegetable B-sides. I don't think it's any coincidence that flavors began to amp up and compete for attention during the recent explosion of the digital age, but I do know that home food—with its soothing, untrendy side dishes—is an antidote to all of that.

All of the dishes in these menus are intended to be served at once, bowls and platters lined up in a row on the counter (unless it's a holiday, which feels more celebratory when the dishes are passed hand-to-hand around the table). On a special night, I might serve a classy green sipping soup in coffee mugs or kick off dinner with a stand-up seafood graze—and I always serve lettuce salad in individual bowls because, my god, I'm not a heathen—but I generally plate everything else on wide platters and let people serve themselves.

After a long day of cooking, it feels good to hang up my apron and embrace the buffet. An overcrowded plate is the emblem of a proper home-cooked meal. There's no prettier sight than a crispy roast potato getting sodden with juices from a hot, pink sliced steak, or a hill of creamed corn sliding into a pile of mashed squash. That juxtaposition, the point where the corn juices mingle with the squash mush, is what gives home food a clear and powerful advantage over restaurant food.

In fact, all of my favorite restaurants, the idiosyncratic, dimly lit ones that are ambitious about their food, work really hard to re-create the atmosphere of a perfect dinner at home with friends. What they're selling—in addition to wine—is intimacy. Home cooks who aspire to create a restaurant-like experience tend to forget about that home-field advantage. Any chef would love to shop the market in the morning for that night's dinner and then leisurely cook it, in their slippers, while listening to their favorite playlist. We should keep that in mind and feel free to improvise and make mistakes. Live on the edge; no one's paying us to be consistent.

Most of these menus follow the standard meat-and-three middle-American formula: a central protein, a starch, and at least two vegetables (one cooked, one raw), plus dessert, if you can still take one down after all of that. My dinner parties are often carnivorous—because meat feels celebratory, and I play to the crowd. But the flora here still outnumbers the fauna two to one. In summer, vegetables come from farmers' markets or my own garden; in winter, from a standard midsized grocery store. Some recipes hinge on top-quality ingredients and can be hustled up in an hour or two, while others that build layers of flavor on top

of regular grocery-store stuff will meet your desire to putter around in the kitchen all day long.

Fast, cheap, or good—you can pick two. What's true for carpentry is also true for cooking. The meal can be fast and cheap, but it may not be particularly memorable. Or it can be fast and absolutely delicious, but the ingredients will probably cost you. Or you can have it cheap and good—but be prepared to be cooking all day. For me, the key to a regular, sustainable, open-door dinner-party habit lies in balancing money with time, and extravagance with thrift.

I'm not sure who first said "Perfection is the enemy of good," but the last person to say it in real life was my friend Bruce, in reference to my chocolate cake. We all agreed that it tasted amazing, like a 12-dollar single-origin chocolate bar, but it was too fragile to cut in neat wedges. So we piled the soft, crumbling chunks of cake onto plates, blanketed them with whipped cream, and then scrabbled like raccoons in a compost pile over the clumps left on the cake plate. This imperfect cake didn't puncture the balloon of my perfect dinner party; it made it more real, and more memorable. (I've since shored up the recipe—see page 279—but I can't guarantee you that serving it in neat triangles will seem as delightfully gluttonous.)

This is all to say that the best dinner parties are always a little off. They hit both high notes and low notes. They swing. The missteps make us human, and cause the understanding to flow around the table, unbroken, like good conversation.

So you can call cooking a compulsion or you can call it an art or you can call it a drag, but you can't call it a waste of time. A meal with friends or family is nothing more, and nothing less, than a fleeting event that fills a momentary spiritual need. If you think about it that way, nearly every inconsequential occasion calls for one. The sweet corn's hit peak ripeness? Let's get together and eat it. It's the shortest day of the year? Let's roast a chicken and talk about the spooky velvety depths of the 4 o'clock darkness. A late-winter week of endless gray skies that runs into a weekend of more of the same drizzle? Let's call some people, tromp out into the slush in rubber boots, grill out-of-season vegetables, and stand around drinking frosty glasses of rosé.

And I probably shouldn't say this, because this is a cookbook and I'm supposed to be selling the culinary dream or something, but when you're having people over, the food doesn't really matter. Specifically, I mean, no one else will ever care about the food as much as you and I do. If we do this thing right, aligning people and season and mood (under soft, gentle lighting), the food will fade into the background. The next day, it will resurface as an idyllic sense memory of flavors and textures that everyone will remember as better than they actually were. That's just how it works. The real hostess gift is the fact that everything— absolutely everything—tastes better at someone else's house.

A Few Notes Before We Begin

I don't want you to feel pressured to make these menus in their entirety from start to finish.

Of course, if you're looking for guidance, follow the menus. They're loyal and well-worn, and they contain the kind of knowledge that is born out of many, many mistakes. From experience, I know that the dishes will balance out on the plate. Tart against hot, cool against earthy, crispy versus creamy, complementary colors, and that sort of thing.

But if I've learned anything from cooking and writing recipes over the past fifteen years, it's that many home cooks are born nonconformists. And, I confess, I'm one of them. My friend Beth makes my own cookies better than I do. ("Because I *follow* the *recipe*.") An appetite for reading (or writing) cookbooks doesn't necessarily translate into a hunger to follow instructions.

Like many of you, I come from a long line of proud cooks who cooked intuitively, by pinch and by feel. My grandma Addie Dion's typical response to newspaper food columnists was not a cheerful, "My, that sounds good!" but a murmured, "Who in the hell does she think she is?" (*with that 20-dollar honey-walnut cake*, or whatever). Back in the day, reputations were made or lost on the quality of the formulas copied onto 3 × 5 index cards stored in one's little recipe treasure box, often without attribution. And they were guarded. Not traded freely, exactly, but bestowed.

My mom, her daughter, inherited that same sense of recipe ownership—and skepticism. "Oh, that'll never be enough chestnuts for one cup of rice," she said as we paged through magazines

in the clinic waiting room one day, scowling at a recipe for crown roast of pork with chestnut dressing. "And that's not *near* enough butter," she said, really turning the knife into that poor defenseless food editor. But then—in an act that was at once defiant and deferential—she tore the double-page spread right out of the magazine and folded it into her purse. From that day forward, we had pork with chestnut dressing for Christmas dinner, with more butter and more chestnuts, of course. What I learned from this episode and others like it was that: one, my mom was the kind of cook who could read a recipe in a glance and see what it would need; two, she was kind of an outlaw; and three, that the finest quality a cook can possess is a well-developed sense of discernment.

I tell you this story only to give you permission to tamper with these recipes to fit your own needs, tastes, resources, and moods. I organized them as menus, with main courses, a starch, and a couple of flanking vegetable sides, to reflect the way we actually eat; but they're just a guide. If you'd rather build your own menu, check out the individual recipe index on page 337. It sorts the recipes into more traditional cookbook categories (dips and spreads, meat, fish, vegetables, dessert) with nods to specific textural cravings and needs—crispy starches, juicy salads, room-temperature vegetables, and so on.

Many of these recipes are tied to my location in the rural north, which is another reason not to follow the menus to the letter. You'll want to

12

adjust them to fit your own place, with its specific set of surpluses and deficits. When I lived in New York, for example, good-quality olive oil was easy to find but good-quality pork was rare (or ridiculously expensive); where I live now, the reverse is true. In some cases, the variation in vegetable seasonality between the southern and northern United States is so stark that they might as well belong to different hemispheres. I don't see peas in my garden until the end of June, when the zucchini plants start producing, and I won't have red tomatoes until the middle of August; by that time in Georgia, gardeners have cleaned up their wilted tomato plants and are waiting for their second harvest, in late fall. Overlooking the differences between growing zones, vegetables themselves, with their natural variables, have a way of tanking even the best-laid plans. Your juicy beefsteak tomato might be soupier and more tender than my homegrown Hungarian Heart roma tomato, and will take longer to reduce down into sauce. Just as human relationships change over time, you can't make chicken cacciatore the same exact way twice.

When you can't find nice zucchini in the store, make green beans (page 231) instead. If there's no time to make, say, the Smoky Tomato Terrine (page 34), just make the simpler Tomato-on-Tomato Salad (page 213). If you're really short on time, you can swap out a complicated recipe with a really simple boiled-and-buttered vegetable side—something like Sopped Greens with Butter-Roasted Walnuts (page 43). I like how Italians refer to vegetable sides as the contours of a meal, the *contorni*. In a large meal, the vegetables not only pad out the offerings, they also tone down the noise coming from the main and the sauces and give the palate some rest. Besides, almost no one serves these grandma-style vegetable sides anymore, which makes those stir-fried garlic greens or the creamed carrot coins—an antique dish by most metrics—feel oddly novel. Guaranteed, someone will come up to you and say that the creamed carrots were their favorite part of the whole meal.

So take these trusted battle plans of mine and change them, mark them up, and make them your own. Nothing would give me greater joy than if you gave one of these recipes to a friend and took full credit for the invention—and it would thrill my dearly departed grandmother.

As for yields, I've leaned generous, because leftovers are usually welcome and I don't want to short-sheet anyone's dinner party. (Keep in mind that I was raised by a woman who thought of running out of food as the eighth deadly sin. To see a guest scrape the bottom of the dish was not taken as a sign that it was delicious, but as a cause for alarm—proof that there wasn't enough.) Since we eat with our eyes, a surplus of food puts everyone at ease and encourages momentary indulgence.

The suggested number of people that each menu serves varies, but is noted in its title. Generally, the menus in Saturday Night serve a group of 6 to 8 people and the menus in Holiday serve a table of 8 to 12. Perennial Parties has two buffets that serve 8 to 10 and two that serve 6 to 8. The menus in Casual Walkabouts feed larger groups: one serves up to 15, the other at least 20, with added potluck dishes.

Your vegetable sides are the bellows of your meal. Use them to swell or contract the menus, according to your guest list. A party of 12 suddenly blooms to 16? No need to panic and run to the store to buy more fish; just make another side dish. Or two.

Have you ever heard of the concept of the "good-enough mother?" A term coined by D. W. Winnicott, the early twentieth century's first-ever pop psychologist, it argues that children do better emotionally when their mothers aren't unattainably perfect, but just "good-enough"—in other words, when the mothers demonstrate that they're human. Dinner parties benefit from the same logic. At some point it's time to drop the knife, stop prepping, go take a shower, put on a clean shirt, and throw some daisies into a jar. The kitchen may not be in perfect order, but then, productive, creative workspaces rarely are. They're flexible, chaotic—and fun. And when people start arriving, that's the vibe they'll catch and follow.

MAKE A HABIT OF COOKING AHEAD

Since we're already cooking, we might as well get ahead on tomorrow.

Sometimes I forget that I did a seven-year tour of duty as a line cook in New York City's best-known food churches—padded pews, saintly ushers, ingredient worship, the whole sacrosanct, intimidating deal. Since I've returned home, my knife skills have atrophied and my time management has gone to hell, but I've hung onto one professional habit from that time that occasionally saves me from dinner party disaster: the habit of breaking complex recipes down into more doable base recipes. I think of it as "component cooking."

Many people are amazed by how chefs make so many complicated dishes seemingly all at once, but I know the secret: they don't. A line cook's chicken roasts at the same speed as anyone else's. In fact, the professional roast chicken takes longer, because it's massaged with salt and herbs the day before, it's coddled, it's basted, it's rested before slicing. But here's where chefs diverge most dramatically from home-cooking civilians: they cook all day long, from eleven in the morning until eleven at night. And during that time, they divide the large, complicated recipes into smaller tasks to be checked off on the prep list.

These base recipes aren't necessarily complicated. Usually, they're pretty plain: Beets cooked in salt water until tender and slipped out of their skins, ready to go for that night's bass dish. Halved winter squash, salted and roasted face down, ready for tomorrow's squash soup. Meat sauces that keep for a few day in the walk-in fridge. That sort of thing.

At home, you don't need to have a week's worth of menus written out to cook in component fashion. While you're standing at the stove cooking dinner, you might as well make something else too for the future. It can be as simple as peeling a whole head of garlic when you need only two cloves, presoaking dried beans, baking off some potatoes, or making twice the amount of rice you need for dinner and saving the leftovers for tomorrow. All of these things are like putting money in the bank. Maybe the extra rice will end up sitting in the fridge for four days, but on the fifth you'll use it for fried rice. Or maybe you'll stir some eggs and milk and sugar into it, just eyeballing, not measuring, and bake a rice pudding. It may turn out, or not, but if you eat it warm from the oven and slather it with homemade jam, it will be your delicious companion while sitting on the couch in front of the TV. Having precooked inventory in the refrigerator is reassuring. Personally, I sleep better knowing that I won't be facing a blank slate every single morning.

Of course, I say this as someone who lives in a rural area and rarely goes out to eat. But even if you cook just one or two meals a week, a habit of keeping the pistons greased and pumped for the near future will make even the loneliest of kitchens feel alive. And if that roasted half of a squash doesn't rise to any occasion beyond being microwaved with butter and brown sugar, at least you didn't let it go soft on the counter. At heart, every kitchen wants to be a working kitchen, full of life and tomorrows projects and, occasionally, yes, even lackluster stop-gap meals. A working kitchen loves the revolving motion so much, it will forgive you.

WE SHOULD PROBABLY TALK ABOUT MONEY

A little hidden penny-pinching makes it all possible.

In any cookbook, food cost is the elephant in the room. But I want to address it—especially in this book, with its hopelessly carnivorous menus that serve such large numbers of people. The photos on the pages may show otherwise, but the truth is, I'm secretly thrifty. Some people—ahem, Aaron—might even call me cheap. I walk around the grocery store with a ticker tape of dollars and cents and price-per-pound nerdery running through my head, not only because I've fantasized about being a contestant on *The Price Is Right* since childhood (though I have), but because I cook for big groups all the time and know the pain of a long receipt. So when the lady next to me at the produce case whispers, "Lemons are so dear," I know she doesn't mean that they're precious as in cute; she means that they've gone up by almost a dollar per pound. Since last week. We both raise our eyebrows and I cross that lemonade for fifteen people off my list.

Since I began writing this book, the price of pork shoulder roast (Boston Butt) has risen from $1.99 per pound ($1.00 per pound when on sale) to $3.99 per pound. The price of beef has tripled; a steak that once cost twelve dollars will now set you back almost thirty. The situation in the produce aisle isn't much better—a full bag of cherries costs more than a bottle of decent French wine—but the sticker shock for vegetables still pales in relation to protein. Our weekday meals have become less decadent, and I've been raising my ratio of veg-to-meat for dinner parties, but I haven't sidelined meat completely. A large hunk of protein still feels celebratory to me, both to cook and to eat. If anything, higher prices correct our long American history of cheap meat and make it more appropriately precious. I feel like we Americans have staked our identity on abundant, cheap meat, culminating in dishonorable animal husbandry practices and corporate subsidies, and

what we're facing now is the real cost of doing business. Meat *should* be expensive. It should feel dear to us.

If you weren't already eagle-eyed in the grocery store, recent inflation should activate that latent hunter-gatherer instinct. The good news is that increases in the prices of conventional meat, fish, dairy, vegetables, and fruit have brought them closer to the well-deserved prices of local farm-raised ingredients, which certainly encourages me to buy better and more ethically raised food. Like many of my neighbors, I was already driving 30 miles to buy chickens from the Amish—and now we're all getting twice as many, and stretching them to two meals, or even three. My beloved high-fat butter from the natural foods co-op costs basically the same as my everyday butter from the grocery store. I'm buying beautiful locally grown cabbages from the farmer's market, wrapping them in tight plastic, and storing them for months in my refrigerator drawers.

If anything, this is the time for all of us secret value-hoarders to come out of the closet. In comparison to many countries around the world, our food has been unnaturally inexpensive. I've been long disturbed by the suspicion that for many well-off Americans, thrift has been more of an ethic than a truism. Some of the stingiest people I've known have also been the most flush. The most generous are almost always the most broke. But the committed cooks who live to feed, from high-end restaurateurs to food-pushing grandmothers, have always been secretly frugal. In the grand tradition of cooking and giving it away, the rules remain the same: serve the best you can afford, with plenty of cheap starches and simple seasonal vegetable sides to pad it out, and always err on the side of too much food. You want to hide your thrift behind a multicolored facade of surplus.

SALT AND SEASONING

The abridged version of this section is this: liberate your salt from the shaker.

It's not just surface decoration, it's your main seasoning: salt makes every ingredient taste more like itself. So when seasoning, add salt from a measuring spoon, or the crease of your palm.

For most purposes, I use **fine sea salt**, usually the kind with added iodine. I prefer the flavor of natural sea salt but can't quite shake my mom's lifelong warnings against non-iodized salt. ("You're going to get a goiter!") About five years ago, iodized sea salt began showing up regularly on the shelves in my hometown grocery store, so now everyone's happy.

I also keep some **natural sea salt** (without iodine) on hand, because my preferred brand, Baleine, comes in an easy-to-hold canister with a shaker top that can distribute a sane, even dusting of salt over the surface of a whole chicken. The Baleine salt brings out a lovely flavor in everything it touches.

You can taste the difference between sea salt and all the others: if picked up on a wet fingertip, sea salt will taste rounder and deeper. The fine sea salt scatters more evenly and melts more easily into ingredients than the coarser salt, which is important when seasoning delicate things like salad greens.

For quantities larger than a tablespoon, I use **kosher salt**, which has become pretty standard in American recipes lately because it's decent and cheap and coarse—the grains are easy to pick up by the pinch and large enough to be seen by the naked eye. If you like kosher salt and substitute it in these recipes, the good news is that because fine sea salt has a smaller flake—meaning that it packs more saline punch per cubic inch than the coarser kosher—you will never overseason any dish in this book. If anything, you may need to add more salt, which is a lot easier than taking salt away.

Fancy **coarse sea salt**s, the kind that glow like iridescent fish flakes, are for finishing; but the purist's choice is plain gray French sea salt. Maldon brand is a more affordable version of flake salt and looks equally glam on a steak.

Except when pumped up with naturally salty ingredients like soy sauce or fish sauce or anchovies, almost everything we cook will need salt. Some people consider salt level to be a matter of personal preference, but I believe in a common mean, a universally standard level of seasoning that the great majority of human palates will recognize as correct.

A person could argue that this universal salt-threshold is just a snobbish myth, but if that were true, restaurants would go out of business. Cooks-in-training don't always hit it right away, but veteran cooks know how to season food to the common mean with instinctive accuracy. No one notices it, because perfect seasoning is invisible; when it's done right, salt fades into the background, letting the ingredients shine.

If you're still learning to locate that sweet spot, you may overseason occasionally, but be nice to yourself. It's easy to overseason, say, a soup. Sipped in small amounts from the wooden cooking spoon, highly seasoned soup tastes great. But halfway through a full bowl, it starts to bite back. In general, it's better to err on the side of too little rather than too much, because desalination is a tough game. You can dilute an offensively salty sauce or broth by adding more liquid—read: a *lot* more liquid—but once you've added too much salt, you can never really go home again.

With more layered recipes, like stews and braises, I think of seasoning as a progressive dinner: you lay down a foundation at the first house, pick up speed at the second and third, and eat lightly at the fourth.

16

For example, when I'm making a pot of Yellow Split Pea Soup with Spareribs (see page 96), I salt it four or five times. First I rub salt into the ribs, to season the pork, and then I season the water they cook in, to drag the umami meatiness out of the simmering bones. Then I add salt to the vegetables while sautéing them, and maybe to the soup again as it begins to simmer—just enough to make the liquid taste alive, but still holding back a bit, because the soup will continue to reduce and concentrate as it cooks. The fifth addition, if there is one, issues a final correction. If I had added most of the salt to the soup at the end, the brothy liquid would taste salty and the pork and vegetables mysteriously bland.

Naturally, this incremental approach to salting can be a nightmare for those who write recipes, and for those who follow them. Visually, I go along with the standard recipe-writing convention that condenses the salt into a single measurement. This streamlines the text and *seems* easier, but it doesn't follow the natural rhythm of salting a dish. So, for all but the simplest recipes, I've split the salt into stages—e.g., "½ teaspoon plus ¼ teaspoon salt, plus more to taste"—just as I write it as I'm developing the recipe. (Baking, obviously, is an exception.) If all of those piddly measurements rub you the wrong way, just total out the salt needed for the recipe, put it in a small bowl, and add it when the mood strikes you. I assume that the intuitive salters will glance at the quantities I've listed, ignore them, and be on their way. I've seasoned everything at the lower end of what I judge to be the universal salt level, adding a "plus more to taste" to account for personal preference. I lean on the side of caution because I'd hate to ruin your dinner. I know you'll add more salt if you think it needs it.

ON DRINKS

When it comes to drinks, I'm pretty hands-off.

A batched cocktail is always a smart move—see Cilantro Lime Juleps, page 202, or Whisky-Sour Gelatin Shots with Potted Sour Cherries, page 248—but when I know the dinner will be long and langurous, I hesitate to kick it off with something so high-octane. The regulars here know where the liquor cabinet is. And most of them arrive with either a bottle of wine or a six-pack of their favorite beer anyway. It's part of our unspoken contract: I spring for the food, they bring the drinks. Everyone puts their wine, beer, and soda in our outside summer-bev fridge, where they find a reassuring top-of-the-line box of white wine on backup.

Don't get me wrong: I love good wine and have even been lucky enough to drink some of it. But where I live, a decent bottle of wine in my preferred twelve- to fifteen-dollar range is hard to find. Consequently, because of budgetary concerns and how often I entertain, I've become something of a connoisseur of cheap wine. A snob of it, you could say. Over the years I've compiled a quick, inexpert, idiosyncratic guide to this lower register.

My local liquor store stocks some very nice high-range wine but populates the affordable aisle with more dubious stuff: big, fruity high-alcohol reds and syrupy, oaky whites with catty-sounding names. Many of these wines are chaptalized, or pumped up with added sugar at the last minute. Winemakers do this to bring out the grape's berry-juice-box flavors, which they call fruitiness, but it raises the alcohol content to a head-spinning level.

For me, a wine with 14- or 15-percent alcohol had better be well made and highly structured, or it can burn a little going down the throat and tends to dominate the food.

With the exception of the occasional enormously impactful high-alcohol Cabernet paired with premium beef, neither of which are very affordable, I like to drink mellow wine with my food. I want my wine to sidle up against the flavors on the plate like a cat. I hunt the aisles for affordable imported bottles—especially from France, Italy, and Spain—and domestics made in the more austere European style. Bigger is not always better, especially at the lower-priced end. For reds, I have learned that the lighter varietals, like Pinot Noir and Côtes du Rhône and Austrian Zweigelt, are more trustworthy. When poured into the glass, they're generally more translucent— think wood stain rather than paint.

For whites, I search for Sauvignon Blancs with simple, classy labels, such as minerally whites from Burgundy or Bordeaux or Albariños from Spain, and in the summertime, I stock up on perennially cheap but decent Portuguese Vinho Verde, a high-acid white wine with a very faint effervescence. Low in alcohol—10 percent, usually—it's my host drink of choice. I can sip it slowly and look like I'm joining in the revelry but still stay sharp enough to get the food to the table on time.

But if faced with red wine that's too big and burning, or whites that are too oaky, I'm not above watering them down: a splash of cold water in the red, or a single ice cube in the white.

How many bottles of wine should you buy? You know your friends. Better to have too much than too little. The truth is, I hide one occasionally so that when someone upends the last dribble into their glass, I can tiptoe dramatically off to the pantry and return triumphantly with another surprise bottle. When I uncork it, people cheer and clap—"Oh, there's another bottle of wine?"—as if I'm some sort of hero rather than just a stingy host.

This is my one and only party trick. Of course, by revealing it I've killed it forever, so it is now yours.

Saturday

Night

Menus

supper club night: steak and sides

FOR SIX TO EIGHT — 25

grilled pickled half-hots — 26

wood-fired rib eyes with fava butter — 27

salt potatoes — 30

boiled zucchini with herb oil — 31

smoky tomato terrine — 34

a lazy day's summer lunch

FOR SIX — 38

homemade Boursin with grilled bread — 38

nightshade confit — 39

sopped greens with butter-roasted walnuts — 43

black currant finger Jell-O — 44

New York City Chinese barbecue at home

FOR SIX TO EIGHT — 46

Mei's ginger-glazed baby back ribs — 46

smashed garlic cucumbers — 49

jasmine rice — 50

bok choy salad with ramen-almond brittle — 53

stir-fried peas and their greens — 54

homemade chitarra pasta work party

FOR SIX TO EIGHT — 56

steamed eggplant with chile oil, lemon,
and 'nduja — 59

chitarra pasta with roasted cherry tomatoes — 61

winter white salad — 64

apple fritto misto with peels, lemons,
and sage — 68

a creative more-time-than-money sort of menu

FOR SIX — 70

crispy smashed chicken breasts with
gin-and-sage jus — 70

matafans: raised potato and cabbage pancake — 72

bacon fat–roasted cauliflower with herb salad — 74

pastis du Quercy — 75

all-you-can-eat fish fry

FOR SIX TO EIGHT — 82

deep-fried sour cream walleye — 83

iceberg plate salad with green chile dressing — 86

steamed and glazed white sweet potatoes — 88

garlic and coconut–scented rice — 89

Pavlova with winter citrus, good olive oil,
and sea salt — 90

a Nordic backcountry ski supper

FOR SIX TO EIGHT — 92

sardines with lardo and Parmesan on bran
crispbread — 93

yellow split pea soup with spareribs — 96

warm wilted spinach with caramelized celery
root and crispy shiitakes — 97

coffee with Chartreuse and smoked
almond praline — 99

pent-up winter grilling

FOR SIX TO EIGHT — 102

deviled egg dip — 102

Bundt pan chicken with bagna cauda butter — 105

Fun House baked potatoes — 109

sweet-and-sour marinated peppers with
Swiss chard — 110

It's almost 2 o'clock and I'm just getting home from town, schlepping grocery bags from the car to the front door—two trips' worth of provisions. It's one of those gusty fall days when the wind cleans the front walk like an angry sweeper, pushing the wet birch leaves into clumps and scattering the dry loose ones across my path. The leaves and the wind at my back, pushing me toward the kitchen, give me that Yes-I-Can energy to get this dinner on the table before 7:30 p.m. I've told people to show up at 6 or 6:30, but this being the rural Midwest, where being on time actually means being early, I figure I need to have the counters wiped and the ice bucket filled by 5:55. Most of my friends know by now to expect a ridiculously long cocktail hour, and often bring slippers in anticipation of settling in, but I know that if I want to keep the preamble to two drinks, I'd better hustle.

I hope this explains why all my dinner parties are Saturday night parties. I've given up trying to have one any other day. On Friday nights, the will to kick back is strong, but post-work prep time is tight. Sunday's a school night. Thursday night dinner parties, popular when I lived in New York in my 20s and 30s, don't play the same in the country. Saturday night dinner parties give me a week to gather inspiration and the whole day to cook. In theory, I would have the entire week to shop for ingredients, too, but in reality I wake up on Saturday morning with only a vague idea (a thawed farm chicken, maybe) and a blank index card and sit down with a cup of coffee to sketch out the menu. To

be honest, this is my favorite moment in any dinner party, when the menu is still in my head and everything is pure potential. Sometimes, I'll anxiously overwrite the menu, if I'm cooking for someone I want to impress, and then start crossing it out before beginning again with a simple question: what am I hungry for? The pressure to please others falls off when you cook to please yourself. And the food, now relieved of what my son would call "cringe-y effort," is better, too.

Locating the exact coordinates of your own hunger is surprisingly difficult. Those of us who tend to think first and feel later will have to push our brains aside for a second and ask the body what it craves. Something fruity? Dark and meaty? Light and loose? Comforting and starchy? Spicy? Like getting up in the middle of the night for a bowl of ice cream, writing a menu is an indulgent moment that feels like it exists outside the flow of normal time. We dream it. Pudding-soft potatoes meet running beef juices, tomatoes roasted to the sweet, dark edge of burnt sit alongside fresh pasta with a perfectly stiff chew, a melting pad of broiled cheese . . . a menu is a whole private world.

Until it hits the plate, in the real world, where it has to make sense and go together. What makes a menu hang together on the plate, and in our memories?

We are unapologetic carnivores in my house, but as I learned from my mom—a wiz with the sides—a central chop does not make a meal. The vegetables flanking it aren't mere accessories; the juices of all should mingle in an intentional way. Successfully predicting how the flavors, textures, and juices of each dish on the plate will interact with one another is what distinguishes a great dinner plate from a mediocre one.

Cooking dinner for friends shouldn't be a source of anxiety. We may be cooking, but it's our party, too. I want to share my food, not serve it with perfect grace and well-veiled effort—and I know that my friends don't want to feel like paying guests, either. Truly, just like yours, they want to feel like family.

supper club night: steak and sides

FOR SIX TO EIGHT

— grilled pickled half-hots

— wood-fired rib eyes with fava butter

— salt potatoes

— boiled zucchini with herb oil

— smoky tomato terrine

The area of northern Minnesota where we live was once known as the "cooling off zone" for mobsters from Minneapolis and Chicago, and many of our local supper clubs, hidden on the shores of secluded lakes, began this way—as secret forest hangouts, rural speakeasies.

When I was a kid, my parents frequented every out-of-the-way supper club within a fifty-mile radius. With their giant white pine log posts and soaring fieldstone fireplaces, they were like churches to us—or at the very least the church of brunch that we attended after church—and I was raised to be reverent in them. My mom also taught me, as every rural Midwestern mother did, that you could never eat as well in a restaurant as you did at home. Yet all of these, even the grungy, poorly managed supper clubs on the skids, were accepted like difficult members of the family. They were allowed to coast on past kindnesses. Given many chances. At the table, when the server asked how everything was tasting, we all nodded and said, "Pretty good." My parents grilled better steaks at home, but we weren't allowed to break the fourth wall of the restaurant experience by dropping judgement—at least not until we got into the car. So for this party, I invite friends and neighbors who share my nostalgia for these now-shuttered places and the ones who appreciate fat, beautiful, 2-inch-thick medium-rare rib eyes cooked at home.

Cooking steak for a large party is pretty much the symbol of wanton generosity. In fact, I'd say that if buying a couple of precious hunks of marbled beef *doesn't* feel like a reckless expenditure, some of this menu's joyful extravagance may be lost on you. Buy the best-quality beef you can afford, and keep in mind that you'll be serving it in fairly small portions alongside a lot of vegetable sides.

I agree it sounds like a lot of food—peppers, zucchini, tomatoes, *and* potatoes—but this menu is easy to pull off in real time. The grilled peppers and tomato terrine should be made in advance, and the zucchini and potatoes are both unusually simple. Vegetables picked at their peak, boiled on the stovetop, and slicked with herb-infused fats require little more than supervision.

To curb that excess, I don't make a dessert for this one. Meat or sugar. You can't string them both along forever; eventually we all have to pick the one we love best. Personally, I like to put this meal to bed with another glass of red wine (sweetness enough) and maybe by picking up one of the meaty steak bones left on the platter. And there's another reason to cut the steak off the bone in the kitchen. After the fat planks of steak disappear, you're left with a platter of crisscrossed rib bones, and the last nuggets of meat hugging the bones are basically like lollipops.

grilled pickled half-hots

These pickled cheese-stuffed peppers take inspiration from the deeply tanned jalapeño poppers served at my local roadhouse burger bar, but they're grilled instead of fried so as not to kill one's appetite for dinner. I use a rainbow mix of semi-hot peppers (aka half-hots or Italian frying peppers) and stuff them with tangy melting cheese, but it's the light pickling cure that really makes all the stuffing and wrapping and tooth-picking required worth your time. The vinegar both kicks the chile heat into gear and takes its edge off, like a chaser.

Originally I didn't wrap these with bacon, but when I made them for my mom, she cocked her head to the side and said they looked "a little naked." I knew instantly what she meant: that the stuffed peppers would look better—i.e., more spiritually complete—if I girdled them with bacon.

Pickle the peppers ahead of time, and let them hang out in their brine for a few hours on the stovetop, or refrigerate them for up to 12 hours. Lacking a grill, you can roast these peppers in a 400°F oven until they ooze, about 15 minutes.

Makes 16 stuffed peppers, serving 8 as an appetizer

16 small semi-hot frying or pickling peppers (Hungarian wax, Italian frying peppers, or mild jalapeños; about 1½ pounds)
2½ cups apple cider vinegar
1½ cups water
⅓ cup sugar

5 tablespoons fine sea salt
2 bay leaves
4 garlic cloves, smashed
8 ounces Havarti or Fontina
16 slices thick-cut smoked bacon
Canola or peanut oil for grilling

Rinse the peppers. With a paring knife, cut a long slit down one side of each one, making a long pocket that stops short of the end. Poke the tip of the knife into the belly and gently pull out the seedpod, taking care to leave the stem intact. You want to remove the wooly interior to make room for the cheese, but a few seeds left behind are fine.

Combine the vinegar, water, sugar, salt, bay leaves, and garlic in a medium saucepan and bring to a simmer. Add the peppers and cook at a slow simmer until they just begin to soften, 10 to 15 minutes, depending on their size. Remove from the heat, submerge the peppers in the brine with a plate, and let sit for at least an hour at room temperature; once cooled, the peppers can be refrigerated for as long as 12 hours.

Drain the peppers in a colander and transfer them to a baking sheet; blot dry.

Cut the cheese into 16 fat finger-width logs and insert one into each pepper cavity. Trim the bacon to lengths that will wrap around the peppers with a bit of overlap, and suture them shut with a toothpick.

Prepare a medium fire in a grill. Rub the peppers with a thin layer of oil and grill, carefully turning them occasionally, until they pick up a bit of char and the cheese begins to leak out through the slits.*

Serve immediately, with a reminder to remove the toothpicks.

---

*The bacon will cook to a crisp in some places but not others, and with high-quality bacon, that's perfectly fine. We've been conditioned to think of uncrisped bacon as inedible, but my bacon-making cousins at the family meat market in Pierz, Minnesota, tell me differently: by law, bacon is a fully cooked smoked product. If you're using bacon from a butcher shop, and it feels firm and has an opaque "cooked-looking" sheen to it, there's no need to make sure it all crisps up.

wood-fired rib eyes with fava butter

I've come to think that the standard one-inch-thick rib eye sprawling across the American dinner plate is both too thin and too much to eat. It's fine if you don't mind your beef cooked medium-well or beyond (but some of us do mind). To cook a steak to the ideal medium-rare, it needs to be at least 1½ inches thick. You need to sear it fearlessly over a punishingly high heat to get that dark exterior bark and then move it to a cooler spot to drive the heat slowly toward the center. The interior should be livid pink from edge to edge, and when you put the first piece in your mouth, the hot metallic juices will run down your throat.

I now buy two 2-inch-thick bone-in rib-eye steaks for a table of 6 to 8 people. I bathe them with a garlicky brine to keep them from drying out, rest them well after grilling, and cut into fat pink slices to serve.

This marinade, my go-to, is very similar to the magical brown sugar–and-soy mixture used to season Korean bulgogi. The maple syrup helps with caramelization, but doesn't linger. By the time you've basted the meat repeatedly with the brine, the sweetness will have faded into a thick, savory crust.

Given their rarity, and the time it takes to shuck them, you want to make a show of the fava beans. I blend the shiny green beans with butter, garlic, Parmesan, and lots of fresh mint—which has been the fava's best friend since forever—and spread the butter on the hot rib eyes right after they come off the grill.

Serves 6 to 8

Two 2½-inch-thick bone-in rib-eye steaks (about 3½ pounds total)
3 garlic cloves, finely grated
3 tablespoons light soy sauce
1½ tablespoons maple syrup

Fine sea salt and freshly cracked black pepper
½ batch Salmuera (salt-garlic brine; page 294)
1 cup Fava Bean Butter (recipe follows)
Coarse sea salt for finishing

Unwrap the steaks and scrape them with a butter knife to remove any bone grit left from their trip through the buzz saw; put them on a platter. Combine the garlic, soy sauce, and maple syrup in a small bowl and rub into the steaks. Let the steaks marinate on the counter for at least 30 minutes; they cook more evenly to the center if they've shaken off some of their chill.

Transfer the salmuera to a squirt bottle if you have one; or just swab it onto the steaks with a pastry brush as you cook them.

Prepare a hot two-zone fire in your grill: one side screaming-hot for searing, the other medium-hot for slower cooking. With a covered gas or charcoal grill, 500°F is good, but higher is better. If you're grilling over an open wood fire (as I usually do), the temperature is right when the heat from the coals feels almost unbearable to your outstretched hand and the meat sizzles loudly the second it hits the metal grate.

When you're ready to cook, sprinkle the steaks with a generous dusting of fine sea salt, rubbing it into the bones and over the fat cap, and follow with a lot of freshly cracked black pepper.

Clean your grill grates really well, and rub with a bit of canola oil. Add the steaks to the hottest part of the grill. Don't move them until they start to brown deeply. After a couple of minutes, rotate the steaks 90 degrees and keep cooking over high heat until the underside is deeply caramelized. (Cooking the steaks longer on the first side ensures a dark-brown charred top crust, so take your time.) Tip the steaks to caramelize the sides (even the bones), then flip and cook until the second side browns, another 2 minutes or so. Once you've caramelized every exterior inch and the interior still feels rare and bouncy,

recipe continues

move the steaks to the cooler part of the grill to finish cooking. For 2-inch-thick steaks, you want to start testing for doneness after about 8 minutes by pressing your finger into the fattest part of the steak. If the meat feels soft and yielding, it's still raw or very rare; if it begins to stiffen, as if it's gained a little muscle tone, it's getting closer to medium-rare. When the steaks begin to bulge just ever so slightly, indicating that the heat has reached the center of the meat, it's time to take them off the grill. You can check the progress with an instant-read thermometer—120°F on the grill will rest to a perfect 125° to 127°F medium-rare though I usually just press the thermometer's metal stem against my bottom lip: cool means black-and-blue rare, hot shower–hot is medium-rare, and boiling-hot is overcooked. If you need to see, slice a little piece from one end to check, taking into account that the edge will look more done than the center. Unlike slicing into the center of the steak, trimming off the end won't release a floodgate of precious juices. And you can just put the cut end back on the grill to seal over the evidence.*

Transfer the steaks to a wide platter that holds them fairly snugly and rest for at least 10 minutes.

To serve, roll the steaks in their exuded juices, which the meat will continue to absorb, and sprinkle lightly with coarse salt. If the steaks have cooled down, reheat them quickly on the still-hot grill to warm, then return to the platter. Smear the tops of the steaks with a liberal amount of fava bean butter. Wipe the edges of the platter—you want to serve the steak in a puddle of the juices but not a bloodbath—and transfer the steaks to a cutting board. Separate the bones from the meat, and then cut the steak into 2-inch-thick slices; transfer both to the platter. The melting fava bean butter will run sloppily, lusciously, down into the seams.

---

* It's always better to undercook than overcook, so if things get hairy in the kitchen with the rest of the menu, just take the steaks off the grill at any point of doneness and let them hang out until you're ready to finish cooking them, just like they do in restaurant kitchens. I've pulled steaks from the grill when rare and let them sit at room temperature for 30 minutes before returning them to the grill, and they were perfect.

fava bean butter If there's an underdog vegetable that requires nimble handwork and has just barely survived extinction, then count me as its greatest fan.

Fava beans grow in leathery, oversized pods, each bean encased in a thick, inedible skin. The beans need to be first slipped from their pods, then blanched in boiling water so you can remove their skins; in other words, they need to be shelled twice. The truth is, fava beans are a royal pain, but then we've known this about them since the Roman era. If they weren't so good, they'd be gone. Tender and bright green, favas taste like a sweet pea with nonconformist tendencies. Compared to shell peas, favas are classier, not as sugary—more austere, you could say—and more interesting.

This recipe makes enough fava butter to accompany twice as many steaks, but it freezes beautifully rolled up tightly in a heavy plastic bag. The butterfat insulates the delicate favas and the butter will stay fresh in the freezer for months. Fava butter gives a summery green gloss to winter risottos, pastas, and potatoes.

Makes 2 cups

3 cups fava beans (shucked from 2½ pounds fava beans in the pod)
1 garlic clove
1 teaspoon minced fresh rosemary
Leaves from 3 sprigs mint
6 tablespoons butter, at cool room temperature

⅔ cup (about 1½ ounces) freshly grated Parmesan
Grated zest of ½ lemon
½ teaspoon fine sea salt, plus more to taste
¼ teaspoon freshly ground black pepper, plus more to taste
Fresh lemon juice to taste

Bring a large saucepot of water to a boil and salt it fairly heavily. Add the fava beans and blanch, uncovered, at a rolling boil until one tests tender to the bite, about 2 minutes, or a little less if they're small. Drain the favas and set them in a bowl of ice water until they're cool to the touch, then drain.

Peel the fava beans by breaking the skin at the top of each one with your fingernail and squeezing out the slippery, bright green bean. (If doing this ahead of time, put the skinned fava beans in a small bowl, cover tightly, and refrigerate.)

Combine the favas, garlic, rosemary, and mint in the bowl of a food processor and process to a medium-coarse texture.

Paddle the butter with a rubber spatula in a small bowl until soft, then add to the processor, along with the Parmesan cheese, lemon zest, salt, and pepper. Process until just blended, then scoop into a small bowl, scraping out every last bit of the precious fava bean butter, and taste for seasoning. Add a squeeze of lemon juice and more salt and/or pepper if needed. If not using the butter right away, store in the refrigerator, with a piece of plastic wrap pressed directly against its surface; bring to room temperature before using. Or freeze, well wrapped, for up to 3 months.

SHELLED GREEN PEA VARIATION

You can substitute freshly shelled green peas for the favas (but not frozen peas, which aren't sweet enough).

salt potatoes

Years ago, I sat down at a table in a small-town café somewhere in Germany and had the best potatoes of my life. There were just three of them, bright yellow and perfectly oval. When I cut into them, the texture was as smooth as cold waxy butter, but it was their sheen that I couldn't get over. How did they pop these potatoes out of their skins, leaving the shiny epidermal layer and all the tiny nipple-like bumps still intact?

For one thing, they were an especially dense and lovely German variety, and it was August, so they were freshly dug. But it was also the way that they were cooked, which I later learned from an Austrian chef friend.

Newly dug potatoes are fragile. If you boil them, their skins will burst and water will flood their insides. But if you poach them slowly in heavily salted water that hovers just under the radar of a boil for over an hour, they'll be creamy and will slip out of their skins. You don't really have to peel them—the skin of freshly dug potatoes is as thin as hosiery, and delicious—but the butter will seep into their pores more easily if you do.

When I have it, I'll toss these potatoes with a few handfuls of tart purslane. Purslane's succulent-like padded leaves have a lovely sour flavor, like sorrel; they pop gently in the teeth in between bites of creamy potato. Purslane is also an annoying garden weed that army-crawls beneath my tomatoes and peppers all summer long. I have spent lots of time pulling it out, but always let a few patches live, mostly for this dish.

Serves 6 to 8 as a side (fingerlings are richer than they look)

2½ pounds fingerling potatoes (or any small waxy early-season variety; Nicola and Carola are my favorites)

3 bay leaves

2 large sprigs rosemary

1½ teaspoons black peppercorns

About 1 tablespoon fine sea salt

8 tablespoons (1 stick) butter

1½ cups purslane trimmed of stems (or substitute a handful of sliced fresh chives or 1 cup freshly shelled peas)

Rub the potatoes under running water to remove any dirt, taking care not to rub off the skin. Transfer to a large wide-bottomed saucepot, add water to cover by 4 inches, and bring to a very gentle simmer. Skim any foam that rises to the surface, then add the bay leaves, rosemary, and peppercorns. Add the salt 1 teaspoon at a time, tasting the water after each addition, until the water tastes frankly salty—a beat past seawater.

Lower the heat, adjusting it as necessary, until the water rumbles and steams. Cook the potatoes, uncovered, until tender. Depending on freshness and size, this will take between 40 and 60 minutes. Test both larger and smaller potatoes by slipping a thin meat fork or paring knife into the center; they're done when the fork or knife slips in easily but the potato is still firm. (If you need to, you can turn off the heat and hold the potatoes in the hot water for up to an hour.)

Just before serving, drain the potatoes in a large colander. If you want to peel them—totally optional—hold the hot potatoes in a paper towel and twist to remove their skins, then take off what remains with a paring knife.

Heat a large sauté pan over medium heat and add the butter. When the butter begins to foam, whisk it with a fork and keep cooking until it turns a rusty brown color, another minute or so. Add the potatoes to the pan and shake to coat them with butter, add the purslane, toss swiftly, and pour into a deep heavy serving bowl. Serve immediately.

boiled zucchini with herb oil

Another extremely simple boiled vegetable side, since you're already standing at the stove minding the potatoes. This platter of boiled, herb oil–slicked zucchini takes its power from two things: first, the warm extra-virgin olive oil, so heavily infused with summer herbs it turns the color of green tea, and secondly, the quality of the zucchini. Ideally, it's a dense, firm Italian heirloom variety like Costata Romanesco— the striped ones with the raised ribs.

When the water boils, you'll want to watch the zucchini like a hawk. Pull it from the water the very minute it gets tender. The skin should be shiny, the insides like firm clay.

The herb oil is best when made ahead of time and steeped off-heat at the back of the stove for a few hours. If making ahead, refrigerate it (with its solids), and gently rewarm before serving.

Serves 6 to 8 as a side

¾ cup extra-virgin olive oil
5 garlic cloves, smashed and peeled
½ teaspoon fine sea salt, plus more to taste
½ teaspoon hot pepper flakes
½ cup fresh mint leaves, plus tiny leaves for garnish
2 sprigs rosemary

¼ cup fresh basil leaves
3 wide strips lemon zest
4 medium zucchini (1½ to 2 pounds), preferably a firm Italian variety
Freshly ground black pepper
A small handful of shaved Parmesan (about 1 ounce)

To minimize the damaging effects of high heat on the delicate olive oil, you want to split the olive oil into two additions, using just enough oil to infuse the herbs and then adding the remainder to steep. Heat ¼ cup of the oil with the garlic in a small skillet over medium-low heat and cook gently until the garlic turns golden at the edges, about 10 minutes. Add the remaining ½ cup olive oil, the salt, hot pepper flakes, mint, rosemary, basil, and lemon peel and bring to a very gentle simmer. Immediately remove from the heat and let the herbs macerate for at least 30 minutes, preferably longer. The oil can sit and infuse on the countertop for most of a day, but it should be refrigerated if made further in advance.

Fill a wide 3-quart saucepan with water and bring to a boil. Salt the water until it tastes frankly saline.

Meanwhile, trim the bottoms of the zucchini but leave the tops intact. Slice the zucchini lengthwise, and then cut each half on a deep bias into 2- to 3-inch lengths. Add the zucchini to the boiling water, reduce the heat, and simmer at a bubbling pace until just tender when pierced with the tip of a knife, 6 to 7 minutes.

Drain the zucchini and blot dry, arrange on a platter, and sprinkle with salt and pepper to taste. Tip up the pan of flavored oil, pushing the solids up to the top, and spoon the oil over the zucchini, including the hot pepper flakes and some small bits of herbs. Garnish with a few tiny leaves of fresh mint and the shaved Parmesan.

smoky tomato terrine

In my childhood memory, most of the salads were sweet and gelatinized and served in common-sense 3-inch squares on wide pads of iceberg lettuce. They were assembled in rows well before dinner was served, like a fleet of pastel-colored rafts.

In tribute to those colorful jellied salads, this smoky tomato terrine salad looks very midcentury, but its smoky paprika treatment tastes very now. Peak-of-summer beefsteak tomatoes encased in their own gelatinized juices are a near-perfect textural match. If the jelly is the right strength—not bouncy, but still firm enough to slice—a fork glides through the tomato and the jelly equally, not able to tell one from the other.

The terrine can be made up to 3 days in advance. It takes 2 (largely inattentive) hours to assemble and at least 4 hours to deep-chill before it's ready to be sliced.

Safeguard any leftovers: a slice of wobbly tomato terrine set on a piece of hot buttered toast makes the best late-summer breakfast I know.

Serves 8, with leftovers

tomato-water jelly
2 pounds ripe tomatoes (beefsteak or Roma)
1 large bunch (6 sprigs) basil
4 garlic cloves
1½ teaspoons fine sea salt
1 teaspoon sugar
¼ cup fresh lemon juice
1 cup water
7 teaspoons unflavored gelatin
2 tablespoons extra-virgin olive oil, plus more
    for the mold

1½ teaspoons smoked paprika
A shake of cayenne pepper

tomato terrine
3 pounds absolutely beautiful ripe beefsteak
    tomatoes
2 balls fresh mozzarella (about 8 ounces each)
2 heads iceberg lettuce

For the tomato water, quarter the tomatoes, transfer to a bowl, and toss with the basil, garlic, salt, sugar, and lemon juice. Puree the tomatoes in a blender in two batches, adding the water as needed to get the blender going and processing until you have a smooth, frothy pink liquid.

Pour the tomato mixture into a large fine-mesh sieve set over a 6-quart measuring cup or a bowl and leave to drip until all the liquid has been expressed, about 1 hour.

Gently move the solids around in the sieve with a rubber spatula to free the remaining liquid, but don't bear down on them; discard the solids. You should have about 4 cups of clear liquid. Using a ladle and a circling motion, skim off the froth from the top of the tomato water. Refrigerate until cold.

For the tomato-water jelly, rub a 6-cup terrine mold (or a 9½ x 4½-inch loaf pan) with a thin layer of olive oil and set aside. Measure the gelatin into a small bowl, stir in ⅔ cup of the cool tomato water, and set aside.

Combine the olive oil, smoked paprika, and cayenne in a large saucepan and heat briefly over medium heat for about a minute, until the the specks of paprika detonate and bloom. Immediately add half of the remaining tomato water and cook gently until the liquid begins to steam. Remove from the heat, add the gelatin mixture, and whisk until melted. Whisk in the rest of the tomato water and let cool to room temperature.

recipe continues

Bring a large pot of water to a boil for blanching the tomatoes, and set up a bowl of ice water to chill them. Cut a cross in the bottom of each tomato and submerge a few of them in the boiling water just until the skins begin to peel back, about 30 seconds. Lift the tomatoes out of the boiling water, drop them into the ice water to chill, and then promptly fish them out and peel them. Repeat with the rest of the tomatoes. Set the peeled tomatoes aside until you're ready to assemble the terrine.

Pour a ¼-inch-thick layer of the cooled tomato-water jelly into the prepared mold and refrigerate. After 30 minutes, check the set: It should be bouncy. (If it's too soft, you may need to add more gelatin. Combine another 1 to 2 teapoons gelatin with 3 tablespoons of the cool tomato water in a small dish and set aside for 2 minutes to bloom, then melt in 2 more cups of the tomato water over low heat before stirring it back into the rest of the tomato water. Chill and carry on.)

Cut a peeled tomato into ½-inch-thick slices and cover the bottom of the mold completely, tearing and fitting the tomato pieces into a single even layer. Nap the tomatoes with enough jelly to cover generously and chill until it's firm enough to bounce back when poked, about 20 minutes.

Repeat the process—slicing tomatoes and making layers, covering them with jelly, and chilling—until you've used up all of the tomatoes and you have about an inch of room left in the terrine mold. Make sure you've got a thin membrane of jelly between each layer of tomatoes, or they will slide around when you slice the terrine.

Slice the mozzarella into ½-inch-thick disks and layer evenly over the last round of tomatoes. Pour in a final layer of jelly to reach at least ¼ inch above the mozzarella, to form a sturdy jellied footing for your terrine. Refrigerate the terrine for at least 4 hours to allow the jelly to set up completely before slicing.

To unmold the terrine, pour boiling water into a container that's larger than your mold. Set the mold in the hot water for 20 seconds, take it out, and slide a thin knife around the perimeter to start to loosen the seal. Repeat this operation until you see the jelly release from the sidewalls.

Find a platter long enough to hold your terrine. Blot the bottom of the mold dry, to keep water from dripping onto the platter. Holding the mold sideways above the platter, wedge the tip of your knife into the space between the jelly and the mold to release the suction. As soon as it makes that gasping sound, quickly invert the mold onto the platter. Tap on the top of the mold and lift it off. If it doesn't release, cycle through this routine again until it does. If the terrine has melted a bit during unmolding, return it to the refrigerator to firm up.

To serve, rip or cut the iceberg lettuce into roughly 3-inch pads, two layers thick, and set them on small plates. Slice the terrine with a sharp knife and carefully transfer each slice to a lettuce raft. If the gelatin feels bouncy, let the terrine sit at room temperature for a while to warm and soften; if not, serve when you can. There's no hurry.

<table>
<tr><td>

a lazy day's summer lunch

FOR SIX

</td><td>

— homemade Boursin with grilled bread

— nightshade confit

— sopped greens with butter-roasted walnuts

— black currant finger Jell-O

</td></tr>
</table>

The centerpiece of this menu, the nightshade confit, is best when the zucchini, eggplant, pepper, and tomato harvests converge during the hot early part of August.

The menu really belongs to a still, breezeless late lunch on the porch, one of those things that lingers on because the air temperature is so temperate, so perfectly suited to the human condition, that you feel almost buoyant in it. One minute you're setting the table and thinking, "We'll be done here by two o'clock . . . ," and then suddenly the day is gone.

Bake the vegetable confit in the ambitious cool hours of morning and set it on the countertop to cool its heels and settle until lunch. Start with the homemade Boursin and leave it on the table while you retrieve the confit and loaf of crusty bread. In fact, I'd be ready with two loaves, one for the cheese and another for swabbing through the vegetable confit's shiny blaze-orange juices. The confit is pretty and substantial enough to constitute lunch, but visually, the vegetables need some company on the plate. Tender boiled collard greens topped with pan-roasted walnuts will cook in the time it takes you to dip back into the house and change the music on the stereo. Serve the greens hot from the pot, the rosé straight from the fridge.

homemade Boursin with grilled bread

Every region of France claims a slightly different version of this herbed fresh cheese spread, made from the fragments of the previous night's cheese plate. In Lyon, it's called *cervelle de canut,* but lately mine takes more direct inspiration from the box of Boursin found in the "finer cheeses" section of my local grocery store.

Now's the time to make use of all of the orphaned cheese in your cheese bin, those mystery lumps mummified in yards of looped plastic wrap. Unfurl them, and lop off the old dry sides. Plop some soft goat cheese in a bowl, add sour cream or crème fraîche, paddle until soft, and then start grating in your stash of cheeses, adding shallots, chives, garlic, and a splash of Cognac as you go. The booze brings the competing cheeses together into one coordinated Gaelic unit.

Once after a lard-rendering project, in a brazen act of decadence, I threw a few tablespoons of crushed pork cracklings into this spread. The granular pork detonated on the tongue like Pop Rocks. If you happen to have a plastic bag of frozen pork cracklings left over from a lard-rendering project—and I know you do—it will be a truly meaningful addition.

3½ ounces fresh goat cheese, softened

½ cup sour cream or crème fraîche

2 tablespoons minced shallot

1 garlic clove, finely grated

2 teaspoons minced fresh thyme

1 packed cup finely grated miscellaneous semi-hard cheeses (aged cheddar, Gouda, Parmesan, blue, whatever you have)

Grated zest of ¼ lemon

¼ teaspoon fine sea salt, plus more to taste

¼ teaspoon freshly ground black pepper, plus more to taste

2 teaspoons Cognac or whiskey

2 tablespoons crushed pork or duck cracklings (optional; see headnote)

Put the goat cheese in a wide mixing bowl and paddle with a sturdy rubber spatula until soft and smooth. Add the sour cream and mix until combined, then add the shallots, garlic, thyme, grated cheeses, lemon zest, salt, and pepper, and paddle everything together. Taste for seasoning, then stir in the Cognac and cracklings, if using. (*The Boursin can be made up to a day in advance, covered, and refrigerated. Bring to room temperature, at least an hour, before serving.*)

Transfer the Boursin to a small serving bowl, smooth the top with a butter knife, and serve with crusty bread.

nightshade confit

Whether shopping in your own garden or your neighbor's, or at a farmers' market, look for small vegetables for this. You want baby eggplant, either long Asian-style or smaller Italian globes, picked when the skin is still shiny and the interior seeds are still small. Skinny Italian frying peppers. Sweet garden onions with the green tops still attached. Thin-skinned cherry tomatoes and zucchini picked well before they explode. I'd avoid those tiny, bland "baby zucchini"; in my experience, zucchini doesn't develop any personality until adolescence.

Confit is the French term for vegetables cooked in a long, slow, luxurious fat bath. This technique is kind of like a fluid transfusion: as the low heat pulls the vegetables' natural juices into the sauce, they in turn draw the olive oil up into their veins. Arrange the vegetables artfully into a colorful mosaic after you've sautéed them all, because eventually they'll become too tender to move, and take the cooking slow. After forty-five minutes, the vegetables will glaze over with exhaustion and be so tender that they can only be shaken in the pan, not stirred. The confit will look like an oil painting—so shiny and deep and saturated that it can't absorb another drop.

Don't let the amount of olive oil scare you off; you can skim it off where it pools at the edges if it feels like too much, but it will function as a preservative if you make this in advance, or store leftovers in the fridge. It keeps for at least a week, getting better by the day. And when you find yourself rushing out the door with a few cold slices of eggplant and pepper riding on a slice of hot toast, the oil dripping down into the gaping bread holes, I truly doubt you'll regret a single teaspoon.

recipe continues

Serves 6 generously as a main, or 10 as a side

2 medium globe or 3 Asian-type eggplants
    (1 pound)
2 medium zucchini (about 14 ounces)
5 sweet or semi-hot frying peppers (about 6
    ounces)
2 spring onions, greens trimmed
¾ cup extra-virgin olive oil
½ teaspoon fine sea salt, plus more for the
    initial vegetable cooking

Freshly ground black pepper
4 garlic cloves, sliced
1½ teaspoons minced fresh rosemary
1 pint cherry tomatoes
2 tablespoons water
1 tablespoon honey
3 bay leaves
2 cinnamon sticks

Preheat the oven to 350°F.

If the eggplants are the globe type, cut them into quarters and then again into eighths; if they're the long Asian type, halve lengthwise and then cut crosswise into long bats. Cut the zucchini lengthwise into quarters. Halve the peppers if they're larger than a kid's fist. Quarter the onions.

Heat an extra-large ovenproof sauté pan over medium-high heat, then add a thin layer of the olive oil. Quickly brown the surfaces of the vegetables in batches (they'll cook to tenderness later), seasoning them with salt and pepper just before putting them in the hot pan: first the eggplant, then the zucchini and the peppers, and then the onions. Don't crowd them, or they'll steam instead of sauté, and add a bit more oil if needed. Transfer the browned vegetables to a sheet tray.

Add the remaining olive oil, the garlic, and rosemary to the pan and cook briefly, just to take the bite out of the garlic, then add all of the sautéed vegetables, nestling them into a nice formation, and drop the cherry tomatoes over the top. Season the vegetables with the ½ teaspoon salt and pepper to taste, then stir together the water and honey in a small dish and drizzle it over the vegetables. Tuck in the bay leaves and cinnamon sticks and bring everything to a simmer. Cook the vegetables until juices begin to accumulate, about 5 minutes, then tip the pan and baste the vegetables with a large spoon.

Cover the surface of the vegetables with a circular lid of parchment paper cut to fit the diameter of the pan, to trap in the flavor and moisture. Transfer the vegetables to the oven and bake for 30 minutes, stopping halfway through to baste the vegetables again. Remove the paper cover, baste the vegetables with the juices again, and bake, uncovered, for another 10 to 15 minutes, until the liquid clings thickly to the vegetables and the exposed surfaces begin to burnish.

Remove from the oven and let settle and cool before serving, right from the pan.

sopped greens with butter-roasted walnuts

Butter-roasted walnuts are a staple in my house, and they're leagues better than oven-toasted walnuts. As they slowly cook in butter and olive oil, the milk fat in the butter clings to the nuts, toasting them from the outside in, all the way to their crispy hearts. Your entire house will smell like a roasted nut stand on a crowded city street. It's intoxicating.

Any kind of leafy green can be used here, but I prefer big-boned greens, like collards or dinosaur kale. Cook them in a large pot of violently boiling water under a watchful eye just until they go pleasantly slack and their leaves soften to velvet. Any less than that, and they won't absorb the buttery walnut juices.

If you think there are too many walnuts here, that's my subconscious at work. You'll want to hold back a few for your morning oatmeal.

Serves 6 to 8 as a side

butter-roasted walnuts
1 cup walnuts
2 tablespoons butter
2 tablespoons olive oil
1 garlic clove, smashed and peeled
2 small sprigs rosemary
Fine sea salt and freshly ground black pepper

greens
2 large bunches collard greens
4 tablespoons butter
2 tablespoons olive oil
3 garlic cloves, minced
Fine sea salt and freshly ground black pepper

1 lemon, cut into wedges or cheeks, for serving

For the walnuts, combine the nuts, butter, olive oil, garlic, and rosemary in a small sauté pan and set over low heat. Season with salt and pepper and cook slowly, distractedly babysitting the pan and overturning the walnuts with a large spoon every once in a while, until they're evenly amber brown. This should take about 20 minutes. Remove from the heat and set aside.

For the greens, bring a large pot of water to a boil while you clean the greens. Strip the leaves from the stems and wash them in a large bowl of cold water. Drain and tear into 2-inch pieces.

When the water boils, salt it heavily and add the greens. Boil, uncovered, until the greens are soft to the bite, 4 to 5 minutes. Drain the greens in a colander. Toss them with a pair of tongs and press them gently against the sides of the colander to remove excess moisture. You don't want to squeeze the greens, but they shouldn't be dripping either.

Heat a large frying pan over medium heat and add the butter, olive oil, and garlic. Stir the garlic, and when it starts to turn light gold, add the greens. Season lightly with salt and pepper and cook, tossing with a pair of tongs, until the greens are hot.

Pile the hot greens onto a wide platter, arranging the leaves with your tongs so they stand up and curl loosely. Sprinkle with a bit of salt and pepper and spoon the walnuts and olive oil/butterfat over the greens. Serve with lemon wedges.

black currant finger Jell-O

When I was a kid, we called these Knox Blox. Aunt Renee made them, using the recipe on the back of the Knox gelatin box. The formula is solid, so I follow it now, but I use black currant juice and roll the squares in citric-acid–spiked sugar, in Sour Patch Kids fashion.

You can also just cut off a hunk of the Jell-O® with a knife and walk around the house with it as you pick up clutter, letting it melt slowly on your tongue. That's the more sacramental way to eat these—especially if you leave the knife in the pan. The whittling butter knife abandoned in a gleaming metal brownie pan feels like a Midwestern childhood icon.

> **NOTE**
> Gelatin doesn't respond consistently to highly acidic mediums; acidity interferes with the set. So if your black currant juice tastes extra-tart and your Jell-O doesn't firm up, just remelt it, add another package of gelatin, throw the steaming pan onto a rack in your fridge, and go do summer: Lope down Main Street. Eat an ice cream cone. Spring for a new pair of flip-flops. And don't worry. The harder the Jell-O sets, the more the kids will like it.

Makes an 8 × 8-inch pan

5 cups black currant juice (lightly sweetened
    store-bought or homemade; recipe follows)
    or grape juice
5 packages (¼ ounce each) unflavored gelatin
½ cup sugar
Finely grated zest of 1 lime
¼ teaspoon citric acid (see page 331)

Measure 1 cup of the black currant juice into a small bowl and add the gelatin. Stir to combine and let sit for 5 minutes, or until the gelatin is bloomed and solid.

Heat 2 cups of the black currant juice in a saucepan over medium heat, then whisk in the gelatin mixture. Heat gently, taking care not to let the mixture come to a boil, whisking until no lumps remain, about 5 minutes. Pour in the remaining 2 cups currant juice and whisk to combine, then pour into an 8 × 8-inch metal pan. When the mixture stops steaming, transfer the Jell-O to the refrigerator and chill until firm, about 4 hours.

Cut the Jell-O into 1½-inch squares. Combine the sugar, lime zest, and citric acid in a small bowl. Roll the squares in the sugar and serve on a platter.

black currant juice If you happen to have a source for fresh black currants, here's my juice recipe. You can freeze it in jars or process it in a boiling-water bath* to pull out in the winter. It's pretty concentrated stuff: Mix it in a 1:1 ratio with sparkling water to make a black currant fizz, or dribble it straight into cocktails.

Makes 2 quarts

3 pounds ripe but firm black currants
4 cups water**

1¾ cups sugar, plus more to taste
Juice of ½ lemon

Pick through the black currants for stems and leaves, put in a large bowl, and cover generously with cold water. Swish the berries with your hands, then let them settle. Carefully pour off the excess water, fill the bowl again, and repeat until you've removed the remaining stems and leaves.

Drain the currants, combine with the 4 cups water in a wide, heavy pot (or jam pot) set over medium heat, and bring to a simmer. Smash the berries with a potato masher to rough them up and get their juices flowing, then add the sugar. Simmer, stirring occasionally, until the liquid tastes strong, 10 to 15 minutes. The sugar should bring out the flavor of the currants but not mask their natural tartness. If the juice is astringent or if the berries were a little on the unripe side, add a little more sugar to taste. Stir in the lemon juice and remove from the heat.

Pour the mixture into a strainer set over a large container and lightly press on the berries to extract as much juice as possible. Pass the liquid again through a finer strainer, and this time let it drip freely to get a clear juice, without pressing on the pulp. Let the juice sit for at least 3 hours, refrigerated, for the sediment to settle. Then pour the clear juice into clean jars (rinsed with boiling water), leaving ¼ inch of headspace, cap, and refrigerate for up to 1 week. If freezing the juice, leave ½ inch of headspace, cap, and freeze up to 6 months.

* To safely process currant juice in a boiling-water-bath canner, follow the formula for grape juice (which has a comparable pH, or acidity) at the University of Georgia's National Center for Home Food Preservation website: www.nchfp.uga.edu.

** As with most recipes for making juice, your water measurement may vary a bit depending on the pot you use and how much surface area it exposes. You want the water to come *nearly* level with the berries, but not over them. Too much water dilutes the flavor of the juice; too little, and it will be wastefully concentrated.

New York City Chinese barbecue at home

— Mei's ginger-glazed baby back ribs

— smashed garlic cucumbers

— jasmine rice

— bok choy salad with ramen-almond brittle

— stir-fried peas and their greens

FOR SIX TO EIGHT

Years ago, I worked in a Chinese restaurant in New York City, where I spent my days prepping in the basement next to a guy named Mei (pronounced *moy*) who worked the seven-foot-tall gas-fired barbecue oven. A sweet guy whose resting expression was a wink, Mei was responsible for the Peking duck (*siu yaap* in Cantonese), the crispy-skinned roast pork bellies (*siu yuk*), and the chile-glazed (*char siu*-style) barbecued ribs, and I knew his choreography by heart. He began his day dipping ducks into a sugar-vinegar brine and swinging them onto meat hooks between the walk-in cooler and the tall rectangular metal roaster. Next he moved on to poaching his ribs, and then to stabbing the skin side of the pork bellies with a sharp metal stippler—it looked like a floral pin frog—before hanging them in the roaster over the propane jets. The fat would run out of the tiny pinpricks and the skin would bubble up volcanically. Standing next to Mei as he flopped hot racks of ribs and crispy pork bellies onto his board was delirious torture. I tried not to stare, or to beg, but eventually he began to slide me choice scraps on the regular.

I can't imagine trying to make Mei's crispy pork belly or Peking duck at home—both need to hang over the encircling jet fire of a Chinese barbecue roaster—but I've been making his caramelized baby back ribs for years. With a recipe made for restaurants (and dinner parties), the work is split into two parts. The ribs poach in slow, unattended fashion for a few hours and then are basted with gingery chile-red *char siu* sauce before heading into the oven for last-minute glazing. To help curb our baser instincts to gorge on sugared pork, I fill out the menu with an assortment of green things: smashed garlicky cucumbers, a quick and spicy dish of stir-fried peas and their greens, and a cold bok choy salad with ramen-almond brittle. It could have sprouted from the imagination of a blond home-ec major working in a Midwestern corporate test kitchen for all I know, but let's not knock it. This recipe single-handedly brought a regular supply of Napa cabbage to northern grocery stores in the 1980s, and it's pretty damn delicious.

Mei's ginger-glazed baby back ribs

I watched Mei make these poached and carmelized pork ribs day in and day out for a year, and I think this recipe for gingery char siu sauce comes pretty close to his version—minus the small spoonful of red dye number 5 he used to tint his ribs neon red. Add it if you're looking for drama. The Chinese chile bean paste called *toban djan* or *doubanjiang* is not so optional. The spicy, salty, umami-rich paste,

recipe continues

made from long-fermented hot chiles and soybeans, adds backbeat to an otherwise straightforward sweet glaze.

These ribs poach in a light soy brine on the stovetop for 2 largely hands-off hours. They come out tender and moist and as defatted as a rib can be before heading into the oven for their appointment with the sticky-sweet glaze. Incredibly easy, these ribs can be scaled up to feed an actual throng—graduation parties, reunions, what-have-you. You can make as many ribs as you have pots to cook them in.

And note that this simple rib-poaching technique can be used to cook other cuts of pork and poultry you intend to glaze with any kind of sauce, Asian-inspired or not. Chicken legs, pork butt steaks, halved ducks, game birds . . . let your imagination run wild.

Serves 6 to 8 (the recipe is easily doubled)

for the ribs
2 racks baby back ribs (4 pounds)
½ cup light soy sauce
8 dried red chiles
One 4-inch piece ginger, sliced (unpeeled is okay)
1 teaspoon fine sea salt, plus more to taste
1 orange, halved

ginger glaze
2 tablespoons finely grated ginger
¼ cup rice wine vinegar
¼ cup toban djan (or doubanjiang; fermented Chinese chile bean paste)*
⅔ cup packed brown sugar
3 tablespoons light soy sauce
1 tablespoon toasted sesame oil

Wash the ribs under cold running water and cut each rack in half. Put them in your largest pan (I use a two-handled roaster set across two burners) and add water to generously cover, about 3 quarts. Bring to a simmer and skim off and discard the foam that rises. Add the soy sauce, chiles, ginger slices, and salt and simmer the ribs for about 2 hours, until they're tender but not quite falling apart. As they cook, the ribs will rise above the surface of the liquid, so you'll want to turn them over every 30 minutes or so, or keep them submerged with plates. When they're tender, transfer the ribs to a platter and discard the poaching liquid (or save and reduce later to make ramen broth).

Meanwhile, make the glaze: Combine all the ingredients in a saucepan, bring to a boil, stirring to dissolve the sugar, and then simmer until thick and sticky, about 15 minutes. Check the consistency by dropping some sauce on a plate and pinching it between your fingers. Taste for seasoning. Depending on your brand of toban djan, you may want to add another tablespoon or so to pump up the heat.

Preheat the oven to 425°F.

Place the ribs on a rack set over a foil-lined baking sheet. Paint the ribs thickly with the glaze and roast for 10 minutes. Reapply the glaze, mopping up any excess that pooled onto the pan with your brush and brushing it back over the ribs. Return to the oven to roast, stopping halfway through to reapply the glaze again, until the sauce fuses onto the surface of the meat and caramelizes to a dark, ruddy red-brown, another 20 minutes or so.

Remove from the oven and let the ribs cool for a few minutes, then slice between the bones and stack them loosely on a large platter.

---

*Lee Kum Kee (LKK) makes a good, if somewhat mild, toban djan, and is a fairly common find in large grocery stores. For more traditional Sichuan heat, head to an Asian market and look for jars labeled doubanjiang or Sichuan chile broad bean sauce. Toban djan varies widely by brand, so keep watch on the spiciness and saltiness of the finished dish.

smashed garlic cucumbers

The thought of these chilled garlic cucumbers sitting in a pool of sesame oil and their own melony, saline juices can motivate me to make this whole menu. The cucumbers are gently smacked with a cleaver to crack their backbones, then liberally salted. The salt gets their juices going, and grated garlic and nutty sesame oil infuse them with flavor. Use thin-skinned Persian cucumbers or English cucumbers—not waxed supermarket slicers—for this recipe. They're crunchy and firm and have smaller seed boats.

This is a make-and-serve dish, but if you'd like to serve it chilled—I usually do—you can make it up to 4 hours ahead.

Serves 6 to 8 as a small side

1½ pounds thin-skinned Persian cucumbers
(7 or 8) or 2 large English cucumbers
¾ teaspoon fine sea salt
2 small garlic cloves, finely grated

1 tablespoon sesame seeds
2 tablespoons toasted sesame oil, preferably a
Korean brand such as Kadoya
1 tablespoon sliced fresh chives

Wash the cucumbers and trim the ends. If their skin is tight and bright green, peel it off in long wide stripes, leaving the cucumbers half jade and half evergreen. If the skins are dark and dull, remove them completely. Halve the cucumbers lengthwise. Persian cucumbers will have small seed pods, so you can leave those intact. English cucumbers have wider seed cavities and their moisture will dilute the sauce, so you'll want to scrape them out roughly with a teaspoon, although you needn't go crazy here. A little bit of extra moisture is fine.

Lay the cucumbers face down on the cutting board and whack them gently with the side of a large heavy knife, just enough to crack them. Then slice them roughly on the bias into ¾-inch-wide pieces and transfer them to a bowl. Add the salt and grated garlic, stir, and leave them to sweat at room temperature for 30 minutes.

At this point, the cucumbers should be wet with their own brine, but not swimming in it. If the cucumbers are particularly juicy or seed-heavy, discard all but 2 tablespoons of the brine.

Toast the sesame seeds briefly in a small frying pan over medium heat until lightly browned.

Add the sesame seeds, sesame oil, and chives to the cucumbers, stir to combine, and scrape into a small serving dish. Chill deeply before serving.

jasmine rice

I was sent off to college knowing ten good ways with potatoes, but I couldn't have made a simple pot of white rice to save my life. That changed when I worked at 66, a French American chef's Chinese restaurant in New York City. Every afternoon at 4:30, the back waiters would make the rice for dinner service, and because they had more time to spare and were chattier than the line cooks, I got the running tutorial. The abridged version of the recipe is: "It's complicated. You can't think in cups!" Followed by, "You should just get a rice cooker." The rice-to-water ratio is calculated spatially, not mathematically, and changes according to the quantity of rice and the surface area of the pot. Essentially, there is no recipe, just a method, a feeling, and, eventually, a knack.

First, buy good rice. My go-tos are jasmine and short-grain round rice (like Kohuyo brand)— the round rice when I want a chewier, stickier grain, the jasmine when I want one that's looser and more delicate. Generally, the rice at Asian markets is fresher and of better quality than the stuff that's distributed commercially to large American grocery stores. Asian stores sell recognizable Asian brands, and the brands have reputations to uphold. Buy a five- or ten- or even twenty-five-pound bag of Chinese jasmine rice, preferably new-crop (freshly harvested) if you can get it. Rice dries out and becomes more brittle as it sits on the shelf from season to season. New-crop rice requires a little less water, but it has a plusher texture. And, I should say, I'm talking about white rice, not brown rice. The texture is superior, it absorbs sauces better, and, personally, I think it's easier to digest. I always feel better after eating white rice than I do after eating brown—but maybe that's just me. That said, my favorite rice in the world is the

semi-milled Japanese rice called haiga mai, or koshikigari, polished enough to remove the bran but not the germ. It's the best of both worlds, really.

Pour however many cups of rice you'd like to cook into a fine-mesh sieve and run it under cold water to remove excess starch and any grit left from the polishing process. You want to really scrub the rice between your hands and flush it with water until the water runs clearer than when you began. Drain, shaking off the excess water, and transfer to a heavy-bottomed saucepan. Rice steams more evenly in a pan with a wider circumference, so if you're cooking a large batch—4 to 5 cups—reach for a wide-bottomed sauté pan with a lid or an enameled cast-iron brasier.

Add water in a straight cup-to-cup ratio to start: for 3 cups rice, add 3 cups water. Rake the rice flat with your hand. Then add enough water to rise ⅝ inch above the surface of the rice (this is the numerical equivalent of the "add enough water to come up to your knuckle" rule). Two cups of rice will require more water per cup than 4 cups of rice, and tall pots will take more than wide pots, so it's best to go by inches.

My Chinese coworkers didn't salt their rice, and unsalted rice tastes almost sweet. To make it more savory, add about ⅛ teaspoon salt per cup of rice. Swish in the salt, then let the rice soak for at least 30 minutes, or as long as 3 hours. Presoaked rice cooks to a more even chewiness.

Bring the water to a vigorous boil over medium-high heat. Stir swiftly with two chopsticks or a fork, then clamp a tight-fitting lid onto the pot and reduce the heat to its lowest-possible simmer setting. The rice should simmer gently, with occasional soft curls of steam. On a gas-fired stovetop, you may need to use a diffuser (see page 326).

Steam the rice for 15 minutes if it's a small quantity, and up to 20 minutes if you're cooking more. The grains should be tender but have some give left in them. If for some reason all the water has evaporated but the rice is too al dente, poke a few holes into the rice, dribble in some water, cover, and cook another 5 minutes. When the rice is tender, remove it from the heat and let it steep, covered, for at least 15 minutes. This last steam bath is essential if you want that characteristically buoyant jasmine-rice texture. Stir the rice with a fork to fluff it up and serve. The rice can also be held in the covered pot for up to an hour, and reheated.

As for serving sizes, 1 cup of raw rice will feed 3 people, without leftovers; 2 cups will feed 4 to 6; 3 cups will feed 8; and 4 cups will feed 12. To cook 3 cups or less, use a heavy-bottomed 3- to 4-quart saucepan, preferably wider than it is deep. For 4 cups rice, use a large wide (straight-sided) sauté pan. To cook 5 to 7 cups of rice, divide the rice between two wide sauté pans, or cook it in a rice cooker. (Zojirushi is the Rolls-Royce brand, the rice cooker that you will include in your will. But any rice cooker will work.)

Makes 8 cups, serving 8

3 cups jasmine rice   ½ teaspoon fine sea salt (optional)
4¼ to 4½ cups water

To cook the rice, follow the method described above, but here's the quick cheat sheet: Scrub the raw rice in a colander under cold running water until the water runs clear. Transfer to a 4-quart saucepan, add the water and salt, if using, and soak for at least 30 minutes. Then bring the water to a boil, cover tightly, and reduce the heat to its very lowest simmer settting; you may need to use a diffuser on a gas stove. Steam for 15 to 20 minutes, and check for doneness. Once the rice is tender, fluff with a fork and let sit, covered, for 15 minutes before serving.

The rice can be made up to an hour in advance and reheated in the same pan or transferred to a heatproof serving dish, covered, and reheated in the microwave or a low oven.

bok choy salad with ramen-almond brittle

I grew up eating some bad takes on this salad, with chalky, raw ramen noodles and dressings so sweet they made your teeth shake, but even bad ramen salad is pretty good. When my friend Amber brought a much better rendition to a potluck a few years ago, I knew she'd found the way forward. She used baby bok choy instead of napa cabbage, and she baked the crumbled ramen with almonds and sugar until it crisped into a sweet, addictive brittle. It tasted like savory sesame granola meets childhood.

During the summer months, I like to add tatsoi or small fava leaves to this salad for a little textural interest and beauty, but they're optional.

Makes 9 cups, serving 8 generously

ramen-almond brittle
Two 3-ounce packages ramen noodles
1½ cups (6 ounces) sliced almonds
3 tablespoons sugar
2 tablespoons water
5 tablespoons neutral oil, such as peanut or canola
¼ teaspoon fine sea salt
Freshly ground black pepper

sesame dressing
1 tablespoon finely grated ginger
3 tablespoons maple syrup
3 tablespoons fresh lime juice
1½ tablespoons light soy sauce
2 tablespoons neutral oil, such as peanut or canola
2 tablespoons toasted sesame oil, preferably a Korean brand such as Kadoya
1 teaspoon unseasoned rice vinegar
½ teaspoon fine sea salt
¼ teaspoon freshly ground black pepper

salad
10 cups rough-chopped bok choy (about 1½ pounds) or napa cabbage (about 1 pound), or a mixture of the two
1 bunch scallions or chives, thinly sliced on the bias
2 cups tatsoi or fava bean leaves (optional)
2 tablespoons sesame seeds

Preheat the oven to 325°F.

For the brittle, split the ramen in half and break it into bite-sized pieces. Combine the broken ramen and almonds in a bowl; set aside.

Combine the sugar and water in a small saucepan, bring to a boil over medium heat, and cook, stirring, for 1 minute, or until the sugar dissolves. Add the oil and salt, and remove from the heat.

Pour the sugar syrup over the ramen and almonds and toss to coat. Spread out on a baking sheet, sprinkle with a little pepper, and bake until the noodles and almonds have turned an even shade of caramel brown, about 20 minutes. Remove from the oven and let cool.

For the dressing, combine the ginger, maple syrup, lime juice, soy sauce, peanut oil, sesame oil, vinegar, salt, and pepper in a small jar and shake until emulsified.

For the salad, toss together the bok choy, scallions, and tatsoi or fava bean leaves, if using, in a large bowl. Add the sesame seeds, then add enough dressing to coat the ingredients thickly without drowning them and toss. Mix in half of the toasted ramen-almond brittle and toss again, then pile the rest on top.

This salad can wait for up to 20 minutes to be served. After that, the ramen brittle starts to get soggy. But since I've enjoyed the leftovers in that state so many times, I can't condemn it.

stir-fried peas and their greens

Just barely touched with wok fire and bathed in the barest slip of a garlic sauce, this electric mixed pea stir-fry is one of my favorite warm-weather sides. I like to use a mixture of shell peas, snow peas, and sugar snap peas, preferably so young and fresh that they feel almost rubberized, along with a few handfuls of young pea green tendrils. Use any peas that are fresh at the market—out of season, even frozen petite peas will work—but slice the podded peas lengthwise on the bias, bisecting the pods and peas. Look for pea shoots at the farmers' market, or in a friend's garden, and use only the most tender tips.

Before you start cooking, pull a serving dish close. You want to cook the peas just long enough to threaten a wilt, because they'll continue to slouch on the platter. Hustle this to the table.

Serves 6 to 8 as a side

1½ pounds mixed snow peas, snap peas, and shell peas

2 cups tender pea shoots (or spinach, tough stems removed)

2 tablespoons chicken stock or water

1 teaspoon soy sauce

2 garlic cloves, finely minced

½ teaspoon fine sea salt

Large pinch of sugar

¼ teaspoon freshly ground black pepper

1 tablespoon cornstarch

1 tablespoon toasted sesame oil

2 tablespoons canola or peanut oil

Rinse the snow peas and snap peas and remove their strings by bending them back at the blossom end. (If they're really young or immature, there may not be any strings to remove.) Slice each one lengthwise on the bias into three long strips. If using fresh sweet shell peas, set them aside in a bowl.

Go through the pea shoots to remove any hard stems, rip into 3-inch lengths, and wash them (or the optional spinach) in a large bowl of cold water. Drain in a colander and tap it against the sink to shake out any remaining water.

Combine the chicken stock or water and soy sauce in one small bowl, the minced garlic in another, and the salt, sugar, and pepper in a third, and set these next to the stovetop. Mix the cornstarch with enough cold water to make a soft, gluey slurry, and set it next to the stove, along with your bottle of sesame oil.

Heat a large wok or a large cast-iron skillet over high heat. When it starts to smoke, add the canola or peanut oil and then, immediately, the peas. Season the peas with the salt and sugar mixture and stir them in the hot pan until they turn bright green, about 1 minute. A little darkening at the hot spots is fine—delicious, actually. Add the pea shoots (or spinach), toss to combine, and then immediately dump in the soy sauce mixture and the sesame oil.

Move the peas and greens out to the sides of the pan, leaving the liquid to pool in the center. Dribble in a small amount of the cornstarch slurry (about ½ teaspoon) in a thin stream to slightly thicken the sauce. As soon as the liquid boils and thickens, toss the greens with sauce, then quickly tip everything out onto a platter and serve immediately.

homemade chitarra pasta work party

FOR SIX TO EIGHT

— steamed eggplant with chile oil, lemon, and 'nduja
— chitarra pasta with roasted cherry tomatoes
— winter white salad
— apple fritto misto with peels, lemons, and sage

Making fresh pasta for a large party sounds like one of those innocent good ideas that could end in disaster. But I promise it will be smooth sailing, if: one, you invite friends who like to get their hands dirty; two, you make it clear that this will be a work party; and three, you make chitarra.

Chitarra means "guitar" in Italian, and in this case the name refers not to the pasta shape but the machine used to make it. A rectangular wooden loom–like structure strung with a tight network of metal wires, a chitarra maker resembles a hollow guitar body. You simply lay a sheet of rolled-out homemade pasta over the chitarra strings and roll over it with a rolling pin. Out fall masses of long square-cut strands, skinny like spaghetti but a touch thicker. To release any pasta that gets stuck in the strings, just strum them. The chitarra maker plays a music of sorts—although it sounds to me more dulcet than twangy, more like a harp than a guitar.

A chitarra maker* is simpler and more space-efficient than a hand-cranked pasta machine, and it's also faster. Almost too fast. The last time I threw this party, my friends were setting down their wineglasses and begging to have a turn at it before all the pasta dough was used up—which barely gave me enough time to make the sauce and salad. Just be sure to have some pasta drying racks ready, or broom handles hung between two chairs, or you'll be quickly overwhelmed with noodles.

The rest of this mostly vegetarian menu can either be thrown together quickly or made in advance. The vegetables for the winter white salad can, and, in fact, should be shaved ahead of time and refrigerated, next to the Parmesan cream dressing. All the ingredients for the apple fritto misto can be prepped ahead so that you can calmly fry a few batches after dinner with your friends at your side.

Given the overall richness of the menu, I like to begin with some kind of vegetable matter. Baby eggplants, steamed until soft enough to spread like butter on toasted bread, feel almost virtuous.

★ Good-quality wooden chitarra makers can be found quite easily, and cheaply, online.

steamed eggplant with chile oil, lemon, and 'nduja

The flavor of eggplant is subtle; its charms are largely textural. This not a vegetable that benefits from a coddling, peace-loving treatment. It should be cooked over a vigorous, driving heat to full collapse. In season, I usually grill eggplant over high heat until charred on its face and sulking-soft inside. But steam, which is technically even hotter than a flame, will reduce the eggplant to a pale, creamy heap in about eight minutes flat, leaving its cleared pores open and ready to absorb the spicy, lemony vinaigrette.

This is an active appetizer that demands participation: you want to track the bread through the chile oil, smash some of the steamed eggplant into it, and top it with a wrinkly, meaty oil-cured black olive. Carnivores—who will otherwise strike out with this vegetarian menu—may want to supplement their eggplant mash with some charcuterie. 'Nduja, a spicy, spreadable cured pork sausage from Calabria, would be my first choice.

This recipe is best made with freshly picked summer eggplant. Whether buying from the grocery store or the farmers' market, seek out eggplants that feel firm and heavy for their size, with taut, shiny skins. Dull skins indicate age, as do a grayish cast to the interior and a thick clod of bitter seeds—the reason why many recipes call for presalting and blotting, to draw out the seeds' bitterness. Fresh eggplant will be pale ivory inside, with a faint, tight trail of small seeds, and it doesn't need presalting. Eggplant will stay perfectly fresh at room temperature for up to 3 days; to buy it more time, wrap each one individually in tight plastic wrap and store in the crisper.

Serves 6 to 8 as an appetizer

1 medium or 2 small globe eggplants (about 1 pound)
½ teaspoon fine sea salt

vinaigrette
2½ tablespoons fresh lemon juice
3 tablespoons extra-virgin olive oil
2 tablespoons Homemade Chile Oil (recipe follows) or 1½ teaspoons store-bought Chinese chile oil
½ teaspoon fine sea salt
Freshly ground black pepper

garnishes
A baguette or two, thickly sliced on the bias
1 garlic clove, halved
Extra-virgin olive oil for drizzling
2 ounces 'nduja, or high-quality salami, sliced (optional)
A handful of fresh parsley leaves, roughly chopped*
½ cup oil-cured black olives, pitted
Meyer lemon wedges

For the vinaigrette, combine the lemon juice, olive oil, chile oil, salt, and pepper to taste in a small bowl and stir together, without trying to emulsify it. You want the chile oil to pool in blobs and separate from the olive oil and lemon juice. Set aside.

recipe continues

---

*I have dark memories of picking parsley as a line cook. Leaf by leaf by leaf. It takes forever. And then one day, I saw a fellow line cook stand the bunch of parsley on his board at an angle, leaves faceplanted against the board, and shave them off with broad swoops of his knife. Within ten seconds, he had shorn most of the leaves from the bouquet of stems. It's a little wasteful, but a lot faster. And you can save the stems for making stock.

Prepare a steamer setup by setting a bamboo steamer over a wok full of water and bring the water to a boil. Halve the eggplant(s) lengthwise and hold each half in the palm of your hand, skin side down. Cut the eggplant flesh into ½-inch cubes, slicing deep but not all the way through to the skin, in crosshatched diagonal lines—as you might cube a halved avocado still in its skin. Rub the salt generously onto the surface and into the cut crevices of the halved eggplant(s).

When the water under the steamer comes to a boil, lay the eggplant cut side up in the steamer, cover, and set a timer for 6 minutes. Depending on age and size, the eggplant will take from 6 to 10 minutes to steam to full tenderness; a thin knife should slip easily into the flesh, and the cubes will start to gap open.

Meanwhile, to prepare the garnishes, toast the bread in a toaster or on a hot grill, rub the surface with the cut faces of the garlic clove, and drizzle with olive oil. Arrange it on a large board next to a generous smear of the optional 'nduja, (or coins of salami).

To serve, lay the eggplant halves on a platter, douse with the vinaigrette, and top with the parsley. Garnish the whole spread with a pile of the olives and the lemon wedges. Set out wide butter knives for scooping and smearing.

---

homemade chile oil

homemade chile oil Homemade chile oil is one of my secret weapons, and I try to always keep a jar in the fridge door for spiking leftovers and simple lunchtime soups.

Chinese recipes for chile oil often include Sichuan peppercorns (which give Sichuan food its trademark lip-numbing heat), dark baking spices, and visible flakes of chile seeds. I strain mine, because chile flakes make some people cough, and I tone down the heat because, well, there's hot and then there's something here called Minnesota-hot. And I'm already pushing it with this.

Makes 1½ cups

½ teaspoon fennel seeds
½ cinnamon stick, preferably soft-stick, cracked
1 teaspoon Sichuan peppercorns, cracked
5 garlic cloves, smacked with the side of a knife but not peeled

1 cup dried red Chinese chiles
8 medium-hot dried chiles, such as guajillo
About 2 cups peanut or canola oil
¼ teaspoon fine sea salt
2 tablespoons water

Heat a medium frying pan over medium heat, add the fennel seeds, cinnamon stick, and Sichuan peppercorns, and toast briefly to activate them. Add the garlic, both kinds of chiles, enough oil to just cover the chiles, the salt, and water. Bring the oil to a sizzle, then reduce the heat to the lowest possible setting and cook gently until the water sputters off and the chiles crisp up and begin to darken, turning from barn red to deep burgundy, 30 to 40 minutes. (If your burner setting isn't low enough, this is the time to use a diffuser; see page 326.)

Remove from the heat and let the chile mixture cool on its heels a bit, then transfer everything (if the cinnamon isn't soft-stick, remove it) to a blender. Blend to a fine puree, stopping to scrape down the sides as necessary. Strain the oil through a fine-mesh sieve set over a bowl, pushing it through the mesh with the back of a ladle. Skim off any foam and let the oil cool to room temperature.

Slowly pour the cool oil into a clean glass jar, leaving behind the bottom sediment. Cap tightly and store in the refrigerator, where it will keep for months.

chitarra pasta with roasted cherry tomatoes

The beauty of homemade chitarra pasta is its handmade irregularity. In one single bite you'll get both thick, chewy middles and whisper-thin ends, the part where someone trailed off in thought while rolling out the dough.

With its iconic square edges, chitarra is more rustic than most fresh pastas. To ensure that it has its characteristic giving chew, I enrich my dough with a couple of extra egg yolks for added strength. I make it in the food processor instead of by hand in the traditional manner (eggs cracked into the center well of a pile of flour on the countertop). The whir of the machine isn't as romantic as the eggs-in-the-well method, but it's a lot more foolproof. While I was purchasing my chitarra maker online, I threw a bag of superfine semolina into my cart. The pasta I made with the addition of this flour was simultaneously silky and springy, and very easy to work with.

The traditional sauce for chitarra is a meaty, long-simmered ragù, but I think a sauce of roasted cherry tomatoes sprinkled with a dusting of bread crumbs feels fresher and doesn't upstage the beautiful hand-cut pasta. As the tomatoes roast, the bread crumbs thicken the golden-red juices into an oily, glowing red sauce that clings tightly—almost feverishly—to the chitarra.

recipe continues

Serves 6 to 8 generously

dough

3 cups all-purpose flour, plus more for rolling

1 cup fine semolina flour, plus more for dusting

1 teaspoon fine sea salt

2 tablespoons extra-virgin olive oil

5 large eggs, cracked into a 2-cup (or larger) glass measuring cup, plus enough egg yolks to make 1½ cups (about 5)

2 to 3 tablespoons water

cherry tomato sauce

2½ pounds cherry tomatoes

½ cup extra-virgin olive oil

4 garlic cloves, smashed but not peeled

2 sprigs rosemary

Fine sea salt and freshly ground black pepper

3 tablespoons fine dried bread crumbs

to finish

¼ cup extra-virgin olive oil

3 tablespoons butter

½ teaspoon fine sea salt, plus more to taste

Freshly ground black pepper

1 cup chopped or ripped fresh basil leaves

A squeeze or two of lemon if needed

Pinch of sugar if needed

1½ cups finely grated Parmesan (about 4 ounces)

For the dough, combine the flours and salt in the bowl of a food processor and pulse to blend. Crack the eggs into a measuring cup and add yolks until it reaches 1½ cups. Add the oil to the eggs and yolks and whisk together with a fork.

Turn on the processor and pour the egg mixture through the feed tube, then dribble in 2 tablespoons water. When the dough begins to gather into a clump, stop the machine and begin pulsing, adding more water as needed to make a smooth, slightly sticky, but not wet dough; your finger should come away from the dough mostly clean. Process until the dough ball circles the blade in a single mass, then turn out onto a lightly floured countertop.

Knead the dough until it comes together into a soft ball, then keep kneading for another 3 or 4 minutes, until the dough feels silky—smooth and poreless. Wrap the dough in plastic wrap and let rest at room temperature for up to 3 hours, or refrigerate for up to a day. If the dough has been refrigerated, let it come to room temperature before rolling it out.

Divide the dough into 12 equal pieces and cover them with a clean cloth. Set up a pasta rack situation, or dust some baking sheets with semolina to hold loosely coiled nests of pasta.

On a lightly floured surface, roll out each piece of dough into a rectangle that will fit on the chitarra maker; it should be the thickness of two dimes. Transfer the dough sheet to the chitarra maker and roll over it with the rolling pin, pressing the dough into the strings. If it sticks, rub your fingers up and down the strings and strum them to loosen the dough. When the pasta falls through, dust it with an even coating of semolina flour to prevent sticking, tip it out onto a clean part of the counter, and hang in a single layer on the pasta rack, or arrange in loose nests on one of the baking sheets. Repeat with the remaining dough. (*Any leftover uncooked pasta can be left out to dry completely, about 2 days, and stored in a plastic bag in the pantry.*)

Preheat the oven to 350°F.

For the sauce, combine the cherry tomatoes, oil, garlic, and rosemary on a heavy baking sheet and toss together to coat. Season lightly with salt and pepper. Spread the tomatoes across the pan and sprinkle evenly with the bread crumbs. Roast—without stirring or shaking the pan—until the tomatoes sink into their juices, their skins roll back and blister, and the bread crumbs turn into a fine golden brown crust, about 25 minutes.

recipe continues

Remove the tomatoes from the oven and let cool; add a bit of water to the corners of the pan where the juices may have overreduced and caramelized, because you want all of those pan juices.

Bring a very large pot of water to a boil and salt the water to taste.

Meanwhile, heat a large frying pan over medium heat. Add the olive oil, butter, and roasted tomatoes, scraping out all the juices with a rubber spatula. Bring to a simmer and shake the pan to incorporate the fats into the sauce, then add the salt, some black pepper, and the basil and cook over low heat for 10 minutes. Taste for a balance of sweetness and acidity and add a squeeze of lemon juice if the tomatoes were too ripe or just bland, or a pinch of sugar if they were a little underripe, and remove from the heat (the sauce will hold for an hour or two at room temperature). Just before serving, reheat the sauce over low heat, stirring once or twice.

Cook the pasta in two batches until just tender but still chewy, 3 to 4 minutes (longer if it has air-dried). Scoop out the first batch with a metal spider or small colander, add to the sauce, and toss with a pair of tongs to coat; repeat with the second batch. Add most of the Parmesan cheese to the pasta and toss, dribbling in a bit of hot pasta cooking water if needed; you want the sauce to cling to the pasta but still be loose enough to slide around. Taste for seasoning, and correct with additional salt, pepper, and/or lemon.

Divide the pasta among individual shallow serving bowls and garnish with the remaining cheese.

winter white salad

During the doldrums of winter, when the lettuces in the grocery store all look as if they could use a turn under the sunlamp, it's good to remember that every sad-sack vegetable in the case has a pale, juicy heart. Fennel bulbs, celery hearts, turnips, and radishes of all types can be shaved into a sweet and crunchy winter salad. All three components of this salad—the shaved vegetables, the cream dressing, and the toasted bread crumbs—can be made in advance. If preparing the vegetables in advance, layer them in a large bowl, cover them with a wet paper towel, tightly seal with plastic wrap, and refrigerate for up to 12 hours. The buttery toasted crumbs add a nice crunch but can be replaced with toasted sliced almonds to make this gluten-free. I always plate this salad individually in shallow bowls instead of serving it family-style, to preserve that top crunch.

Makes 6 to 8 individual salads

bread crumbs
2 cups fresh bread crumbs (fluffy medium-
    coarse crumbs from a porous country loaf
    or ciabatta)
5 tablespoons extra-virgin olive oil
2 garlic cloves, smashed and peeled
Fine sea salt and freshly ground black pepper

Parmesan cream dressing
A 2½-ounce chunk of Parmesan
½ cup heavy cream

⅓ cup plain whole-milk yogurt, preferably
    runny (not strained)
½ garlic clove, finely grated
Shy ½ teaspoon fine sea salt
¼ teaspoon freshly ground black
    pepper
Grated zest of ½ lemon
2 tablespoons fresh lemon juice
1 teaspoon unseasoned rice vinegar or apple
    cider vinegar
2 tablespoons extra-virgin olive oil

shaved vegetables

4 cups thinly sliced celery (yellow and pale green parts only, leaves included)

2 cups shaved or thinly sliced fennel (root ends removed and halved)

1 cup shaved or thinly sliced white turnip or kohlrabi (peeled and halved)

1 cup shaved or thinly sliced radish (red globe radishes or peeled daikon)

Fine sea salt and freshly ground black pepper

You can toast the bread crumbs up to an hour or two ahead. Heat a medium frying pan over medium heat and add the olive oil and smashed garlic. Cook until it begins to sizzle and color lightly on both sides. Add the bread crumbs and salt and pepper to taste and cook slowly over lowish heat, stirring often, until the crumbs take on a uniform amber color and crunch between your teeth, 15 to 20 minutes. Remove from the heat and set aside.

For the dressing, grate enough of the Parmesan to make ½ cup. Shave the rest of the cheese into thin shards, cover, and set aside until ready to serve.

Pour the cream into a small bowl. Whisk in the yogurt, garlic, salt, pepper, and lemon zest. Add the lemon juice and vinegar and stir to combine. Within a few minutes, the cream mixture will thicken into a creamy but still pourable consistency. Stir in the olive oil and the finely grated Parmesan cheese. (The dressing can be set aside at room temperature for up to 3 hours or refrigerated, covered, overnight.)

To serve, pile all of the vegetables in your largest mixing bowl and season with salt and pepper, turning them over in your hands. Add most of the cream dressing, toss to coat, and taste to see if it needs more. The salad should be heavily dressed, but not sopped with it. Add the reserved shaved Parmesan cheese.

Line up your salad bowls and divide the salad among them. Top each salad with a few spoonfuls of bread crumbs.

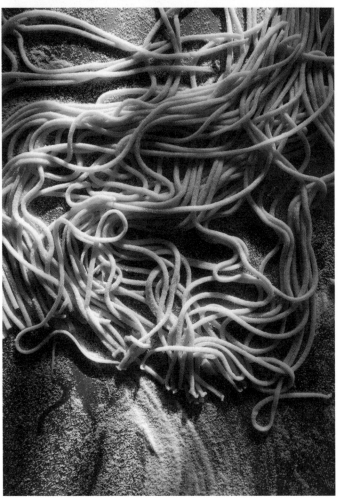

apple fritto misto with peels, lemons, and sage

The classic Italian fritto misto, or "mixed fry," usually consists of a pile of small fish, herbs, and vegetables fried to a bronze crisp and stacked high on a paper-lined plate. Fritto misto is a dish you pick at slowly on a small marble table while working on a cold glass of wine, not quite knowing what you'll get and not really minding. We have a similar dish here in the rural north: it's called a "junk basket," a hodgepodge of frozen appetizers thrown into the deep-fryer at the whim of the griddle chef. My version, a sweet dessert fritto misto, borrows more from Italy than the local roadhouse. And yet, smuggled into the haphazard pile of apples, sage leaves, and lemon rounds are spirals of crispy apple peels, which look an awful lot like onion rings.

The hot-and-fresh nature of frying makes this a casual, communal dessert. Serve it at a table close to the stove, when the apples, peels, lemons, and sage leaves are almost still too hot to handle, so that everyone can decide, as a group, which part is best. The delicate apple peels usually win, with the gushing lemon slices running close second, though there's always someone who votes for the woodsy sweet sage. But this dessert is best when all four components are consumed in quick succession, everyone's fingers coated with fine lemon-sugar sand.

Everything can be prepped ahead of time except for the batter, which should be stirred together while the oil heats up in the pot.

Serves 6 to 8

apples, peels, lemons, sage
2 Meyer lemons, scrubbed
2 tablespoons sugar
1 pound small tart, firm apples (4 to 5)
Leaves from 2 bunches sage
About 4 cups peanut or canola oil for
    deep-frying

batter
1¾ cups all-purpose flour, plus more if needed
¼ cup rice flour
1 teaspoon fine sea salt
1½ cups tonic water, plus more if needed
1 cup white wine
1 large egg

to finish
¾ cup sugar mixed with the grated zest of 1
    lemon

First prepare the lemons: Cut off the ends, slice them ⅛ inch thick, and flip out the seeds with a paring knife. Toss the lemon slices with the sugar in a small bowl and let macerate for about 30 minutes to soften and sweeten.

Meanwhile, peel the apples in a circular fashion, making long looping rings of peel but not worrying about perfection. Slice the apples the width of two stacked nickels, about ⅜ inch thick—I use a mandoline here for uniformity and then cut out the seedy centers with a circular cutter or apple corer (you could even use a sharp knife).

Rinse the sage leaves and blot them dry. Blot the lemon slices on a paper towel.

For the batter, whisk the all-purpose and rice flours and salt in a medium bowl. Pour ¾ cup of the tonic water into a measuring cup, add the white wine, and drop in the egg. Whisk with a fork to combine and then pour all at once over the flour mixture. Mixing with the fork, swiftly work out the big lumps, but don't overmix; fine lumps are okay. Whisk in the remaining ¾ cup tonic water.

Pour 3 inches of peanut oil into a large heavy, high-sided pot and heat over medium until the oil reaches 375°F.

Your frying setup is key. Set a cooling rack on a baking sheet, for draining the fritto misto, with the lemon sugar next to it, for coating, and a paper-lined platter for serving. (Cut Chemex coffee filters make wonderful blotter paper when serving fried food, but paper towels will also work.)

Dunk a couple of test slices into the batter and then into the hot oil. The batter should cling, with the consistency of school glue, the excess dripping off slowly in large drops. Crispness here depends entirely on the consistency of the batter. If it's too thick, the crust will be doughy rather than crisp—you can correct it by adding another tablespoon or two of tonic water. If the batter is too thin, it will recede and not cover the apples, and they'll get greasy—if necessary, sift a tablespoon of all-purpose flour over the batter and mix in with a fork.

Dip an assortment of apples, peels, lemons, and sage into the batter and then into the oil. Not too many at once; you want to give them space to fry, so plan on four or five batches. Fry the fritto misto to a deep brown on both sides, gently flipping the pieces with chopsticks or a fork, then lift them with a metal spider to the cooling rack. Sprinkle immediately with some of the lemon sugar so it clings to the hot surfaces, then transfer the fritto misto to the platter. Serve immediately, while still warm, and continue to fry the rest as the eaters start to eat.

a creative more-time-than-money sort of menu

FOR SIX

— crispy smashed chicken breasts with gin-and-sage jus
— matafans: raised potato and cabbage pancake
— bacon fat–roasted cauliflower with herb salad
— pastis du Quercy

At 4:30 in the afternoon around the time of the winter solstice here in the north, the sun slinks off and the sky turns an eery, deep blue. Within an hour, it will be dense and black, turning the window over my kitchen sink into a mirror. These are the shortest days of the year, but somehow they feel like the longest. The evenings yawn. By Friday night, Aaron and I are popping like popcorn in the pot, anxious for something to happen, and last-minute calls to invite people over are always met with a breathless, "YES!" I can understand why the early pagans celebrated the holiday called Winter Solstice.

The silver lining of these short days is long nights that provide the perfect moody conditions for happy hour. Nothing will knock down an overactive sense of duty quite like a ridiculously early sundown. It's a good reminder to go to someone else's kitchen, with different lighting and different food and different people, to eat chicken in gin-and-sage sauce before going back the way you came, in the dark.

I have to tell you that if you want to serve the pastis du Quercy, you'll have to plan to start it ahead, at least 8 hours, and preferably a full day, ahead. But I promise that rest of the menu takes just 2 hours, from beginning to end.

crispy smashed chicken breasts with gin-and-sage jus

If someone were to stand over a pan of sautéing chicken holding an ice-cold martini and happen to slosh it into the pan, you would have this sauce—basically a liquidy chicken gravy spiked with gin and sage leaves. I'm making it sound sloppy, but in fact there's a lot of craft to it.

You want to cook the garlic-and-sage-marinated chicken on its skin side for what seems an interminably long time, slowly turning the skin into a hard-shell top and dragging out the chicken's juices, which will reduce to a varnish of pure umami on the bottom of the pan. Deglazing that with a bit of chicken stock and gin makes a thin but potent natural jus. But it's the crumbly fried sage leaves that make this dish fit for company. Be prepared to stand stoveside and watch the bottom of the pan with predatory focus, because if you let yourself be called away, the precious browned foundation will burn and the whole sauce will be thrown.

recipe continues

Serves 6

24 sage leaves
3 large skin-on chicken breasts
6 garlic cloves, smashed and peeled
½ teaspoon fine sea salt
½ teaspoon freshly ground black pepper
3 tablespoons olive oil

3 tablespoons butter, cold
¼ cup gin
¾ cup chicken stock, preferably homemade (page 259)
1 to 2 tablespoons fresh lemon juice (to taste)
Lemon wedges for serving

Rinse the sage leaves and dry thoroughly with a towel.

If the chicken breasts have the rib cage attached, remove it—and any other bones—with a sharp knife. Don't trim off any skin or fat. Set each chicken breast skin side down on a cutting board and pound with a large meat mallet to even out the hump, flattening the chicken to an even thickness.

Put the chicken in a bowl and add the garlic cloves, 12 of the sage leaves, the salt, and the pepper. Cover and marinate for at least 1 hour, and up to 6 hours, refrigerated.

Heat the olive oil and 1 tablespoon of butter in a very large stainless steel sauté pan over medium-low heat. When the butter melts, add remaining 12 sage leaves and fry, moving and flipping them gently with a fork, until crisp, about 3 minutes. Remove the crispy sage to a plate.

Turn up the heat slightly and add the chicken, skin side down, to the oil, along with its marinade aromatics. Gently cook the chicken over medium heat, slowly but steadily, taking care not to burn the oil, until the skin crisps and turns a deep caramel color, 25 to 30 minutes. Be prepared to stay stoveside, moving the chicken around in the pan, pressing on it with a spatula to force contact with the pan, and moderating the heat as necessary, until the white sign of doneness creeps two-thirds of the way up the sides of the breasts. As you sauté, remove any garlic cloves that threaten to burn and save them for the sauce.

When the chicken skin has turned dark amber, flip the chicken, lower the heat, and cook gently until the internal temperature reaches 140°F degrees on an instant-read thermometer. The temperature will carry over to a safe but still juicy 150°F while you finish the sauce. Transfer the chicken to a serving platter and add the gin to the pan, off the heat. Return it to the burner and simmer for 30 seconds to burn off the sharpness, then add the chicken stock and cook, scraping at the browned residue on the bottom of the pan to loosen it, until the liquid has reduced by half. (You should have about ½ cup of sauce.) Add the lemon juice, any reserved garlic cloves, and the remaining 2 tablespoons cold butter, remove from the heat, and swirl the pan to emulsify the butter.

Move the chicken breasts to a cutting board and slice crosswise, taking care to cut neatly through the skin, then return to the platter. Pour the sauce around the perimeter of the platter—not over the chicken, which would dampen and soften the crispy skin—and top with the crispy sage leaves. Serve immediately, with a fork for spearing the meat and a serving spoon for the sauce. Garnish with lemon quarters.

matafans: raised potato and cabbage pancake

I found this recipe in Madeleine Kamman's excellent *Savoie* cookbook, but I've taken so many liberties with it—adding cabbage and leeks, and more potato—that the lineage is nearly gone. The core idea remains, though: a delicate raised pancake of cooked potato, cabbage, and leeks that gets an impressive lift from whipped egg whites. Leftover wedges are delicious fried in butter the next day, the fluffy center surrounded by a fragile cage of crisp.

Serves 6 to 8 as a side (or 3 as a main)

1 large russet potato (12 to 14 ounces), peeled
   and cubed

¼ cup hot water

¼ cup cold milk

3 large eggs, separated

½ teaspoon fine sea salt

7 tablespoons all-purpose flour

2 tablespoons butter, melted, plus 2
   tablespoons cold butter

¼ green cabbage, cut into large, irregular
   shapes, including any green outer leaves
   (about 2 cups)

½ large leek, cut into large diamonds,
   including the light green leaves

Put the potatoes in a large pot, cover with water, and bring to a boil. Lightly salt the water, reduce the heat, and simmer until the potatoes are tender, about 15 minutes. Drain the potatoes in a colander and return them to the hot pot over low heat to dry out for a minute.

Lightly mash the potatoes. Measure out 1 lightly packed cup and reserve.

Preheat the oven to 375°F.

Combine the hot water and milk in a liquid measuring cup and then pour into a large bowl. Separate the eggs, putting the whites in another large mixing bowl and add the yolks to the tepid milk mixture. Add the salt and flour to the milk mixture, whisking until it's smooth and no lumps remain. Add the melted butter and mashed potatoes and stir to combine.

Whip the egg whites until soft peaks form. When you lift up the whisk, the egg whites should be shiny and hold a fat peak that droops over at the top. You want to whip them enough for the foam to hold up the pancake but also leave a little lift in them. Immediately fold half of the whites into the potato mixture with a wide rubber spatula, then fold in the rest until no streaks of egg white remain.

Heat 1 tablespoon of the cold butter in a 10-inch cast-iron skillet or carbon-steel frying pan over high heat and add the cabbage and leek. Cook at a driving pace until the vegetables brown on the edges, about 4 minutes. Flip the vegetables over and add the potato mixture to the pan. Shake the pan to even out the mixture and reduce the heat to medium-low.

Tear the remaining tablespoon of butter into small bits and dot them around the edges of the pan. Cook the pancake until the bottom browns and fine bubbles break across the surface, about 20 minutes. As it cooks, slide a thin knife around the edges of the pancake and occasionally lift it to check the bottom for overbrowning. Just watching the edges will be misleading; the edges brown more quickly than the bottom, and you want the bottom to be uniformly acorn brown.

When it's there, pop the pan into the hot oven to briefly set the top of the pancake, about 5 minutes.

Remove the pan from the oven and invert a large shallow plate over the top. Holding the pan with two pot holders, with your thumbs on the plate, quickly turn the pancake upside down onto the plate. Set the pan back over the heat, slide the pancake back into the pan, and cook briefly on the

recipe continues

other side, about 3 minutes. Invert the pancake again to present it show side up, and serve immediately, on a platter or back in the pan, cut into wedges.

Alternatively, you can make the pancake up to an hour ahead of time and reheat in a bit of butter in the hot pan. What the made-ahead pancake loses in loftiness, it gains in extra-crisp edges.

bacon fat–roasted cauliflower with herb salad

When roasting cauliflower, or really any vegetable, bacon fat is my lipid of choice (although substituting coconut oil will make this vegetarian). Bacon fat has a high smoke point, never tastes burnt, and frizzles the ragged cauliflower edges into smoky vegetable candy. After moving the roasted cauliflower to a platter, I take a cereal spoon to the crumbs left behind on the pan to rescue the treasure trove of blackened cauliflower bits from the oily corners. Airy and junky, they're like the marshmallows in a bowl of Lucky Charms. Cook's treat.

Moisture is the enemy of roasted vegetables, so I mop off any residual water from rinsing the cauliflower with a clean towel, and let it air-dry for a while. Preheating the baking sheet helps too, and will put a jump on the browning. When the cauliflower hits the pan, it should sizzle instantly—a happy sound to hear when roasting any vegetable.

Serves 6 to 8 as a side

1 large cauliflower (about 2 pounds)
2 shallots, halved and cut into thick arcs
6 tablespoons bacon fat or coconut oil
½ teaspoon fine sea salt

herb salad
Leaves from 1 bunch parsley
¼ cup sliced fresh chives or thinly sliced
    scallion greens
½ teaspoon freshly ground black pepper
Grated zest of ½ lemon
2 tablespoons fresh lemon juice
1 tablespoon extra-virgin olive oil

Throw a heavy baking sheet into the oven to preheat and preheat the oven to 425°F.

Rinse the cauliflower, pat dry, and break it into florets. Cut the large ones into ½-inch-thick slabs, and the smaller florets into bite-sized pieces. Transfer the cauliflower to a bowl and add the shallots.

Warm the bacon fat to a liquid state, pour half of it over the cauliflower, and season with the salt.

Pour the rest of the bacon fat onto the preheated baking sheet, then dump out the cauliflower, spacing out the pieces to give them room to roast rather than steam. Roast the cauliflower until dark and appealing, browned at the edges, and tender but not mushy at the center, 20 to 25 minutes. Midway through, take the pan out of the oven to flip the cauliflower and move the more rapidly darkening outliers at the edges to the center.

Meanwhile, combine the parsley and chives in a small bowl. Season with the pepper and toss with the lemon zest, juice, and olive oil.

When the cauliflower is darkened at the edges and tender, pull it from the oven. Scatter the dressed herbs over the cauliflower and quickly toss with a pair of tongs to lightly wilt the herbs. Transfer to a shallow bowl and serve hot or tepid; both are good.

pastis du Quercy

Pastis du Quercy is like an Austrian apple strudel crossed with the French need to push everything to lighter, crispier, boozier heights, even further beyond the reach of mere mortals. After I made this cake for the first time, it became my obsession. My calling. I got into it the way other people get into transcendental meditation. The day of the first snowfall, the only thing I wanted to do was put off everything and just pull strudel dough. For no occasion at all but to help me ease into winter.

You can't rush the "pulling," as the Europeans say. It should take at least 45 minutes, and anything quicker than that won't give a good result. As you walk around the table, reaching beneath the dough and stretching it thinner and thinner, you can feel the dough tensing up at first and then slowly releasing.

The old adage about pulling the dough until it's thin enough to read a newspaper through isn't quite right. You need to keep going until it begins to feel like newspaper itself, lightweight and easily torn. You need to stretch the dough so thin that a palm reader could read your future through it.

recipe continues

There's no question, this is a hard recipe. I give it a ten for difficulty. The only way to realistically serve it for a party is to make the dough the night before and clear an hour-wide-hole in your morning schedule. Also, you'll need space to pull it. A large countertop island is ideal, but a dining room table (covered with a sheet if you don't want to fling flour all over) will also work.*

Makes one tall 9-inch cake, rich enough to serve 10

2¾ cups (400 g) all-purpose flour
¾ cup (100 g) bread flour
½ teaspoon fine sea salt
½ cup plus 1 tablespoon canola oil
2 large egg yolks
1 cup plus 2 tablespoons warm water
1 pound tart apples (2 large or 3 small)
3 tablespoons kirsch (cherry brandy)

2 tablespoons dark rum
⅔ cup plus 3 tablespoons sugar, plus another
⅓ cup or so for finishing
12 tablespoons (1½ sticks) unsalted butter, plus
softened butter for the pie plate
Vanilla ice cream or Sour Cream Whip (page
189) for serving

Combine the all-purpose and bread flours; the mixture should weigh exactly 500 grams (or 17½ ounces)—favor weight over cup measures, and adjust as needed. Transfer the flour mixture to the bowl of a stand mixer fitted with the paddle attachment and add the salt. (You can also make this by hand in a wide mixing bowl.)

Pour the oil into a large measuring cup or a bowl, add the yolks and the warm water, and whisk with a fork to combine. Paddling the flour at medium speed, add the liquid mixture in a steady stream. The dough should form a single soft clump around the paddle. If it doesn't, add another tablespoon of water to pull in all of the flour, making a soft, but not wet, dough. Mix for another 2 minutes to develop the gluten.

Transfer the dough to the countertop and knead by hand for 2 minutes. Cover loosely with plastic wrap and let rest for 3 to 5 minutes to hydrate the flour, then knead until the dough is pliant, smooth, and silky to the touch, another 3 minutes or so.

Wrap the dough in plastic wrap and let rest for at least 3 hours at room temperature, and up to 2 days in the refrigerator. If it has been refrigerated, give the dough 2 hours to come to room temperature.

Peel and quarter the apples and remove the cores. Slice each quarter crosswise twice or three times to make 1-inch fat chunks. Toss the apples with the kirsch, rum, and 3 tablespoons of the sugar in a bowl, and set aside.

To clarify the butter, heat it in a sauté pan over medium heat until it foams and turns golden and crusty at the edges. Let settle a minute, then tilt the pan and spoon the crusty foam into one bowl and the clear golden butter into another, taking care not to include the milky residue at the bottom. Reserve the browned milk solids for another use (you can fold them into scrambled eggs, among other things).

Preheat the oven to 350°F. Rub a 9- or 10-inch glass pie plate thickly with soft butter.

Sprinkle a very large work surface (see headnote) with flour, spreading it evenly over the surface. If

*I spent a lot of time developing this recipe, researching strudel flours from Austria, testing and cross-checking against recipes from pastry chefs I used to work with, and what I learned, in a nutshell, is that many strudel recipes written for the American market have lost something in the translation. The flour is different. The wheat is different. You can't make the dough with bread flour—it's much too tightly wound. A dough made entirely with all-purpose flour is too soft, not resilient enough to withstand the stretching. Austrians use a dedicated "strudel flour," a finely ground white flour with a bit more of that high-protein spring to it, which makes sense. I've found that a ratio of five parts all-purpose flour to one part bread flour is the ticket, giving the dough a gentle strength. For the best result, the flour for this recipe should be weighed, and since I began with European recipes, I've kept the metric units of measure.

you're wearing sharp rings or bracelets, take them off now, as they'll rip the fragile dough. The entire stretching operation will take at least 20 minutes and shouldn't be rushed. It's awfully nice to have two people stretching, each pulling from opposite ends, but I usually do it solo, walking around my kitchen island.

Unwrap the dough and pat it into a rectangle. With a rolling pin, roll it to a rectangle about the size of a 13 × 17-inch baking sheet, throwing flour underneath the dough to prevent sticking as you go. Now begin to pull the dough from the center, reaching underneath and stretching it over the back of your hands. Tug at the edges with your fingertips to thin them, then stretch again from the center, traveling around the table and sending air beneath the dough as if it were a tarp, and pitching more flour beneath it. The dough will feel muscular, and you'll be pulling gently to break up its thick knots. After you've pulled it to the size of a large suitcase, let it rest for a few minutes to relax it. Then continue stretching the dough to about a 6 × 4-foot rectangle, until it's thin enough that you can see the veins in your hands through it. If you tear the dough, pull both sides of the dough over the tear and then roll over it with your pin to get it to hang together, or just ignore it and keep going. You can patch big gaps later, and tiny tears won't matter.

Trim off the thick cords at the edges of the dough with a knife and set aside. (You can sprinkle these with sugar, coil up, and bake into a special treat.) Then trim the thin dough to roughly 6 feet by 4 feet—harvesting some of the extra-thin pieces to lay over any holes and saving the rest for the topping. Don't worry if this takes so long that parts of the dough look to be drying out; the dried parts will be extra-crispy.

Warm the clarified butter to a liquid but cool state. Drizzle it in long thin lines over the dough, reserving 2 to 3 tablespoons for the topping. No need to brush the butter: the dough is too fragile. Sprinkle the remaining ⅔ cup sugar evenly over the dough.

Drain the apples, reserving the juice. Lay down half of the apples in a single row near the bottom long side of the rectangle, spacing them out at roughly 3-inch intervals. Fold the bottom edge of the dough up over the apples to cover them, and then, using a bench scraper or metal spatula, flop the roll over twice to make a fat, bumpy rope. Resist the urge to roll it tightly or neatly, as the air trapped inside will keep the pastry delicate. Lay down the second row of apples, staggering them with the first row. Then continue rolling the dough, flopping it over itself, all the way to the top. If the dough is papery and the apples break through in spots, don't worry; by the end, they'll be covered. Beginning at one end, coil the pastry loosely into a spiral.

Gently lift the pastry into the buttered pie plate. Sprinkle the reserved thin scraps of dough with some butter and sugar and arrange in abstract waves on top of the pastry. Distribute the remaining clarified butter, and another couple of tablespoons of sugar, across the top of the cake.

Bake for 1 hour and 10 to 15 minutes, until the internal temperature measures 200°F on an instant-read thermometer and the entire surface of the pastry has turned deep amber brown. It might look done after 1 hour, but baking it to a full 200°F will fully firm the moist interior and ensure separation between the layers. Bring the reserved apple liquid to a simmer for a minute, or less, as long as it takes to become a light syrup.

Remove the pastry from the oven and pour the reserved apple liquid over it. After a minute or two, run an offset metal spatula around the perimeter of the pastis, and beneath it, to loosen the caramel. Let it sit for a few minutes, twisting the pan occasionally to keep the pastry from sticking to it. As soon as the pastis is cool enough to touch, transfer it—lifting it with two metal spatulas—to a cake platter.

Serve tepid or at room temperature, cut into wedges, with a poof of Sour Cream Whip or a ball of vanilla ice cream—hard to say which is better.

recipe continues

NOTE

If you'd like to make this in advance, you can bake the pastis until nearly done and then freeze it. Pull the cake from the oven after 1 hour, when the internal temperature is 185 to 190°F and cool completely. Wrap tightly in plastic wrap, then foil, and freeze. (I haven't frozen it any longer than a week, but a month or two shouldn't hurt. I'm curious, so if you try it, let me know.) To serve, thaw the cake at room temperature for an hour or so and then bake at 325°F until the internal temperature reaches 200°F and the surface is dark golden brown, about 30 minutes.

Kicking off a meal with a complicated starter when dessert is something as heroic as the Pastis du Quercy might look like overachieving. That said, people sitting at my counter having a drink and keeping me company deserve to be given a few flavors and something to do with their hands while they wait. Cheese, cured meats, pickles and nuts easily fill the void. Here's my shortlist of trusted appetizer hustles.

Arrange these snacks on platters or boards and in small bowls that hug them tight. A cup of toasted snack nuts sitting in the bottom of an oversized bowl looks lonely and picked over, but the same amount piled into teacup-sized pottery looks adorable.

Toasted nuts. Almonds, cashews, or pecans, seasoned and tossed in a little olive oil, baked until they darken one shade and the oil clings to their skins, and served warm from the oven. You can add minced fresh rosemary or anise seeds or cayenne pepper or cinnamon (or all of these together). But plain dry-roasted hazelnuts, skins rubbed off and piled in a small bowl, are my favorites, especially if the nuts are fresh and sweet. (Better if they're really fresh, sold in bulk, preferably from a refrigerated case.)

Pickles. Pickled green beans, asparagus, dilled cucumber pickles, fermented pickles, carrots, and/ or beets, served crowded into small dishes.

Whipped plain cheese with something poured on top of it. Throw goat cheese and cream cheese in nearly equal amounts (I like more goat cheese) into a food processor along with a tiny lump of butter and a scrap of salt. Process until smooth and then spoon onto a decorative plate, smoothing it into a dome-like shape before making a well in the center. Top with some kind of fancy condiment from your pantry: spicy honey mixed with toasted walnuts, or good chutney. In the fall, you can fill the center with a pool of fresh Concord grape

juice, reduced to a syrup, or imported saba, or cherry tomatoes roasted in lots of olive oil, garlic, and herbs—or my favorite solution: sage leaves slowly sautéed in a bath of butter and olive oil until crisp. Spoon the warm, brittle sage leaves, butter and all, over the cheese.

See also: a lump of blue cheese (that almost overripe chunk of Gorgonzola will be perfect) pureed with an equal amount of cream cheese and a dollop of butter to mellow it out.

Warm squash-mascarpone puree with crisp sage, spooned onto hot toast. Whip a cup or two of leftover baked buttercup squash (or sweet potato) with a large spoonful of mascarpone or cream cheese or ricotta until perfectly smooth. Warm it up with a lump of butter, season to taste, pour into a shallow bowl, and top with the above-mentioned crisped sage leaves. Set it next to a pile of grilled bread, and the suggestion to use it as a spread will be obvious.

Warm bean dip. Fry some cubed bacon or chorizo in a frying pan, and then add some onions, diced poblano peppers if you're feeling ambitious, and sliced garlic cloves. When the vegetables turn soft and sweet, add a cup or two of leftover cooked beans. Mash roughly, until the beans start to form a puree. Season with salt and smoked paprika, ground cumin or coriander, or ground chipotle as needed. Transfer to a baking dish, dot the top with butter, and bake in a hot oven until bubbling at the edges, about 30 minutes. Crumble some queso fresco on top and serve with tortilla chips and sliced radishes.

Giant grilled cheese sandwich. Set 2 large, relatively thick pieces of country bread on your board and swipe one with some kind of hot chile sauce (harissa or a bit of Sriracha) and the other with a soft cheese, like goat cheese. Top the goat cheese with slices of aged cheddar and alpine cheese, like Gouda. (Some require one slice of American cheese to hold the sandwich together, and I don't disagree.) Slather both sides of the bread with butter and fry the sandwich slowly, until the bread turns completely crisp and the cheese melts through the holes. Rub the surface of the sandwich with a cut garlic clove, toss it onto the cutting board, and cut it into 1-inch squares, like you would for a toddler. Adults, of course, love this.

Olives. A variety of green and purple olives of various sizes is nice, served mixed on a shallow bread plate without too much pooling brine and your tiniest cup for the pits. No need to coat them in olive oil unless you're doing marinated olives— but that's another dish and it requires a serving spoon. If you're going to be finger-picking, a rubbery surface is better than an oily one.

Potato chips. Your favorite variety (mine: thick salt-and-pepper kettle chips) with a sidecar of plain sour cream.

Creamed feta with curried dried fruit. Dice a large handful of dried fruit—apricots, figs, dates, currants, raisins, sour cherries, whatever—and marinate in a lot of extra-virgin olive oil, fresh lemon juice, salt, some cracked black pepper, a dimespot of honey, and a half-teaspoon or so of good curry powder, all to taste; set aside to soften. Sometimes I splash some sherry into this.

Break half of a standard 4-inch block of feta roughly (into both chunks and crumbles) into a bowl. Pour in some heavy cream—2 to 3 tablespoons—and stir once or twice to coat. Pour the creamy broken feta onto a platter and top with the curried fruit and a decorative drizzle of olive oil. Serve with crackers or bread.

Cucumbers, radishes, and fresh cabbage. At the height of the growing season, quarter fresh pickling-sized cucumbers and bright red radishes and pile into a shallow bowl that holds them snugly.

Cheeses. There's little to do here but serve these at the correct temperature. Most cheeses should be served at cool room temperature, so take them out of the refrigerator about 30 minutes before. Small disks of cheese with washed or bloomy rinds, as

well as wedges of firmer cave-aged cheese, have a pretty natural shape, so you can just set them onto the cheese board and serve each one with its appropriate knife—a wide spreader for soft cheeses, a short sharp knife for the firm. Dry-aged cheeses like Parmigiano-Reggiano, Manchego, and Mahon are usually served in rough clods; an oyster knife is the perfect tool for these. If serving ordinary rectangular blocks of grocery store cheese, it will look better if you cut it into perfectly square overlapping slices to, you know, make the most of its blocky industrial shape. Grocery store cheddar is also best served cold, in my opinion.

Charcuterie (prosciutto, speck, or cotto ham) or salumi, sliced. If the salumi comes covered in a tight, bloomy rind, I like to remove it. Wet the salumi briefly to dampen the rind, and it will peel right off. I often pre-slice the first half before putting it on a cutting board, because it seems to disappear faster that way, but it's up to you.

Toasted baguette slices on the side. Slice the bread on the bias into thirds or fourths, and then again lengthwise, and toast them on a hot grill, if you have one ready, or in the toaster. Rub a cut garlic clove across the surface of the bread and brush with a mixture of melted butter and olive oil.

Garlic-rye crisps. You can make these with any moist sort of rye bread, but it's a good use for those small, rectangular pre-sliced pumpernickel cocktail loaves. If using a larger loaf, thinly slice, about ¼ inch thick, the same as a slice of cocktail loaf pumpernickel. Heat a bunch of smashed garlic cloves in what seems like an overgenerous amount of neutral oil (substituting some bacon fat here would be correct) until the garlic browns lightly. Discard the garlic, pour the oil over the rye bread in a bowl, and toss together with salt and pepper to taste. Spread out on a baking sheet and bake in a 325°F oven until the bread crisps and browns at the edges. Very finely chop another few garlic cloves, along with some chopped chives or parsley, if you have it, and throw that mixture onto the hot croutons when they come out of the oven. Toss and serve. Beware: these are dinner-spoilers.

all-you-can-eat fish fry

FOR SIX TO EIGHT

— deep-fried sour cream walleye
— iceberg plate salad with green chile dressing
— steamed and glazed white sweet potatoes
— garlic and coconut–scented rice
— Pavlova with winter citrus, good olive oil, and sea salt

Deep-frying fish in the middle of the winter will make your house smell like a muggy, beloved Midwestern roadside tavern that never closes. But, oh, that helps create the *thee-ah-tre* of the Friday-night fish fry. Those in the know wear wool rather than cotton to this party. One cold night spent on the porch will air a wool shirt right out.

Most of this menu can be made during the quiet hours before the party. The individual Pavlovas can be prepared a full day in advance and the orange topping a few hours before. On the day of the party, you can make the green chile dressing, portion the fish, and prep the fish-breading station well ahead of time, then make the rice and the sweet potatoes an hour before serving. Wait to fry the fish until all guests are present and the collective hunger is fully stoked.

deep-fried sour cream walleye

As a rule, I side with the underdogs of the lake—northern pike, eelpout, and smelt—but I can see why walleye is considered the king of fish here in the north. A 2-pound walleye stretched out in my sink corner-to-corner is positively regal. Pointed sharply at both ends, mouth and tail, its skin glows like real silver against the dull stainless steel.

As all northerners know, winter is walleye's downfall—and our windfall. They drop their guard during ice-fishing season, and taste better then too. After a few months of swimming in dark, icy waters, the walleye have put on a layer of insulating fat. The normally lean, athletic fish look pearly under the lights. I'm sure it's quite embarrassing for them, but who are we to judge, walking around in heavy wool sweaters to cover up our cheese addictions?

recipe continues

This crumb coating takes its inspiration from cold-weather layering: first a thin wicking coat of flour, then a dip into sour cream–thickened egg, and then a roll in a mixture of fine and coarse seasoned bread crumbs. The breading is as light as fleece but impermeable. It doesn't crack until you break a fish fillet in half to reveal its juicy white interior.

It's very difficult to remove the pin bones from a walleye fillet with a set of tweezers, as you do with salmon, because the lean, delicate flesh tears easily. Instead, slice out the bones by running your knife narrowly along both sides of the center bone line, which will leave two long flaps of boneless fish joined only at the top three inches or so. Separate these sections, then cut each long boneless fillet into two or three 4-inch-long fish fingers. I'd much rather serve a parade of hot four-bite pieces of fish than a single curling fillet.

Serve the fish hot from the frying oil, in batches, with extra bowls of green chile dressing (which you've made for the salad; page 86) for dipping.

Fresh walleye or freshwater finfish will taste much better than fish that's been previously frozen and thawed. The best walleye in this area, and maybe anywhere, comes from Red Lake Nation Fishery, line-caught by members of the Red Lake Band of Ojibwe. When they ship whole fish from that morning's catch, they're fresh—sometimes alarmingly fresh. *Miigwetch.*

It's nice to have a deep-fry/candy thermometer for this recipe.

Serves 6 to 8 in generous portions

2 pounds skinless walleye or freshwater fish
    fillets
1 cup all-purpose flour
½ teaspoon plus ¾ teaspoon fine sea salt, plus
    more for lightly seasoning the fish
3 large eggs
⅔ cup sour cream
1½ cups panko bread crumbs
1½ cups plain dried bread crumbs

1½ teaspoons garlic powder
1½ teaspoons paprika
Two or three shakes of cayenne pepper
Grated zest of 1 lemon
Lots of freshly ground black pepper
At least 4 cups peanut or canola oil for
    deep-frying
Green Chile Dressing (page 86) for serving

Rinse the fish fillets and pat dry. Remove the skin if necessary: Pitch your knife at a 45-degree angle at the tail end of each fillet, shoving your blade between the skin and the flesh, and grip the tip of the tail with a towel. Swoop your knife underneath the flesh, shimmying the tail back and forth to help it along, and cut off the skin in one fell swoop.

Run your fingers along each fillet to feel for the center bone line, and slice along either side of it to free and remove it. Halve the fillets lengthwise, then slice each piece in half or into thirds, to make fairly equal 4-inch-long pieces. Lay out the fish on a baking sheet and refrigerate if not cooking right away.

For the breading, set up three bowls: Mix together the flour and ½ teaspoon of the salt in the first; the eggs and sour cream in the second; and the panko, dried bread crumbs, ¾ teaspoon of salt, the garlic powder, paprika, cayenne, and lemon zest in the third. Grind some black pepper into both the flour and the bread crumb mixtures and stir to mix.

When ready to fry the fish, pour 5 inches of oil into a heavy high-sided pot, such as a medium enameled cast-iron saucepot. Strap a deep-fry/candy thermometer to the interior wall and heat over medium heat until the oil reaches 375°F.

Meanwhile, set up a draining station by placing a metal rack on a baking sheet. To bread the fish, work in batches. Season the fish fingers with salt and pepper on both sides and drop piece by piece into the flour. Shake off the excess flour and drag the fish through the egg mixture, holding each one up to

allow the excess to drip off, then drop into the bread crumb bowl and shake the bowl to coat. Reach under each piece of fish to flip it, press a handful of crumbs on top, and move the fish to a large plate.

When the oil reaches 375°F, fry the fish, 4 or 5 pieces at a time, until deeply golden brown. Scoop out the fish with a metal spider and set on the rack to drain. When all the fish has been fried, transfer to a serving platter and serve with small dipping cups of green chile dressing on the side.

iceberg plate salad with green chile dressing

Equally welcome at both garage parties and gilded steakhouses, iceberg is refreshing, and cool to the touch, even in the summer. But I like it better in winter, when the firm, ridged surfaces resemble compressed snow—thick and molded and, yes, close to tasteless. You could say it's bland—that's true—or that it's a willing subject for our creativity. Strong, thick, aggressive dressings that overwhelm leaf lettuce find their match in crunchy iceberg.

Its best asset is its tight, closed-up fist shape. A head of iceberg cannot, and should not, be washed— or spun, or air-dried. It will never ask you to do anything that resembles doing the laundry, ever. Just remove the wilty outside layers and give the head a quick rinse. In the grocery store, check for coppering at the root, a sign of age, but otherwise, just toss it into the cart without thinking about it for another second.

I call this a "finger salad," one meant to be picked from the plate, which works well for iceberg, because it gets soggy if dressed before serving. Assemble it on a shallow salad plates or in pasta bowls, in an abstract pattern: on one side, lay down a wide puddle of green chile dressing, then fill the other side with arcs of pale iceberg, a few coins of radish, and a fantail of sliced kohlrabi. At the table, just pick up the vegetables with your fingers and swab them through the dip.

Serves 6 to 8 (with extra dressing for serving with the fish)

green chile dressing

4 to 5 Anaheim chiles or similarly semi-hot
　　Italian frying peppers (6 ounces)
3 tablespoons extra-virgin olive oil
1 teaspoon fine sea salt, plus more for
　　seasoning the peppers
2 large garlic cloves
2 cups roughly chopped fresh cilantro,
　　including tender stems
¾ cup lightly packed fresh basil leaves
¾ teaspoon sugar
¾ cup sour cream

¾ cup full-fat yogurt
3 tablespoons fresh lemon juice
1½ teaspoons apple cider vinegar or wine
　　vinegar, or to taste
Cayenne pepper (optional)

salad

1 large head iceberg lettuce, cut into 6 to 8
　　wedges
1 bunch radishes, thinly sliced
1 large kohlrabi, peeled, halved, and thinly
　　sliced

For the dressing, rinse the peppers, blot them dry, and halve them lengthwise. Heat a large frying pan over medium heat and add the olive oil. Add the peppers cut side down and season with a little salt. When they sizzle, add a dribble of water, cover the pan, lower the heat, and let the peppers steam-cook until tender when prodded with a fork, about 5 minutes.

Transfer the peppers to a blender and add the garlic, cilantro, basil, sugar, the 1 teaspoon salt, the sour cream, yogurt, lemon juice, and vinegar. Puree until smooth. Taste for seasoning and adjust as needed, adding a bit of cayenne if the peppers fail to bring the heat. The dressing should be cool and hot and floral all at once.

Spoon a generous puddle of dressing into the middle of each salad plate and drop a wedge of iceberg to one side of it. Prop slices of radish and kohlrabi in between the lettuce and plates and serve immediately. (Reserve the remaining dressing to serve with the fish.)

steamed and glazed white sweet potatoes

I learned to steam sweet potatoes years ago from a friend, a big-hearted strictly devout vegan. After we'd eaten dinner, he stood devotional watch at the stove over a bamboo basket full of cylinders of sweet potato. Then, uncorking the steamer, he gently transferred the sweet potatoes to plates, garnished each one with a rolling bead of tamari, and served them for dessert. They were plenty sweet, and the texture was pure velvet.

I've been an advocate for steaming sweet potatoes ever since. Where roasting concentrates their sugars and shrivels their edges, steaming opens up their pores—which is particularly nice if you want to eventually gloss them with a little spiced coconut glaze. The glaze comes together quickly from a base of browned butter and caramelized ketchup. I'm not a huge fan of the red stuff, but reducing ketchup with brown butter rids it of its industrial tang and fully redeems it.

I like to use white sweet potatoes, sometimes called Jersey sweet potatoes, for steaming because they're denser and smoother and not as up-front-sugary as the orange kind. They're less competitive with the fish.

To make this ahead, steam the sweet potatoes, transfer them to a baking dish, nap with the glaze, lightly cover, and store at room temperature for up to 3 hours. Finish them in the oven right before serving.

Serves 6 to 8 as a side

3 pounds white (Jersey) sweet potatoes (about 4 large)

½ teaspoon fine sea salt, plus more for seasoning the sweet potatoes

5 tablespoons butter

2 heaping tablespoons ketchup

2 teaspoons paprika

½ teaspoon cayenne pepper

¼ teaspoon ground cumin

Pinch of ground cinnamon

⅓ cup coconut milk

2 tablespoons maple syrup

Peel the sweet potatoes and cut crosswise into 1½-inch-thick cylinders. Season on both sides with a light sprinkling of salt and arrange them in a single layer in a bamboo steamer—this will take two levels—and set the steamer over a wok filled with a few inches of water. Bring the water to a boil over high heat, cover, and steam until the sweet potatoes are very tender when tested with the tip of a knife, 15 to 20 minutes.

Meanwhile, preheat the oven to 425°F.

Heat a small saucepan over medium heat and add the butter. Cook until it foams and starts to brown, then add the ketchup and cook, stirring, until it thickens and caramelizes, about 2 minutes. Immediately add the spices and the ½ teaspoon salt and stir to bloom the spices in the fat. Whisk in the coconut milk and maple syrup and simmer until the glaze thickens slightly, just about a minute. Remove from the heat.

Arrange the sweet potatoes in a single snug layer in a large oval baking dish. Nap with the glaze and pop into the oven. Roast until the sweet potatoes begin to darken at the edges, about 10 minutes. Remove from the oven and repaint with the glaze that has pooled in the corners of the dish, then return to the oven to roast until deeply caramelized, another 10 minutes. Serve warm, straight from the dish.

garlic and coconut–scented rice

I love the way that garlic sidles up to coconut when trapped in the steamy rice pot. Ginger with coconut is out with me now; garlic is in.

Use your heaviest saucepot for cooking the rice, preferably one wider than it is tall. The larger the surface area of the rice, the better it turns out (see page 50 for more on jasmine rice).

Makes about 8 cups, serving 8 to 10

3 cups jasmine rice
2 tablespoons butter
3 garlic cloves, smashed and peeled

1 cup coconut milk
½ teaspoon fine sea salt

Put the rice in a fine-mesh sieve and run it under cold water, scrubbing it with your hands until the water runs perfectly clear; set aside to drain.

Heat the butter in a 3- or 4-quart saucepan, or a short stockpot, and add the garlic cloves. Cook the garlic until it turns lightly golden, about 2 minutes, then add the rice, coconut milk, 3½ cups water, and the salt and shake to level the rice. (If your pan is narrow and tall, you may need slightly less water. The water should rise to ⅝ inch above the rice.) Bring the water to a simmer and clamp on a tight-fitting lid, reduce the heat to low, and cook slowly for about 20 minutes, checking the progress during the last 5 minutes.

When the rice is tender, let it sit off the heat, covered, for 10 minutes to fully hydrate. Fluff with a fork and serve, or keep warm until ready to serve.

Pavlova with winter citrus, good olive oil, and salt

I have a soft spot for Pavlova, especially when topped with softly whipped cream and a drooping mess of tart syrupy fruit that rivers down to the flaking meringue. The difference between baked meringue and Pavlova is slight but key. A baked meringue is a light, crisp shell, whereas a Pavlova has more weight to it; its middle has a more forgiving roasted-marshmallow chew. Even though fruit-topped Pavlovas contain an official boatload of sugar, they never feel heavy, even after a big dinner. Here that collection of oranges, tangerines, and limes that have been slouching on the counter all week will be just fine when macerated with a fresh vanilla bean* and garnished with a few loops of fruity green olive oil and some coarse salt.

White sugar has become so unfashionable that I've taken a renewed, perverse pleasure in it. Its trademark lack of flavor never competes with the subtle fragrance of seasonal fruit. Its glittery surface also reminds me of the disciple-like relationship that many of us had with sugar in childhood, back when if we asked for juice, our mothers stirred up a batch of Kool-Aid—when we still had that kind of faith. In stars, or sparkles, or whatever else—this was the honeymoon phase of our sugar addictions. In any case, I know that a Pavlova temporarily restores it.

And if you're looking for things to knock out early in the day, you can make the Pavlova shells up to 12 hours in advance, and the citrus fruits and their syrup 2 or 3 hours ahead.

Makes 8 individual Pavlovas

Pavlova shells
½ cup egg whites (about 4 large)
¼ teaspoon cream of tartar
¼ teaspoon fine sea salt
1¼ cups sugar
1 tablespoon cornstarch
2 teaspoons apple cider vinegar
1 teaspoon pure vanilla extract
⅛ teaspoon lemon extract
3 drops extract or other flavoring of your choice: almond or vanilla extract, rosewater, orange blossom water, etc.

citrus in vanilla syrup
6 oranges (preferably a mixture of Cara Cara, Valencia, and tangerines)
2 limes
1 vanilla bean
2 tablespoons dark rum
½ cup sugar
2 tablespoons fresh lemon juice

Whipped Cream (page 281)
2 to 3 tablespoons best-quality extra-virgin olive oil
Fancy coarse sea salt for garnish

For the Pavlova shells, preheat the oven to 250°F.

Combine the egg whites, cream of tartar, and salt in the bowl of a stand mixer fitted with the whisk attachment. Measure 1 cup of the sugar into a bowl and reserve. Whisk together the remaining ¼ cup sugar and the cornstarch in a small bowl and set aside.

Whip the egg whites at medium speed until they're white and fluffy and hold medium peaks—past soft-peak, but before firm-peak—and then begin adding the reserved 1 cup sugar: Gradually add the

---

*If you're like me and tend to miser your precious vanilla beans so long that they become too stiff to slit open, just blitz them in the microwave—in 5-second intervals—to plump them back up.

sugar, ¼ cup at a time, over the course of 5 minutes. Sprinkle in the the sugar-cornstarch mixture, and then the vinegar and extracts, and continue to whip until the meringue is stiff and glossy, another 3 minutes or so.

Line a baking sheet with parchment paper and secure the paper to the pan by dabbing a bit of meringue underneath the corners.

Dollop the meringue into 8 individual poofs, going for height over width, and then make a deep divot in the center of each. Bake for about 45 minutes, or until the shells are firm and pale and opaque and the surface cracks when pressed in the middle. The interiors should appear opaque but remain a bit chewy at the center. Remove the Pavlovas from the oven and let cool.

Meanwhile, to make the macerated citrus, lop the tops and bottoms off all the citrus fruits so they sit up securely on the cutting board. With a sharp knife, shear off the peel and white pith, curving your knife from top to bottom as you work around the fruit. Trim off any lingering white pith. Working over a fine-mesh sieve set over a mixing bowl, cut the oranges and limes into segments: Slip your knife down either side of the thin membranes, cutting in a V-shape to free the citrus segments, and drop them into the sieve. Transfer the orange and lime segments to a bowl. Squeeze the juice from the citrus carcasses into the sieve and then measure ½ cup of collected juices; save the rest for another use.

Put the sugar in a small bowl. Slit the vanilla bean down the center, scrape out the seeds with the point of a paring knife and rub them into the sugar, then toss in the spent pod as well.

Combine the vanilla sugar, the juice, and the rum in a small saucepan and bring to a simmer over medium-high heat. Simmer until the bubbles grow large and a drop or two of cooled syrup feels sticky when pinched between your fingers, about 2 minutes, then add the lemon juice. The syrup should taste bright and frankly acidic, but not unbalanced. Chill the syrup over ice or in the refrigerator until cool, and then pour the cooled syrup over the citrus segments. Macerate for at least 30 minutes, but no longer than 2 hours.

Fill each Pavlova with a generous cloud of whipped cream and top them with the macerated citrus, letting the syrup drip down the sides. Garnish each one with a generous swirl of olive oil and a heavy sprinkle of coarse sea salt.

a Nordic backcountry ski supper

FOR SIX TO EIGHT

— sardines with lardo and Parmesan on bran crispbread
— yellow split pea soup with spareribs
— warm wilted spinach with caramelized celery root and crispy shiitakes
— coffee with Chartreuse and smoked almond praline

In winter here, the hibernation is real. The constant stream of summer company dries up. Time hangs in the blank white page between the snow and the sky. Sometimes in late winter, after months of eating bread and cheese, I'll notice that my appetite starts to drag. I wake up one day to a blunted hunger and feel sick at the thought of eggs for breakfast, my usual ride. It will be disorienting, in a jet-lag kind of way, and mildly worrying. Hunger is normal; deadened instincts are not.

That's when I know I've been hanging out too long in the cave and it's time to invite some friends over for cross-country skiing and soup. We strap on our skis and follow Aaron on his daily route, our skis cutting well-defined tracks in the powdered-sugar snow. Out on the frozen creek, my nose hardens in the wind and picks up no scent at all. The air is thin, like another atmosphere. It smells like rock-cold well water tastes—sharp, minerally, hygenic.

But as we ski through the woods, awkwardly herringboning up the hills and barreling down them, my body heats up, and something flips. Now anything warm enough to live in this tundra takes on a new intensity, as if drawn up through a funnel. The balsam branches underneath my skis smell like rosemary crushed in my palm. The smoke from our wood stove, chugging out two miles away, is strong. The cold heightens our faculties so much that I can empathize with dogs, both gifted and cursed with sensitivity.

As I come into the creaky porch from the outside, cracking my skis against each other to shake off the sticky snow, shucking my wet clothes in the doorway of the humid house, my freshly dilated senses are overwhelmed by the pot of soup simmering on the stove. The scent of long-simmered pork under a blanket of split peas fills the house with its thick, muggy perfume, and suddenly we're all very, very hungry.

Knowing how skiing can rile up the appetite, this menu is engineered to be ready to go. The soup is done, the sardine appetizer just needs assembly, and the chocolate sauce for the dessert was made two days ago, freeing me now to focus solely on making the warm, earthy platter of wilted spinach, caramelized celery root, and crispy shiitakes.

sardines with lardo and Parmesan on bran crispbread

Very rarely do I plate individual canapés (miniature morsels give me bad catering flashbacks), but I make an exception for this sardine-lardo-Parmesan appetizer carefully assembled on shattered puzzle pieces of bran crispbread.

For this, you'll need a tin of top-flight plump, silver-skinned sardines. Pink and meaty, they find their deadly delicious match in cured pork lardo, especially when bridged with curls of Parmesan cheese.

Smash the bran crispbreads with the butt of your knife into a bunch of jagged, irregular pieces. Then build these bites slowly—a shard of Parmesan followed by a petal of lardo, a sardine, some olive oil, and a few bright pinches of Aleppo pepper.

recipe continues

Serves 6 to 8 (or more) as an appetizer

Two 4-ounce jars or tins whole sardines packed in extra-virgin olive oil

2 large Bran Crispbreads (homemade, recipe follows, or substitute store-bought Wasa or large round Finn Crisp)

A 2-ounce chunk of aged Parmesan

3 ounces lardo, very cold (just omit if it can't be sourced)

Aleppo pepper or smoked paprika for garnish

Extra-virgin olive oil for drizzling

Pull the sardines carefully from their oil and lay on a plate. Pinch each one gently at the fattest part to split it into 2 fillets. Pluck out and discard the spines, and lay the sardines on a plate, skin side up.

Lay the crispbreads on a serving board and crack them with the blunt end of a knife to break into approximately 2 × 2-inch abstract shards. Shave the Parmesan into thin curls with a vegetable peeler and lay one on each cracker. With a sharp knife, shave off thin pieces of lardo, and drape over the Parmesan, then top each one with a broken chunk of sardine. Arrange the canapés on a platter, dust with Aleppo pepper, drizzle with olive oil, and set within reach of people.

bran crispbread This recipe for Norwegian bran flatbrød, or crispbread, comes from my friend Bruce Engebretsen, whose Auntie Sarah made it once a week. He remembers breaking off shards of it from her bottomless kitchen-table basket during coffee breaks on the farm, to use as—in his words—"a vehicle for butter."

Bruce is an EMT by day and a master hand weaver by vocation. He's the kind of friend who calls at 7 o'clock in the morning because he just came across a fascinating 100-year-old recipe for pickled beef hearts that I might want. I treasure him. When he's not weaving or spinning, he's rescuing old recipes and hand tools from near extinction. If there was ever a more difficult way to do something, Bruce knows about it, and can pinpoint the exact place where domestic skills and scarcity came together to make something slightly more delicious or more beautiful than we usually see today. "I worry sometimes that the next generation is romanticizing hardship," he says as he sweeps excess flour off my countertop with a giant bird feather. The rich history of deprivation and the creative recipes it produced is one of our favorite topics, but I can't resist teasing him about the bird feather. "So practical!"

The Scandinavian docked rolling pin Bruce uses to roll out the crispbreads is essential, though. The knobby surface imprints the dough in alternating thick-and-thin intervals, preserving both its strength (so it can be transferred to a baking sheet) and its lightweight delicacy. You can use a regular rolling pin and dock the dough with a meat mallet—or, if you're desperate, a Lego.

Makes 6 large crispbreads
(more than you need for this recipe, but they keep for weeks in an airtight tin)

8 tablespoons (1 stick) butter, softened
½ cup hot water (boiled, not hot from the tap, and slightly cooled)
½ cup buttermilk or runny whole-milk yogurt

½ teaspoon baking soda
3 tablespoons sugar
1 teaspoon fine sea salt
2 cups all-purpose flour, plus more as needed
2 cups wheat bran

Put the butter in a large bowl and pour the hot water over it. Whisk in the buttermilk, baking soda, sugar, and salt.

Mix the flour and wheat bran together in another bowl and then add to the buttermilk mixture, stirring with a wooden spoon until it comes together into a soft, collected lump. If the dough feels too loose, add a bit more flour.

Knead the dough lightly—not so much as to develop the gluten, just enough to form it into a ball. Transfer to a bowl, cover tightly, and refrigerate for at least 2 hours, and as long as overnight.

Preheat the oven to 325°F. Have two large baking sheets at hand.

Divide the dough into 6 equal pieces. Dust the countertop lightly with flour. Pat the first lump of dough into a disk and rub the top with flour. Using a docked (or smooth; see headnote) rolling pin, roll the dough with a light touch, lifting and rotating as you go to make sure it clears the countertop, until it reaches the size of a large modern dinner plate.

Flop the dough in half, swiftly transfer it to one of the baking sheets, and unfold it. Bake the crispbread for 10 to 12 minutes, flipping it over once, until the edges just threaten to brown. The surface should look dry but will remain pale; these crispbreads aren't so much baked as dried. Transfer the baked crispbread to a rack to cool and repeat with the remaining balls of dough.

When all of the crispbreads have been baked, turn off the oven, spread the crispbreads across the two baking sheets, and put them back in the oven with the door propped open to let steam escape for about an hour, until crisp and brittle.

Cool the flatbreads completely and store them in a dry tin or a cake carrier, where they will keep for a very long time.

yellow split pea soup with spareribs

Scandinavian split pea soup is more often made with yellow peas than green, and I'm pretty sure the affection for them is partly visual. Their tender straw color is more appetizing than the usual combat-fatigue green. But the eye can be very convincing, and when it tells me that yellow split peas taste spicier and feel less floury in the mouth, I believe it. To capitalize on this, I add a pinch of curry powder—not enough to steer the soup anywhere geographically, but just enough to haunt the background.

Either kind of split peas should be cooked nearly forever, until they disintegrate completely and lose their famously gritty texture. If you simmer pea soup long enough, it will eventually give up and turn glossy and sleek.

After a lifelong reflexive habit of throwing smoked ham hocks into pea soup, I've converted to the Nordic way and now believe wholeheartedly in the use of fresh spareribs. Unlike the sharp tang of smoked pork, the fresh doesn't compete with the earthiness of the peas.

Makes approximately 10 cups, serving 6 to 8

2½ pounds pork spareribs

½ teaspoon plus 1½ teaspoons plus 1 teaspoon fine sea salt

Freshly ground black pepper

1 pound (2 cups) yellow split peas, rinsed

Water to cover

1 head garlic

3 bay leaves

2 to 3 dried red Chinese chiles

2 tablespoons extra-virgin olive oil

1 tablespoon butter

2 cups diced sweet onion

1½ cups diced carrots

1 cup diced turnip

¾ cup diced celery

1½ teaspoons curry powder

Rinse the spareribs, pat dry, and season with ½ teaspoon of the salt and a few turns of freshly ground black pepper.

Combine the ribs and peas in a big stockpot and add water (about 11 to 12 cups) to cover by 2 to 3 inches. Bring to a simmer, standing by to catch the rising foam. Skim off all of the foam and discard it.

Meanwhile, trim the head of garlic, scrape the dried root end to remove any grit, and slice about ¼ inch from the top to expose the cloves. Add the garlic to the pot, along with the bay leaves, dried chiles, and 1½ teaspoons salt (enough to lightly season the broth). Cover the pot with an offset lid and simmer the soup slowly until the rib meat is nearly falling off the bone and the peas have disintegrated into a slurry, about 2 hours. Remove from the heat. (*At this point, you can either finish the soup or let it cool, cover it, and refrigerate until tomorrow before proceeding.*)

Pluck out the spareribs, and when they're cool enough to handle, pick the meat from the bones, discarding fat and gristle. Dice or crush the meat into bite-sized pieces. Run a slotted spoon across the bottom of the soup pot to make sure you haven't left any small bones behind.

Combine the olive oil, butter, and onions in a wide sauté pan and heat over medium heat until it gradually comes to a sizzle. (Heating the cooking fat and onions together gradually keeps the onions from browning too quickly.) Continue to cook until the onions turn translucent and start to soften, 5 to 10 minutes. Add the diced carrots, turnips, and celery and season with the remaining 1 teaspoon salt. Raise the heat a bit and sauté the vegetables, stirring often, until their edges soften and take on some golden color and they taste sweet, about 15 minutes.

Add the vegetables and all of their cooking juices to the cooked pea soup base. Add the curry powder and diced pork, bring the soup back to a simmer, and simmer for 10 minutes. Adjust for seasoning and add water if needed to thin to a pourable consistency. Serve steaming hot, no garnish.

warm wilted spinach with caramelized celery root and crispy shiitakes

This warm platter salad is best served mid-wilt, the spinach hanging in suspense between upright and collapsed, the smoky bacon dressing pooling in the crevices. The bacon fat lends a lot of flavor to the cubes of celery root and the crispy mushrooms that sauté in its smoky wake, but you can replace it with coconut oil to make this dish vegetarian.

I'm always glad when I can create a recipe that puts celery root in a lead role, because it's the produce aisle's shrinking violet. It is in fact a shy, mild vegetable, with the soft flavor of celery and the textural meatiness of a beet. Caramelizing celeriac slowly in bacon fat helps it find its voice.

Knobby and rough, and sometimes even still dirty from the ground, celery root should be pared with a paring knife, not a peeler.

recipe continues

Serves 6 to 8

12 lightly packed cups young spinach (about 11 ounces)

1 large knob celeriac, cut into large dice (1½ cups)

4 slices thick-cut bacon (or 2 tablespoons coconut oil)

6 tablespoons butter

¼ teaspoon fine sea salt, plus more for the vegetables

2 teaspoons sugar

5 ounces shiitake mushrooms, thinly sliced

½ teaspoon freshly ground black pepper, plus more to taste

2 tablespoons water

¼ cup apple cider vinegar or mild wine vinegar, plus more to taste

Thoroughly wash and spin the spinach; set aside to air-dry.

Bring a small saucepan of water to the boil and season it heavily with salt. Add the celery root cubes and simmer until the tip of a knife slips into the celery root with no resistance, about 10 minutes. Drain the celeriac in a colander, shaking it to remove excess water, and set aside.

Slice each strip of the bacon lengthwise in half, and then crosswise into ½-inch pieces. Heat a large sauté pan—large enough to later accommodate the celeriac—over medium-low heat and add the bacon. Cook, stirring, until the bacon turns bronze at the edges but is not yet crisp. Remove the bacon with a slotted spoon, leaving its fat behind, and deposit it in a large salad bowl for serving.

Add 3 tablespoons of the butter to the pan (plus the 2 tablespoons coconut oil if you skipped the bacon) and then add the celeriac cubes. Sprinkle them evenly with salt and sauté over medium heat until the celeriac turns brown at the edges and is tender within, about 10 minutes. During the last 2 minutes, sprinkle the celeriac with 1 teaspoon of the sugar to boost the caramelization. The bottom of the pan will brown, but take care not to burn it, because that's the flavor foundation for your vinaigrette.

Remove from the heat, remove the celeriac from the pan with a slotted spoon, and drop into the salad bowl. Add the remaining 3 tablespoons butter to the pan (the celery root will have absorbed most of the first addition) and then add the mushrooms. Sauté them over medium-high heat until the liquid they release evaporates. Season with salt and some freshly ground pepper and continue sautéing until the mushrooms become light and crispy, another 3 to 4 minutes. Transfer the mushrooms to the bowl with the celery root and bacon.

Set the pan over medium heat, immediately add the water and vinegar to deglaze the pan bottom, and bring to a simmer. Add the ¼ teaspoon salt, the ½ teaspoon pepper, and the remaining teaspoon of sugar and scrape the bottom of the pan with a wooden spoon to release the flavor skirting the bottom. Taste the sauce for balance. The vinegar should match the fat just enough for the sauce to teeter between sweet and savory.

Add half of the spinach to the pan, season lightly with salt, briefly roll it in the hot dressing until its stems begin to bend, and then lift it with a pair of tongs onto the celeriac, bacon, and mushrooms. Add the rest of the uncooked spinach to the bowl, and scrape the pan with a rubber spatula so you can pour out every last bit of hot vinaigrette over the greens. Toss well to coat, and taste for seasoning, adding salt and/or a dribble of vinegar if needed.

Using the tongs, lift the greens to a platter, then top with the celery root, mushrooms, and bacon lingering at the bottom of the bowl. Although this salad tastes liveliest if served within a few minutes, it does have a relatively long hang-time.

coffee with Chartreuse and smoked almond praline

Is serving coffee at the conclusion of dinner a stroke of class or a hint to leave? I lean toward thinking coffee is a buzzkill, maybe because the orders around my table usually call for decaf, but I can get behind a sweet chocolate-and-booze-spiked coffee dessert like this one.

A post-ski drink should be strong, so I spike mine with Chartreuse, a potent French herbal liqueur, but skip the candy shenanigans.

There are two kinds of Chartreuse, both of which have been made by Carthusian monks in the Chartreuse Mountains since the eighteenth century. Green Chartreuse is high octane and ridiculously expensive. Yellow Chartreuse is sweeter and more affordable. Both are made from a proprietary mix of wild herbs and roots foraged from the subalpine forest and, like any secret recipe, both taste rare and mysterious. Feel free to substitute your preferred liquor—bourbon is never a bad idea—or to skip the alcohol altogether.

The smoked almond praline and chocolate syrup are useful base recipes. The chocolate syrup keeps for months in the refrigerator. Store it on the door, where it can be easily found when someone wants to make a glass of chocolate milk.

Just once, make the almond praline with Barsy's almonds, which come by their subtle smoke honestly, over a bed of hickory wood. But even a packet of liquid-smoked almonds bought at the gas station will make good almond praline.

for each drink
¾ cup hot strong black coffee (pour-over or French-press)
3 tablespoons Chocolate Syrup (recipe follows)
1 ounce (2 tablespoons) Chartreuse

3 tablespoons Whipped Cream (page 281) for garnish
2 teaspoons finely chopped Smoked Almond Praline (recipe follows) for garnish

Brew a pot of black coffee, at extra strength, or prepare shots of espresso for each drink. Fill each mug with ¾ cup hot black coffee. Then add the chocolate syrup and Chartreuse and stir to mix. Garnish each mug with a generous lid of whipped cream and a heavy dusting of chopped almond praline.

---

chocolate syrup You can make the syrup ahead of time; it keeps well in the fridge for months.

Makes 3½ cups

1½ cups water
⅓ cup Lyle's Golden syrup or light corn syrup
1½ cups sugar

½ cup Dutch-process cocoa
1 teaspoon fine sea salt
6 ounces semisweet chocolate, finely chopped

Combine the water, corn syrup, sugar, cocoa, and salt in a saucepan and bring to a simmer over medium heat. Cook gently, whisking, until the sugar crystals dissolve, about 2 minutes. Remove from the heat, add the chopped chocolate, and let stand for 3 minutes to melt.

Starting from the center, gently whisk the mixture in a whirlpool motion to incorporate the chocolate and then stir until completely smooth. Let the syrup cool, then pour it into a clean class jar. Keep it at room temperature for a few hours, until needed, or cap tightly and refrigerate for up to 3 months. The syrup will thicken slightly when cold, but it should remain pourable.

recipe continues

smoked almond praline

Makes about ½ cup

3 tablespoons sugar   ½ cup smoked almonds
½ teaspoon butter

Prepare a nonstick surface for the caramelized nuts to land on—i.e., a silicone baking mat or an oil-rubbed baking sheet.

Heat a small frying pan over medium heat. Sprinkle the sugar across its surface and shake the pan to even it out. Cook undisturbed until the sugar melts and progresses from clear to light brown to dark walnut. Add the butter and toss in the almonds. Stir in just a few quick strokes to coat the nuts with caramel and immediately pour the caramelized almonds onto the waiting liner or baking sheet. With a silicone spatula, corral any leftover caramel in the pan onto the almonds, and spread them out to cool for at least 30 minutes. Don't touch them until cool, or the caramel will stick to your fingers and burn.

Transfer the almond brittle to your cutting board and finely chop, leaving a few pieces the size of corn kernels but reducing most of it to smaller particles. Store the smoked almond brittle in a covered container at room temperature for up to a week (the praline will seize into a sticky clump if refrigerated).

pent-up winter grilling

FOR SIX TO EIGHT

— deviled egg dip
— Bundt pan chicken with bagna cauda butter
— Fun House baked potatoes
— sweet-and-sour marinated peppers with Swiss chard
— sopped greens with butter-roasted walnuts (page 43)

Outsiders marvel that we northerners grill outside all year round, but they don't quite understand how grueling a six-month winter can be. By March, the sun is higher in the sky, and less aggressive; it no longer ricochets off the snow to shoot you straight in the eyes. Those piles of snow lining our paths have been part of the yard since December, and they're aging. If I squint, they look like beaches, slowly receding. When you start to see mirages in the snow and feel emotionally attached to them, you know that winter has gotten to you. Six months would be way too long to go without cooking over live fire.

The general consensus that summer is the best season for grilling stands on the same reasoning that eating a spicy bowl of chile-spiked soup on a sweltering day will bring you some relief. Sure, spicy food makes you sweat, and in theory, when the wind hits, it will cool you off. But it's a penitent comfort, and pretty meager given that what you really want, what your hot rising soul craves, is a bowl of cold, calming cucumber yogurt soup, a couch in a dark room, and a fan.

Winter grilling spares you this indignity. A true northerner will always say that warming up is easier than cooling off. Standing out in the Arctic wind in front of the grill in the middle of winter doesn't make you warm per se. But if you have the boots for it, and the chops, you will stay perfectly comfortable by rotisserie-ing yourself in front of the fire, first the back, then the front, turning yourself like a chicken.

deviled egg dip

If you're the sort of person whose inner child sucks the yellow part out of the deviled eggs and the white cream from the oreos, licking the chocolate shells clean, I think you'll forge a real pact with this dip.

Discovering that I could poach the eggs instead of hard-boiling them the usual way, since they'd be pureed anyway, made this dip 200 percent easier. But if hard-boiling is your habit, go ahead and follow your favorite method for just-cooked boiled eggs with flaky, powdery yolks. (I prefer a cold start, adding the eggs to a pot, covering them with cold water, and bringing to a high simmer for 2 minutes before steeping them off heat, covered, for 12 minutes.)

Serve with bread or crackers (or Bran Crispbread, page 94) or thinly sliced radishes, carrots, and kohlrabi for dipping.

recipe continues

Serves 6 to 8

8 large eggs

1 teaspoon white vinegar (rice, wine, or distilled)

5 tablespoons mayonnaise

2 tablespoons fresh lemon juice

1 tablespoon Dijon mustard

1 tablespoon Worcestershire sauce

½ teaspoon fine sea salt

1 tablespoon salt-packed capers, soaked in cold water and drained

Aleppo pepper or paprika for garnish

Extra-virgin olive oil for garnish

Partly fill a deep wide-bottomed saucepan with cold water and bring to a boil. Add the vinegar and a pinch of salt and, one by one, crack the eggs into the simmering water. Gently troll the bottom of the pan with a spoon to make sure the eggs don't stick, and cook just until the yolks feel hard to the touch, 5 to 6 minutes. Remove the eggs with a slotted spoon and drain them on a paper towel–lined plate.

Drop 2 whole poached eggs into the bowl of a food processor. Pop out the rest of the yolks and add them to the processor as well. Finely chop 2 of the egg whites for garnish; reserve the rest for another use. (I'm sorry I couldn't incorporate the extra whites into the recipe; I hope you'll find a use for them.)

Process the whole eggs and yolks to a fine fluff. Add the mayonnaise and process again until smooth, stopping once to scrape down the sides of the bowl. Add the lemon juice, mustard, Worcestershire, salt, and pepper and pulse to combine. Don't overmix, or the mixture will become tough—you want it to be soft and luscious.

Spoon the deviled egg dip onto a platter. Chop the capers, and sprinkle across the top. Scatter the reserved chopped egg whites over the dip and garnish with a few strong shakes of Aleppo pepper or paprika and a thin swirl of extra-virgin olive oil.

Bundt pan chicken with bagna cauda butter

I was slow to embrace the beer-can chicken phenomenon. I couldn't see how a steaming can of Budweiser would add much flavor, but clearly I was thinking too literally. The magic doesn't come from the beer, but from the positioning. A chicken sitting on its haunches will cook more evenly than one that's lying on its back on the grill. The squatting posture brings the dark meat (which takes longer to cook) closer to the heat and pitches the white meat (which cooks more quickly) farther away from it.

A few years ago, I started roasting chickens on the grill in a ceramic Bundt pan that I'd received as a wedding gift but never used. The genius of the Bundt pan is that its well, or its moat, will catch and hold all the chicken juices. And you can toss all of your aromatics into it to flavor your bird, and your eventual sauce. Because I love a melting, buttery anchovy sauce with chicken, I add the components of a warm Italian bagna cauda dip to the pan. By the time the chicken skin burnishes and the meat feels tender, the garlic, lemon halves, and anchovies will have sunk in their salty, sour, fishy teeth.

The added wood chips give the chicken a subtle smokiness, but they're just for flavor. We want a roast chicken with just a hint of smoke, not a preserved smoked chicken; roast this chicken in any large charcoal grill. If using a gas-fired grill, add the wood chips to the smoke box or a foil pouch.

The chicken will need to be salted and refrigerated at least 4 hours in advance, preferably the night before.

recipe continues

Serves 6 to 8

One 4- to 5-pound chicken
¾ teaspoon fine sea salt
½ teaspoon freshly ground black pepper, plus
  more for the chicken
1 Meyer lemon, scrubbed and cut in half
¼ cup extra-virgin olive oil
10 fresh sage leaves
2 bay leaves

1 head garlic, separated into cloves, not peeled
5 anchovy fillets, rinsed in warm water
⅓ cup white wine
3 tablespoons butter
¼ cup milk

1 cup apple or maple wood chips

Wash the chicken in a large bowl of water and pat dry with paper towels. With a sharp paring knife, cut off its little tail, so that it will be able to sit up straighter. Rub the salt and some freshly ground pepper into its skin and into the cavity and set on a rack on a baking sheet. Put it in the refrigerator, uncovered, to dry out in the fan wind. The smoke will cling better to a dry-skinned chicken.

When ready to cook the chicken, prepare a hot fire in your grill. Put the wood chips in a bowl, drizzle a little water over them, and toss with your hands to moisten; set aside. Once the grill is hot, rake the hot coals to one side (to make a hot spot and a cooler spot) and then bring the heat down to an even 325°F by covering the grill and cutting off the oxygen.

Rub the halved lemon all over the chicken and swab with half of the olive oil. Toss the lemon halves, sage, garlic cloves, and 2 of the anchovies into the well of the Bundt pan, and then sit the chicken on the center pivot, haunches down, breasts up. Dribble the white wine into the well and add the butter.

Set the pan on the grill grates, over the hot part of the fire, and close the lid. Cook the chicken for 30 minutes, then baste it with the juices from the well, and toss on half of the damp wood chips (see headnote if using a gas grill).

Maintaining a temperature between 300 and 325°F, cook the chicken for another 30 minutes. Baste it again and add the remaining wood chips. (More is not more when it comes to wood chips in this case; adding too many too late in the game will make the sauce taste too smoky.) Continue to cook until the skin is burnished, the wings feel loose in their sockets, and an instant-read thermometer inserted into the thickest part of a thigh reads 160°F. A 4½-pound chicken will need to grill/smoke for a total of approximately 1½ hours, a 5-pounder up to 2 hours.

Transfer the chicken to a platter to rest and tip the sauce from the Bundt pan into a saucepan. Remove the sage and discard. Fish out the garlic and squeeze the cloves from their papery skin into the sauce. Add the remaining 3 anchovies and mash against the bottom of the pan with a wooden spoon. Squeeze the juice from the hot lemons into the sauce (discard their carcasses) and add the ½ teaspoon pepper. Add the milk, bring the sauce to a rolling simmer for 1 minute, and remove from the heat. Add the remaining olive oil and stir the sauce together, but don't try to emulsify it until smooth; I think the sauce tastes better when rustic and broken. Taste the sauce for seasoning and add lemon and salt as needed.

Cut the dark-meat chicken into pieces for serving and transfer to a platter: 2 drumsticks, 2 thighs, 2 wings. Cut away the breast meat from either side of the breastbone and slice fairly thin. Flip the chicken over and gouge out the sweet nuggets of dark meat (the "oysters") from the pocket where the thigh meets the back and add them to the platter.

Pour some of the bagna cauda sauce over the sliced meat and the rest onto the platter and serve.

Fun House baked potatoes

My mom, Karen, tells me that this recipe was inspired by watching the ladies in her hometown cook at the Pierz Fun House, a social club used for weddings and other public functions. They would make these potatoes by the hundreds: halved russet potatoes, sandwiched with butter and onions and bay leaves, smashed back together, and baked in foil. When you unwrapped your potato, the onion would lie pallid in the middle, and the butter would pool in the foil.

Smartly, my mom pivoted to baking each potato half open-face, so that the onions crisped into dark toupees on top. She also scored the potato flesh deeply before baking, so that the butter knew where it was supposed to go: down the cracks to the bottom skin. After an hour or so in the oven, the skin bakes to a dark brown callus. When I was a kid, I'd capsize my potato boat so that the soft cubes of potato fell out and I could fold the shatteringly crisp bottom around a piece of meat, like a taco.

Yellow or red (or even purple) potatoes, not russets, are best for this recipe.

Serves 6 to 8

1½ pounds yellow potatoes (about 5 large), scrubbed and halved
¼ teaspoon fine sea salt, plus more to taste
Freshly ground black pepper
8 tablespoons (1 stick) butter, softened

1 garlic clove, grated
½ teaspoon paprika
¼ teaspoon smoked paprika, plus more for garnish
1 small sweet onion

Preheat the oven to 350°F.

Hold each potato half in your palm and crosshatch the flesh deeply with a sharp knife, cutting about halfway through the potato, then set cut side up in a 9 × 13-inch baking dish. If the potatoes wobble, shear a thin layer from their bottoms so they sit upright. Season the potatoes with the salt and pepper to taste, rubbing it into the cuts.

Mash the butter with the garlic, paprika, and smoked paprika in a small bowl and divide it in half. Divide half of the compound butter evenly among the potatoes, smashing it into the potatoes. Cover the pan tightly with aluminum foil and bake until the potatoes are just tender when poked with a knife, 30 to 40 minutes, depending on the size of the potatoes.

Uncover the baking dish and raise the temperature to 450°F. Slice the onion lengthwise into thin arcs, and season with salt. Divide the remaining compound butter among the potatoes and top each with fantailed slices of onion. Roast the potatoes, uncovered, until the edges darken and crisp and the onions toast at their thinnest points, about 25 minutes.

Garnish with a sprinkle of smoked paprika shot across the surface of the potatoes and serve hot or warm, right from the dish.

sweet-and-sour marinated peppers with Swiss chard

If you can find an assortment of sweet and semi-hot peppers in a bunch of different colors, this dish will be a stunner. The glowing technicolor tangle of peppers, sweet onions, and curling greens cooked in their own juices is nudged right to the sweet-sour edge with a few drops of honey, vinegar, and extra-virgin olive oil.

Conveniently, this dish tastes best when tepid. Cook it on the early side, turn it out onto a wide platter, push it across the counter to look pretty and settle into itself, and cross it off the list.

Serves 6 to 8 as a side

¼ cup extra-virgin olive oil
1 pound mixed sweet frying peppers
¼ teaspoon plus ½ teaspoon fine sea salt
1 large sweet onion, halved lengthwise and cut into fairly thin arcs
1 tablespoon butter
Freshly ground black pepper
1 heaping teaspoon minced fresh rosemary

1 large bunch Swiss chard (about 10 jumbo leaves, stripped from the stems)
1 teaspoon honey
1 tablespoon red wine vinegar
¼ teaspoon hot pepper flakes, or to taste
1 tablespoon fresh lemon juice
⅓ cup fresh basil leaves, torn if large

Heat 2 tablespoons of the olive oil in a large (12-inch) stainless steel or cast-iron skillet over medium heat. Add the peppers, season with ¼ teaspoon of the salt, and fry, flipping them with a pair of tongs, until beginning to brown on both sides, about 5 minutes. Cover the pan tightly, reduce the heat to medium-low, and cook, checking often, until the peppers have browned on all sides and gone slack, about 20 minutes. Remove the pan from the heat and transfer the peppers to a bowl.

Return the pan to medium-high heat and add the onion, butter, the remaining ½ teaspoon salt, and a few turns of ground black pepper. Fry the onion until the tips start to brown deeply, then reduce the heat to medium and cook until lightly caramelized, about 15 minutes.

Add the rosemary and Swiss chard to the pan and cook briefly, just until the greens wilt. Return the peppers to the pan and add the honey, red wine vinegar, hot pepper flakes, lemon juice, and the remaining 2 tablespoons olive oil. Reduce the heat to medium-low and cook, uncovered, for a minute or two to meld the flavors, turning the peppers and greens over in the sauce with a pair of tongs. Add the basil, then turn out onto a shallow dish or platter and serve—warm, tepid, or at room temperature.

Holiday

tables of eight to twelve

Menus

Thanksgiving

FOR TEN TO TWELVE 118

crab legs with spicy black vinegar
dipping sauce 119
lardo-crisped roasted turkey with
mushroom gravy 124
classic buttery dressing 126
sour orange cranberry jelly 127
spiralized roast potatoes 129
turnip-date gratin 130
baby greens with glassy pecans
and Pecorino 131
buttercup bourbon pie 133

Holiday baking 136

Bohemian poppy seed coffee cake 138
mincemeat baklava 140
sesame pralines 143
olive oil thumbprints with lemon curd 144
lacquered walnuts 145

Thielen family Christmas

FOR TEN 148

pâté grandmère 149
cast-iron garlic shrimp with chorizo and
green olives 152
smoked prime rib with celery-leaf salsa verde 154
aligot (stretchy mashed potatoes with cheese) 156
creamed poblano spinach 158
caramelized carrots 159
watercress and Bibb with smoky
blue cheese dressing 161

Spangler family Christmas Eve

FOR EIGHT 162

baked spiced quince with soft cheese 164
sylta 165
spiced meatballs with cream gravy 168
mascarpone whipped potatoes 169
citrusy braised red cabbage 170
crispy curried cauliflower with mustard seeds 173
cranberry cookie tart 174

St. Patrick's day

FOR TEN TO TWELVE 176

green cabbage sipping soup 177
slow-smoked brisket pastrami
with creamy zhug 179
quick-steamed pastrami 182
yuca fries persillade 183
creamed carrot coins 184
marinated roasted beets and grapes with
radicchio and hazelnuts 184
green salad with invisible vinaigrette 187
sticky date olive oil cake 188

Easter feast

FOR EIGHT 190

deviled eggs with Roman Jewish
fried artichokes 190
ham cooked in milk, honey, and sage 193
wok-fried black pepper asparagus 195
creamy baby turnip salad with dill 196
hot water rolls 197
rhubarb-almond envelope tart 199

Fourth of July

FOR EIGHT TO TEN 202

cilantro lime juleps 202
reformed dill dip with iced garden vegetables 204
homeground burgers with hot-and-sauer
pub cheese 207
three-bean salad with salumi, celery hearts,
and smoked provolone 208
milk corn 210
tomato-on-tomato salad 213
rhubarb-raspberry pie 214

In my memories of many a hectic family holiday, the wall-mounted phone starts to jangle just as someone at the card table rakes in a giant pot of poker chips. The crowd around the table boos and hoots in dramatic outrage, and the TV in the living room, which is tuned to the big game, coincidentally bursts into cheers of response. Meanwhile, the cook is on her hands and knees searching the darkest reaches of her lower cupboards for the gravy boat. The roast is ready to come out of the oven any minute now, and her voice is muffled, but it sounds like she's saying, "Who is it?" or maybe, "Where is it?" In any case, she's clearly begging for help. Finally one of us, a giggly kid or a slightly buzzed adult, answers on the eighth ring with one of Grandma's schticks, just as unfunny now as it was in the Eisenhower era: "Grand Central Station, how can I help you?"

That I remember my mom on her hands and knees rather than standing in glory next to her magnificent roast says it all: I didn't understand the work she put into making everyone else's holiday light, fun, and joyous. And to think all she wanted was for someone to pick up the phone.

I think we should promise ourselves that we'll never be too busy cooking the holiday meal to take a phone call or to hop in for a round of poker. That we will get up early in the morning, tie an apron on over our pajamas, and start making the stuffing, giving ourselves that whole morning to enjoy the ritual of cooking the holiday meal. We will be untroubled by what people are going to eat for breakfast, or lunch, because they can make toast or eat jumbo marshmallows for all we care—or better yet, just wait for the grand feast we are so pleasurably pulling together.

Being in closer proximity to the food, we have more snacking privileges. Personally, I like to taste-test a single-serving ramekin of baked stuffing chased with a swallow of cold, black chocolatey coffee for breakfast, followed by a plate of sugared baked pie crust scraps for lunch.

Those are the holy moments, when we're alone in the kitchen in our apron, eating scraps while everyone else is happy and otherwise occupied. The stockpot on the stove is contentedly gurgling away, the pie is in the oven, half of the prep list has already been crossed off, and we're buzzed on coffee and anticipation of the real cooking action that still lies ahead. Cooking for a holiday crew is a swirling, intoxicating, forty-eight-hour sensory experience. At no other time of year do the sweet smells of pie crust and roasted meat drippings crisscross so thickly in the air.

But we can't forget that as camp cooks, we are also chief appointed memory-makers. We make the menu, we are responsible for the future nostalgia. And yet, there's no rule that we stick to the traditional family holiday menu. For Thanksgiving, when I have access to venison, I cook it without guilt. And five years ago, I replaced Great-Aunt Helen's port-walnut Jell-O with a translucent citrusy cranberry gelatin, because the wet walnuts were becoming a polarizing issue.

The truth is that any family recipes from the post–World War II period that embraced cans and boxes are endangered in my kitchen— and, in fact, with my entire generation. What we treasure are the really old family recipes, the ones that are weird enough to spook the next generation—the bloodier and fishier and more primitive, the better. Extra points if one of my relatives actually made it for the holidays, although anything I find is fair game. I'm all for comfort foods, but do we remember the details of those recipes, or just the blurry safe feeling they gave us? I have a hunch that the recipes born out of hardship are the ones that stick through the generations. Chances are, one of these picky young skeptics will take a bite of reconstituted lye-preserved cod, or rich pork liver pâté, and bolt off in disgust— ironically fixing it in their memories forever in vivid, sensory detail. One day they're running fast away from their heritage, and the next, thirty years have passed and they're foisting the same dish off on their own friends and family.

The irony is, it can be hard to know for sure if those "family holiday recipes" are even rooted in truth and tradition. It would be so easy to start a new one and invent a backstory. Someone did, once.

Thanksgiving

FOR TEN TO TWELVE

— crab legs with spicy black vinegar dipping
  sauce
— lardo-crisped roasted turkey with mushroom
  gravy
— classic buttery dressing
— sour orange cranberry jelly
— spiralized roast potatoes
— turnip-date gratin
— baby greens with glassy pecans and Pecorino
— buttercup bourbon pie

In my experience, the pressure to make a flawless, earth-shattering, one-for-the-books Thanksgiving meal rarely comes from others; usually, the call is coming from inside the house. I toggle between embracing traditions and making new ones, but usually find a 14-pound turkey in my sink anyway. It's larger than I need, because to me, Thanksgiving means leftovers, and those hinge on the bird.

Grocery stores hawk piles of affordable brined turkeys, and they're fine, but a farm-raised turkey that has never seen the inside of a freezer is just a phone call away. (Or a short drive away, if I buy one from the Amish.) I could take this fresh bluish-skinned Amish turkey and dunk it in brine myself, but why? A salty dry rub adds just as much flavor.

So let's tie on those aprons and start working backward, starting four days in advance, to give our farm-raised bird time to chill and relax, or our frozen birds a chance to thaw in the refrigerator. Although, if I'm being honest, we should really start in October, when we hang a bundle of sage to dry from a kitchen cupboard knob, thinking about homemade rubbed sage for the Thanksgiving dressing. It dries within a week, and when rubbed between your fingers, the leaves dissolve into a woodsy, lichen-colored dust.

crab legs with spicy black vinegar dipping sauce

For my birthday years ago, we met some friends at a tiny gem of a restaurant in a hip area of Los Angeles, the kind of place you hope to find when traveling. The space was fashionably cramped, and cluttered in a Sunday-at-home sort of way. A rainforest of overexcited houseplants was splayed against the front window in a state of benign neglect. After putting our BYOB wine and beer in the kitchen's produce refrigerator to chill, I understood that whoever ran the kitchen wasn't worried about the plants. They were concentrating on the food. We ordered a blue crab appetizer with a spicy vinegar dipping sauce—rich and sour and jet-black—and I've never forgotten how it sluiced through the sweet crab.

When I got home, I tried using just about everything on my condiment shelf to re create it— dark soy sauce, light soy sauce, balsamic vinegar. Nothing came close until I added Chinese Chinkiang vinegar, which is inky black like balsamic but has none of its residual sweetness.

Crab legs are the triple-dollar splurge I reserve for very special occasions. Pre-cutting the legs with kitchen scissors before steaming means less work for the guests, and ensures that all of the precious crabmeat leaves the shell. When you lift off the top shell, the meat lies pristinely on the bottom one.

Steam the crab legs in a covered large, low-sided pan. When they're ready to serve, set the whole pan on a trivet in the center of the appetizer table. Cover again as needed to keep them warm.

Serves 12 as an appetizer

spicy vinegar dipping sauce
4 garlic cloves, minced
1 teaspoon hot pepper flakes
½ cup water
3 tablespoons black Chinkiang vinegar
3 tablespoons light soy sauce
2 teaspoons mirin
1 teaspoon toasted sesame oil

crab legs
4 to 5 pounds frozen crab legs, thawed in the
    refrigerator overnight
3 thick slices ginger, crushed
8 dried red Chinese chiles

recipe continues

For the dipping sauce, combine the garlic, hot pepper flakes, water, vinegar, soy sauce, and mirin in a small bowl and whisk together with a fork. Float the sesame oil on the top, then pour the sauce into individual dipping cups, as many as you have eaters.

Use a pair of heavy-duty kitchen scissors to cut the crab: Starting at the thicker end, make two lengthwise cuts down each side of the leg—I think of them like pant seams—so that after steaming, you can lift off the tops and serve them on the half-shell.

Lay the crab legs in a large shallow braising pan and add the smashed ginger and chiles. Add enough water to cover the bottom by ½ inch. Bring the water to a simmer, cover the pan tightly, and reduce the heat to medium or medium-low, until a steady rivulet of steam leaks from the pan. Steam for 10 minutes, or just until the crab is hot through and through.

Bring the covered pan to the appetizer table, set out the individual dipping cups, and lift off the lid. Serve with small forks and lots of napkins.

Thanksgiving timeline

If you want to follow this menu as written, realize that it's very turkey-centric. Both the dressing and the gravy call for homemade turkey stock (though you can substitute chicken stock), so you'll have to make that first, preferably a few days in advance. Taking the sides out of the equation for a minute, you will want to tackle three turkey projects before Thanksgiving Day, in this order.

First, make the stock (from the neck and trimmings from the turkey and extra turkey legs) and pick the meat from the bones for the dressing. Second, air-dry the bread for the dressing. Third, salt-rub the turkey.

Here's a more detailed schedule:

Five days before Thanksgiving:
— Thaw the turkey if frozen

One to three days before:
— Cube the bread for the stuffing and leave out to dry
— Make the cranberry jelly
— Make the turkey stock
— Dry-rub the turkey and refrigerate it

The day before:
— Make the pie dough, roll it out and fit it into the pie plate, and refrigerate
— Make the buttercup bourbon pie filling and refrigerate
— Thaw the crab legs, and stir together the black vinegar dipping sauce
— Make the vinaigrette and the pecans for the salad
— Uncover the turkey if necessary to let the skin dry out in the refrigerator

Thanksgiving Day:
— 9:45 a.m. Put the pie together and pop into the oven
— 10:00 a.m. Make the turkey dressing
— 10:30 a.m. Assemble the turnip gratin; set aside
— 11:00 a.m. Shove the lardo under the turkey skin, fill the cavity with the dressing, tie the legs together, and put on a rack set in a roaster
— 11:30 a.m. Start roasting the turkey
— 12:15 p.m. Bake the turnip gratin
— 12:30 p.m. Wash and spin the greens for the salad
— 1:00 p.m. Steam the crab legs and set out for the appetizer
— 2:00 p.m. Make the spiralized potatoes and pop into the oven to roast
— 3:30 to 4:00 p.m. Pull the turkey from the oven, set it aside to rest, and make the gravy

turkey logistics

which one to get

— **A fresh, never-frozen turkey.** In my area, I buy these from specialty grocery stores or butcher shops, or directly from the Amish. A truly fresh farm-raised turkey can sit in the refrigerator (on a rimmed baking sheet; leakage is the worst) for up to 5 days. Keep in mind that you may have to pre-order a fresh turkey. Generally, all-natural or organic turkeys will not be brined, and will need a dry salt rub (see below).

— **A thawed previously-frozen turkey.** In the week leading up to Thanksgiving, you'll find thawed fresh turkeys galore in the meat case. If it's been recently thawed, a fresh turkey can sit in the refrigerator on a baking sheet for 3 or 4 days. Often the turkey will be brined, in which case, you want to skip the salty dry rub. If the turkey has been removed from its original bag, ask about its brining status, and the percentage of salt solution. Brined turkeys usually range from 4- to 9-percent added salt solution; 4-percent is plenty for added moisture, 9-percent is almost as salty as lunch meat.

— **A frozen turkey.** This will likely be the cheapest option, but you'll need a few days to thaw the bird. If it's brined, make sure to note the salt solution percentage, as above, and skip the salty dry rub.

how big?

— If you want to lean conservative and not have leftovers, figure 1 pound of turkey per person. (Because small birds have a lower meat-to-bone ratio, you should think more generously. For example, a 10-pound turkey usually serves 8 people.)

— A ratio of 1½ pounds-per-person is standard. You'll have leftovers, but not much to give away.

— If you only cook turkey once a year and intend to try some new recipes for leftovers, or if you want to send people home with generous stashes, figure on at least 2 pounds per person.

how to thaw

If you buy a frozen turkey, make sure to plan ahead, because these take forever to thaw, and a bird that's still icy at the core won't cook evenly or safely, and will be impossible to stuff. There are two ways to thaw: in the refrigerator or submerged in cold water.

To thaw the turkey in the refrigerator, put it on a large baking sheet to catch the juices and wait: 2 days for a 10- to 12-pound turkey, up to 5 days for a 20-pounder.

But I usually thaw my turkey—and actually, all frozen meats—by submerging the vacuum-sealed or heavily bagged bird in cold water. To do this, you'll need to find a container that's larger than the bird to hold it. Water-bath canners and commercial kitchen storage containers work well, but sometimes a scrubbed clean sink will have to do. Fill the container with cold water and some ice cubes, and submerge the turkey. Turkeys tend to bob, so you'll need to figure out a way to weight it down. Flip the turkey every couple of hours, and add more ice as it melts. A small turkey will thaw in about 6 hours, a large one in 12 or so. With a really large bird, I generally start thawing it in cold water in the afternoon, move it to the refrigerator overnight, and either let it continue to thaw there or finish thawing it in water the next day.

lardo-crisped roasted turkey with mushroom gravy

To make the turkey skin extra feast-worthy, I like to push very thin layers of cured lardo—or, alternatively, seasoned slices of fresh pork fatback—beneath the skin. The pork fat has two important jobs. First, it protects the breast meat from drying out in the tanning bed that is your oven. Theoretically, shoving cold butter under the breast skin should do the same thing, but in real life, the butter melts within the first 20 minutes and runs down between the legs of the turkey. Subdermal fatback, on the other hand, softens but doesn't melt; it self-bastes the turkey for the duration. More important, though, fatback doesn't contain any water, as butter does, which means that the skin will fry in both directions, from the top and the underside, and become as light and flaky as a wafer. Basically, the fatback turns the skin into one giant chicharrón.

You can often buy frozen uncured fatback from pig farmers at the farmers' market, or just buy cured lardo from a butcher shop. If you don't have access to either, substitute bacon fat or even rendered lard or duck fat; any kind of dense animal fat will bring the same magic.

As I see it, there are two keys to the kingdom when it comes to feeling like you've won Thanksgiving: doing your best not to overcook the turkey and making a nice rich, runny gravy. You'll never regret the time you take during the rush of pulling the whole meal together to stand at the stove and carefully scrape up all of the accumulated bits of caramelized meat and juice stuck to the bottom of the roasting pan with your wooden spoon.

Serves 10 to 12

roast turkey

One 12 to 14-pound turkey

1½ tablespoons fine sea salt, plus more for the lardo

1 tablespoon freshly ground black pepper, plus more for the lardo

3 ounces lardo or fatback (see headnote), thinly sliced

Grated zest of 1 lemon

2 tablespoons chopped fresh thyme

8 garlic cloves, grated

2 tablespoons extra-virgin olive oil

Classic Buttery Dressing (page 126)

mushroom gravy

Makes 4 cups

2 tablespoons butter

10 ounces mixed mushrooms (cremini, button, wild, whatever you can swing)

2 garlic cloves, minced

Fine sea salt and freshly ground black pepper

2 teaspoons minced fresh thyme

1 cup dry white wine

Reserved defatted juices from the turkey

5 cups turkey stock or chicken stock, preferably homemade (page 259)

3 to 4 tablespoons dry sherry

2 tablespoons cornstarch, mixed with enough water to make a slurry

One to two days before Thanksgiving, set the turkey in a deep sink and pull the giblets (neck, liver, heart, and gizzard) from the cavity. Rinse it inside and out (remembering where those flying juices go, for sanitizing later), transfer to a baking sheet, and blot dry. Look at the bird. If the neck is long and sticking out, lop it off short. Run your fingers under the skin over the breast to loosen it, and then dig down to loosen the skin over the thighs. Combine the salt and pepper in a dish and sprinkle all over the turkey, rubbing it into the skin, around the joints, and inside the cavity.

Slice the lardo or fatback into thin, wide petals with a sharp knife and put into a bowl. Season it with salt and pepper, then add a pinch each of the lemon zest, thyme, and garlic, along with a little of the olive oil, and mix with your hands. Cover and refrigerate.

Combine the remaining lemon zest, thyme, garlic, and olive oil in a small bowl and rub all over the outside of the turkey. Set the turkey in a roaster or on a baking sheet and refrigerate for at least 10 hours, and as long as 36. If you are refrigerating the turkey more than 12 hours, put it in an oven bag or cover with plastic wrap; uncover for the last 12 hours to let the skin air-dry.

When you're ready to cook the turkey—at least 4½ hours before dinnertime—preheat the oven to 375°F.

Blot the turkey to remove any excess brine. The exposed skin should be nice and air-dried, which will help crisp it in the oven. Push the lardo slices underneath the turkey skin, placing some over the thigh meat and covering the breast meat with a single layer. Bend the wings back at the elbow and tuck them behind the back, then crisscross the legs at the ankles and tie them together with kitchen string. Stuff the cavity of the turkey with most of the dressing—but very loosely, don't pack it in. If the neck skin is intact, stuff some more dressing into the neck cavity, and roll the skin underneath to tuck it in. Set the turkey on a low rack set inside a heavy turkey roaster.

Roast the turkey at 375°F for 45 minutes to jump-start the browning, then brush it with its juices and reduce the heat to 325°F. Baste the turkey every 20 minutes for the first two hours, then stop basting it, to let the skin dry out and crisp up, and continue to roast until an instant-read thermometer inserted into a thigh tests 160 to 165°F, another 1 to 1¾ hours. Total roasting time will be around 4 hours or so, depending on size. (To slow down the turkey, take it out when the thermometer hits 150°F and reduce the oven temperature to 250°F. Then return the turkey to the low oven and let it slowly rise to temperature while everything else comes together.)

Transfer the turkey to a platter to rest for 20 minutes. Strain the pan juices through a sieve into a small bowl; when the fat rises to the surface, skim off the fat with a small ladle and reserve it.

Add a spoonful of turkey fat back to the roasting pan, along with the 2 tablespoons butter, the mushrooms, and garlic. Season the mushrooms with a little salt and pepper and cook over medium-high heat until they brown on the edges, about 5 minutes.

Add the white wine and deglaze the pan, scraping the bottom and edges with a wooden spoon to gather up all caramelized bits. Add the reserved turkey cooking juices, the turkey stock, and a shot or two of sherry. Tip the pooling juices that have accumulated around the resting turkey into the sauce and bring to a simmer. Taste for seasoning and correct the salt as needed.

Stir the cornstarch slurry and dribble half of it into the gravy, whisking to combine. Keep adding rivulets of slurry and whisking until the gravy thickens to a thin, pourable, cream-like consistency. Pour the gravy into a small pitcher or a gravy boat.

Some like to carve the turkey right on its platter as a holiday table centerpiece, but cutting it up in the kitchen is neater and also allows you to moisten the meat with a little gravy.

Remove the string and slice through the skin between the legs and breasts. Open the legs and run your knife around the nuggets of meat in the small of the back, then bend them backward and and pop the joint; cut through it and remove the leg. Divide the legs into thighs and drumsticks by slicing diagonally through the cartilage at the joints. Cut the thighs into thick slices, but leave the drumsticks whole on the platter for visual appeal. (They can be sliced at the table.) Bend back the wings, slice through the joint cartilage to separate them from the bird, and set them on the platter. Remove the crispy turkey skin from the back of the turkey and set aside. Free the breast meat by running your knife along the sides the breastbone and thinly slice it across the grain. Chop the crispy back skin into wide pieces and lay over the meat. Pour a little gravy over the white meat and some more around the perimeter of the dark meat and bring the platter to the table, with a sauce spoon and a meat for.

NOTE

More post-game theory: I've found that leftover turkey keeps best when stored in liquid, where oxygen can't get to it. So I now bury large chunks of leftover white and dark meat in my surplus turkey stock. When I want to make a sandwich, I pull the meat out of the jellied stock, warm it just enough to melt off the stock, and slice away. Sandwiches made with stock-stored meat are much fresher tasting and more luscious.

classic buttery dressing

This recipe is stubbornly old-school, but it's a stickler for the details. The turkey stock is made with turkey thighs, drumsticks, and the neck from the bird. The butter starts in the pan with the onions and celery and emerges celery-flavored. Like my mom, I mix my dressing in a veritable trough, using the strength of both shoulders, yielding enough to cook both inside the bird and in a baking dish on the side.

Turkey dressing should be made with honest-to-goodness bread, a country loaf with a stiff crust and gaping holes in the crumb—basically, any bread that will go stale. It needs that structure. And all the holiday glory will be yours if you toss the bread cubes in butter first before you add the moistening stock, because some of those cubes will rise in peaks to the top as buttery turkey-scented croutons.

Makes enough to serve 10 to 12, with leftovers, but is easily halved

3 loaves ciabatta or country bread (about 14 ounces each)

1 pound fresh loose chorizo or pork sausage

¾ pound (3 sticks) butter (or more, if you like)

3 sweet onions, cut into small dice

7 celery stalks, cut into small dice

1 large leek, including the tender green parts, cut into small dice

1 teaspoon plus 1½ teaspoons fine sea salt, plus to taste

1 teaspoon plus 1 teaspoon freshly ground black pepper

2 tablespoons minced fresh thyme

2 tablespoons rubbed dried sage (see page 119) or 3 tablespoons minced fresh sage

1½ teaspoons freshly grated nutmeg, or 1 teaspoon ground nutmeg

3 to 4 cups Turkey Stock (page 259), or as needed, plus 3 cups roughly diced meat left over from making the stock

Dice the bread into 1-inch cubes, crust included (you should have about 26 cups). Spread it out on three baking sheets and leave to dry for 1 to 2 days at room temperature, until dry to the touch but still pliable at the center. To speed-dry it, bake the bread cubes at 275°F until no longer soft to the touch, 15 to 20 minutes. Place the bread cubes in a large roaster.

Fry the chorizo in a large high-sided sauté pan, stirring occasionally, until browned. Scoop out with a slotted spoon and transfer to a bowl.

Add the butter to the pan, along with the diced onions and celery. Season with 1 teaspoon each of the salt and pepper, and cook over medium heat until the vegetables soften, about 15 minutes. Add the leek and cook until tender, another 10 minutes or so. Add the thyme and sage and remove from the heat.

Pour the vegetables over the bread cubes, scraping the pan to get all of the butter. Add the pork sausage, the turkey meat, the nutmeg, and the remaining 1½ teaspoons salt and 1 teaspoon pepper and toss to combine.

Heat the stock to a liquid state and pour it, cup by cup, onto the dressing, tossing to combine. You want to add enough stock to make a moist, but not wet or sticky, mixture. It's not a contest to see how much stock the bread will absorb; the bread should bounce back like a wet sponge. Handle with a lightness; you don't want to press it down—you want it to be light and crusty when baked. Taste for seasoning and correct as needed.

Stuff some of the dressing into the cavity and neck of the turkey as directed in that recipe (page 125), and transfer the rest to a heavily buttered baking dish. Bake at 375°F until brown, about 45 minutes.

sour orange cranberry jelly

This is a clear cranberry jelly spiked with the liquor of the season—ruby port—and brightened with a medley of citrus juices. You can use any combination of citrus you might have—mandarins, Cara Caras, limes, and/or Meyer lemons—as long as they mix to make a pleasing sweet/tart juice. Ideally, I think, the Thanksgiving cranberry jelly should be firm enough to unmold but start to look a little shaky on its feet after sitting on the table while waiting for the rest of the feast to arrive.

Serves 10 to 12 as a side/condiment

5 cups (20 ounces) fresh or frozen cranberries
3 thick slices ginger
2 cups water
¾ cup ruby port
5 whole cloves

6¾ teaspoons (3 envelopes) unflavored gelatin
¾ cup sugar
½ cup tart citrus juice (a mixture of freshly squeezed mandarins, Cara Cara oranges, limes, and/or lemons)

Combine the cranberries, ginger, water, port, and cloves in a large saucepot and bring to a simmer. Cook gently for 20 minutes, or until the cranberries have burst and released their liquid.

Remove from the heat, crush the cranberries with a potato masher, and then strain through a fine-mesh sieve set over a bowl, shaking the sieve to release the liquid but not pressing on the solids. You should have 2½ cups cranberry juice; if you're short, add water to make 2½ cups.

Pour ½ cup of the cranberry juice into a small bowl and chill until cold. Sprinkle the gelatin across the top of the juice, whisk with a fork to combine, and let sit until it blooms and turns sandy, about 5 minutes.

Pour 1 cup of the juice into a saucepan, add the sugar, and cook over low heat, stirring to dissolve the sugar. Add the gelatin mixture and heat gently until steaming, stirring to dissolve it. Add the remaining cup of cranberry juice, along with the citrus juices, to the pan and whisk to combine.

Prepare a 3- or 4-cup-capacity mold. It can be anything—a bowl with ridges, a small soufflé dish, a small bread pan—but should preferably be deeper than it is wide, so the jelly sits upright after unmolding. Rub the inside of the mold with a thin fingertip coating of neutral oil. Pour in the cranberry mixture and let cool to room temperature, then transfer to the refrigerator and chill until set and firm, at least 4 hours. (*The jelly can be made days in advance and kept refrigerated, tightly covered.*)

To unmold the jelly, pour hot water into a large bowl. Run a thin knife around the perimeter of the jelly and set the mold in the hot water for 30 seconds to loosen it. Invert the mold onto a serving plate, wedging your knife into the space between the jelly and the mold to release the suction. If the jelly doesn't immediately release, warm the mold and try again. Run a clean towel around the plate to mop up any drips, and serve.

spiralized roast potatoes

If you're already ladling gravy over the meat and the dressing, do you really need mashed potatoes too? Wouldn't it be just as nice to set a caramelized coil of potato between your turkey and the jellied cranberry sauce? Maybe just this once.

I made these buttery roast spiralized potatoes after Aaron and I had spent a marathon evening peeling bushels of apples for applesauce—him working the countertop apple corer we'd bought at the farm-and-fleet store, and me stirring the sauce. For dinner, I tossed him some potatoes to roast. After roasting them with butter and herbs, magically, they came out looking like this.

Serves 10 to 12

6 cups water
3 tablespoons sugar
8 tablespoons (1 stick) butter, softened, plus
  more for the baking dish

12 medium yellow potatoes, more or less, to fill
  a 9 × 13-inch baking dish
Fine sea salt and freshly ground black pepper
3 sprigs thyme
1 sprig rosemary

Preheat the oven to 350°F.

Combine the water and sugar in a bowl and whisk until the sugar dissolves, to make a dip for the potatoes to keep them from oxidizing to a gray cast. The light sugar solution will also boost their caramelization when they're in the oven.

Rub a heavy 9 × 13-inch baking dish generously with butter and set aside. Put the potatoes through a hand-cranked apple corer, adjusting the control to make sure that you're not peeling them too deeply or too thinly. Swish each stacked potato coil through the sugar water as you go and transfer to the buttered baking dish, continuing until you have enough potatoes to fit comfortably in a snug but not crowded single layer.

Season the potatoes with an even, generous dusting of salt and pepper and scatter the herbs around them. Pour a very thin layer of sugar water into the bottom of the pan, to create a little steam. Cover tightly with foil and bake until the potatoes test tender when poked with a paring knife, about 30 minutes. Keep an eye on them, because different varieties and sizes of potatoes cook at different rates, and you don't want them to become so tender that they collapse.

Melt the stick of butter. Uncover the baking dish and spoon the melted butter over the potatoes, basting them until every inch is covered. Raise the oven temperature to 375°F and roast the potatoes until caramelized at the edges, basting once more with the butter, about 25 minutes.

Serve warm, directly from the dish.

turnip-date gratin

This buttery gratin of turnips, layered with cream and a few torn Medjool dates, was the breakout hit of my Thanksgiving last year. The sides are always so numerous at Thanksgiving that they tend to run together, but more than a few people asked, *"What is that awesome mystery potato gratin thing?"*

Years of trial and error (mostly error) have taught me that creamy vegetable gratins should be baked at 325°F for a long time, under a cover of light cream. Heavy cream is almost too rich; it clogs vegetables' pores and prevents them from softening. Milk isn't rich enough; it will break into curds under the heat.

Unfortunately, this isn't France, and we can't always buy light cream in stores, so we have to make our own with a ratio of 80-percent heavy cream to 20-percent milk. In this case, because turnips express so much liquid, I increase the cream by a few points. But if you ever you want to shoot from the hip and make a sliced potato or root vegetable gratin without measuring, just eyeball a 5:1 cream/milk ratio in a measuring cup and pour it over the shingled vegetables until nearly covered. Bake at 325°F until the vegetables are tender and the surface is deeply caramelized.

Serves 10 to 12 as a side

2½ pounds turnips (6 to 8 medium)
½ teaspoon plus ½ teaspoon plus ¼ teaspoon fine sea salt
3 tablespoons, plus 2 tablespoons softened butter
1 small sweet onion, thinly sliced

Freshly ground black pepper
10 large Medjool dates (6 ounces), pits removed and torn in half
1¼ cups heavy cream, plus more if needed
¼ cup milk, plus more if needed
¼ teaspoon freshly grated nutmeg

Peel the turnips thickly to remove the possibly woody outer layer and slice them on a mandoline, about the width of a nickel. Layer the turnip slices with ½ teaspoon of the salt in a large bowl to draw off their moisture. Let sit for 15 minutes to sweat, then blot the slices dry.

Preheat the oven to 325°F.

Melt the 3 tablespoons butter in a large frying pan over medium heat. Add the onion, ½ teaspoon salt, multiple turns of black pepper and cook, stirring occasionally, until the onion is soft and golden brown, about 20 minutes. Remove from the heat.

Rub a large oval baking dish with half of the soft butter, holding back the last tablespoon for the top. Cover the bottom of the baking dish with a layer of about one third of the turnips, slightly overlapping, followed by half of the onions, and half of the dates. Repeat for the second layer, and end with a layer of overlapping turnips. Combine the cream and milk in a measuring cup, season with the remaining ¼ teaspoon salt and the nutmeg, and pour over the turnips. Press the turnips down into the cream. The liquid should be level with the top of the turnips layer, but depending on the dimensions of your baking dish, you may need to dribble in a little more cream/milk mixture.

Bake, uncovered, until the surface sports golden brown blister caps and the turnips are tender, about 1 hour and 10 minutes; check after the first 30 minutes to poke down any floating turnips or dates.

Serve warm, straight from the dish.

baby greens with glassy pecans and Pecorino

Just a simple green salad, made with care and garnished with a fine blitz of salty Pecorino and some glassy stovetop-caramelized pecans. I sometimes think that in our collective pursuit of interesting recipes we forget that the end goal of a green salad is very basic: to refresh the palate. By design, Thanksgiving is a celebration of dizzying abundance, but it can feel like a flavor-chasing rat race. The palate needs somewhere to go to rest and recharge. So this is just a simple green salad.

To make it special, zero in on the lettuce. Buy multiple small heads of soft lettuces, or some nice mesclun, or whatever looks best that day. Tatsoi, arugula, cress, all are good. If I'm not finding much inspiration in the baby greens section, I buy a couple of large-leaf lettuces and use only their tender, sweet hearts, saving the bigger, floppier leaves for a later date.

If you're not already in the habit of making quick pan-caramelized nuts with a dry caramel—what pastry chefs call praline—these nuts may be life-changing. Whenever I need a little pick-me-up, I caramelize a little sugar in a hot frying pan, toss in some nuts and an acorn of butter, and then immediately tip out the nuts onto a silicone mat to cool. The caramel sets to hard-shell within minutes. You can leave the nuts whole and use them to top salads or to snack on, or you can finely chop them and sprinkle over oatmeal, or baked squash, or a midnight bowl of whipped cream and yogurt, and on and on.

recipe continues

Serves 10 to 12

glassy pecans

¼ cup sugar

1 teaspoon butter

1 cup pecans, lightly oven-toasted if you have time

Fine sea salt and freshly ground black pepper

salad

10 cups mixed baby greens (see headnote), washed and spun

About ¼ cup extra-virgin olive oil

¼ teaspoon fine sea salt

Freshly ground black pepper

2 tablespoons fresh lemon juice

2 teaspoons red wine vinegar or balsamic vinegar

A 1-ounce chunk of aged Pecorino, finely grated

For the nuts, lay out a nonstick landing pad: a silicone baking mat, buttered parchment or foil, or even a buttered dinner plate. Heat a medium stainless steel frying pan over medium-high heat for a few minutes, then sprinkle the sugar evenly across the bottom. Standing by with a silicone spatula, cook until the sugar melts and turns dark amber brown. Once most of the sugar has melted, lift the pan from the heat and stir the caramel until no lumps remain.

When the caramel is smooth, return the pan to low heat, add the butter and the nuts, and immediately fold the caramel over the nuts to coat. Spread the nuts in one layer on the nonstick surface, sprinkling lightly with salt and pepper and breaking up clumps and friendships with your spatula before they cool.

To assemble the salad, pile the crisped-up lettuces in a large salad bowl and toss with a tablespoon of olive oil to lightly coat. Season with the salt and a little freshly ground pepper, then sprinkle the lemon juice and vinegar over the salad, along with the rest of the olive oil, and toss lightly until mixed. Garnish the salad with handfuls of the glassy pecans and shower it with the grated Pecorino, not mixing it in, but letting it pile up on top. Serve immediately.

buttercup bourbon pie

If you've reached the end of this menu as frayed as the end of a rope, you can pop open a can of unsweetened pumpkin and proceed from there (you'll need 3 cups puree). But if you have the time, try making the pie with squash, preferably a dry, sweet, cakey variety like kabocha or, my favorite, buttercup.

Conveniently, this filling tastes best if made a day ahead and refrigerated, to give the spices time to ripen and bloom. I generally make both the filling and the pie crust in advance and chill them separately so that I can bake the pie first thing in the morning. The scent of the spicy pie baking in the oven goes really well with a few cups of hot coffee, and it signals to all in the house that today is Thanksgiving.

Makes one 9-inch pie

buttercup bourbon filling
1 extra-large buttercup or kabocha squash (approximately 4 pounds)
½ teaspoon fine sea salt, plus more for the squash
Neutral oil, such as canola or peanut, for brushing the squash
4 ounces full-fat cream cheese, at room temperature
3 large eggs
¾ cup packed brown sugar
¾ cup heavy cream
3 tablespoons brandy or bourbon
1 teaspoon ground ginger
½ teaspoon ground cinnamon
½ teaspoon freshly grated nutmeg
½ teaspoon ground cardamom, preferably toasted and freshly ground
Pinch of ground cloves

pie pastry
⅓ cup almonds or pecans
1½ cups plus 2 tablespoons all-purpose flour
½ cup confectioners' sugar
½ teaspoon fine sea salt
9 tablespoons (1 stick plus 1 tablespoon) unsalted butter, cold, cubed
4 to 6 tablespoons ice water

meringue
2 large egg whites
¼ cup packed brown sugar
½ cup white sugar
1 tablespoon fresh lemon juice
¼ teaspoon fine sea salt

For the squash, preheat the oven to 350°F.

With a heavy knife, cut the squash in half; if the skin is tough, use a big knife and pound it through with a meat mallet, hitting the knife on the tang. Scrape out the seed cavities with a large spoon. Rub the interior of the squash with a bit of salt and a thin coat of oil and lay it cut side down on a baking sheet.

Bake until the squash feels very tender when poked, anywhere from 40 to 60 minutes, depending on the size and age of the squash. It's better to overcook squash than to undercook it, because the sugars keep increasing as it bakes. When done, remove from the oven and let cool, then scrape the cooked squash out of the skin. Measure 3 packed cups of squash for the pie and reserve the rest for another use.

Add the cream cheese to the bowl of a food processor and process until soft and whipped. Add the squash, eggs, and brown sugar and process to a smooth puree. Scrape down the sides and add the cream, brandy, the ¼ teaspoon salt, ginger, cinnamon, nutmeg, and cardamom and process to blend. Transfer it to a bowl, cover, and refrigerate. (*You can refrigerate the filling for up to 2 days.*)

recipe continues

To make the dough, first process the nuts in the clean dry food processor bowl until finely ground. Transfer to a large bowl, add the flour, confectioners' sugar, and salt, and mix well. Add the cubed butter and cut it in with a pastry blender until the largest pieces are the size of large peas and the mixture begins to clump on the pastry blender. For pastry that's both tender and strong, push most of the mixture up one side of the bowl and cut in the butter more finely in the portion of dough that remains at the bottom. Then shuffle through the mixture with your hands to mix and to break up any large clumps. Drizzle ¼ cup ice water over the mixture and stir together quickly with a butter knife. Squeeze the dough in your hand; if it clumps together, it's hydrated enough. If not, add another tablespoon or two of water, until you can form a single rough ball, packing it together like a snowball.

Turn the dough out, pat it into a disk, wrap, and refrigerate for at least 30 minutes, and as long as 2 days.

When ready to bake the pie, preheat the oven to 350°F. If the dough feels rock hard, let it sit at room temperature for about 20 minutes before rolling.

Dust a countertop with flour and roll the dough to a 13-inch diameter, about ¼ inch thick. Because this is a sweet, rich dough, you may find it easier to roll it between two sheets of parchment paper or plastic wrap.

Sweep excess flour from the dough, fold it in half, and transfer it to a 9-inch pie plate. Flop the dough open and press it into the corners and up the sides. Trim the edges to a ½-inch overhang, then roll the overhanging dough into a cord and pinch it against the edges of the pie plate to crimp the edges. Refrigerate until chilled before baking.

Press a square of aluminum foil against the bottom of the crust and cover with a layer of raw beans to weight it; bake until the crust begins to take on a shade of color, 20 to 25 minutes. Remove the pie shell from the oven and reduce the oven temperature to 325°F. Lift out the foil and pie beans.

Pour the filling into the crust and return to the oven. Bake, uncovered, until the filling no longer jiggles when shaken, 45 to 50 minutes. Remove from the oven and let cool to room temperature before topping with the meringue.

For the meringue, combine the egg whites, brown and white sugars, lemon juice, and salt in the bowl of a stand mixer or another heatproof mixing bowl. Set the bowl over a pot of simmering water to make a double boiler and heat, stirring with a rubber spatula, until the mixture feels quite hot to the touch, 130 to 140°F, about 5 minutes. Transfer the bowl to the mixer stand—or get out your hand mixer—and beat the egg whites until they turn very glossy and stiff.

Dollop the meringue onto the pie and shape it how you like. I tend to pile most of it in the middle and pull the meringue into points—but only because it's not really Thanksgiving until someone pinches off a browned peak of meringue. But if you want to scrape the meringue into a plastic-bag piping bag and make little rosettes or baubles or whatever, go for it.

To toast the meringue, hit the tips with a blowtorch held at a 6-inch distance, or pop it under a hot broiler and keep a close watch on it.

holiday baking

— Bohemian poppy seed coffee cake

— mincemeat baklava

— sesame pralines

— olive oil thumbprints with lemon curd

— lacquered walnuts

Any celebration that falls roundabout the winter solstice, the feasting will likely revolve around one thing: the sweets. The cookies, candies, cakes, and confections that we make just once a year for such occasions often represent the strongest tethers to our traditions and taste memories. For many of us, baking is the lifeblood of the holiday season.

My grandma Addie Dion's poppy seed coffee cake is best when consumed within four days, although it freezes beautifully, to be thawed when needed. Addie's rich, buttery milk dough and generous hand with the streusel elevates this coffee cake to holiday status. But it's the dark, weaving river of poppy seed filling, black and rich and slightly forbidding, that feels like a throwback to Christmases past.

Like many other cooks of her generation who learned to bake by eye and by teacup, my grandma never fully trusted the cup-measure system. She rightly thought of it as inferior to instinct. So when it came to reproducing her coffee cake, I wasn't surprised that her recipe didn't result in the family heirloom that I remembered. I couldn't go by the metrics she wrote down on the card she gave me. I had to *think* like her. I had to remember how she measured yeast (instinctively) and flour (judiciously) and butter (devotionally). She was positively squanderous with the butter.

The way my grandma measured could also describe the way she was as a person: generous with her praise, loud and extravagant and the life of every party, but protective of her secrets. She told fanciful stories that began in everyday life and then veered into fantasy without warning whenever they came too close to a vulnerable edge. Widowed at age thirty with three kids under the age of four, I would guess that she felt the bittersweet darkness of her Bohemian side's poppy seeds acutely.

It's easy to focus on the glitter and sparkle-sugar and red ribbon bows of the Christmas season, but there are two sides to this holiday that falls so close to the shortest, darkest day of the year. These are heightened times. The joys are greater, but the losses—money, stability, family, lost loves, lost hopes—cut deeper too.

Back in grandma's day, before forced cheer overtook the holiday, when loss was rolled into the season and perhaps more acceptable, poppy seeds ruled. If you wanted to make a poppy seed coffee cake, you had to crush them yourself to release their perfume, the seeds rolling out of the grinder like black soil, smelling like overripe plums. Recipes like these represent the unlit, melancholic corners of the season. The heavy black poppy seed filling gushing up through the slashes in the sparkly sugar streusel topping brings us back to earth. It's almost as if the dark, wry Bohemians lurking back there in Addie's family history want to point out that all of this sugar, butter, and joy would taste somehow cheap without that sweet darkness.

Bohemian poppy seed coffee cake

My Grandma Addie Dion pulled this recipe from her mother's Bohemian side and served it with a lot of fanfare each Christmas. Even though we call it poppy seed coffee cake, the texture of the pale, milky dough hovers between sponge cake and sweet bread. After baking, the dough remains damp and lovely, almost subservient to its potent poppy seed filling.

Addie's original recipe made three rectangular cakes, which she wrapped individually, froze in her mammoth deep freezer, and brought up from the basement at the first indication of any social action. I've scaled the quantities down to a single square cake, half of which goes into my freezer in anticipation of a party, and half of which I end up eating all by myself in the days that lead up to Christmas Eve, piece by piece for breakfast. Coffee cake lives for coffee. (Although this one could also live for a tiny glass of black currant liqueur.)

I call for instant yeast because I've found it to be the most reliable of the grocery store options. Addie used fresh cake (or compressed) yeast, or course, which she bought from the town bakery. If you take that route, break off a ⅔-ounce chunk, and crumble it into the warm water to proof.

Makes one 8 × 8-inch cake; serves 25 in small portions

sweet dough
½ cup whole milk
3 tablespoons lukewarm (110°F) water
2 teaspoons instant yeast
¼ cup sugar, plus a pinch
2½ cups all-purpose flour, plus more for kneading
½ teaspoon fine sea salt
8 tablespoons (1 stick) cold unsalted butter, cubed
1 large egg

poppy seed filling
¾ cup poppy seeds
⅓ cup water
½ cup port
¼ cup sugar
3 tablespoons honey

⅓ cup heavy cream
2 teaspoons red wine vinegar or balsalmic vinegar
2 tablespoons unsalted butter

3 tablespoons unsalted butter, softened, for assembly

streusel
½ cup all-purpose flour
6 tablespoons sugar
Pinch of fine sea salt
5 tablespoons unsalted butter, at cool room temperature

Heavy cream for brushing
Softened butter for serving (optional)

For the dough, first scald the milk: Bring it to the brink of boiling in a small saucepan, remove from the heat, and let cool until tepid.

Meanwhile, combine the water, yeast, and pinch of sugar in a small bowl and let stand until the yeast foams, about 10 minutes. (If it doesn't look activated, begin again with new yeast or with cooler water.)

Mix together the flour, the ¼ cup sugar, and the salt in a wide bowl and add the cold butter. With a pastry blender, cut in the butter as you would for pie crust, reducing it to the size of petite peas.

Whisk together the egg and the milk, add the yeast mixture to it, and pour the egg mixture into the flour. Mix swiftly with a rubber spatula until combined. The dough will be soft and sticky. Toss a towel over the top and let it rest for 5 minutes to hydrate the flour.

Turn the dough out onto a generously floured countertop and begin to knead, using a pastry scraper or wide rubber spatula, because the dough is soft. Reach beneath the dough with your scraper, fold it in half, lift it up, and slap it down on the counter; repeat at least 10 times, adding flour as needed to form a ball. Give it another five-minute rest, and then keep kneading in this manner until the dough starts to look smooth and clears the countertop (leaving just an imprint of dough behind), about 5 minutes. The surface should still feel slightly tacky.

Put the dough in a clean oiled bowl and let rise until doubled. This will take anywhere from 2 to 4 hours, depending on the temperature of your room and the vigor of your yeast.

Meanwhile, make the filling: Combine the poppy seeds and water in a blender and process to

recipe continues

a thick paste. Add the port and blend again. The mixture will loosen and then thicken again as the machine pulverizes the poppy seeds. Add the sugar, honey, cream, and vinegar and blend to a thick, dark puree.

Scrape the poppy seed mixture into a wide-bottomed saucepan, add the butter, and bring to a simmer over medium-low heat. Cook gently, stirring occasionally and lowering the heat as necessary, until the mixture thickens enough to show the bottom of the pan when stirred, about 20 minutes. Remove from the heat and let cool. (If not using it right away, press a sheet of plastic against the surface of the filling and store in the refrigerator for up to 4 days. Bring to room temperature before using.)

Line an 8 × 8-inch square baking pan with a sling of parchment paper, leaving at least 2 inches overhanging on two opposite sides. Lightly butter the paper and the two exposed pan sides and set aside.

Pat out the dough on a lightly floured surface and roll into a 8 × 20-inch rectangle, lifting and dusting flour beneath it to keep it loose. Position the dough so that one of the 8-inch sides is facing you. Brush the dough with the soft butter, and then spread the poppy seed filling evenly across the bottom half of the dough. (I prefer a lopsided ratio of filling to cake, so that the poppy seed mixture oozes thickly from the center of the finished cake but tapers off toward the edges.) Starting at the bottom, loosely roll up the dough into a fat cylinder. Press down lightly on the dough to flatten and widen it and transfer to the prepared pan. Cover with a light towel, and let the dough rise for 1 to 2 hours, just enough to give it some time to fill out to the edges and rise an inch or so but not so long as to double in height. (The cake will spread further in the oven.) You want the sweet dough to remain moist and rich after baking, not lofty, and curtailing this second rise is key.

Preheat the oven to 375°F.

For the streusel, mix the flour, sugar, and salt in a medium bowl. Pinch off chunks of the butter and drop into the flour, then quickly work in the butter, shuffling and twisting it lightly between your fingers until the butter is fully incorporated and the streusel holds together when squeezed.

With a sharp knife, cut a few shallow slits across the surface of the dough and brush it with a little cream. Pile the streusel on top of the cake, pressing lightly to help it adhere. Slip the coffee cake into the oven and turn the heat down to 350°F. Bake until the coffee cake is dark golden brown and an instant-read thermometer inserted in the center reads 190°F, about 50 minutes. Let cool to room temperature before lifting the cake from the pan for cutting and serving.

My grandma always cut the cake into rectangular pieces and spread the long sides with a thick coat of butter before arranging them on a serving platter, but the butter frosting is optional.

mincemeat baklava

A layer of mincemeat puts baklava in a dark-spiced holiday mood, and it holds up remarkably well throughout the whole ten-day marathon.

Any decent jar of mincemeat will do, but this is a good use for that gift jar of homemade mincemeat. The best version of this recipe was made with my friends Bruce and Budd's venison mincemeat. For one week each fall, they turn their kitchen into a mincemeat factory, grinding apples and spices and suet and, yes, venison hearts, to make forty-odd quarts of the finest old-school mincemeat I've ever had. I'm usually lucky enough to score two jars.

But given that even Bruce and Budd struggle to source venison hearts and suet most years, I've pivoted to meatless mincemeat, accepting the fact that it's probably more accessible—even if it is slightly less compelling. Commercial mincemeat varies in moisture, so be sure to drain it in a fine-mesh sieve before measuring it, as you would drain moist ricotta.

Makes a 9 × 13-inch pan, serving dozens

syrup
2 cups sugar
¼ cup honey
1¼ cups water
2 tablespoons fresh lemon juice

baklava
2¼ cups (8 ounces) walnuts
½ pound (2 sticks) unsalted butter
1 pound phyllo dough, thawed
1 shy cup prepared mincemeat

Confectioners' sugar for sprinkling

Preheat the oven to 325°F.

Make the syrup first to give it time to chill. Combine the sugar, honey, and water in a saucepan and bring to a simmer. Cook, whisking, until all of the sugar has dissolved, about 5 minutes. Add the lemon juice, remove from the heat, and set aside. When cool, refrigerate until needed (the syrup can be made up to a week in advance).

For the baklava, spread the walnuts on a baking sheet and toast in the oven until lightly browned, about 15 minutes. Let cool, then chop the nuts to rough bits, the size of small lentils, and set aside. Turn the oven up to 350°F.

To clarify the butter, heat it in a frying pan over medium heat until it foams and then until a thin layer of brown crust forms around the perimeter of the pan, about 4 minutes. Remove from the heat and let the butter settle for a few minutes. Tipping the pan, carefully skim off the surface froth with a serving spoon and deposit it in a small bowl. Pour off the clear, clarified butter into another bowl, and then pour the milky liquid and browned milk solids at the bottom into the bowl of froth. You will now have about ⅔ cup of clarified butter and a small dish of browned butter "lees," which can be added later to soups, beans, mashed potatoes, scrambled eggs, etc.

Brush a 9 × 13-inch baking pan with a thin layer of the clarified butter.

Unfold the phyllo dough and trim it to fit the pan, lopping off about an inch from a short side. Cover the phyllo with a towel if you think you might be called away from the process, to keep it from drying out. If the clarified butter has solidified, warm it to liquefy.

Lay 2 sheets of phyllo into the baking pan and brush with a thin layer of clarified butter. (You can layer the dough singly, but two-by-two is faster and it will still be perfectly crispy.) Repeat until you have used about half of the phyllo, stacking the sheets with a light hand, to keep the baklava crispy and airy.

Stir the mincemeat into the walnuts and spread it across the phyllo dough in an even layer, making sure not to press down on the pastry below. Continue layering butter-brushed phyllo sheets, two-by-two, on top of the mincemeat until you've used them all. Brush the rest of the clarified butter over the phyllo. Cut the baklava diagonally, at roughly 1½-inch intervals, into a diamond pattern, making sure to cut all the way to the bottom of the pan.

Bake the baklava for 20 minutes, or until it begins to take on color. Reduce the oven temperature to 325°F and bake for another 50 to 60 minutes, until the baklava is deeply browned.

Remove the pan from the oven, cut it again through the fault lines, and pour the cool syrup over the hot baklava. Let cool, then transfer the baklava pieces to a plate. Sprinkle with confectioners' sugar before serving. Store leftover baklava in an airtight tin for up to 2 weeks.

> **NOTE**
> Warm baklava, served fresh from the oven with a ball of vanilla ice cream, makes for a ridiculously good dessert.

sesame pralines

When I worked as a line cook at Bouley in Tribeca, I'd swipe one of these sesame praline sandwich cookies from the pastry cooling rack every single day, and I wasn't alone; we all had our favorites.

That two lacy, eggshell-thin sesame tuile cookies could hold back the rich, gooey tahini–peanut butter filling seemed like a feat of culinary architecture to me. I loved how the delicate cookies shattered, glass-like, into the nut butter—and I justified my theft by telling myself that it was research. I was never able to nab the recipe, though, so I had to re-create it from taste memory. After much trial and error, I think these come really close.

The cookies are fragile until they've cured and set up, so assemble them with a light hand.

Makes about 25 sandwich cookies

sesame praline batter	nut-butter filling
6 tablespoons unsalted butter	4 tablespoons unsalted butter, at room temperature
½ cup white sugar	6 tablespoons creamy peanut butter
⅓ cup packed light brown sugar	2 tablespoons tahini
1 large egg white	2 tablespoons heavy cream
½ cup all-purpose flour	1 teaspoon pure vanilla extract
1 tablespoon water	A hefty pinch of fine sea salt
½ teaspoon fine sea salt	¾ cup confectioners' sugar
⅓ cup white sesame seeds	

For the batter, melt the butter and pour it into a large cold bowl to cool.

When the butter looks opaque, add the white sugar and mix with a rubber spatula, whipping for a minute or two to lighten. Then mix in the brown sugar, beating until the batter is soft and floppy. Add the egg white and beat until the batter stiffens a bit, then mix in the flour. Add the water, salt, and sesame seeds and stir until the batter is smooth. Cover the bowl and refrigerate until thoroughly chilled.

Preheat the oven to 325°F. Line two baking sheets with silicone mats or parchment paper.

Pinch off ½ teaspoon-sized chunks of the batter, roll them between your palms into rough balls, and arrange on the baking sheets, leaving about 4 inches between them—about 9 cookies per baking sheet.

Bake the cookies for 8 minutes, or until they turn fully, deeply amber brown from edge to edge. Remove from the oven and let the cookies cool on the pan until they're stiff enough to lift with a metal spatula, then transfer them to a parchment- or waxed paper-lined landing sheet to cool. (You should have about 50 small cookies.)

For the filling, paddle the butter in a bowl with a sturdy spatula until smooth, then add the peanut butter, tahini, cream, vanilla, salt, and sugar and beat until the mixure is soft and fluffy. Transfer the filling to a small plastic bag, usher it into one corner, and snip off the tip to make a piping bag.

Before filling the cookies, pair them by size. Line them up two by two, and turn one of them upside down to make the bottom cookie. Working directly on the flat countertop, pipe a thin layer of filling onto each bottom cookie, in concentric circles and cover it with its matching top. Gently press the sandwiched tuile cookies together, then slide them offstage to set up.

After 2 hours, the filling will have firmed up and the cookies can be stored in a single layer in an airtight tin. The cookies will keep for up to 2 weeks; they won't get soggy, but eventually will dry out.

To serve, arrange the cookies in overlapping fashion on a cookie plate or, to be fancy, stand them up side by side in a long narrow cracker or relish dish.

olive oil thumbprints with lemon curd

Adding a healthy glug of olive oil to shortbread dough causes what are already tender cookies to dissolve to crumbs in your mouth. When you're mixing it together, the dough will feel crumblier than a butter dough, but have faith: it seizes together nicely in the oven.

You can fill these thumbprints with jam or melted chocolate or maple-flavored confectioners' sugar icing, but I like to lean into the Italian spirit of the rosemary-scented olive oil cookie and fill them with a spot of lemon curd. To me, lemon curd is one of those recipe marvels. It doesn't matter when you add the butter, at the beginning or the end; it turns out either way. The only trick is to stir with two alternating utensils: a whisk to prevent clumping, and a rubber spatula to clear the sides of the bowl. Beyond that, the process is an immersive, intuitive, lemon-scented experience.

Makes 55 cookies

lemon curd
Makes 3 cups
1 cup fresh lemon juice (from 7 to 9 lemons, preferably Meyer lemons)
1½ cups sugar
2 large eggs
6 large egg yolks
10 tablespoons (1¼ sticks) cold unsalted butter, sliced into tablespoons
Pinch of fine sea salt
1 teaspoon elderflower liqueur (optional)

cookie dough
2½ cups all-purpose flour
¼ cup sugar, plus another ½ cup for rolling cookies
½ teaspoon fine sea salt
½ teaspoon finely minced fresh rosemary
6 tablespoons unsalted butter, cubed, at cool room temperature
½ cup extra-virgin olive oil
1 large egg yolk
4 tablespoons milk, plus a little more if needed

Sugar for finishing

For the lemon curd, fill a saucepan with a few inches of water, for a double boiler, and bring to a simmer over medium heat. Whisk together the lemon juice, sugar, eggs, and egg yolks in a medium heatproof bowl until smooth. Set the bowl over the pan of simmering water and reduce the heat to low. You want heat, but not steam that huffs out through the cracks.

Cook the curd slowly, over low heat, stirring continuously with the rubber spatula in a figure-8 motion, scraping down the sides of the bowl, and occasionally whisking. It should take about 2 minutes to feel hot to the touch, and 5 minutes for the curd to start to thicken. After 8 to 10 minutes, the curd will look shiny, smooth, and jelled. Add the salt and the optional liqueur, then whisk in the cold butter one tablespoon at a time. The curd should look like a soft pudding and taste like warm, hyper-lemony butter. If using, add the elderflower liqueur.

Pour the curd through a fine-mesh sieve into a bowl and stir it to release the steam. After it cools down, press a small piece of plastic wrap against the surface of the curd and refrigerate. (*You can make the lemon curd up to 4 days in advance.*)

For the cookies, combine the flour, ¼ cup sugar, salt, and rosemary in a wide bowl. Add the butter and work it into the flour mixture with a pastry blender until the butter is reduced to fine bits and nearly disappears. Add the olive oil in a thin stream and quickly stir in with a fork, keeping the flour mixture light and fluffy.

Combine the egg yolk and milk in a small bowl and drizzle over the flour mixture. Immediately whisk the dough together with a fork, rotating the bowl to evenly distribute the moisture, until the dough holds together when pinched. It will be a little crumbly, but it should be able to form a rough ball; if the dough feels too dry, dribble in a little more milk. Press the dough down against the bottom of the bowl to hydrate and let sit for 10 minutes.

Arrange the racks in the upper and lower thirds of the oven and preheat to 325°F. Put the sugar for finishing in a small bowl.

To keep the bottoms of the cookies from coloring too much, bake them on doubled-up cookie sheets—the air gap between them acts as insulation.

For each cookie, pinch off a small wad of dough—about 2 teaspoons' worth—and form into a flattened ball. Press and turn the dough between your thumb and forefinger to make a rounded puck shape. (Don't overwork the dough in pursuit of perfectly round balls; this is a rustic cookie.) Toss the balls in the bowl of sugar to coat and arrange on the baking sheets in rows, leaving about 2 inches between them. Press the butt end of a wooden spoon into the center of each cookie to make a fairly deep, fillable depression.

Bake the cookies for 15 to 17 minutes, until the bottoms are light golden brown and the tops just barely bronzed at the edges; these cookies are best when only lightly browned. Transfer the cookies to a rack to cool.

Spoon the cold lemon curd into a quart-sized plastic bag and snip off a corner. Fill the center wells of the cooled cookies with the lemon curd and set aside for at least 4 hours for the lemon curd to fully set.

The cookies can be stored in a covered tin, in single layers separated with parchment paper, for up to a week.

lacquered walnuts

I'm going to stick my neck out and say that all other candied nuts pale in comparison to these. Where some are heavily upholstered in sugar, these are just cleverly slipcovered. It has everything to do with the technique—a perfect example of Chinese culinary ingenuity.

Twice a week during my time at the Chinese restaurant in lower Manhattan, the chefs would bring two large pots of water spiked with a half-cup of baking soda to a boil to make crispy sweet fried walnuts. The initial boil in baking-soda water is genius; it removes nearly all of the wispy walnut skin, which is especially nice for those who dislike their tannic taste. After draining the nuts, the chefs heated up a large wok full of frying oil and proceeded to pour in two containers of maltose, a Chinese inverted sugar that's similar to light corn syrup but heavier. In went the nude walnuts, to bob around and fry in the sweetened oil. When the walnuts turned the color of dark caramel, the chefs lifted them out with large spiders and tossed them onto sheet trays, and we all hurried to separate the burning-hot walnuts with chopsticks before they could stick together. The deep-frying seemed to toast the nuts from the inside out, and they felt lighter in the hand than they'd been before. Each walnut was encased in a miraculously thin hard-shell layer of caramel, as shiny as varnish.

I've made these at home using the same method, but when I ran out of maltose, I began rolling them in dark corn syrup and baking them—instead of deep-frying—to finish. They're as shiny and light as I remember, and less sweet tasting than they look. For Christmas, I always sprinkle the walnuts with freshly ground aniseeds right after they come out of the oven. These are also fantastic in salads.

recipe continues

Makes 3 cups

1½ teaspoons aniseeds or fennel seeds (the anise is better, more subtle)
1½ teaspoons baking soda
3 cups (about 11 ounces) walnut halves, as unbroken as possible

¼ cup dark corn syrup
¼ cup canola oil
2 tablespoons sugar
Fine sea salt and freshly ground black pepper

Preheat the oven to 325°F. Line a baking sheet with parchment paper.

Toast the aniseeds or fennel seeds in a small frying pan over medium heat until just fragrant. Cool, then transfer to a spice mill (or a mortar and pestle) and grind medium-fine. Set aside for sprinkling on the hot walnuts when they come out of the oven. (You won't need all of this.)

Combine 6 cups water and the baking soda in a medium saucepot, add the walnuts, and bring the water to a boil, stirring often. Cook until the bubbles grow in size and the water begins to look like frothy chocolate milk, about 10 minutes. Drain the walnuts in a colander and rinse well to wash away their skins.

Blot the walnuts dry, put them in a medium bowl, and toss with the corn syrup, canola oil, and sugar. Arrange the walnuts evenly on the lined baking sheet and bake for 20 to 25 minutes, until they turn a dark chestnut-honey brown. To check the doneness, move a walnut to your board to cool, and slice it in half; the interiors should be light brown, no darker.

Remove the nuts from the oven and immediately sprinkle them with a fine dusting of the ground anise or fennel seeds. Season lightly with salt and pepper as well. Separate any fused-together walnuts with chopsticks and let them cool completely.

Transfer the cool, dry walnuts to an airtight tin, where they will keep for up to 6 weeks (although they taste freshest during the first 2 weeks).

Thielen family Christmas

FOR TEN

— pâté grandmère
— cast-iron garlic shrimp with chorizo and green olives
— smoked prime rib with celery-leaf salsa verde
— aligot (stretchy mashed potatoes with cheese)
— creamed poblano spinach
— caramelized carrots
— watercress and Bibb with smoky blue cheese dressing

When my parents split up, they divided the traditional Christmas meals down the middle. Quite peaceably, too, considering. My mom, the cook, took her side's traditional German pork roast and homemade noodle dinner. At Christmas at her house, we eat her love and labor, sighing to bursting as we pass around the mushroom gravy that is at once boundary-testing and yet also never too much. We take more noodles, and more gravy, because it is saintly and we believe in it. (And then we collapse.)

My dad took with him his mother's prime rib roast, with customary shrimp to start, the reverence for a good sharp steak knife, and also, let's be honest about it, his checkbook. For Christmas dinner now, I order a six-bone prime rib beef roast from the Thielen family butcher shop—endlessly debating with my cousins over the phone about whether I should get a ten-pound roast or a twelve pounder, bone-in or boneless, virtually hand-picking the roast from the hanging meat hook— because my dad is coming to my house for Christmas, and that's what we do: he loves prime rib. This is time well spent. Prime rib roasts to feed 10 don't come cheap, and they're only getting dearer.

In any case, buy the best-quality prime rib roast you can get, preferably on the bone, which imparts more flavor and moisture to the roast. Dry-aged roasts are ideal, but harder to find; these days, most are wet-aged.

A beautiful roast of prime rib needs nothing more than a hot oven and a cook's confidence, so I don't want to muck it up with superfluous rubs or strained attempts at originality. But I do prefer to cook it in a covered grill with a few handfuls of damp fruitwood chips to give it a little smoke. I fill in the rest of the meal with variations on classic steakhouse sides: spicy creamed spinach, caramelized long carrots, a salad of chilled greens and smoky blue cheese, and mashed potatoes pureed with masses of melted stretchy cheese. We have shrimp to start, of course—and oh, there's pâté too. Honestly, one appetizer would probably be enough, but the pâté can be made at least 5 days in advance . . . and it is Christmas.

Much of this menu can be made ahead. To split the work over two days, marinate the shrimp and make the spinach, the salsa verde, and the smoky blue cheese dressing the day before. That clears the day of the dinner for prepping and smoking the meat, making the potatoes and the carrots, and, finally, just before everyone arrives, baking the shrimp.

pâté grandmère

In the world of French charcuterie, pâté grandmère is the most rustic of them all. This is the creamy, boozy, livery, delicately spiced pork terrine that your imaginary great-grandmother used to make in the family farmhouse outside Lyon, the one she hid on a cold high rafter to cure for a week before slicing at the candlelit wooden table.

A pâté is little more than a fancy meat loaf, although sourcing fresh pork belly and liver may require some expert sleuthing on your part. (Check with local hog farmers; they're usually flush with frozen pork livers.) A good pork pâté lives and dies on the texture, most of which depends on the starchy porridge you use for the binder. Most recipes call for milk-soaked bread, but I prefer swollen milk-cooked rice. It makes for a lusciously smooth pâté that can be smeared in a long contrail across a hot piece of toast.

The pâté can be consumed as soon as it chills enough to firmly slice, but with a few days to cure in the refrigerator, the liver flavor mellows and fades to the background. This is nature's way of giving us the green light to make the pâté well in advance.

You'll need a few pieces of equipment for this recipe: a heavy 2-quart rectangular terrine mold (see page 324 for more on that) or a 9 × 5-inch bread pan; a meat grinder (or a very kind butcher to grind the mixture for you); a spice grinder for buzzing up the whole spices; a bored kid to shell the pistachios. And this is where my attempt to pass this off as an "easily doable recipe" officially dies: sure, you could use pre-shelled pistachios, but since we're going all out anyway, why not pry them from their little shells by hand? They taste fresher.

recipe continues

Makes 1 large pâté, enough to serve 10 as an appetizer, with leftovers

8 ounces fresh pork liver*

2 pounds boneless fatty pork, preferably a
   mixture of shoulder and meaty pork belly**

1 teaspoon plus ¼ teaspoon fine sea salt, plus
   a pinch

¼ teaspoon pink curing salt (optional, but
   keeps the pâté appealingly pinkish; see
   Pink Salt, page 166)

¾ teaspoon freshly ground black pepper

¼ teaspoon ground cardamom, preferably
   toasted and freshly ground

½ teaspoon freshly grated nutmeg

¼ teaspoon ground cinnamon

⅛ teaspoon ground cloves

Pinch of sugar

2 tablespoons Cognac or whiskey

3 tablespoons port

¼ cup round sushi rice

1 cup whole milk

2 tablespoons butter

½ cup finely diced sweet onion

1 heaping teaspoon minced fresh thyme

⅓ cup chopped fresh parsley

2 large eggs

¼ cup shelled pistachios

Bread or crackers, Dijon mustard, and
   cornichons for serving

Wash the liver well in a large bowl of water, drain, and pat dry. Trim away any membranes and bits of gristle, and cut the liver into 2-inch cubes. Cut the pork shoulder and/or pork belly into 2-inch cubes as well.

Mix the pork and livers in a large bowl. Add 1 teaspoon of the salt, the pink salt (if using), ground spices, sugar (sounds strange, but trust the French here), and Cognac to the meat and toss well. Cover and marinate in the refrigerator for at least 6 hours, and as long as 36.

The next day, bring a small saucepan of water to a boil, add the rice, and par-cook it for 5 minutes. Drain the rice, return it to the pan, and add the milk and a pinch of salt. Simmer the rice over very low heat, partially covered, stirring occasionally, until the grains are soft and overblown and the milk has nearly evaporated, 30 to 40 minutes. Transfer the rice pudding base to a bowl and chill thoroughly.

Preheat the oven to 325°F.

Heat a large frying pan over medium heat. Add the butter, onion, and the remaining ¼ teaspoon salt and cook gently, stirring occasionally, until the onion is golden and tender, about 15 minutes. Add the thyme and parsley and heat briefly, then scrape the mixture onto a plate, let cool, and refrigerate.

When the onions are cold, add them to the the pork mixture.

Set up your grinding operation, fitting the grinder with the coarse die and positioning a large bowl beneath it to catch the falling meat. Push the chilled pork-liver-onion mixture through the grinder, and then feed in clumps of cold rice pudding. (If you're not grinding your own meat, pulse the cold onions and rice pudding to a soft mush in a food processor, then combine with the 2 pounds of ground fatty pork.) Add the eggs and mix well with your hands. Fold in the pistachios.

Rub a heavy 2-quart rectangular terrine mold or a 9 × 5-inch bread pan with a thin layer of neutral oil, and fill it with the pâté mixture. Smooth the top.

Bake the pâté for 20 minutes, then reduce the oven temperature to 225°F. Continue to bake the pâté for 40 to 60 minutes, until an instant-read thermometer inserted in the center reaches 155°F. Baking time varies widely depending on the size and shape of your mold. In a traditional skinny terrine mold like the one I use, the pâté will reach the final temperature within 40 minutes, but a wider bread pan may require

---

* You can probably get away with using chicken livers, but don't quote me.

** What you really want for this pâté is a fatty, pastured pork shoulder with a thick cap of fat, but you can approximate that by mixing fresh pork belly with leaner conventional pork shoulder, in a 60/40 ratio of pork shoulder to pork belly. If not grinding your own meat, substitute 2 pounds of fatty ground pork, preferably freshly ground at the butcher counter.

another 20. Gauge by internal temperature, not time. If you don't have a thermometer, stick a thin metal skewer into the fattest part of the pâté for 30 seconds, and then press it against your bottom lip. If it's uncomfortably hot and the liquid burbling from the hole you just made runs yellowish clear, not pink, the pâté is done. Remove the pâté from the oven and let cool to room temperature.

It's traditional to press a pâté with a weight to make a denser loaf that slices cleanly, and if you have a terrine press, I salute you. If not, track down a board or a piece of thick cardboard cut to fit inside the terrine and wrap it in a few layers of aluminum foil. Set the board over the pâté and weight it down with a few heavy cans. An unpressed pâté will be just as delicious but a bit more crumbly. Pressed or not-pressed, refrigerate the pâté for at least 12 hours before slicing, and perferably as long as 48.

When ready to serve, remove the pâté from its mold. Cut it into ½-inch thick slices and arrange on a platter. Serve with bread or crackers, Dijon mustard, and tiny cornichons. Leftover pâté can be wrapped tightly in layers of plastic wrap and refrigerated for up to a week, or wrapped well and frozen in a tightly sealed plastic bag up to 2 months.

SHRIMP SHOPPING

Nearly all shrimp is frozen immediately after harvesting, right on the boat, and for good reason. All crustaceans—shrimp, crab, langoustines—start to disintegrate the minute they stop moving. A refrigerated raw, split lobster tail will turn to ghostly goo within two days. If you can find live, flopping shrimp with curious feelers at a fish market, buy them; live shrimp are buttery, and simply the best. But back at the grocery store, I pass over the fresh shrimp (i.e., frozen and recently thawed) lying in the case and head straight to the freezer section. Pawing through the packages, I'm searching for shrimp in-the-shell, which protect them from bloomy freezer burn. The numbers on shrimp labels indicate how many shrimp it takes to make a pound: The U10s, sometimes called prawns, are the biggest at just 10 to make a pound. Next are 11–15s, which are quite large, the size that steakhouses hook over martini glasses for shrimp cocktail, then 16–20s, which are pretty standard (and also, the size you want to use for this recipe.) 31–35s, which are small, the size of pinkies, are perfect for cocktail platters.

At home, transfer the shrimp to a bowl and thaw in the refrigerator overnight, or thaw them more quickly in a deep bowl of cold water. When the shrimp are soft enough to bend, you can remove the shells; but leave the tails intact. They should smell shrimpy but oceanic, like a shiny shell at the beach. If I detect a whiff of "fish washed up on the beach," I put the shrimp through a quick treatment I picked up in my line cook days. Dump the shrimp into a colander and mix them with a teaspoon of baking soda, swishing them against the colander until a slurry forms. Then set the colander inside a larger bowl and turn on the cold water tap. Let the water run through the shrimp and like a waterfall over the sides of the bowl for almost 5 minutes. (During a drought, 2 minutes will do.) This trick will purge the funkiness and restore the snap to any shrimp.

cast-iron garlic shrimp with chorizo and green olives

A dinner like this has so much going on, and so many multiple moving parts, that you don't want to worry about a complicated appetizer. This rustic baked shrimp dish is almost prefab: so easy. Marinate the shrimp the night before, with garlic and smoked paprika and tangerine peels, and then an hour or two before dinner, when people are starting to look hungry, pour the shrimp into a cast-iron skillet with some green olives, sliced chorizo, and a boatload of extra-virgin olive oil, and pop it in the oven. Five minutes later, the pan of sizzling smoky shrimp and warm olives seems to just materialize, the way it does when you're sitting at the counter of a dim, garlic-scented Spanish tapas bar. Serve with plenty of bread for dipping, because this dish hinges on that pool of smoky olive oil.

Serves 10 as an appetizer

1 Valencia orange or tangerine

1 pound large shrimp (about 20), shells removed but tails left on (see Shrimp Shopping, page 151)

7 garlic cloves, minced

6 bay leaves, preferably fresh

1 teaspoon minced fresh rosemary

½ teaspoon fine sea salt, plus more to taste

¼ teaspoon freshly ground black pepper

¾ teaspoon sweet paprika

¼ teaspoon smoked paprika

⅔ cup extra-virgin olive oil

2 ounces hard chorizo, thinly sliced (or substitute 10 dried red chiles)

16 large green olives, such as Cerignola or Castelvetrano

Remove 3 wide strips of zest from the orange and set aside. Halve the orange and squeeze the juice into a small bowl; reserve.

Combine the shrimp, garlic, orange zest, bay leaves, rosemary, salt, pepper, and both kinds of paprika in a mixing bowl and drizzle the orange juice over all. Toss to combine. Cover and marinate the shrimp in the refrigerator for at least 2 hours, and as long as 24.

When you're ready to cook the shrimp, preheat the oven to 350°F.

I bake the shrimp in two batches because they need to cook in a single layer, but feel free to cook them all at once in one enormous pan.

Heat a heavy ovenproof sauté pan over medium-low heat and add ⅓ cup of the olive oil. When it feels warm to the touch, add half of the shrimp, including half of the orange peels and bay leaves. Add half of the chorizo and olives and toss to coat. Pop the skillet into the hot oven and bake for 5 minutes, then flip the shrimp. Continue to bake until the garlic sizzles and the shrimp have curled into loose C shapes, another 3 to 5 minutes, depending on their size. Keep a close watch on the oven to keep from overcooking them; when you think you can smell the garlic hitting the smoky olive oil, they're pretty close.

Set the pan on a trivet and serve with plenty of bread for dipping into the rusty, garlicky oil. When the shrimp have disappeared, add the remaining ⅓ cup olive oil and then the rest of the shrimp and aromatics to the same pan, building on the compounded flavor, and cook the second batch.

smoked prime rib with celery-leaf salsa verde

A proper holiday roast beast. I'll just say it: everyone's counting on us to not screw it up.

This recipe specifies a smoker grill, but a large charcoal grill will work too.

Serves 10 (³⁄₄ to 1 pound per person)

One 8- to 10-pound bone-in prime rib roast
Olive oil
2 to 3 tablespoons kosher salt
1½ tablespoons cracked black peppercorns
    (milled in a spice grinder or store-bought)
1 tablespoon finely minced fresh rosemary,
    plus a couple of sprigs for flavoring the
    juices
8 garlic cloves, smashed and peeled
6 tablespoons butter

3 cups fruitwood chips, like apple or cherry

celery-leaf salsa verde
2 garlic cloves
2½ tablespoons capers, preferably salt-packed
3 anchovy fillets
1 cup roughly chopped flat parsley
¼ teaspoon fine sea salt
⅓ cup sliced chives
2 tablespoons chopped pale celery heart leaves
1 teaspoon Dijon mustard
½ cup extra-virgin olive oil
3 tablespoons fresh lemon juice
1 tablespoon water

Flaky sea salt for serving

At least a few hours ahead, or preferably the night before you want to cook it, unwrap the roast. If it was vacuum-sealed, wipe it down with a damp cloth. Trim away any grayish oxidized fat and clean up the sides and the rib bones if they're shaggy, but be careful not to trim away any precious hard white fat. Rub the meat with a thin layer of olive oil. Sprinkle the roast with an even layer of salt, then apply the black pepper and minced rosemary. Set the roast on a rack set over a baking sheet and refrigerate for at least a few hours, or, preferably, overnight. (Even just a few hours of drying in the cold air of the refrigerator will help the meat to form a skin, or pellicule, which will help the smoke adhere to it.)

As for timing, budget approximately 4 hours for the prime rib roast—3 hours to cook it plus at least 30 minutes to rest the meat and pull the dinner together—and then work backward from there. When you're ready to start the prime rib, preheat a covered smoker grill to 400°F, or prepare a hot fire in a large charcoal grill.

Set the beef in a heavy low-sided roasting pan that holds it comfortably. (Too snug or too deep, and the meat will steam; too roomy, and the bottom juices may burn.) Toss the rosemary sprigs, garlic cloves, and butter into the pan, and set it in the middle of the grill.

Lower the cover and roast the prime rib for 45 minutes, or until the beef begins to brown, then baste it with the pan juices and lower the grill temperature to 325°F. Meanwhile, toss the wood chips with a little water to dampen.

When the temperature reaches 325°F, throw half of the damp wood chips onto the charcoal fire and close the lid. Continue to roast the beef, basting the meat with its juices every half hour and adding the rest of the wood chips when the smoke peters out. (Check the level of the coals; you will need to add more charcoal periodically.) Cook the prime rib until an instant-read thermometer reads 125°F for medium-rare. Depending on the weight of the roast and the consistency of the grill temperature, this will take anywhere from another hour and a half to 2½ hours. (As you time the readiness of the beef with the rest of the meal, know that you can pause the cooking at any point. Pulling an underdone prime rib out to sit next to the grill in order to give the sides time to catch up and then returning it to the heat won't hurt it in the least.)

When the temperature nears 120°F, start paying close attention; 124° F may be the official number for medium-rare, but in my experience, 128 or 129°F is a more accurate reflection of a roast that will be hot, dark pink, and juicy from end to end after resting. To make sure, cut off a thin truth slice, keeping in mind that the interior will be less done. When you hit your number, baste the meat with the accumulated juices and let the beef rest at room temperature for 20 to 30 minutes before slicing. As it rests, the juices will settle and the temperature will rise 5 to 10 degrees.

Meanwhile, at any point during this process, make the salsa verde: You can use a food processor, but I prefer a mortar and pestle. If the capers are salt-packed, rinse them and soak briefly in warm water to desalinate. If the anchovies aren't prime, rinse them quickly under warm water. Pound garlic to a fine paste, add the capers and anchovies and pound until smooth. Add the chopped parsley and salt and pound until the parsley begins to break down. Add the chives and then the celery leaves and reduce to a paste. Stir in the Dijon, olive oil, and lemon juice, taking care to avoid emulsifying the sauce, then add the water. The salsa will taste sharp at this point but should hang in the balance between tart lemon and buttery olive oil and tangy Dijon. It will mellow as it sits on the counter, so you should adjust it as needed before serving. If making the sauce more than 3 hours in advance, cover and refrigerate, but bring back to room temperature before serving.

To serve the prime rib, cut the meat away from the bones in a single swoop. Cut the rib bones apart by slicing in between them and stack them on one side of the serving platter—for those of us who would rather chew on a rib than take a second piece of meat. Lay the roast on a large cutting board and slice the beef crosswise into portions. Generally I like roasts thinly sliced, but I think that prime rib slices should be more slab-like. Slide your knife underneath the meat and transfer it to the platter. Pour any accumulated juices around it and sprinkle lightly with coarse salt (or save it to pass). Serve the prime rib with the salsa verde.

aligot (stretchy mashed potatoes with cheese)

This is not everyday fare, but it is just sinful with the beef.

In L'Aubrac, a region of flat steppes, tiny white wildflowers, and many, many cows in the middle of France, cooks have been making this rich puree of potatoes and cheese for centuries. Years ago in Laguiole, I watched a grandmother toss handfuls of grated local cheese (Tomme d'Auvergne) into a pot of mashed potatoes, beat it soundly with a wooden spoon, and then stretch the cheesy puree high into the air, strings of melted cheese dangling, before letting it snap back to the mass. She did it again and again until the aligot got springier, tauter, and began to look alive. On the plate it tasted like pure butter and tangy mountain cheese with just a hint of potato to bind.

This dish is so deeply regional, so dependent on Aubrac potatoes and cheeses, it can hardly be replicated, but we can try. Commercially grown American potatoes generally fall into just two categories—waxy/buttery or starchy/flaky—but aligot needs something in between, a potato that has starch for strength and a rich, buttery density. Russets are too fluffy and bland. Red potatoes are too sticky. Yukon Golds are a bit waxy. They will work if given sufficient butter and a light touch, but the multi-purpose potatoes grown by small farmers and CSAs—like Kennebec, or Bintje, or German Butterball—would be better. The cheese is hard to find here too, but I'm happy with this mixture of three: an Alpine Gruyère-type for nuttiness, cheddar for tang, and mozzarella for stretch.

You'll need a stick (immersion) blender or a fine-holed potato ricer for this recipe.

Makes about 6 cups, serving 10 to 12 (it's rich)

3 pounds yellow potatoes (Yukon Golds, or a starchy, multi-purpose potato; see headnote)

1½ teaspoons fine sea salt, plus more to taste

2 bay leaves

3 garlic cloves, smashed and peeled

12 tablespoons (1½ sticks) butter, cut into slices

½ cup milk

½ cup heavy cream

8 ounces aged white cheddar, coarsely grated

8 ounces Gruyère, coarsely grated

8 ounces fresh mozzarella, coarsely grated

Peel the potatoes and cut into large cubes. Put them in a saucepot, cover generously with water, and bring to a simmer. Add the bay leaves, garlic, and salt. Simmer the potatoes, uncovered, until very tender when poked with a fork, 30 to 35 minutes. Drain the potatoes in a fine-mesh sieve and shake to remove excess moisture. This is one of those times that the potatoes cannot wait or otherwise cool off; to be creamy, they need to be mashed immediately. Have either a stick blender or a fine-holed potato ricer ready.

Just before the potatoes are done, heat the milk and cream in a small saucepan or microwave-safe container until steaming. Remove from the heat and cover to keep warm.

Return the potato pot to medium-low heat and add the butter. When the butter has melted, return the potatoes to the pot and mash quickly with a hand masher to coat them with the butter. The richness of the butter, together with the heat of the potatoes, will prevent them from turning gluey. Then puree the hot, buttery potatoes with the stick blender—very, very briefly, being careful to stop before they get gummy, just 30 seconds or so—until creamy. Or, if using a ricer, move the potatoes to a bowl and feed them back through the ricer into the pot with the melted butter. Stir in enough of the milk/cream mixture to make a well-knit but floppy puree. Reserve any remaining milk/cream mixture.

If the potatoes aren't perfectly smooth, pass them again through a sieve: Set a large fine-mesh sieve over a large bowl, and working in batches, push the potato mixture through the sieve, pressing on the puree with the back of a ladle. This is not necessarily easy, but the silken texture makes it worth the effort.

Scrape the puree into a clean saucepan. (*If you're not ready to serve the aligot, it can be held for a couple of hours. Dribble some of the reserved milk/cream mixture around the puree to keep it moist, press a butter wrapper against its surface, and cover the pan to keep it warm. Before serving, reheat the potato puree, stirring with a spatula until smooth and adding more of the milk/cream mixture as necessary to loosen the puree.*) Add all of the grated cheese to the potatoes, folding and stretching the puree over low heat until all of the cheese has melted. Pull up on the puree and stretch it high into the air, drop it back into the pan, and stir it up again. Keep repeating this until the mass gets tighter and shinier. Scrape the aligot into a warm serving bowl and serve immediately.

creamed poblano spinach

Incredible shrinking spinach. What looks like a bushel when raw will reduce after blanching to just two fistfuls of dark green mineral charge. I'm always so relieved to see the same clump spread out its wings and plump back up as it simmers in its cream sauce.

I think that creamed spinach should be slippery enough to slither off a serving spoon, rich with cream but not clotted with it, and have a faint sweetness coming from the butter-cooked onions. Poblano peppers have a nice smoky edge to them, and for grocery-store peppers, they're reliably semi-spicy. A single diced poblano should add a perfectly stealthy amount of heat.

This dish can be made ahead, cooled, refrigerated, and reheated just before serving.

Serves 10 as a side

3 large bunches (about 1½ pounds) fresh leaf spinach (not baby spinach)
5 tablespoons butter
1 large sweet onion, cut into small dice (2 cups)
½ teaspoon plus ¼ teaspoon fine sea salt, plus more if needed

1 large poblano pepper, cut into small dice
2 garlic cloves, minced
⅓ cup white wine
Freshly ground black pepper
1 cup heavy cream
¼ teaspoon freshly grated nutmeg

Bring a large pot of water to a boil over high heat and season with a small palmful of salt.

Meanwhile, without untying the spinach bunches, chop the spinach into 2-inch lengths until you reach the stems. Untie the bunches and spend a few minutes picking out any particularly long or thick stems that remain. Submerge the leaves in a large bowl of cold water to remove the grit, and transfer to a colander to drain. If the spinach is sandy, wash it twice.

Heat a large frying pan over medium heat. Add the butter, onions, and ½ teaspoon of the salt and cook until the onions turn soft and golden (but not caramelized) at the edges, gradually lowering the heat as they soften, about 20 minutes. Add the diced poblano and garlic and cook until the poblano is tender, 10 minutes or so. Add the white wine, bring it to a simmer, and remove from the heat.

Add half the spinach to the boiling water and blanch it until it's tender at the stem, about 1½ minutes. Fish it out with a metal spider and drain it in a colander set over a bowl. Briefly run the colander under cold running water to cool off the spinach (without rinsing away all its flavor) and toss it with tongs to aerate. The more quickly it cools, the greener it will remain. Repeat with the remaining spinach.

When it's cool enough to handle, pick up baseball-sized clumps of spinach and gently press them between your hands to remove excess water. Don't put muscle into it; the leaves should retain *some* moisture. Set the spinach on your cutting board and slice them thinly one way and then the other, for a medium-fine chop. (*If making this the day of the dinner, you can prep both the onion base and the blanched spinach in advance and reunite them for final cooking about 15 minutes before serving. If you want to make it the day before, finish it, spread the creamed spinach thinly on a baking sheet to cool, and then store in a covered bowl in the refrigerator; gently reheat when needed.*)

Add the spinach and cream to the pan of sautéed onions and set over medium-high heat. Add the cream and bring to a simmer, stirring the spinach with a pair of tongs to encourage it to unfurl in the sauce. Reduce the heat to medium and cook, uncovered, until the spinach swells and the cream thickens, 5 to 10 minutes. Add the grated nutmeg, taste for salt and add if needed, and pour out into a serving bowl. Serve hot.

caramelized carrots

For smaller parties of just 4 to 6, I make glazed carrots in old-school French fashion by filling my widest sauté pan with a single layer of slim carrots and cooking them gently in just the water clinging to them—along with a pinch of sugar and a godly amount of butter. But ten to twelve carrots will never feed a hungry holiday horde, and stacked carrots won't cook evenly, and working two large pans of carrots on the stovetop is the last thing any of us need. Thankfully this is not one of those "impossible situations" I was so fond of when I was younger, but instead what my dad would call a "can-do opportunity!" (Picture an arm up, and a finger pointed, to indicate that the sky is the limit.) You can sear fourteen or sixteen carrots—or more!—well ahead of time, caramelizing and parcooking them a bit before piling them up in a large pan and glazing them right before dinner. Everyone at the table will be able to perch a whole cinnamon-colored caramelized carrot across their plate, and some will even get two.

Look for firm, elegant, tapered carrots with the tops still attached for this recipe.

Serves 10 as a side

2 pounds (3 bunches) slim, mature carrots
½ teaspoon plus ¼ teaspoon fine sea salt, plus
    more to taste
1 teaspoon sugar
2 tablespoons coconut oil

2 teaspoons maple syrup
1 sprig rosemary
A 1-inch piece of ginger, peeled and smashed
3 tablespoons butter

Peel the carrots and trim their tops and tails. If you want to be fancy—this is a holiday, after all—leave half of an inch of green stems at the top but scrape them down to clean, green nubs with a paring knife.

Toss the carrots with ½ teaspoon of the salt and the sugar—rub them in with your hands—and let the carrots sit and sweat for about 30 minutes. Pre-seasoning brings out a lot of flavor—although if you're pressed for time, feel free to skip it.

Heat a large—12 to 14-inch—sauté pan over medium-high heat, and when hot, add the coconut oil. Sear the carrots in batches, leaving lots of space between them, until dark brown on both sides; transfer to a plate as they are done. It will take at least 5 minutes for the first side of the carrots to brown, but the second side will go more quickly.

When you've seared all the carrots, discard the fat and wash the pan. Coconut oil can take high heat better than butter or olive oil, and it will have lent its perfume to the carrots, but now you're going to replace it with butter. Return the carrots to the pan, gently toss them with the remaining ¼ teaspoon salt, the maple syrup, rosemary, ginger, 2 tablespoons of the butter, and ¾ cup water. (*At this point, you can cover the carrots with a lid and hold them until you're ready to finish cooking them right before serving.*)

Bring the carrots to a boil over medium heat. Lower the heat to a steady simmer, cover tightly, and cook until the carrots are just tender when pierced at the core, about 10 minutes. Lift the lid every few minutes to rotate the carrots and to make sure the water hasn't evaporated; add a little if it has.

Uncover the pan and cook over medium heat until the reduced juices cover the carrots with a glaze; you want just enough liquid to cling. Remove the ginger, swirl in the final tablespoon of butter, correct for seasoning, and serve.

watercress and Bibb with smoky blue cheese dressing

This creamy blue cheese dressing doubles-down on the smokiness (blue cheese plus smoked paprika) but eases up on the acidity. Hank doesn't like a sharp dressing, so I'm forever trying to invent new ones for him—and others who might share his vinegar sensitivity.

If you wanted to go full-on supper club, you could add cherry tomatoes and shaved red onions and croutons and all manner of salad bar toppings that have ever glowed under the fluorescent lights, but I choose simplicity. There are a lot of big-personality flavors in this menu, and we don't want a war.

Serves 10 as a side salad

10 cups mixed trimmed watercress and Bibb lettuce (or other small soft-head lettuce)

dressing
½ cup heavy cream
½ cup thick Greek-style yogurt
1 small garlic clove, finely grated
¼ teaspoon fine sea salt, plus more to taste
½ teaspoon freshly ground black pepper, plus more to taste

2 teaspoons fresh lemon juice, plus more to taste
2 tablespoons extra-virgin olive oil, plus more for the greens
3 ounces smoked blue cheese, crumbled
½ teaspoon smoked paprika
Pinch of cayenne pepper
Milk to thin

Lay the washed and spun out watercress and lettuce on a large clean dishtowel in a single layer, tie up into a loose bundle, and refrigerate. If holding for any longer than 3 hours, put the bundle into a plastic bag (you may need to divide it between two bags) before refrigerating, to prevent wilt.

For the dressing, stir together the cream, yogurt, garlic, salt, pepper, and lemon juice in a bowl. Add the olive oil, whisking with a fork to emulsify it. Add the blue cheese and paprika and stir together, mashing any large chunks with a fork, until the flavor of smoked blue cheese permeates the dressing. Add the cayenne to bring up the smoked paprika flavor, check for salt level and acidity, and adjust to your taste.

To serve, fill an extra-large salad bowl with the greens and toss with a fine drizzle of olive oil to coat lightly, which will prevent the cream dressing from sogging the delicate greens. Sprinkle the greens lightly with salt and pepper.

Stir the dressing, which can stiffen when made ahead of time. Its consistency should be hefty but still liquidy on the spoon, so thin it with milk if necessary. Drizzle the greens with large spoonfuls of dressing, tossing until thinly coated. To keep the salad from feeling weighed down, it's best to go a little light and then drip a little more over the top just before serving. (Any leftover dressing keeps for about 10 days in the refrigerator, tightly covered.)

Spangler family Christmas Eve

FOR EIGHT

— baked spiced quince with soft cheese
— sylta
— spiced meatballs with cream gravy
— mascarpone whipped potatoes
— citrusy braised red cabbage
— crispy curried cauliflower with mustard seeds
— cranberry cookie tart

The locals of Norwegian heritage around here like to talk a big game about eating lutefisk, but few would say exactly that they love it.

Imagine a piece of colorless fish that has been soaked in a barrel of lye solution until the bones dissolve and the flesh turns to gelatin. Many months later, after being brought back to life via multiple purgings in fresh water, the lutefisk arrives on your doorstep. The traditional recipe calls for boiling the lutefisk in nothing but water before transferring it to a platter, and then to your plate, where it tastes only of the melted butter ladled on top of it.

To be clear, I didn't grow up eating lutefisk; I grew up lutefisk-adjacent, you could say, and married into a pro-lutefisk family. Minnesotans from Norwegian-immigrant families (like Aaron's mother's side) take a pervish delight in eating this reconstituted poverty food of their homeland, even though modern-day Norwegians stopped eating lutefisk generations ago and are trying to put it behind them. What outsiders don't understand, though, is that Minnesotan-Norwegians eat plates of the stuff every year *in jest*. It took me a while to get this too, because the trademark earnestness throws you off. Lutefisk is a collective cultural reenactment, and as stunts go, this one is airtight—everyone's in on the joke but you.

They all know it stinks. That's why the Bemidji Lutheran church pulls up an open cargo trailer next to the church hall for cooking it, so the lutefisk fumes don't get trapped inside the walls of the church. Again, this proves my theory: you don't eat lutefisk because it's so good; you eat it because it's so bad. It's sacramental. Old-school. Liturgical.

Aaron's mom, Carolyn, is Norwegian—she grew up in a small farm town called Norseland—and his family has served as my sponsors in lutefisk. They're very nice about it, not too pushy, no oaths or vows. But I do have the responsibility of cooking it. Every Christmas Eve, about fifteen minutes before we're about to sit down and eat dinner, Carolyn tosses me the package of lutefisk from the backroom fridge and says, "We can't forget the lutefisk!" It's an afterthought every year, but she always slips it in just before the bell.

I've tried to be creative with it, I really have. I've baked it, I've simmered it, in water and in milk. Strangely, it doesn't really react to different treatments but just remains stubbornly itself. So we poach it in salted water and pull it out to a platter, and I pour a large stream of rosemary-infused brown butter over it. I must admit, it's grown on me. When it's mixed into the potatoes, you can't even really taste it.

That's what they always say! "You can't even taste it." For a clear, almost see-through gelantinous fish, invisibility is the highest compliment.

What this traditionally monochromatic white meal could really use are a few pops of color; something like blood-red braised cabbage and curried fried cauliflower. I also like to kick it off with an old-fashioned cured pork loaf called *sylta* that I shamelessly pulled from someone else's Scandinavian tradition. The baked quince, sometimes made with fruit that arrives in the mail from a California friend with an overactive tree, further distances things from the original Norwegian Christmas plate. But I don't dare mess with the spiced meatballs bobbing in cream gravy, because they are luscious and one step too rich to be considered everyday fare. They feel even fancier when rolled small, the size of large marbles.

Three of these dishes—the quince, the sylta, and the red cabbage—can be made up to 5 days in advance. You can press the tart dough into its pan a full day ahead (covered and refrigerated) to bake first thing the next morning. The meatballs can be rolled the morning of the dinner, but no earlier, or they'll become tough. This schedule leaves just the mascarpone whipped potatoes and the crispy cauliflower with curry and mustard seeds to knock out before dinner.

baked spiced quince with soft cheese

Uncooked quince is dense and fibrous, but when it's baked in a bath of sugar and white wine, the fruit's toughness slowly melts away. It glows bright salmon pink and develops a hypnotic perfume, as if an apple tree were blooming next to a rose bush in full flower and the two just happened to cross. Baked quince is the perfect companion to your holiday cheese splurge—a small full wheel of cow's-milk or sheep's-milk cheese with a creamy paste and a bloomy rind.

Some people stop cooking quince when it reaches tenderness, but I like to leave it in the oven a little longer. If you cook quince with the seed cavities intact, without coring the fruit first, the color just keeps getting deeper, from blush pink to bright coral. Quince is nearly impossible to overcook—it would take a real feat of inattention to bring it slouching to its knees.

You can bake the quince days before you need it and reserve it chilled in its syrup. Take it out of the refrigerator to temper when you bring out the cheese, and serve both on the same board. I often serve this as an appetizer, in step with the American custom to serve cheese before dinner, but this pairing is calling out to be served after dinner, sometime between wine and coffee.

Serves 8 to 10 as an appetizer

3 quince (about 1½ pounds)
½ cup sugar
¾ cup water
½ cup white wine
2 wide strips lemon zest from a Meyer lemon
2 tablespoons fresh lemon juice

1 teaspoon black peppercorns
8 allspice berries
1 small sprig rosemary
A small wheel of bloomy-rind sheep's- or
    cow's-milk cheese

Preheat the oven to 325°F.

Rub the quince in a towel to remove any gray fuzz clinging to the skin, then peel, dropping each one into a bowl of cold lemon water as you go to keep it from oxidizing. Cut the quince in half and flick away any loose seeds, but leave the seed cavities intact. Lay them cut side down in a baking dish that holds them snugly. (Cooking them with their cores gives them more flavor and a prettier color, and you can always cut the cores out later, or just slice around them.)

Combine the sugar, and water, and wine in a saucepan and bring to a boil. Cook, stirring, until the sugar dissolves, the syrup thickens, and bubbles cover the surface, about 2 minutes. Add the lemon juice and remove from the heat.

Pour the syrup over the quince and add the lemon zest, peppercorns, allspice, and rosemary. Cover tightly and bake for 1 hour.

Take the quince out of the oven and baste with the juices, then return to the oven to bake until tender, approximately 1 hour more. Remove from the oven and let cool, then store in the syrup until ready to serve. (If making the dish in advance, submerge the quince in its syrup and store in a tightly covered glass container in the refrigerator for up to 2 weeks.)

To serve, let both the quince and the wheel of cheese come to room temperature. Pull a couple of the quince halves from the syrup and scoop out their cores with a sharp-edged measuring teaspoon. Thinly slice the quince, transfer to a serving dish—its own, or a wooden board to be shared with the cheese—and nap with a bit of the syrup to moisten. Serve alongside the wheel of cheese. It may seem natural to add a cracker or baguette to this spread, but I like the pairing as-is.

sylta

Sylta is a traditional Scandinavian home-cured jellied ham mosaic that hails from the days when pork aspic terrines weren't reserved for special occasions, but respectfully made and consumed with relish any ordinary day of the year. Sylta is not my Christmas tradition, nor is it my in-laws', but I make it for a number of reasons. One, although it takes some foresight, the active working time is ridiculously short, and it can be made up to a week in advance. Two, when cut with a hot sharp knife, the sylta looks like a sliced geode, the meat trapped in amber gelatin. The thin rectangular slices are gorgeous arranged in careful overlapping domino fashion on a fancy crystal cake stand. Three, adults think it looks impressive and the kids all think it looks intimidating (even though it tastes just like ham), which just means more for us. We eat the leftovers on toast for breakfast for a week afterward.

This recipe makes enough sytla to fill a clean 3-pound Folger's coffee can—what I've been told is the traditional yield. It will also fit into a 2-quart terrine mold or two small loaf pans. The yield always varies a bit depending on the leanness (or fattiness) of the pork, and if I don't have an empty coffee can or terrine mold I can use, I just go hunting in my cupboards for two vessels to divide it between. Loaf pans, vintage baking or storage dishes, anything taller than it is wide will work.

Sylta doesn't need any adornment, but I often serve it with a little dish of Dijon mustard on the side, next to the crackers.

Note that the sylta needs 3 to 4 days to cure before cooking, and then at least 8 hours to chill before slicing.

Serves a crowd

2 quarts water
½ cup (5 ounces) kosher salt
½ cup sugar
1 teaspoon pink curing salt (see Pink Salt, page 166)
One 2-pound piece pork belly, cut in half
4 pounds pork butt, cut into 2-inch-thick slabs

3 bay leaves
12 allspice berries
10 juniper berries
3 whole cloves
1 tablespoon black peppercorns
8 teaspoons unflavored gelatin (from 4 packages)

For the brine, pour 4 cups of the water into a large stockpot, add the kosher salt, sugar, and pink salt, bring to a simmer, whisking, until the salt and sugar have dissolved. Remove from the heat and add the remaining 4 cups water. Chill thoroughly.

Submerge the pork shoulder and belly in the cold brine, cover, and refrigerate. Leave to cure for 3 to 4 days, checking and turning the meat daily to make sure it is submerged.

After it has cured, drain the pork, rinse under cold running water, and soak in a pot of cold water for 30 minutes. Drain, cover again with fresh water, and soak for another hour to remove some of the saltiness.

Transfer the meat to a large stockpot, cover with water by 2 inches, and bring to a simmer. Remove any foam that surfaces with a ladle. Cut a square of cheesecloth to make a sachet, pile the bay leaves, allspice, juniper berries, cloves, and peppercorns in the center, and tie up the four corners tightly, then add to the pork. Simmer, uncovered (adding water to just cover if it evaporates), until the meat is very tender when pierced with a fork, about 3 hours. Remove from the heat and let settle.

Pull the meat from the broth and transfer to a bowl to cool.

Strain the broth through a fine-mesh sieve into another bowl. Let settle for a few minutes, then run a ladle around the perimeter of the bowl, tilting it to skim the fat from the surface; discard. Taste the broth. It should be highly seasoned but not salty. Measure 4 cups of broth into one bowl and 1 cup into another, and reserve the rest for something else (like soup). Chill the 1 cup broth.

recipe continues

Line your chosen mold—a 2-quart terrine, loaf pans, or a clean 39-ounce metal coffee can—with plastic wrap.

Add the gelatin to the cold cup of broth, and stir well. Within a minute, the gelatin should seize up and look sandy.

Warm the remaining 4 cups of broth in a saucepan and add the gelatin mixture, whisking until dissolved. Pour ½ inch of the gelatinized broth into the bottom of the mold(s) and refrigerate until set.

Pick through the meat, discarding any soft, floppy fat and connective tissue but reserving anything marbled or streak-of-lean, along with any solid pieces of meat.

Arrange a layer of meat over the layer of set jelly and cover with a thin layer of gelatinized broth. Continue filling the mold(s) with meat and broth, arranging the meat closely but not packing it together. Finish with enough gelatinized broth to cover the meat by ½ inch. Chill the sylta for a minimum of 8 hours, until set and bouncy.

When ready to serve, warm the bottom of the mold in a pan of steamy water and invert the terrine onto a cutting board, tugging at the plastic to release it. Remove the plastic and cut the terrine into thin slices, and then in half again, to make two- to three-bite portions. Serve with spicy mustard and bread, crackers, or toast.

PINK SALT

The recipes on pages 150, 165, 179, and 253 contain pink salt, or sodium nitrite, which serves to pinken, flavor, and keep meat safe to eat as long as leftovers last in the refrigerator—although my ratio is lower than the standard. The sodium nitrite (or "nitrates," the common term used to reference either sodium nitrite or sodium *nitrate*, the one included in long-cured pink salt formations) also gives the pastrami that tell-tale "corned" flavor. I use Instacure 1, which I bought from my butcher cousins, but it can be easily found online. It looks awfully similar to tinted sanding sugar, and I have nightmares of kids using it to make pink lemonade, so I've marked its bag: POISON—NOT SUGAR!

That said, I am not afraid of pink salt. In some form or the other, nitrate-rich salts, like saltpeter, have been used since the dawn of cooking and meat preservation.

I do wonder if some meat producers overuse nitrates (especially the unregulated ones) out of an abundance of caution, and fear of litigation, but I worry more about giving my family or my guests botulism in the short-term future. While a continuous daily diet of high-nitrate lunch meat could possibly, though no one knows for sure,

contribute to cancer down the road, the botulinum toxin is instantly lethal in large doses. And, undeniably, pink salt gives smoked meats their recognizable "metallic" flavor.

According to my cousins at Thielen Meats, the no-nitrite meats trend is a bit of a scam anyway, wool pulled over consumer eyes. If the meat you buy has been salted and smoked and is pink (not gray) in color, it is most certainly "cured" with nitrates derived from celery powder (long-cured unsmoked charcuterie, like prosciutto, which is traditionally cured without nitrates, is an exception.) Apparently this celery-powder nitrtate business is as unregulated as the wild west, because there are no federal guidelines as to its usage. Having tasted a batch of no-nitrate bacon from the farmers' market that left a low radioactive buzz on my tongue—I immediately wondered if there was too much celery-derivite nitrite—I think that adding a cautiously low ratio of pink salt to meat before curing or smoking is probably the safest thing a person can do.

You can omit the pink salt, of course, although I can't guarantee then that the pâté or the pastrami will keep for as long or taste exactly as it should.

spiced meatballs with cream gravy

I had to resist the urge to add garlic to these. Swedish meatballs might contain a scrap of garlic, but Norwegian meatballs, never.

Properly, the aromatics are allspice, freshly grated nutmeg, and a peppery slush of grated onion. If made with freshly ground pork and beef—avoid meat that has been compacted into blocks or vacuum-packed—and light, soft bread crumbs, these are the most tender meatballs I've ever known. They can be rolled any size, but tiny perfectly round meatballs the size of pinballs give this dish its holiday stature.

I bake them to keep their shape, then heat them up in the creamy spiced gravy in a large covered brasier, which keeps them warm at the table. Though, as is traditional at large Scandinavian-Midwestern family gatherings, you could double the recipe and heat and serve the meatballs from an electric roaster set on the countertop.

Makes about 60 small meatballs, serving 8

1½ pounds ground pork
1½ pounds ground beef
1½ cups soft bread crumbs
⅓ cup grated sweet onion
1 cup milk
3 large eggs
1½ teaspoons fine sea salt, plus more if needed
1 teaspoon freshly ground black pepper, plus
   more if needed

½ teaspoon ground allspice
¼ teaspoon ground ginger
½ teaspoon freshly grated nutmeg
3 tablespoons butter
3 tablespoons all-purpose flour
3 cups beef stock
¾ cup heavy cream

Combine the ground pork and beef in a large bowl. If the meat looks compressed, punch it with your hands to break it up. Add the bread crumbs, grated onion, milk, eggs, salt, pepper, allspice, ginger, and ¼ teaspoon of the nutmeg. Gently mix with your hands until thoroughly combined. (*The meatball mix can be made up to 8 hours in advance and stored, tightly covered, in the refrigerator.*)

Preheat the oven to 350°F.

Rub a large rimmed baking sheet with a thin layer of canola oil. With wet hands, roll the meat mixture into balls the size of mothballs, about an inch in diameter, and line them up on the baking sheet in rows, leaving a bit of space between them. You should have about 60 meatballs.

Bake the meatballs for 40 to 45 minutes, or until the liquid that seeps from them has reduced and caramelized at the edges and the tops of the meatballs are lightly browned. Let the meatballs cool for a few minutes, then transfer to a wide bowl.

Remove and discard any coagulated white matter that remains on the pan and add ½ cup water to the pan. Set the baking sheet across two low burners to warm. Scrape the bottom with a wooden spoon to incorporate the flavorful pan stickings and pour into a bowl for the gravy.

Heat a large sauté pan or braising pan (one that will double as your serving dish) over medium heat and add the butter. When it foams, add the flour and stir until it bubbles and the mixture is smooth. Add the beef stock, deglazed pan liquid, cream, and the remaining ¼ teaspoon nutmeg and bring to a simmer, whisking until smooth. Taste for seasoning, adding salt and pepper as needed.

Add the meatballs to the sauce, reduce the heat to medium-low, and stir gently with a rubber spatula to coat the meatballs with sauce. Continue to cook them at the lowest simmer for another 15 minutes or so to give the meatballs and sauce time to fuse together.

Just before serving, rewarm the meatballs if necessary and baste again with the sauce.

mascarpone whipped potatoes

It doesn't feel like a family holiday until someone gets out the hand mixer to whip the mashed potatoes. This is their chance.

The texture here is old-school, lofty and almost synthetically smooth. Whipped into tall peaks, the mashed potatoes look like soft-serve. Pile the potatoes into a deep heavy pottery bowl or some other thick ceramic thing. Deep serving bowls keep starches warmer longer at the table.

Use starchy russet-type potatoes for this recipe, nothing too waxy.

Serves 8 as a side

2½ pounds russet potatoes
1 teaspoon fine sea salt, plus more to taste
3 bay leaves
6 tablespoons butter (or more)

½ cup milk
½ cup mascarpone
Freshly ground black pepper

Peel the potatoes and cut into 2-inch chunks. Put in a large saucepot, cover with water by 2 inches, and add the salt and bay leaves. Bring the potatoes to a simmer and cook until very tender when pierced with a knife, about 25 minutes.

As the potatoes cook, melt the butter in a frying pan set over medium heat and cook until it foams up and turns golden at the edges. Give it a stir to mix in the browned bits and then keep cooking until the liquid butter turns amber brown. Reserve. Heat the milk in a saucepan until just steaming; keep warm.

Drain the potatoes in a colander, return them to the dry pot, and heat over medium heat, shaking the pot, to dry out the potatoes. Add the browned butter. With a hand mixer, whip the potatoes and butter until smooth, stopping often to scrape down the sides of the pot. Add the mascarpone and mix until combined. Add the warmed milk little by little, whipping the potatoes until they're soft and lofty and hold stiff peaks. Taste for seasoning and add salt and pepper as needed.

Although these potatoes are best made right before dinner, they can be kept warm for up to an hour. Transfer them to a heatproof serving bowl, press a butter wrapper (or piece of plastic wrap) against the surface of the potatoes, cover tightly with plastic wrap, and keep warm by setting the bowl over a pan of hot water.

citrusy braised red cabbage

I learned to make this dish from some crazy Austrian chefs who were not afraid to reduce two bottles of very good Blaufränkish to make braised red cabbage. In their hands, this traditionally rustic dish was so saturated and rich that it seemed to bleed out on the plate. They taught me that braised red cabbage balances on the top of three poles: sweetness from the caramelized onions and burnt sugar, acidity from the citrus juices, and dark, buttery earth from the reduced chicken stock, wine, and the cabbage itself. The cabbage needs to cook in this slurry for a long time, until it doesn't have any spring left in it and turns wine-sodden red.

Its intensity increases the longer it sits, so you can—and should—make it well in advance. And use half duck fat/half butter if you can get your hands on duck fat.

To spin this dish Scandinavian, I add a handful of frozen lingonberries.

Serves 8 as a side, generously

1 large head red cabbage (4 pounds)
½ cup fresh tart orange or tangerine juice
½ cup fresh lemon juice, plus more to taste
1 teaspoon plus 1 teaspoon salt, plus more to taste
3 tablespoons sugar
2 large sweet onions, cut into small dice
6 tablespoons butter, plus more to taste
2 cups red wine

1½ cups chicken stock, preferably homemade (page 259)
3 tablespoons red wine vinegar, plus more to taste
¼ teaspoon ground ginger
⅛ teaspoon ground allspice
½ teaspoon freshly ground black pepper
2 bay leaves
1 cup fresh red lingonberries or red currants

Preheat the oven to 350°F.

Shred the cabbage, aiming for strips the thickness of a nickel and 3 to 4 inches long. Put the cabbage in a large bowl and toss with the orange juice, lemon juice, and 1 teaspoon of the salt. Massage the juices and salt into the cabbage and leave to sit while you caramelize the onions.

Heat a large enameled cast-iron brasier or a wide high-sided sauté pan over medium heat and sprinkle the sugar evenly across the bottom of the pan. When the sugar liquefies and browns, add the onions and butter and cook over low heat, stirring occasionally, until the onions are deeply caramelized, about 45 minutes.

Preheat the oven to 350°F

Add the red wine to the onions and reduce until it clings to them, about 15 minutes. Add the chicken stock, cabbage, and all of its citrusy juices to the pan and cook, stirring, until the cabbage wilts.

Add the vinegar, ginger, allspice, pepper, bay leaves, and the remaining 1 teaspoon salt to the pan and bring to a simmer. Cook for 10 minutes, or until the cabbage begins to slump. Cut a large square of parchment paper into a circle to fit inside the pan, snip a hole in its center, and press down on the cabbage. (Or partially cover the cabbage with a lid.)

Transfer to the oven and bake the cabbage for 1 to 1½ hours, until dark and rich and fully collapsed, stirring once or twice. Add the lingonberries or red currants and continue baking until they burst, about 15 minutes.

Remove from the oven and taste for seasoning, correcting the balance with additional salt, vinegar, and/or butter. Leave the cabbage to sit with itself for at least 30 minutes, and rewarm just before serving. (*To make the cabbage ahead, cool, store in the refrigerator, and reheat gently when needed.*)

crispy curried cauliflower with mustard seeds

This menu needs some texture to counter all of the soft comfort. Quickly seared cauliflower with scallions and a touch of curry will keep everyone alert.

I always prefer to make this dish last, and to bring it to the table when the curry scent is in full bloom. But to save your sanity, you can cook it ahead of time and spread the cauliflower on a baking sheet to cool. To reheat, fry the cauliflower in a hot pan until steaming, or transfer to a serving dish and blitz in the microwave (uncovered) until hot.

Serves 8 as a side

1 large head cauliflower (2 pounds)
3 tablespoons coconut oil
½ teaspoon fine sea salt, plus more to taste
Freshly ground black pepper
2 tablespoons butter

4 garlic cloves, minced
1 teaspoon curry powder
2 teaspoons yellow mustard seeds
1 bunch scallions (or 1 thin leek), trimmed and
   sliced

Rinse the cauliflower and pat it dry. Separate it into large florets and slice them moderately thin, a little less than ½ inch thick. Cut the wider florets in half, so that you have a mixture of one-bite pieces and nibbly little cauliflower crumbs.

To ensure that the cauliflower browns rather than steams, you'll need to cook it in your largest, widest, heaviest pan, like a wok or a 14-inch sauté pan or cast-iron skillet. Preheat the pan over medium-high heat, and then gather all of your materials around you, because the cooking will go fast.

Turn up the heat to its highest setting, and when the pan is hot, add the coconut oil, immediately followed by the cauliflower. I start with handfuls of the largest pieces first and save the crumbly bits for later. Season the cauliflower with the salt and pepper and cook over high heat, turning often, until both sides have browned. Add the small cauliflower bits, then push the cauliflower to the edges of the pan to make some room in the center and add the butter and garlic. Cook the garlic briefly, then add the curry powder, mustard seeds (they will pop briefly), and the scallions (or leek). Continue cooking the cauliflower over high heat, giving the scallions their turn to brown, tossing every 20 seconds or so, until the cauliflower is tender.

Taste to correct the seasoning, turn out into a shallow bowl or platter, and serve.

cranberry cookie tart

This tart was born when I found myself with an extra lump of sugar cookie dough and one too many bags of cranberries in the fridge—that's what two-for-a-dollar will get you—and decided to bake them together just to see what would happen. Let me tell you, the bottom crust sets to crisp, hard sand, the middle turns into a chewy warm sugar cookie, and the cranberries bloat into sugar-coated balloons. Unlike most fruit tarts, the dough supplies more of the sweetness than the fruit. The cranberries, tossed with just a bit of sugar and some chopped fresh thyme, stay tart, which amplifies their woodsy nature. All of which makes this a very difficult dessert to decline, even after a very filling meal.

You will need an 8-inch fluted tart pan with a removable bottom for this recipe.

Makes one 8-inch tart, serving 8 who want a full piece, or 10 who agree to just a sliver

tart dough and streusel
14 tablespoons (1¾ sticks) unsalted butter, at coolish room temperature
⅔ cup plus 7 tablespoons sugar, plus more for garnish
2 large egg yolks
1 tablespoon fresh lemon juice
1 teaspoon pure vanilla extract
1¾ cups plus 2 tablespoons all-purpose flour
½ teaspoon fine sea salt
Grated zest of ½ lemon

cranberry filling
2¾ cups (10 ounces) fresh cranberries
⅔ cup sugar
1 teaspoon minced fresh thyme
1 teaspoon grated lemon zest
1 tablespoon fresh lemon juice

Vanilla ice cream for serving

In the bowl of a stand mixer fitted with the paddle attachment, paddle the butter until light. Add the 7 tablespoons sugar and paddle until creamed: iridescent and fluffy. Add the egg yolks one at a time and mix until incorporated. Add the lemon juice and vanilla and whip to lighten the mixture.

Wisk together the flour, salt, and lemon zest in a medium bowl. Add to the butter mixture and mix just until it comes together.

Loosely fill a ½-cup measuring cup with dough for the streusel topping, and refrigerate.

Lightly butter an 8-inch fluted tart pan with a removable bottom. Scatter the rest of the dough into the tart pan and press it evenly over the bottom and up the sides of the pan. The pastry will be relatively thin, which is what will make this tart crisp and delicate, so take your time to distribute it evenly. Refrigerate until chilled.

Preheat the oven to 350°F.

For the filling, combine the cranberries, sugar, thyme, and lemon zest and mix to coat the berries. Pour the filling mixture into the chilled tart shell, raking the berries to fill it level. Scatter the reserved dough across the top in haphazard lumps and sprinkle with a couple of tablespoons of sugar.

Bake until the cranberries bubble and the topping turns golden brown, 45 to 50 minutes. Cool on a rack, then remove the tart ring, cut the tart into wedges, and serve—ideally just warmer than tepid—with vanilla ice cream.

RED CURRANT VARIATION
This tart is also delicious made with fresh red currants in the summer. Use 2 cups (12 ounces) fresh red currants in place of the cranberries and add 1½ teaspoons cornstarch along with the sugar to soak up their abundant juices.

St. Patrick's day

FOR TEN TO TWELVE

— green cabbage sipping soup
— slow-smoked brisket pastrami with creamy zhug
  (*or* quick-steamed pastrami)
— yuca fries persillade
— creamed carrot coins
— marinated roasted beets and grapes with radicchio and hazelnuts
— green salad with invisible vinaigrette
— sticky date olive oil cake

I have not a drop of the Irish inside me, but I will happily take other people's holidays as an excuse to throw a party. Celebrating a day that doesn't figure into your heritage is very freeing; it means that you're beholden to no tradition. I can even construct a St. Patrick's Day menu that omits potatoes, because wouldn't yuca fries be better than fried potatoes? The crunchy exterior; the flaky, velvety middle; the sweet burnt shards at the bottom of the bowl. Yes, yes they might.

The centerpiece of this feast is—surprise!—a large hunk of meat. Corned beef may feel pretty conventional on St. Patrick's Day, but curing and smoking your own beef brisket and then rubbing it in pastrami spice is so exciting. It also provides me the opportunity to use my new favorite tool, the brine injector. With a giant steel cylinder and a thick needle, it looks like a comically large cartoon syringe. You can just soak the brisket in the curing brine, of course, but injecting the cure into the meat is more precise and can shorten the curing time from a week to 3 or 4 days.

You might ask, what's the benefit to spending 5 days (albeit mostly inactive working time) making your own corned beef when flats of corned beef beckon from the store—and they're on sale?

Well, you don't have to. You can skip the curing and the smoking and just rub a prepared corned beef roast with the same pastrami spices and go on from there; see page 182. But the number one reason to cure your own is to turn down the salt volume to a healthier, more pleasant level. Most commercial corned beef is cured hard enough to withstand a round-the-world voyage—too salty, in my opinion.

And it's fun. Smoking meat at home begins for many people as a personal challenge that blooms into a hobby and then into a vocation. Conveniently, it enforces leisure, making a case for sitting and doing nothing that we, good members of workaholic culture, usually cannot. It requires an entire day of inattentive babysitting, but the rewards are huge: 10 pounds of wobbling, pink, spice-crusted brisket, so tender it folds over onto the knife as you slice it. And opening the smoker to let out a cloud of meat smoke just as your friends are arriving is the best welcome signal there is.

green cabbage sipping soup

In lieu of a snacky appetizer, sometimes it's nice to make a drinkable vegetable soup. Hot and bacon-scented and poured into mugs, green cabbage sipping soup calms down an active hunger without filling you up too much, and when you're standing outside around the smoker, it also warms the hands.

This cabbage and leek soup was originally my private "reducing" broth—i.e., what I make for myself to counter the heaviness I feel after eating too much rich food for days on end. Some may not trust a maintenance regimen that includes bacon—just two slices!—but it lends a dirty smokiness that keeps the soup from feeling too virtuous. Dairy-free except for the butter, which can be replaced by olive oil, and containing just a whisper of starch to thicken, this soup is pretty much liquid vegetable.

Prep all the ingredients before you start cooking, and gather your equipment around you, because this one comes together quickly.

Makes 6 cups, serving 10 to 12 in small coffee cups

2 slices thick-cut bacon, cut into thirds

5 tablespoons butter

2 cups thinly sliced leeks (mostly light and dark green tops)

3 garlic cloves, minced

6 packed cups thinly shredded green cabbage, including dark green outer leaves (about half of a medium cabbage)

1 teaspoon plus 1 teaspoon fine sea salt

½ teaspoon freshly ground black pepper

1 packed cup chopped parsley

5 tablespoons fine polenta or cornmeal

6 cups water

Freshly grated nutmeg

6 ounces bocconcini (small mozzarella balls) for garnish

3 to 4 tablespoons Chive Oil (recipe follows) for garnish

Set your largest, widest sauté pan or enameled cast-iron braiser over medium heat and add the bacon. Cook until browned around the edges but not crisp through. Transfer the bacon to a bowl, reserving the fat in the pan.

Turn the heat up to high, add 3 tablespoons of the butter and the leeks, and cook briefly, until they turn bright green. Add the garlic—quickly stirring to coat it in the fat—followed immediately by the cabbage. Keep the heat high so that the moisture steams off quickly and the cabbage browns a bit on the bottom of the pan, which will keep both its color and bright flavor. Add 1 teaspoon of the salt and the pepper and cook, stirring to keep the cabbage moving, until fully wilted but still green, about 3 minutes.

Add the parsley and cook briefly to wilt, and then add the polenta. Stir until the polenta is evenly distributed, and add the water. Bring to a fast boil, reduce to a lively simmer and cook for 5 to 8 minutes, until the cabbage is just tender. Add the nutmeg and remove the pot from the heat.

Working in two batches, scoop the soup into a blender, along with the remaining 2 tablespoons butter, and process until finely pureed. Pour the soup through a fine-mesh sieve into a wide bowl, pushing on the puree with the back of a ladle to force it through the sieve. The soup should be smooth, as thick as heavy cream, and a soft lime green.

If not serving right away, chill the soup in a metal bowl set over a bowl of ice, stirring until cold, and reheat just before serving. Otherwise, pour straightaway into small coffee cups, each garnished with 2 or 3 floating bocconcini and a spoonful of chive oil.

chive oil Look for a fresh bundle of chives, or borrow some from a neighbor's clump, because this oil is best when made with in-season spring or summer chives, because that's when they're sweetest. In fact, go ahead and make it when the chives are fresh and freeze it for later, stored in a tightly rolled heavy plastic bag.

Chilling the oil helps to keep the chive oil cool while it's in the blender and maintains its trademark bright electric green.

Makes 1 cup

1 cup thinly sliced fresh chives
¾ cup canola oil, chilled

Pinch of fine sea salt

Combine the chives, oil, and salt in a blender and process on high speed until well combined and bright green. Pour into a metal bowl set in a larger bowl of ice water and stir until cold. Store in the refrigerator for up to 5 days, or in the freezer for 1 year.

slow-smoked brisket pastrami with creamy zhug

At minimum you will need to start this recipe 4 days before serving—you need at least 3 days to cure the brisket and a full day to smoke it. I generally stretch it out over a week.

Also, take this precise recipe for times and temperatures with a grain of salt, because every piece of meat is different, and so is every cooker. In general, you want to smoke the meat over wood chips at a range of 225 to 250°F until the internal temperature hits 200 to 205°F—which can take anywhere from 6 to 10 hours—plus an hour to let it rest before slicing. In a pinch, I've cooked a brisket at 300°F to get it done in 6 hours, but rushing sort of defeats the point. Some people cook their briskets more slowly and at a much lower temperature (185°F), camping out by the cooker through the night, but I've found that 225°F is the sweet spot if you, like me, want to start your brisket in the morning and serve it for dinner that night.

There are two commonly sold cuts of brisket: the thicker, fat point cut and the thinner, leaner flat cut. The point cut is richer and more succulent (and the one I prefer) but the flat cut will absorb the brine more quickly. You could brine and smoke a whole 12-pound brisket if you wanted (there's enough brine here to cure it), but I've found that 8 to 10 pounds is enough for most parties.

Green sauces of one sort or another rotate in and out of my kitchen all year long. Throw any combination of fresh-cut herbs from the garden and toasted whole spices into the blender, they're always good. I briefly notate the recipe on an index card before throwing it into my kitchen junk drawer, and rarely make these the same way twice. But this one, based on spicy Israeli green zhug, smoothed out and lengthened with sour cream, was special from the start.

Note that you will need a brine injector to make this recipe.

Serves 12, with leftovers

One 8- to 10-pound beef brisket (preferably from the point-cut end)

cure
1 gallon water
11 ounces (1¼ cups) kosher salt
1 cup packed brown sugar
4 teaspoons pink curing salt (see Pink Salt, page 166)
2 tablespoons black peppercorns
1 teaspoon fennel or anise seeds
8 whole cloves
8 bay leaves
2 heads garlic, tops sliced off to expose the cloves
6 dried red Chinese chiles

3 to 4 cups fruitwood chips, such as apple

pastrami spice rub
3 tablespoons lightly toasted and coarsely ground coriander seeds
¼ cup cracked black peppercorns
2 tablespoons coarsely ground yellow mustard seeds
2 tablespoons garlic powder (not garlic salt)
1½ teaspoons ground allspice
1 teaspoon ground ginger

Creamy Zhug (recipe follows)

recipe continues

Four days before you intend to serve it, brine the brisket: Combine half of the water—2 quarts—with the salt, brown sugar, and pink salt in a large stockpot and bring to a simmer, whisking to dissolve the salt and sugar. Add the peppercorns, fennel or anise, cloves, bay leaves, garlic, and chiles, then remove from the heat and add the remaining 2 quarts cold water. Cool the brine to room temperature, then refrigerate until chilled.

Find a vessel large enough to hold the curing brisket—a stockpot or very large storage container. (I use a deep 2-gallon lidded enameled metal roaster that I found in a thrift store and, yes, it's one of my prized possessions.) If you have a point-cut brisket, you may want to trim some of the shaggy fat on top. I leave it ½-inch thick because I generally buy the regulation grocery-store-grade beef, and the fat cap gives it necessary moisture, but if you're using a more marbled piece of beef you could trim it a little more closely.

Put the brisket in your container of choice, draw some of the brine up into the barrel of the brine injector, and inject the brisket at 2-inch intervals, coming at it from every side. Pour the rest of the brine over the brisket. Weight down the meat with a large plate to submerge it into the brine, and refrigerate overnight.

The next day, inject the brisket again with brine, drawing up the brine pooling in the container. Cure for at least 2 more days, although the meat can hang out in the brine for as long as 7 days.

When you're ready to smoke the brisket, make the rub by combining all the spices in a small bowl.

Drain the brisket, brush off the spices, and rinse well under cold running water. Pat the brisket dry and set on a rack inside a low-sided roasting pan that will fit into your smoker. Sprinkle the rub spices evenly over all sides of the brisket, pressing so they adhere. Refrigerate for at least 3 hours, and as long as 24 hours.

Prepare a fire in your outdoor smoker and steady the temperature at 275°F. (I use a Big Green Egg for smoking meat, but any kind of smoke-fueled barbecue cooker will work.) You'll want to smoke the brisket at about 225°F, but the smoker generally drops in temperature when you open it to put the meat on, so I start high. Toss the wood chips with a little water in a bowl to moisten, then add a handful to the coals. Set the roasting pan that contains the brisket in the smoker, shut the lid, and steady the temperature again to hover between 225 and 250°F. Don't worry if it fluctuates a bit, but take care not to let it rise about 300°F for too long, or the brisket will brown too quickly. Cook the brisket, adding fresh wood chips whenever the smoke stops coming, until the internal temperature reads 190°F. It should be tender when stuck with a fork, but not quite jiggly. Depending on the thickness of the brisket and the consistency of the temperature, smoking the brisket will take anywhere from 5 to 7 hours.

Remove the pan of brisket from the smoker and preheat the oven to 200° F. Wrap the brisket in parchment paper and set on a baking sheet. Put the brisket in the low oven and leave it there for at least 30 minutes, or until the internal temperature reaches 201 to 203° F. Turn off the oven; you can hold the brisket in the warm oven for up to an hour before serving. (Alternativeely, wrap the brisket in paper and finish resting it in a small insulated cooler, although this really works better when you have multiple briskets.)

Thirty minutes before serving, drop the oven rack to the bottom third and turn on the broiler. Unwrap the brisket (save the juices), put it in the oven, 10 inches below the broiler, and stand by as the exterior caramelizes and darkens. Transfer the brisket to a cutting board and let rest for 20 minutes before slicing.

Slice the brisket across the grain into thin slices, arrange on a serving platter, moisten with the reserved juices, and serve with the sauce.

---

creamy zhug You can make this fragrant sauce while the meat is smoking. The heat of serrano chiles from the grocery store is pretty consistently hot but not blistering, so don't hold back. This sauce should be spicy.

If time allows, toast whole spices in a hot dry pan until aromatic and grind separately in a spice-dedicated coffee mill. Coriander, cumin, and cardamom all taste stronger when toasted and freshly ground.

Makes about 1½ cups

1½ serrano chiles, sliced
2 garlic cloves
1½ cups roughly chopped fresh cilantro,
    including tender stems
1 cup roughly chopped fresh parsley
2 teaspoons ground coriander (see headnote)

½ teaspoon ground cumin
¼ teaspoon ground cardamom
½ teaspoon fine sea salt
¼ cup fresh lemon juice
¼ cup extra-virgin olive oil
⅔ cup sour cream

Combine the serranos, garlic, cilantro, parsley, ground spices, and salt in a blender and blend on high to grind them to a paste (medium, not finely ground). Add the lemon juice, olive oil, and sour cream and blitz until combined.

Scrape the sauce out into a serving bowl. It can be held at room temperature for up to 4 hours; if making it further in advance, cover and refrigerate.

recipe continues

quick steamed pastrami An alternative to the home-smoked brisket pastrami if you're too busy to think that far ahead. In truth, I often make this a few weeks after March 17, to take advantage of all of the corned beef on sale. (And if there's any extra spice rub, save it to make hot buttered pastrami popcorn. Believe me, people go nuts for that pastrami corn.)

Serves 10 to 12

One 5- to 7-pound corned beef brisket roast,   Pastrami Spice Rub (page 179)
     preferably point cut

Rinse the corned beef and trim off any soft, ropy fat, preserving as much of the top fat cap as possible. Soak it in cold water for 1 to 2 hours, refrigerated, to desalinate a little.

     Drain the corned beef and pat dry.

     Fit a large stockpot with a metal steamer basket, filling the bottom of the pot with water to reach about an inch below the basket, and set over high heat. Sprinkle the spice rub thickly over all sides of the meat—you may not use all of it—pressing it into the meat to adhere.

Transfer the corned beef to the steamer basket, cover, and steam until the meat is very tender when tested with a fork, about 4 hours. Keep watch on the water level, and replenish before it evaporates.

Preheat the oven to 425°F.

Carefully transfer the meat to a roasting pan and roast until the surface of the meat caramelizes and darkens to the color of black coffee, about 15 minutes. Let rest for at least 20 minutes before slicing.

yuca fries persillade

Fried yuca emerges from the hot oil with sharp, brown craggy edges, looking like the world's best steak fries. It's almost sacrilegious not to make potatoes for an Irish holiday, but dare I say that yuca makes a more interesting pairing with the corned beef. It has a voluptuous, almost waxen interior, and its surface holds its crispness almost indefinitely, even after being tossed with a last-minute persillade, a fine mist of minced raw garlic and parsley.

Buy heavy-feeling yuca roots from a grocery store or market whose clientele keeps it in heavy rotation, store it in a dark place at cool room temperature, and cook it within a few days.

Serves 10 to 12 as a side

fried yuca
Canola or peanut oil for deep-frying
   (at least 6 cups)
2½ pounds yuca (2 large, long yucca)
Fine sea salt

persillade
½ cup tightly packed fresh parsley leaves
3 garlic cloves
¼ teaspoon fine sea salt
¼ teaspoon freshly ground black pepper

Bring a large pot of water to a boil over high heat. Meanwhile, get your frying pot ready: Pour 4 inches of oil into a heavy high-sided pot and set over the lowest possible heat. If you have a candy/deep-fry thermometer, clip it to the side of the pot.

Fill a large bowl with cold water and set it by your side while you prep the yuca, as peeled yuca oxidizes and turns gray almost immediately. Lop off both ends, peel the yuca, cut into 4-inch long sections, and submerge in the water. Cut each cylinder lengthwise into quarters and split the fat quarters again, into eighths. The yuca will flake and be hard to cut evenly, but irregularity is what you want here (think a mix of logs and kindling). The roughed-up split edges will be the crispest. Return the yuca to the bowl of cold water as you go.

When the water boils, salt it generously. Take half of the yuca out of the water, drain on towels, and add to the boiling water. Boil, uncovered, until the yuca is perfectly tender when pierced with a knife, about 15 minutes. Pull out the yuca with a spider or a sieve and transfer to a baking sheet to dry. Cook the second batch the same way; drain and add to the baking sheet.

Raise the heat under the oil and bring the temperature to 350°F. Set a rack over a baking sheet next to the oil pot, to hold the finished fries. Add half of the yuca to the hot oil and fry until it turns evenly dark golden brown, about 5 minutes. Lift the fried yuca from the hot oil to the rack, then toss into a large bowl, add a hefty pinch of the persillade and an even spray of salt, and flip the yuca in the bowl to coat. Repeat with the remaining yuca and seasoning.

creamed carrot coins

Bright soft carrots lounging in a soft blanket of orange-stained cream are luscious, and vintage. This dish would look more modern if the carrots were cut into elongated ovals, but it wouldn't be exactly correct. They should be cut into coins, perfectly round, as thick as a pinkie. When you stir, the carrots should suction down to the bottom of the pot like a penny to the floor.

To peel or not to peel, that is the question, and the answer depends on the state of your carrots. Young summer carrots have thin skins that will nearly disappear during cooking and so need only a good scrubbing. Winter-storage carrots, which is what you'll usually find in the grocery store, are more mature and generally sweeter, but their rough, dry skins should be peeled. Staying in character for the creamed-carrot era, I should probably say that those carrots should be *scraped*.

Serves 10 to 12 in small portions

1¼ pounds carrots, peeled or not (see
    headnote), cut into ½-inch-thick coins
Rounded ¼ teaspoon fine sea salt, plus to taste
4 tablespoons butter

¼ teaspoon minced fresh rosemary
7 to 8 tablespoons heavy cream
2 teaspoons dry sherry or Madeira

Put the carrots in a 12-inch frying pan, add the salt, and massage it into the carrots with your hands to get their juices flowing. Add 3 tablespoons of the butter and 1 cup water and bring to a rolling simmer over medium heat. Cover the pan and cook until a thin knife slips into the side of a carrot without resistance and they are frankly tender, about 15 minutes. Check often to make sure that the water hasn't boiled away—sound cue: it will sound more urgent—and add more if necessary.

Uncover the pan and cook until the remaining liquid covers the carrots like a glaze. If the water has reduced and the butter is pooling at the edges, add a dribble of water to emulsify it. Add the rosemary, 7 tablespoons of the cream, sherry, and the remaining tablespoon of butter and simmer until the cream sauce clings thickly to the carrots, about 3 minutes. (If they need more coverage, add another splash of cream.)

If not serving immediately, keep the carrots warm and covered, diluting the sauce with water on the reheat if most of it has evaporated.

marinated roasted beets and grapes with radicchio and hazelnuts

Tangy sweet-and-sour marinated roasted beets are one of my large-party lifelines, because they're best when made hours (or even a day or two) before. And conveniently, the dark red pool of marinade that collects around them becomes the dressing for the salad. Be sure to roast the beets until their bottoms caramelize deeply. Even after they've been peeled, those charred contact spots will bring the down-to-earth balance that this mixture of sweet roasted grapes and cool, slightly bitter radicchio needs.

The way the broken plum-colored vinaigrette coats and stains pale radicchio hearts makes my heart drum faster, it's so pretty, but you can use any peppery or sweet/bitter sturdy fall green (like endive, tatsoi, mizuna, or arugula).

Arrange this salad on a very large, wide platter to show off its good looks, and shower it with cracked toasted hazelnuts at the very last minute.

Serves 10 to 12 as a side salad

2 pounds beets (about 6 medium-small beets)

4 garlic cloves, crushed and peeled

1 teaspoon minced fresh rosemary, plus 2 sprigs

1 teaspoon fine sea salt, plus more for the beets and grapes

Freshly ground black pepper

2 tablespoons canola oil

2 tablespoons butter

1½ cups (about 8 ounces) purple or red grapes, preferably Concord or a similar wine grape

1 teaspoon sugar

½ cup hazelnuts or Butter-Roasted Walnuts (page 43)

¾ cup red wine

1½ tablespoons red wine vinegar

2 tablespoons finely minced shallot

2 tablespoons fresh lemon juice, plus more to taste

5 tablespoons extra-virgin olive oil

1 large head radicchio

1 lightly packed cup fresh parsley leaves, washed and air-dried

Preheat the oven to 400°F.

Place the beets in a baking dish or roasting pan large enough to accommodate them in a single layer. Add the crushed garlic cloves, a rosemary sprig, the canola oil, and enough water to just barely cover the bottom of the pan. Sprinkle the beets evenly with salt and a few turns of black pepper and shake the pan to coat.

Cover the pan with foil and roast until the beets are just tender at the center, about an hour for medium-small beets. Uncover and roast until the edges of the beets darken a shade and a fork slips in and out of the center easily, another 45 minutes or so, depending on size. Transfer the beets to a bowl and cover tightly. (The steam helps loosen the peel.) Leave the oven on.

When the beets are cool enough to handle, hold each one in a paper towel, trim the tops and bottoms with a paring knife, and then twist off the skin in the towel. The smooth beets should slip right out for the most part, but remove any stuck-on scraps with the paring knife.

Cut the beets into bite-sized pieces and transfer to a bowl. Add the shallots, lemon juice, 1 teaspoon salt, about 10 turns of black pepper, the 1 teaspoon minced rosemary, and ¼ cup of the olive oil. Let the beets sit to soak up the marinade for a few minutes and then taste for seasoning, looking for a balance between sweetness and acidity. Add more lemon juice and a bit of salt if needed. Let the beets marinate at room temperature for up to 4 hours, or refrigerate for as long as 3 days before making the salad. They get increasingly better as they sit, and in my experience, they'll keep up to a week, but at some point the shallots will give away their age. Pull the refrigerated beets out an hour before making the salad.

To roast the grapes, heat a medium frying pan over medium-high heat and add the butter and then the grapes. Season with a little salt and pepper and the sugar. Sauté, tossing occasionally, until the grapes take on a little color, about 3 minutes. Add the remaining rosemary sprig and transfer the pan to the oven to roast until the grapes shrink and caramelize, about 30 minutes. Remove from the oven and reduce the oven temperature to 325°F.

Return the pan of grapes to the stovetop and add the wine and vinegar. Bring to a simmer over medium heat and cook until the wine has reduced to a thin, pourable syrup (it will thicken further as it cools). Remove from the heat, remove the rosemary sprig, and pour the grape mixture over the beets, tossing to coat.

To toast the hazelnuts, put them in a small skillet or baking dish and toast in the oven until their skins lift away and the interiors turn golden brown, about 20 minutes. Dump the hazelnuts onto the center of a clean tea towel, gather the corners together to make a sack, and squeeze and rub the nuts to remove their skins. Unwrap and roll the skinned nuts away from the skins, then usher them into a small bowl. (Shake

recipe continues

185

out the towel over the sink or trash can.) When they are cool, chop the hazelnuts roughly, for a mixture of halved pieces and fine gravel.

To serve, transfer the beet-grape mixture, including all of its juices, to a wide serving bowl. Remove the outer leaves of the radicchio, give it a quick rinse, and slice lengthwise into quarters. Tear the radicchio into large abstract bite-sized pieces and pile on top of the beets. Chop the parsley leaves, leaving them pretty large, and add to the salad, along with the last tablespoon of olive oil. Toss the beets and radicchio together until just mixed, then garnish with the hazelnuts. The salad can sit for about 30 minutes before serving without any problem.

green salad with invisible vinaigrette

Invisible vinaigrette, which I've been making for years, is the little black dress of salad dressings. It has a talent for slipping quietly into the background, for tasting more like lettuce than some lettuces do themselves. I pin it on the tangy salted capers, the dill, and the large volume of chopped parsley, minced to a paste.

Store any leftover vinaigrette in the refrigerator. Always save leftover salad dressing, even if it's just a couple of tablespoons, because you can always pull it out and build a new one on its back sometime soon.

Serves 10 to 12 as a side

invisible vinaigrette
2 teaspoons salt-packed capers
2 small garlic cloves
½ cup chopped fresh parsley
¼ teaspoon fine sea salt, plus more to taste
Freshly ground black pepper to taste
1 tablespoon chopped fresh dill
1½ teaspoons Dijon mustard
3 tablespoons fresh lemon juice
2 teaspoons red wine vinegar
½ cup extra-virgin olive oil
1 tablespoon water

salad
10 cups salad greens (a mixture of pale lettuce hearts and dark green baby greens—like arugula, mizuna, or baby spinach), washed and spun-dry
4 yellow inner celery stalks, thinly sliced, leaves and all
2 tablespoons finely minced shallots or thinly sliced scallions
Fine sea salt and freshly ground black pepper

For the vinaigrette, put the capers into a small bowl and cover with warm water, giving them a quick squeeze to express their salt. Soak for at least 20 minutes, then drain and rinse.

I make this vinaigrette in my mortar and pestle but it can also be made successfully by hand if you're willing to go long on chopping the herbs. Combine the garlic and capers, and pound or chop until finely mashed together, using the flat side of your knife if you're not using a mortar and pestle. Add the parsley, salt, and pepper and pound or chop until the parsley begins to express dark green juice, then add the dill and do the same. Stir in the mustard, lemon juice, vinegar, and olive oil and taste for salt, adjusting as needed. Stir in the water and set the dressing aside to meld and come together.

For the salad, combine all the washed spun greens in a large salad bowl, tearing any larger leaves into bite-sized pieces, and add the thinly sliced celery and shallot or scallions. Season lightly with salt and pepper and toss with just enough of the dressing to coat. Serve immediately.

sticky date olive oil cake

This cake has all the flavors of sticky toffee pudding, just a bit reshuffled. A simple yogurt and olive oil upside-down cake reveals Medjool dates trapped beneath a shiny, sugared top. The cake is perfumed with lemon zest, nutmeg, and a few glugs of earthy Madeira and moistened with enough olive oil to tint the crumb gold. If you pinch this cake between your fingers, it springs back like a new yellow sponge.

If you're not feeling particularly flush with cash at the moment, you can cut the olive oil with something cheaper, like canola or peanut oil.

Makes one 8- or 9-inch square cake, cut into 12 sensible (or 9 healthy) portions

Softened butter for the baking dish
Sour Cream Whip (recipe follows)

date topping
¼ cup white sugar
¼ cup packed brown sugar
2 tablespoons butter
3 tablespoons maple syrup
1 tablespoon water
½ teaspoon fine sea salt
8 large soft Medjool dates (6 ounces)

olive oil cake
2 ¼ cups all-purpose flour
1½ teaspoons baking powder
¼ teaspoon baking soda
½ teaspoon fine sea salt
Grated zest of half a lemon
2 large eggs
1¼ cups sugar
⅔ cup extra-virgin olive oil
½ cup plain whole-milk yogurt (not Greek-style)
2 tablespoons Madeira

Preheat the oven to 350°F. Rub an 8- or 9-inch square heavy metal baking pan (Pyrex is fine too) with a thick coating of soft butter and set aside.

Combine both sugars, the butter, maple syrup, water, and salt in a small saucepan and bring to a boil over medium heat. Cook, stirring often, until the sugar has dissolved and the bubbles grow large, 2 minutes at a rapid boil. Drop a bit of the syrup onto a cold plate to check for thickness; it should feel sticky when pinched.

Pour the hot caramel into the prepared baking pan, scraping the saucepan with a rubber spatula to get every bit and tilting the pan to cover the bottom. Rip the dates in half, remove the pits, and lay them skin side down on the caramel.

For the cake, combine the flour, baking powder, baking soda, salt, and lemon zest in a large bowl and whisk to mix the leavening into the flour, giving it about 30 strokes.

Combine the eggs and sugar in the bowl of a stand mixer fitted with the whisk attachment (or in another large bowl, if using a hand mixer) and whip until thickened and pale yellow, about 2 minutes.

Measure the olive oil in a large glass measuring cup, add the yogurt and Madeira, and whisk with a fork. While the mixer is going, dribble in the olive oil mixture, emulsifying the liquids into the eggs. Add the flour mixture, mixing just enough to form a smooth batter.

Pour the batter over the dates, smoothing it to the edges, and bake until the cake browns lightly and springs back when pressed with a fingertip, about 35 minutes. Remove from the oven and let the cake cool for 5 minutes.

Run an offset metal spatula around the perimeter of the cake to loosen it, carefully reaching below the cake to loosen the dates as well. Then set a serving platter or cake plate upside down over the pan.

Holding onto the edges with two hot pads, quickly flip the cake upside down onto the platter. If any dates or caramel stick to the dish, transfer them to the top of the cake.

Let the cake cool to room temperature before cutting into squares. Serve garnished with the sour cream whip.

sour cream whip If you want to make the kind of whipped cream that will hold for hours in the refrigerator, nearly as well as Cool Whip, use this recipe. The sour cream stabilizes the whipped cream, and it also gives it a tang reminiscent of crème fraîche.

Makes 3½ cups

1½ cups heavy cream
¼ cup sugar
½ teaspoon pure vanilla extract
Pinch of fine sea salt
½ cup full-fat sour cream

You can use a stand mixer or a hand mixer to make this, or you can whip the cream by hand with a whisk. A chilled bowl and a large balloon whisk make short work of it, and I think that hand-whipped cream is denser and more luscious.

Combine the cream and sugar in a large bowl and whip until the cream starts to mound softly. Add the vanilla and salt and continue whipping, pushing it past the soft peak stage to full crinkle—but stop before it loses its sheen and starts to look curdy. Whip the sour cream to lighten it, then fold it in by hand, which will return the mixture to floofy soft peaks. This stores well in a tightly sealed container in the refrigerator for 2 days.

189

Easter feast

FOR EIGHT

— deviled eggs with Roman Jewish fried
   artichokes
— ham cooked in milk, honey, and sage
— wok-fried black pepper asparagus
— creamy baby turnip salad with dill
— hot water rolls
— rhubarb-almond envelope tart

Everywhere else the rhubarb is popping its bring pink heads out of the ground and the crocuses are blooming, right on schedule, but here the world remains stubbornly black and white: papery birch trees, dark mud, trumpeter swans sitting on the half-melted creek. Spring is still just a fermenting thought in our heads, a craving.

I roll through the grocery store looking for fresh flavors to break the long winter fast anyway. I buy asparagus, the thickest stalks I can find, with the least jostled tips. I buy Meyer lemons, their skins smooth and youthful, and two artichokes, fat and wrapped tightly in plastic. Back home, I dig out a bag of frosty frozen rhubarb from my deep freezer and bang it on the counter to knock off the ice crystals. If only this holiday could hold on for two more weeks and wait for northern rhubarb.

In any case, the main structural posts of this meal are not the vegetables, but instead the large double-smoked ham sitting in my refrigerator and the hot water roll dough mushrooming in a bowl on the countertop. So rarely do I make homemade dinner rolls that this old-fashioned boiling-water dough recipe feels like a 36-hour reenactment of life circa 1920. It requires that you sit on a grandmother stool next to the counter to carefully shape the dough, rolling it under the tent of your hand until the surface of the dough stretches taut like skin. Then you must find a place (not too drafty) for the pan of rolls to rise at a snail's pace overnight. In the morning, I rush into to the kitchen to find inflated balls of dough as translucent as balloons. I fear they'll pop, but baking sets them. When they come out of the oven, the light, pale interior will pull out like a sheet of gauze. A heavy swipe of cold butter would squash this roll, but it's ideal for holding a piece of ham to gently swab through the dill cream sauce pooling around the spring turnips, which is really all I ever want out of this spring holiday meal.

deviled eggs with Roman Jewish fried artichokes

Easter is the season to drag out your great-aunt so-and-so's deviled egg platter—you know, that ugly one that your female relatives have creatively "passed on" to you like a game of hot potato (because no one wants to be known as the heartless wretch who sent the thing to the Goodwill). If you're nostalgic like me, you'll get suckered into caretaking all of these treasured family heirlooms. I fill the platter with deviled eggs topped with something that my Great-Aunt Rose would never have: crispy sprays of artichoke fried in olive oil. In Italy, they're known as *carciofi alla Giudia*, or artichokes fried in the manner of Jewish Romans, and they serve them whole and unadorned on a plate like dried sunflowers.

190

Trimming two artichokes down to the hearts seems fiddly, but in this case neatness isn't the goal. The snakier they look, the crispier they'll be.

In my opinion, a soft, luscious room-temperature deviled egg tastes better than one that's cadaver-stiff and straight from the fridge, so wait to fill the eggs and fry the artichokes until just before serving. But both the eggs and the filling can be made up to a day in advance and stored in the refrigerator.

While it may seem a waste to squander 2 cups of extra-virgin olive oil to fry 2 measly artichoke hearts, you can save the oil for future frying, or use it to add a nice musky olive flavor to homemade mayonnaise.

Makes 18 deviled eggs

deviled eggs
9 large eggs
1 tablespoon Dijon mustard
3 tablespoons sour cream or crème fraîche
1 tablespoon extra-virgin olive oil
2 teaspoons fresh lemon juice
1 teaspoon pickle juice
¼ teaspoon fine sea salt, plus more to taste
Dash of cayenne pepper
Freshly ground black pepper

fried artichokes
2 globe artichokes
1½ to 2 cups extra-virgin olive oil
Fine sea salt

Put the eggs in a saucepan, cover with cold water, and bring to a simmer. Softly boil the eggs for 2 minutes, then take the pan off the heat and set a timer for 10 minutes.

Drain the eggs, gently crack the shells against the sides of the pot, and cover with cold water. Shell them immediately.

Blot the eggs dry, cut them in half, and pop out the yolks. Crush the yolks with a fork in a wide bowl until powdery and no lumps remain, then whisk in the mustard, sour cream, olive oil, lemon juice, and pickle juice. The mixture should be soft but not runny. Season with the salt, cayenne, and pepper to taste, and spoon the egg yolk mixture into a plastic quart bag, pressing it down into one corner. (*You can prep the eggs to this point up to a day ahead; refrigerate the egg yolk bag and the egg whites, tightly covered.*)

To clean the artichokes, trim the stem ends to ½ inch. Bend back the outer leaves until they snap off, circling around each artichoke to remove all of the stiff dark green leaves, stopping when they get thin, close to the heart. Lay the artichokes on their sides and cut off their tops, just above the heart, exposing the hairy chokes. Using a sharp spoon, scoop out the chokes. With a paring knife, trim the perimeter of

recipe continues

the artichoke hearts, leaving a few thin layers of leaves. If you are doing this in advance, refrigerate the artichokes in a bowl of cold lemon-spiked water to keep them from oxidizing. If you're cooking them soon, the oxidation won't bother anything—they'll be fried to a frizz anyway.

For optimum crispness, fry the artichokes twice, as for French fries. Pour 2 inches of olive oil into a small saucepan and heat over medium-high heat. When the oil is hot enough to spark a droplet of water (about 350°F), add the artichoke hearts and simmer gently until tender, but try to avoid browning. Pull out the artichokes and drain on paper toweling. To remove any stray bits that will burn on the second fry, strain the oil through a fine-mesh sieve into a bowl.

Pour 4 to 5 tablespoons of the olive oil (reserve the rest for another use) into a wide sauté pan set over medium-high heat. Cut each artichoke in half and then into 9 or 10 triangle-shaped spears. When the oil sizzles on contact (about 375°F), add the artichokes and fry until dark brown and crisp. Drain on paper towels and sprinkle with salt.

Snip the tip of the egg yolk bag and fill each egg white half with deviled egg filling. Top each one with a piece of fried artichoke and serve.

ham cooked in milk, honey, and sage

This ham gets an Italian treatment inspired by *maiale al latte,* or pork cooked in milk. It was an accidental recipe, one driven entirely by the ingredients within my reach—or to be honest, the stuff that was in my way. Unfurling the white paper wrapping around my beautiful double-smoked ham, I pushed away the stray ingredients that had collected on the countertop during the last twenty-four hours—a bottle of vermouth, a dredged-out bear of honey, a jug of milk that some young creative had used to make a glass of splattered Jackson Pollock–inspired chocolate milk. And I decided to work with them. Salty ham loves a sweet glaze, so why shouldn't it come from milk and honey? As the ham bakes, the sage-scented sauce breaks at first into curds but eventually fuses into a soft, milky caramel.

The ham here should be a proper bone-in Midwestern smokehouse beast, lightly brined and cold-smoked over wood. The surface of a double-smoked ham will feel dry to the touch and it will smell up-front smoky, like bacon concentrate. Unlike the everyday mass-produced water-added ham that's plumped with brine, a proper smokehouse ham doesn't drip with saline when you shuck it from its wrapping, or look or taste anything like lunch meat. The ham, or lower haunch of the pig, is by nature a lean cut, so a smokehouse ham should be baked in a low, slow oven until tender and hot at the bone. The center will be juicy, but the caramelized edges will be fragile and crumble a little into the sauce when sliced.

Serves 8, with leftovers

One 7-pound double-smoked ham
2 teaspoons cracked black peppercorns
2 tablespoons butter
10 fresh sage leaves
¾ cup dry vermouth

¼ cup light honey
1 cup heavy cream
4 whole cloves
3 bay leaves
¾ cup whole milk, plus more if needed

Preheat the oven to 325°F.

With a sharp knife, score the rounded surface of the ham in a ½-inch-deep crosshatched pattern. Set it into a heavy low-sided roasting pan, prettiest side up. You need a heavy-bottomed pan, because a thin one will overreduce the milk sauce. A wide enameled cast-iron braiser or a heavy turkey roaster will work well. Rub the black pepper all over the ham, working it into the scored lines.

Heat the butter in a medium skillet over medium heat and add the sage leaves. Cook until the leaves turn bright green and are fragrant, about 2 minutes, then add the vermouth and honey and bring to a simmer. Cook for 1 minute, stirring, then add the cream, cloves, and bay leaves and return to a simmer. Whisk in the milk and immediately remove from the heat.

Pour the milk-honey-sage sauce over the ham, arranging the sage and bay leaves around its perimeter. Cover with a foil lid and bake until the ham tests warm when a thin fork is inserted into its center, about 45 minutes.

Uncover the ham (save the foil for possibly keeping it warm later on) and bake for another 1 to 1½ hours, basting every 20 to 30 minutes, until the outer edges are a dark stained-oak color—some parts suggestively close to burnt—and the juices have reduced to a liquidy dulce de leche–colored caramel. Check on the ham often to make sure that the sauce hasn't evaporated. If the roasting pan is too thin or significantly larger than the ham, this can happen. In that case, whisk more milk into the sauce by the tablespoon to restore it to a pourable condition.

recipe continues

When the ham is done, fish out the bay leaves, cloves, and sage leaves; save the sage for garnish. Impale the ham with two meat forks and lift it to a serving platter. Set the roasting pan over two burners on low heat, run a whisk around the edges of the pan to dissolve the caramelization line, and whisk the sauce into a relatively smooth, pourable cream. If the sauce is too thick, add a dribble of water to loosen it and simmer to combine. It wouldn't be wrong to return the ham to the roasting pan and slice it there, letting the slices fall down into the sauce. But given that it's a holiday, you might want to be a bit more formal and pour the sauce in a moat around the ham on the platter.

wok-fried black pepper asparagus

At Easter, the minds of the devout turn to redemption and the minds of the lapsed turn to sin—specifically, all the crimes ever committed against asparagus. Actually, it's a pretty short and boring confession, because they're all the same: the only way to mess up asparagus is to overcook it.

It's easy to overcook asparagus when you're harvesting your own and the fat stalks are growing next to the skinny stalks willy-nilly, all with different cooking times. Conveniently, though, markets tend to package asparagus by size. For this quick stir-fried pile of asparagus with freshly cracked black pepper, use skinny asparagus. The bacon fat is optional but recommended, and a spoonful of added ham fat skimmed from the pan wouldn't hurt either.

Serves 8 as a side

1½ pounds skinny asparagus
1 tablespoon bacon fat, or canola oil
¼ teaspoon fine sea salt, plus more to taste
3 garlic cloves, minced
½ teaspoon freshly cracked black peppercorns

¼ teaspoon soy sauce
1 tablespoon butter
One Meyer lemon, cut into cheeks or wedges
    for serving

Break or cut the asparagus stalks at the point where they naturally snap, usually about 2 inches from the bottom, and discard the woody stems. Rinse the asparagus in a large bowl of cold water, swishing it around to dislodge any dirt. Drain well in a colander and transfer to a towel to dry, then cut the asparagus into 2-inch lengths.

Preheat a heavy steel wok or a wide cast-iron skillet over high heat. When it starts to smoke, add the bacon fat, immediately followed by the asparagus. Spread the asparagus out across the surface of the pan and cook until it begins to brown. Season with the salt and cook, stirring occasionally, until the asparagus starts to get tender, about 2 minutes. Add the garlic and pepper and stir-fry for another minute, or just until the garlic cooks through. Add the soy sauce and butter, toss to coat, and pour out onto a shallow serving platter. Garnish with the lemon wedges.

creamy baby turnip salad with dill

As round as golf balls, these young turnips—sometimes referred to as Japanese or Hakurei turnips—are juicy, almost fruity-tasting. After popping the first few slices into your mouth, give them the classic, creamy cucumber-salad treatment. What makes this turnip salad special is the addition of minced fronds of spring dill.

    I've been growing Hakurei turnips in my garden for a few years, but I've been seeing them more and more in farmers' markets. They're on the upswing now.

Serves 8 as a small side

1½ pounds young spring turnips (about 9)
½ cup sour cream
1 small garlic clove, finely grated
Grated zest of ½ lemon
¼ teaspoon fine sea salt, plus more if neeeded

¼ teaspoon freshly ground black pepper
1 tablespoon fresh lemon juice
1 teaspoon rice wine vinegar
3 tablespoons chopped fresh dill, plus more for garnish

Trim and peel the turnips, then slice them horizontally (across the globe). You want thin but not transparent slices, the width of a nickel. A mandoline makes this easier. Drop the turnips into a bowl with half a cup of water and two handfuls of ice cubes and let the turnips sit in the melting ice water until they crisp up, about 30 minutes.

Drain the turnips, blot dry on a towel, and transfer to a bowl.

Combine the sour cream, garlic, lemon zest, salt, pepper, lemon juice, vinegar, and most of the chopped fresh dill in a small bowl. Spoon the dressing over the turnips, mixing with your hands to coat. Taste for seasoning and add salt if needed, although the sweet and mustardy notes of turnip should predominate.

Chill the salad until needed—at least 30 minutes, and up to 4 hours. Garnish with the remaining chopped dill before serving.

hot water rolls

I use this old-fashioned recipe to make rolls for the holidays, and soft, cottony hamburger buns all year round. The hot-water technique, which essentially precooks a portion of the dough, has roots in Mennonite, Japanese, and Baltic baking, but my recipe was adapted from Mrs. Harvey Nelson's in the *Lake Park* [Minnesota] *Centennial Cookbook*. Her base of boiled potato water and sugar shortening gelatinizes the flour in the dough, giving it the strength to rise to an airy height. As soft as brioche, this roll doesn't contain any fat or dairy, and it stays soft and fresh for days. For a crusty top, I start the buns in a hot oven and brush them halfway through baking with a cooked cornstarch glaze. When I can, I bake them in my wood stove, which gives the tops a recklessly dark finish.

Lofty rolls like these need time to accumulate air, meaning 6 to 8 hours (sunrise to sunset) of rising time. I usually make the dough in the late afternoon and let the shaped buns rise overnight. The anticipation of seeing how much they've risen during the night kicks me out of bed faster than any alarm clock.

I use a stand mixer to make the dough, but you can certainly make it by hand, using a large bowl and a wooden spoon, as I would bet Mrs. Nelson did. Note that I bake these on doubled sheet pans to allow the tops of the rolls to brown deeply but insulate their bottoms, which means that you will—ideally—need two 13 × 17-inch rimmed baking sheets.

Makes 24 medium rolls (overkill for this menu, but the finished rolls freeze beautifully)

dough
1 small russet potato (4 ounces), peeled and cubed
⅓ cup sugar, plus a pinch
¼ cup vegetable shortening
2¼ teaspoons (1 package) active dry yeast
6¼ cups (2 pounds) white bread flour, plus up to an additional ½ cup as needed
1 large egg

2 teaspoons distilled white or apple cider vinegar
2 teaspoons fine sea salt, plus a pinch

cornstarch glaze
1 teaspoon cornstarch
½ cup water
Pinch of sugar

Put the potatoes in a small saucepan and add water to cover by 3 inches (about 3 cups). Add a hefty pinch of salt and bring to a simmer over medium-high heat. Cover, and cook until the potatoes are very tender when pierced with a fork, about 15 minutes. Drain the potatoes, making sure to reserve the cooking water.

recipe continues

Transfer the potatoes to the bowl of a stand mixer fitted with a whisk attachment and mix briefly, while hot, until smooth.

You will need exactly 2½ cups of potato-cooking liquid, so add fresh water (or pour off excess potato water) as necessary. Scoop ¼ cup of the measured hot potato water into a small bowl to let cool, for proofing the yeast, and pour the remaining 2¼ cups potato water back into the dry potato-cooking pot. Add the ⅓ cup sugar and the shortening, and bring this mixture to a simmer. Cook, whisking, for one minute, to dissolve the sugar.

When the potato water in the small bowl has cooled to baby bathwater temperature (about 110°F), add the yeast and a pinch of sugar and jostle the bowl to mix. Within 5 minutes, the yeast should activate and foam up; if it doesn't, begin again with plain warm water and new yeast.

Pour the hot, sweetened potato-water mixture onto the potatoes in the mixing bowl, whisking on low speed, stopping to scrape the sides, until combined. Add 2 cups of the flour. Increasing the speed to medium, mix until the batter becomes perfectly smooth and cools off a bit, about 4 minutes. (The hot water cooks the first addition of flour, giving the dough a moist, springy base.)

Add 2 more cups of flour, the egg, the vinegar, and the bloomed yeast to the mixing bowl and mix on medium until the dough is stringy and elastic—a sign that the gluten is waking up—about 5 minutes.

Switching to the dough hook, add the remaining 2¼ cups flour at a slower speed, in ½-cup increments. Mix until the dough begins to clear the bowl and look muscular, another 5 minutes. The dough will feel a bit tacky, but if it sticks to your fingertip, add the additional flour bit by bit. Cover the mixer with a dish towel and let the dough rest for 15 minutes to hydrate.

Add the salt to the dough and mix on low speed until fully incorporated. Turn the dough onto a clean countertop and begin to knead. Pull one edge of the dough into a long stretch, fold the tip to the center, press down to secure, turn 90 degrees, and repeat. If the dough sticks terribly to the counter, toss a bit of flour beneath it. Knead until the surface is perfectly smooth and the dough begins to squeak, about 10 minutes. (My kneading time estimates always include pauses to do dishes or wipe countertops, and the dough seems to reward me for my laziness, getting softer and plusher on each return.) Transfer the dough to an oiled bowl and let rise at room temperature until doubled in volume, 3 to 4 hours.

Punch down the dough and let it rise again until doubled. (If you've run out of daylight, the second rise can take place overnight, in the refrigerator. The next morning, you can transfer the dough to the countertop and give it a quick knead to speed its return to room temperature.)

Tip the risen dough out onto the countertop and cut into four equal quarters. Taking care not to deflate the dough, roll each quarter into a fat cylinder, and then divide each cylinder in 6 to make 24 equal portions. Cover the dough with a cloth. (To be precise, you can weigh the dough and divide the total number of ounces by 24. It's usually about 2 ounces each. To make smaller rolls, divide the dough into 36 pieces, and line them up on the baking sheet in rows of 6 by 6.)

One by one, shape the rolls on an unfloured countertop: rotating the dough in a single spot, gently coddle it into a ball between your two hands, twisting until a tight skin stretches across the top. Set the rolls on a 13 × 17-inch baking sheet, in rows of 4 by 6, and then set the pan onto another pan of the same size, doubling them up.

Cover the rolls with a loose, floating lid of plastic wrap—it should prevent the dough from forming a skin but not strap the buns down. Let it rise at room temperature until doubled in size, 6 to 8 hours— roughly overnight, although they may rise faster in a warm summer kitchen.

Preheat the oven to 400°F.

For the glaze, combine the cornstarch, water, and sugar in a small saucepan and whisk to combine. Cook over medium heat, stirring, until translucent and pourable, adding more water if needed. Remove from the heat and set aside.

Carefully remove the plastic wrap from the rolls, and bake them at 400°F for 12 minutes, to jumpstart the browning.

Reduce the oven temperature to 350°F, take out the rolls, and brush them with the cornstarch glaze. Return the rolls to the oven and bake until the tops of the rolls turn deep, dark brown and the internal temperature hits 200°F, another 20 to 25 minutes. Remove from the oven to cool for a few minutes, transfer to a cloth-lined basket, and serve. (If making ahead, briefly rewarm the rolls in a low oven, or just serve at room temperature.)

rhubarb-almond envelope tart

I realize that this chapter (in fact, this entire book) makes quite the case for rhubarb desserts, but call me its public defender. I love the stuff. Rhubarb is early, electrifyingly tart, shockingly beautiful, and, in the Midwest anyway, plentiful and free.

This tart is like a large free-form galette, but with a more common-sense fold. The sugared, spiced ground almond mixture pulls double duty as both a rubbly topping and a starchy pad beneath the fruit to soak up its juices. I serve this on a large cutting board, cut into squares of varying sizes, so that the uncomfortably full can take just a small piece and the kids can grab big slices and run off with them.

I've used this Maida Heatter recipe for quick puff pastry for so long I've started to play around with it, here by adding some rye and whole wheat flours. Classic French puff pastry usually takes two days to make, given the six rollings and foldings—technically called turns—it requires, but this one only asks for four. I ran out of time once and gave it just three turns and then realized I could start it as late as 2:00 for a 7:00 dinner party. It's the procrastinator's puff pastry. A little denser than real puff pastry, this dough splits into fewer layers, but they're more buttery and sturdier—and, actually, I think better.

> **NOTE**
> If using frozen rhubarb in a recipe that calls for fresh, there's no need to thaw it before mixing it with the sugar. Just scrape off any surface ice crystals, add an extra tablespoon of flour—frozen rhubarb is leakier than fresh—and bake it straight from frozen.

Makes a 10 × 12-inch free-form tart, serving 12 to 16

quick puff pastry
1 cup all-purpose flour, plus more as needed
¼ cup rye flour
¼ cup whole wheat flour
1½ teaspoons sugar
¾ teaspoon fine sea salt
½ pound (2 sticks) cold unsalted butter
½ cup sour cream

rhubarb and almond filling
⅓ cup slivered blanched almonds
1¼ cups plus 3 tablespoons sugar
2 tablespoons poppy seeds

¾ teaspoon ground cardamom, preferably toasted and freshly ground
1½ pounds rhubarb, trimmed and sliced into ½-inch-wide pieces (about 5 cups)
2 tablespoons all-purpose flour
1½ tablespoons fresh lemon juice

Heavy cream for brushing the crust
Sour Cream Whip (page 189) or ice cream for serving

recipe continues

For the quick puff pastry, combine the flours, sugar, and salt in a large bowl and stir to blend. Dice the butter, add to the flour, and toss to coat. Using a pastry blender (or two butter knives), cut the butter into the flour until the butter is reduced to pieces the size of coarse grit and starts to clump on the pastry blender. Add the sour cream and stir together quickly with a fork.

Press the dough into the bottom of the bowl until it hangs together, then scoop it out, pat it into a disk, and wrap in plastic. Chill for 1 hour in the refrigerator or 30 minutes in the freezer.

On a lightly floured surface, roll the dough into a rough-hewn rectangle about 16 inches long by 9 inches wide. The dough is really rich with fat at this point, so use a lot of flour to prevent sticking and a bench scraper to move it around. Fold the dough into thirds, forming a 9 × 6-inch rectangle. Place on a baking sheet, cover with a sheet of plastic wrap, and refrigerate for about 1 hour to rest and chill.

Roll out the dough again. Fold in thirds again and refrigerate for another hour or two.

When the dough feels cold and firm to the touch, roll it out and fold it again to give it its third and final turn, and refrigerate.

While the dough chills for the last time, make the filling: Preheat the oven to 325°F.

Spread the almonds on a a small baking sheet and toast until lightly browned, 10 to 15 minutes. Remove from the oven and raise the oven temperature to 375°F.

Combine the toasted almonds, the 3 tablespoons sugar, the poppy seeds, and cardamom in a food processor and pulse to a medium-coarse grind.

Put the rhubarb in a large bowl and add the remaining 1¼ cups sugar, the flour, and lemon juice; set aside.

Roll out the dough, this time a little wider, into a 16 × 12-inch rectangle, and lay it on a rimmed baking sheet.

Sprinkle two-thirds of the almond mixture over the center of the dough in a 12 × 10-inch rectangle, leaving a wide border around the perimeter. Pile the rhubarb on top of the nuts, patting it down evenly. Fold the border dough up over the filling, leaving a windowpane of uncovered fruit in the center. Gently press the corners together to seal the crust. Brush the top of the dough with a thin layer of cream and sprinkle with the rest of the sugared almond mixture.

Bake the tart until the crust turns dark golden brown and the filling bubbles in the center, 45 to 50 minutes. If any of the filling has leaked and caramelized on the bottom of the pan, run a thin metal spatula under the tart immediately, and then again 5 minutes later, to loosen it. When it's cool enough to handle, move the tart, with two bench scrapers or metal spatulas, to a serving platter or cutting board.

Cut into squares and serve warm or at room temperature, with the sour cream whip.

Fourth of July

FOR EIGHT TO TEN

— cilantro lime juleps
— reformed dill dip with iced garden vegetables
— homeground burgers with hot-and-sauer pub cheese
— three-bean salad with salumi, celery hearts, and smoked provolone
— milk corn
— tomato-on-tomato salad
— rhubarb-raspberry pie

Writing the Fourth of July menu always seems to ignite that age-old internal struggle between my own need to make something creative and challenging—because it's a holiday—and the needs of the group, who just want to eat something classic, simple, and All-American at some point after the parade and before the fireworks display. What the people want are burgers. To make everyone happy, give them homeground burgers, thick as hockey pucks, grilled hard enough to char the outsides but keep the interiors juicy and pink, handed off with a drooling, melted topping of spicy pub cheese.

Make the rhubarb-raspberry pie, the three-bean salad, and the cilantro-julep base early in the morning, or the day before. The milk corn and the tomato salad should be prepared closer to the point of serving, but they will take just about five minutes each, which allows plenty of time for practicing your signature in the sky with a sparkler.

cilantro lime juleps

These drinks are pretty but potent—or maybe just pretty potent. They taste the way the herb garden smells after a rain, sweet and spicy, but not nearly as innocent. This is a good use for that patch of cilantro that's bolted to seed, because it makes use of the pearly green coriander buds and all.

cilantro julep base
makes 2 cups, enough for 10 drinks
1 cup Simple Syrup (recipe follows)
2 cups ice cubes
½ teaspoon coconut oil
1½ cups packed fresh cilantro leaves and tender stems (and, if possible, some of the green buds as well)
½ cup packed fresh parsley leaves
Grated zest of 1 lime

for 1 drink
Crushed ice
1 ounce (2 tablespoons) Cilantro Julep Base
2 ounces bourbon
Club soda (optional)
Fresh lime juice

recipe continues

For the cilantro julep base, combine the ice cubes and simple syrup in a small bowl and set aside.

Heat a medium skillet over high heat and add the coconut oil, and then the herbs. Cook just briefly to wilt, then plunge them into the ice and syrup mixture to stop the cooking.

Pour the herb and ice cube mixture into a blender, add the lime zest, and blend until finely ground and bright green. Immediately pour through a fine-mesh sieve into a bowl, pushing on the mixture to express all of the liquid.

Pour the cilantro base into a jar and refrigerate. It tastes brightest when made close to serving time but can be made a day or two ahead.

For each drink, fill a highball glass with crushed ice, piling it high so it mounds up over the top. Mix together the julep base and bourbon and pour over the ice. A traditional julep contains just booze and slowly melting ice, but you can add a few splashes of club soda to lighten it, if you like. Finish with a splash of fresh lime juice.

---

simple syrup Nice to have on hand year-round, but even more so during the lemonade months, simple syrup keeps in the refrigerator for a very, very long time. The ratio is 1:1 granulated sugar to water, so just scale up or down as needed.

Makes 3 cups

2 cups sugar
2 cups water

Combine the sugar and water in a saucepan and bring to a simmer. Cook for a few minutes, whisking, until the sugar dissolves and the liquid turns clear.

Remove from the heat and let cool, then pour into a glass container and refrigerate.

reformed dill dip with iced garden vegetables

There may come a time when you'll be asked to bring a platter of "veg and dip" to an event—a potluck, a birthday, a school meeting. The request will most likely come with rock-bottom-low expectations, as in a platter of pre-cut vegetables and tub of dill dip from the grocery store.

It's true that my initial motivation to make homemade dill dip was fueled by a desire to upend the status quo, but I quickly realized that good old veg and dip is actually the ideal pre-dinner kickstarter. It doesn't weigh anyone down before the heavy meal to come, and I can pull it together in 20 minutes—less time than it would take me to drive to the grocery store.

The dip is really best in the summer, when the dill and chives are so powerful that they stain my cutting board green as I chop them.

If toting this offsite, set the dip in the center of your largest platter (I've even used a turkey roaster), fill the perimeter with piles of vegetables, slap a cover on it, and head out the door. At home, I arrange the platter with a little more care, and I cover it with a fine layer of crushed ice. The ice makes the vegetables sparkle and keeps them crisp. Eventually it melts, but nothing was ever sweeter than that last stiff slice of purple daikon fished out of icy cold waters.

Makes 3 cups of dip, enough for 10, with some leftover to dress salads

dill dip

2 cups sour cream

1 cup plain full-fat yogurt, preferably the
    runny kind

2 small garlic cloves

⅔ packed cup finely chopped fresh dill fronds

⅓ cup thinly sliced fresh chives

1¼ teaspoons fine sea salt, plus more if needed

1 cup finely grated aged white cheddar (2
    ounces)

½ teaspoon grated lemon zest

3 tablespoons fresh lemon juice, plus more if
    needed

2 tablespoons grated fresh horseradish or 1½
    tablespoons prepared horseradish

Shake of cayenne pepper

Heavy pinch of sugar

Drizzle of extra-virgin olive oil

1 cup crushed ice for serving

**use at least 5 of the vegetables listed here, a
    combination of raw and briefly cooked**

raw vegetables

Firm green cabbage

Young turnips

Radishes (a mixture of red globe and fancier
    radishes like watermelon, purple daikon,
    and/or black Spanish is nice)

Kohlrabi

Carrots, the kind sold in bunches, multicolored
    if possible

Ripe cherry tomatoes

briefly cooked vegetables

Broccoli or, better yet, broccolini

Cauliflower

Green or yellow filet or Romano beans

Sugar snap peas or snow peas

Shishito peppers (optional)

Extra-virgin olive oil if using shishitos

For the dip, combine the sour cream and yogurt in a bowl, then grate the garlic into it, using a fine grater (or mince the garlic and add to the bowl). Put the dill on your cutting board and chop madly until it is reduced to an oily green pulp, then add to the sour cream mixture. Chop the chives the same way and add to the sour cream. Stir in the salt, cheddar, lemon zest, lemon juice, horseradish, cayenne, and sugar. Add the olive oil and taste for seasoning, correcting with more salt or lemon juice if necessary. Pour into a small serving bowl, cover, and refrigerate until needed.

For the vegetables, cut the cabbage into arcs. Peel the turnips and thinly slice. Halve the globe radishes. Slice specialty radishes—if their skins look fresh, leave them on, because the color contrast is part of their identity. Cut off the woody bottom end of the kohlrabi, then carefully peel the bulbous top, the most tender part, and slice crosswise ½ inch thick. If you're feeling fancy, scrape the stem ends of the carrots with a paring knife to remove any dirt, rinse well, and serve them with a ½ inch of stem still attached. Leave the cherry tomatoes whole.

Cut the broccoli (or broccolini) and cauliflower into florets. Cut the tips from the beans and snap peas. Blanch these vegetables in salty hard-boiling water just long enough to rid them of their raw bite— in and out. Drain them in a wide colander and toss them onto a baking sheet to cool.

If serving shishito peppers, blister them quickly in a hot pan to bring out their flavor: Cook them in a single layer in very little oil in a hot frying pan over high heat until they pick up spots of blackening on both sides and start to slump.

If you're prepping the vegetables in advance, transfer all the vegetables to a towel-lined dish, cover, and store in the refrigerator.

To serve, arrange the vegetables on a platter with as much artfulness and care as you have time to muster, packing the different varieties snugly but leaving some space. Sprinkle with a fine layer of crushed ice, letting the colors and shapes show through, and serve next with the bowl of dip alongside.

homeground burgers with hot-and-sauer pub cheese

While I really appreciate a panfried thin burger (preferably a double) on any given Tuesday, for special occasions, I want a thick monster of a burger that dominates the plate. I like it to hover between medium and medium-rare, when the juices run wild into the bun and the interior flushes a feverish pink.

Not to fixate on governmental guidelines or anything, but I'm hesitant to serve pink standard-issue grocery store ground beef to a crowd. Unless you have access to freshly ground beef from a trusted butcher shop, the best solution is to grind your own.

It's always a good idea to make friends with your neighborhood meat purveyor, but if there was ever a time to really suck up, this is it. Marbled chuck roasts with thick fat caps contain the ideal ratio of fat to lean, but they don't come cheap. (So if you can only get very lean chuck, add 2 slices of fatty bacon per pound of chuck to balance.) If you can persuade a butcher to sell you clean beef trimmings, this whole project becomes much more affordable.

These burgers get a spice rub before hitting the hot grill, a dark, umami-rich liquid mop while they cook, and, finally, a spicy pub cheese topping. It's kind of like pimento cheese, but hot-and-"sauer," as in sauerkraut. Unlike a slice of cheddar, which always takes longer to melt than you think it will, pub cheese starts to melt on contact.

This amount of meat will make 10 burgers that weigh roughly 7 ounces each, but you can make them any size you like.

Makes 10 large hamburgers

burgers
4½ pounds fresh beef trimmings (roughly 80% lean/20% fat; see headnote)
8 slices thick-cut bacon (optional)
1¼ teaspoons fine sea salt, plus more for seasoning the burgers
Freshly ground black pepper

burger rub
2 teaspoons garlic powder
1 teaspoon dried thyme, crushed
1 teaspoon chipotle or ancho chile powder
1 teaspoon freshly ground black pepper

burger baste
3 garlic cloves, crushed and peeled
2 tablespoons light soy sauce
1 tablespoon fish sauce, preferably Red Boat brand
1 tablespoon maple syrup
1 tablespoon Chinkiang or balsamic vinegar
2 tablespoons water

hot-and-sauer pub cheese
makes 2½ cups
4 ounces cream cheese, at room temperature
4 ounces soft goat cheese, at room temperature
4 jarred piquillo peppers (or 1 red bell pepper, roasted and peeled)
½ serrano chile, minced
4 ounces sharp cheddar, shredded (1 cup)
2 teaspoons sweet paprika
1 teaspoon smoked paprika
½ teaspoon fine sea salt
1 cup sauerkraut, drained

10 hamburger buns, split
Soft butter for the buns

garnishes
Beefsteak tomato slices
Thinly sliced raw onion
Lettuce leaves

recipe continues

For the burgers, cut the beef into 1-inch cubes and blot it dry. Moisture and warmth are the enemies of grinding; the burgers will be juicier if the beef is chilled until firm and dry to the touch. Toss the beef with the bacon, if using, salt, and pepper to taste and spread it on a baking sheet. Chill thoroughly in the refrigerator, at least 3 hours, and as long as 24. Chill your grinder and attachments as well. (I use the grinder attachment that came with my KitchenAid mixer, and it has served me well.)

When ready to grind, fit the grinder with the medium-sized die, and set a bowl under it to catch the ground meat. Start feeding the meat through the grinder. If the meat is cold and the blade relatively sharp, the meat should shoot out of the grinder in pellets. If it starts to smear, stop the machine, detach the grinder, and wash it under cold running water. It's usually a piece of sinew looped around the blade that's holding things up. Then grind all the meat again through the same die, because twice-ground meat hangs together better and makes for juicier burgers.

To portion the burgers, weigh the first few 7-ounce balls on a scale to get a sense of size, and eyeball the rest. Pat the meat into hockey pucks and make a shallow indentation in the center of each one, which will prevent them from bulging during cooking. Make sure not to overhandle the beef, because you don't want to smear the fat.

Make the burger rub by stirring together all of the ingredients in a small dish; set aside. For the burger baste, combine all of the ingredients in a small jar and shake to mix.

For the hot-and-sauer cheese, combine the cream cheese and goat cheese in the bowl of a food processor and process until smooth. Add the piquillo peppers, serrano, cheddar cheese, sweet paprika, smoked paprika, and salt and process until combined. Add the sauerkraut and process to a medium-coarse puree.

Prepare a hot fire in a grill (or preheat a grill pan over high heat).

Season both sides of the hamburgers with an evenhanded fine dusting of salt. (The salt tossed with the beef was there to bring out the flavor of the beef, but the burgers still need surface salt.) Sprinkle both sides of the hamburgers with an even dusting of the rub (you won't use all of it).

When the grill is ready, put on the burgers and cook over high heat until a thick brown crust forms on the bottom, about 5 minutes. Baste once or twice with the burger mop. Flip the burgers, baste again, and cook until the bottoms begin to brown. Move the burgers to a medium-hot part of the grill and continue to cook until they begin to swell, start to feel resilient, and are medium-rare inside (about 125° F on an instant-read thermometer), another 3 to 4 minutes. Rest the burgers on the warming rack for 5 minutes, to let the heat penetrate to the center. Slather the burgers with the pub cheese while they rest.

If you want to toast your buns, now's the time. Butter them and grill them cut side down over medium heat until golden brown, then remove to a serving platter.

When you're ready to eat, slip a burger into each bun, top it with a tomato slice, an onion slice, and a lettuce leaf, and serve.

three-bean salad with salumi, celery hearts, and smoked provolone

Bean salads are surprisingly delicious, especially when made with this-season's dried beans (like those sold by Rancho Gordo) and dressed with a strong vinaigrette—something authoritative enough to get under their skins.

This one takes flavor cues from the Mediterranean, where borlotti beans, green beans, and flinty little lentils would naturally mingle with salumi, smoked provolone, and a bit of colatura, a clear, salty anchovy

tomato-on-tomato salad

Make this at the peak of tomato season, when the beefsteak slicers are so rich and ripe they taste wild, almost gamy. With perfect tomatoes, I find that the usual embellishments—balsamic vinegar, shaved Parmesan, capers—distract from what should be essentially a lightly salted fruit salad. This one is nothing more than pure, luscious tomato-on-tomato action.

If you marinate a few handfuls of halved cherry tomatoes (including yellow ones for visual contrast) with some lemon juice, salt, a shot of good extra-virgin olive oil, and a few choice aromatics and let them sit on the counter, they will express their juices and basically make their own dressing.

Young or small-leaf basil looks and tastes best in this salad, because mature basil gets kind of licorice-y, but use whatever you've got.

Serves 8 to 10

2 large dead ripe beefsteak tomatoes (about 2 pounds)

⅛ teaspoon fine sea salt, plus more for the beefsteaks

6 ounces (1 heaped cup) small cherry tomatoes

Freshly ground black pepper

⅛ teaspoon sugar (optional)

2 teaspoons fresh lemon juice

2 tablespoons extra-virgin olive oil, plus more for drizzling

2 sprigs small-leaf basil, torn

¼ cup shelled pistachios, chopped

Slice the beefsteak tomatoes—thick or thin, whatever's your passion, although I think that soft ripe tomatoes taste better when thickly sliced and firmer ones when sliced more thinly. Shingle the tomatoes on a serving platter and sprinkle evenly with fine salt. Let them sit until moisture beads up on the surface.

Meanwhile, halve the cherry tomatoes and put them in a small bowl. Add the ⅛ teaspoon salt, pepper to taste, the optional sugar (if the tomatoes aren't naturally sweet), the lemon juice, olive oil, and a few torn basil leaves. Mix everything together and let sit on the counter to soften and get saucy, at least 15 minutes. An hour or more would be ideal.

When ready to serve, rub the beefsteak tomatoes to disperse the salt, then spoon the cherry tomatoes and all of their juices over them. Garnish with a few more judiciously placed torn bits of basil, the pistachios, and a fresh swig of olive oil.

rhubarb-raspberry pie

I've never quite understood the widely assumed bond between rhubarb and strawberries. Cooked strawberries shed a lot of moisture, which dilutes rhubarb's flavor and color. I think raspberries are a better match. Their perfume is stronger, and they turn up the color of cooked rhubarb to an agitated pink.

With every new pie recipe, I increase the ratio of butter to flour to push the limits of its fragility, in the hopes it will bring me one step closer to re-creating the mythical pies that my great-grandmother made on the farm in rural Minnesota. Reading old cookbooks, you can chart the transformation of pies through the language. What they called "pie pastry" in the early 1900s gradually began to sound sturdier, shifting to "short crust," and then, eventually, just "crust." The early descriptions of rolling out pie pastry were cautionary, full of instructions for patching holes and fixing rips. There's no mention of rock-hard chilled butter, or ice water to bind. (I know for certain that my Great-grandma Hesch used cellar-cold lard for her pie dough and did not have ice.) They didn't chill the dough to a modeling-clay consistency so they could stamp out cute shapes for decoration; the dough was too fragile for that. This was *pastry*, an exercise in risk. The dough was rolled out quickly, the double crusts were pinched shut at the edges, and the pie was raced to the oven before the juicy fruit could leak through the seams.

For me, using a food processor to make pie dough strips the history and sensory experience from it, and also reduces the butter too evenly. By cutting the butter into the flour with a pastry blender, I can control for a mix of large and small butter pebbles, leaving some bigger ones for flakiness and some smaller ones for strength.

Working by hand, I pretty much have to follow my great-grandma's script and use cool—not rock-hard—butter. Butter that's too cold takes so long to cut into the flour that you risk overworking it and activating its gluten, which is what makes pie dough tough. But if you use butter that's five minutes out of the fridge, you can stand at the counter leisurely cutting it in while talking on the phone, pausing what you're doing to talk, and your pastry will not suffer in the least.

Since this pie's such a throwback, I use flour instead of the more modern cornstarch or tapioca for thickening. It gives the filling a faded, antique look, blurry at the edges.

Makes one 9-inch pie

pastry
2⅓ cups all-purpose flour
1 tablespoon sugar
1 teaspoon fine sea salt
½ pound (2 sticks) plus 2 tablespoons high-fat
    unsalted butter, cold but not hard
6 to 8 tablespoons ice water

filling
1¾ pounds rhubarb, cut into ½-inch-thick
    pieces (5 cups); if using frozen rhubarb, see
    note on page 199
1½ cups (5 ounces) raspberries
1¼ cups sugar
5 tablespoons all-purpose flour
½ teaspoon ground cardamom
1 tablespoon fresh lemon juice
2 tablespoons cold unsalted butter

Cream and sugar for glazing

For the pastry, combine the flour, sugar, and salt in a large wide bowl and whisk together. Dice the butter and mix into the flour with your hands to coat. Start cutting it in with a pastry blender, rotating the bowl as you go and stopping often to clear any clumping butter from the blades with a butter knife. When you've reduced the butter to the size of large brown lentils, push most of the flour mixture to one side and give the rest of it about 10 more strokes.

Dribble in 6 tablespoons ice water and mix the dough together swiftly with your butter knife, shaking the bowl to encourage it to clump together. Pick up some dough in your hand and squeeze it. If it holds the outline fairly well, it should be good. If not, add up to 2 more tablespoons water, but it's better to be too dry than too wet. Gather the dough into a ball, packing it together like a snowball, and divide it in half. Pat into 2 disks, wrap them in plastic, and refrigerate for 20 to 30 minutes, until they begin to stiffen. (*The pastry can be made refrigerated for up to 2 days or frozen for up to 3 months. Let chilled dough stand at room temperature for 20 minutes before rolling.*)

For the filling, combine the rhubarb, raspberries, sugar, flour, cardamom, and lemon juice in a bowl and stir to coat the fruit. Set aside.

Position a rack in the lower third of the oven and preheat the oven to 375°F. Set out a 9-inch pie plate.

On a floured surface, roll out one of the dough disks, stopping often to rub your pin with a thin coat of flour and to lift and rotate the dough to keep it from sticking, until it measures 2 inches larger than your pie plate, with a thickness of about ¼ inch. Fold the dough in half, transfer it to the pie plate, and flop it open. Refrigerate the bottom crust while you roll out the top crust to the same size.

Fill the bottom crust with the rhubarb mixture. Cut the 2 tablespoons of cold butter into thin pats and insert at random just under the top layer of fruit. (My grandma's trick—the butter will mix with and thicken the fruit juices.) Cover with the top crust, trimmed to a ½-inch overhang. (Save the trimmings: Transfer them snugly to a baking sheet, sprinkle with cinnamon- or cardamom-sugar, and bake up for treats.)

Roll the edges of the pastry under and secure to the rim of the pie plate with decorative pinches. Cut a small steam hole in the center of the pie, and then a few slash vents. Brush the top of the pie with a thin layer of cream and sprinkle it heavily with sugar.

Bake—preferably with a baking sheet set on the rack below the pie to catch any potential drips— for 20 minutes. Reduce the oven temperature to 350°F and continue bake the pie for another 40 to 50 minutes, until the crust is evenly caramel brown and the juices bubble thickly from the slits. (The total baking time should be 60 to 70 minutes.) Let the pie cool for at least 3 hours, and, preferably, at least 5 hours, if you want neatly cut wedges.

Serve each slice with a ball of vanilla ice cream.

Perennial

groups of six to ten

Parties

Menus

an outdoor fried chicken party

FOR TEN	222
double-dipped fried chicken	222
coconut creamed corn with basil oil	227
Addie's pepper cukes	229
braised collards with smoky tomato	229
green and yellow beans with garlic	231
lemon nemesis	233

family brunch around the fire pit

FOR SIX TO EIGHT	236
orange Julius with basil	238
grilled garlic bread with bacon fat and smeared tomato	239
potato tortilla	240
smoked sausages with mustard-miso sauce and arugula	242
muskmelon Caprese	244

deer camp feast

FOR UP TO TEN	246
whiskey-sour gelatin shots with potted sour cherries	248
chipotle-cashew salsa with bacon fat	250
apricot snickerdoodles	251
deer liver mousse with pickled grapes on the vine	253
backstrap (venison loin) bordelaise	256
cider-braised red cabbage wedges	260
squash bake with goat cheese custard	262
bitter lettuces with warm brown butter vinaigrette, fried shallots, and duck gizzards confit	263

annual birthday blowout for my brother

FOR SIX TO EIGHT	268
raw oyster bar	270
corn soup with coconut and littleneck clams	271
pork-stuffed barbecued chicken thighs	273
sticky rice	275
stir-fried greens and leeks	276
honeydew and cucumber salad with cilantro-lime dressing	278
single-origin chocolate cake	279

By perennial, *I mean recurring, as in never-ending. These are the kind of parties that you couldn't cancel if you tried.* They usually coalesce around a seasonal food-based occasion (like deer hunting, or summer solstice, or a birthday, or maple syruping time) rather than an official holiday. Asynchronous holidays, the time-marking celebrations that Hallmark knows nothing about, inspire a fervent group loyalty like no other. Come Sunday, the last day after a weekend of ceremonial feasting, everyone gets out their calendars to book the next year's date. So I think it's befitting that this chapter contains some of the most sprawling menus, with the most complex, debaucherous recipes in the book.

When Aaron and I first started living here in the 1990s—in the same rustic cabin we live in today, but without running water or electricity—we moved into a culture rich with annual theme parties. Our neighbors, most of them back-to-the-landers one generation above us, threw ski parties, pig roasts, horseradish-harvest parties as if on the festival circuit, each of them conceived of and kept alive by their owners. But like dried beans in a dusty food co-op, these parties did in fact have shelf lives, and eventually, in 1998, the Fourth of July party fell to us. The invitation was open, passed by word of mouth, as was the local custom. Before cell phones, the game of telephone was quite possibly more reliable than our landline phones, and open-invite ensured that all of your friends, your neighbors, their friends would show up. About a hundred of them did.

When I think back to it now, my heart palpitates. Our 1998 looked and felt more like 1898. We had no electricity (just oil lamps), no running water (just a hand pump down the hill), no refrigeration, no bathroom (but an outhouse!), no disposable cups. I thought that because I had a collection of thirty thrift-store forks and a garden

full of miraculous hanging vegetables, I'd be all set. By 5 o'clock, the growing crowd made it clear that my small spread of precious garden vegetable dishes wouldn't last long, and I was throwing stacks of dirty dishes behind the curtained shelves in my tiny kitchen because I'd run out of water to wash them. It was obvious that I should have called potluck. So I was relieved to see that our local friends had ignored my instructions to "just bring yourselves" and had instead brought reinforcements: coolers full of beer, bathroom towel–wrapped potluck dishes, their own lawn chairs.

Around 3 a.m., when the last logs in the fire pit had burned down to a night-light glow, the remaining campfire creatures crawled into makeshift nests, too drunk to battle the heckling mosquitoes. The next morning, I played short-order cook, handing plates of eggs and hash browns through the open kitchen window to the porch where last night's merry revelers sprawled against the wooden posts, knees hooked over legs, heads on laps. Sunburnt and campfire-smoked as a string of sausages, they were quick to declare it the best party ever.

At that moment, ready or not—mostly not—the neighborhood generational party torch passed to us. From an organizational standpoint, that first party was a disaster, but it taught me some things that have stuck:

One, you can never have too much food.

Two, loud-enough music and low lighting (or better yet, a total lack of electric lighting) cover up all mistakes.

Three, never let your friends see your fear, or your thrift. Hide them both, along with the dirty dishes, in your cupboards.

Four, prep like mad until people arrive, then share the reins. Let them help.

an outdoor fried chicken party

TO FEED TEN

— double-dipped fried chicken
— coconut creamed corn with basil oil
— Addie's pepper cukes
— braised collards with smoky tomato
— green and yellow beans with garlic
— lemon nemesis

This is one of those dinners that looks epic but is secretly easy to pull off, because nearly everything can be made in advance. The menu is full of familiar comfort food hits that all have a little something extra. The chicken is double-dipped for twice the crunch, the braised greens have an unsuspecting kick, the cucumber salad is surprisingly racy, and the lemon nemesis (a frozen lemon silk meringue pie with a junky butter-cracker base) is a knockout in an ordinary 9 × 13-inch pan. The green beans are calm, rational, and seasonal. That is their only function.

Although frying chicken in the open air may look performative, it will allow you to join the party, which feels so much better than standing alone over a pot of hot boiling oil under a low ceiling. Never let them see you sweat. Fans and hoods can only do so much when you're frying twenty-two pieces of chicken.

double-dipped fried chicken

Fried chicken is the most idiosyncratic of iconic American recipes. It starts with basically the same cards—chicken, flour, oil—but everyone throws down a different hand.

There's the minimal, purist Southern thing, enrobing saltwater-brined chicken in a whisper-thin casing of flour. There's the fried-first and baked-second Midwestern style, doused with a gravy constructed from the flavorful pan juices.

Lately I've been into this maximalist version. I brine the chicken in the traditional buttermilk, roll it in spiced flour, dip it in egg wash, and then—going for the gold—send it through the flour again. Double-dipping feels kind of sleazy, but that's not the only reason I like it. When I'm frying chicken for a crowd, the flour coating always soaks in and disappears before I can get the chicken into the oil—so it makes sense to just give the pieces all another roll. I like to fry the chicken at a slow pace, taking it out when the crust has deepened to a rusty dark sienna and the surface has burst into a cluster of amber bubbles. In the places where the crust swells to a glorious half-inch thick—a little cake flour in the dredge keeps it light—it will take two bites to reach the meat.

This recipe involves two chickens cut into eleven pieces each—if you include the backs, which I recommend (see page 226)—giving you a tower of twenty-two stacked pieces. Given that most adults will take two pieces and some kid will take only chicken and no vegetables, this recipe wouldn't be worth a damn if it served more than ten people. With this many pieces, I recommend frying in two pans at once. Do halve the recipe if cooking for a group of 5 or fewer. And if you're short on time or not keen on cutting up whole chickens, just buy bone-in chicken thighs. They're the best piece of the bird anyway.

I used to keep the chicken warm in a low oven until serving, but the heat robbed the crust of its crunch. Now I don't worry about keeping it hot. The flavors are better at ambient temperature, anyway.

recipe continues

Serves 8 to 10

chicken and brine

2½ cups buttermilk (or an equal mixture of
    whole-milk yogurt and milk)

1 tablespoon fine sea salt

1 teaspoon sugar

1 teaspoon freshly ground black pepper

1 teaspoon cayenne pepper

4 garlic cloves, smashed and peeled

1 tablespoon minced fresh rosemary

2 chickens, cut into 11 pieces each (see page
    226; or 22 bone-in chicken thighs)

egg dip

4 large eggs

3 tablespoons water

flour dredge

5 cups all-purpose flour

1 cup cake flour

1 tablespoon fine sea salt

1 teaspoon freshly ground black pepper

½ teaspoon cayenne pepper

½ teaspoon smoked paprika

2 teaspoons garlic powder

About 5 cups canola or peanut oil for
    deep-frying

For the chicken, whisk together the buttermilk, salt, sugar, black pepper, cayenne, garlic cloves, and rosemary in a large wide bowl. Add the chicken, tossing with your hands to coat. Submerge the chicken in the buttermilk brine and marinate, refrigerated, for a minimum of 4 hours, and as long as 36.

When you're ready to start frying the chicken—about 45 minutes before you'll sit down to eat it—prepare your breading setup: Whisk together the eggs and water in a medium bowl. Whisk the all-purpose and cake flours, salt, pepper, cayenne, smoked paprika, and garlic powder together in a large deep bowl.

Transfer the chicken to a wire rack set over a baking sheet to let the excess buttermilk brine drip off. Then roll each piece in the flour dredge and return to the rack. It can sit like this for up to 15 minutes while you get everything else ready.

Set a rack on another baking sheet to hold the chicken when it comes out of the oil. And arm yourself with two pairs of tongs if you can, one for turning the raw chicken and one for turning the cooked chicken.

Pour oil to a depth of 2 to 3 inches into your largest, deepest cast-iron or enameled cast-iron pan (or use two pans if you can) and set over medium heat. Slowly heat the oil to 360°F.

Drop a few pieces of floured chicken into the egg dip, then back into the flour, mashing every exposed inch of it into the flour to coat heavily, and add to the hot oil. Fry only as many pieces of chicken as can fit comfortably in the pan, giving them some wiggle room. The temperature will drop at first, so slowly bring it back so it hovers between 340 and 350°F. (Lacking a candy/deep-fry thermometer, know that the surface of the chicken won't start to really take on any color until the oil hits at least 340°F.) If the temperature races away from you and the oil starts to smoke, lower the heat, add some cold oil to bring it back to par.

Fried at the right temperature, not surging but insistent, each batch of chicken will take anywhere from 12 to 15 minutes. And if you've cut it in such a way as to leave the white meat pieces on the bone, both breast pieces and thighs will cook at nearly the same rate. To test doneness, either slice off an end of a piece—cook's privilege, you know—or pierce the thickest part with an instant-read thermometer or thin meat fork. The internal temperature should measure 160°F, and the fork will feel hot when brought to your lip. Any juices running out of the pierced holes should be clearish-yellow, not pink. Remove the chicken to the clean rack to cool, and cook the remaining batches.

Serve the fried chicken on a platter. Because the breading will make the pieces indistinguishable, pile the dark meat on one side and the white on the other.

For any recipe that calls for chicken on the bone, you'll want to cut the chicken into relatively equal pieces: two thighs, two drumsticks, two wings, four pieces of breast, and, if you like it, the back. If you're making fried chicken, I highly recommend frying the back. It houses two meaty oval nuggets, known as the oysters, which are the most succulent bites on the bird. The back is the part that I keep my eye on as the chicken gets passed around the table. I put an invisible "Reserved" sign on it and hope no one takes it.

In the meat aisle, given the choice between chicken parts and a whole chicken, I buy the intact bird and cut it up at home. Whole chickens are juicier, more flavorful, and, I always think, less manhandled. Cutting up a chicken is just the thing to do in the morning after you've had your coffee and righted the kitchen after breakfast. This may sound strange—*Ah, now let's cut up a chicken*—but I find it restful and satisfying. And because a whole chicken always yields a few extra bits and bones, you can also make a little stock afterward.

Set yourself up with a cutting board, your sharpest knife, a heavy tool to knock the knife through the bones (a meat mallet, or even a hammer), a bowl to catch the scraps for stock, and some paper towels. (When your hands are slick with raw chicken juices and you want to wipe them before pulling out the garbage can or turning on a faucet, paper towels are your friends.) Take the chicken out of its wrapping and drop it into a large bowl for washing. I know that the CDC has warned us all not to wash raw poultry for fear of raw chicken juices cross-contaminating what they shouldn't, but when was the last time this factory chicken was washed? The answer is never. A raw chicken is nothing to fear, but salmonella is actually pretty real, so view flying chicken juices as if they were invisible ink. After washing the chicken, you want to scrub the sink and the faucet and everything it touched with hot soapy water. Scrub the board too, and then toss the cleaning sponge or wad of paper towels into the trash, or the dishcloth into the hamper.

Lay the chicken on its back, splay its legs, and slice through the skin between the breast and thighs to separate them. Flip the bird over and bend the leg backward to pop the joint, then cut around it to remove the leg. Separate the legs from the thighs by cutting right through the soft center cartilage of the knee joint. It's a diagonal cut. To remove the wings, bend the wing backward, and slice generously around the shoulder joint. If you want to capture a bit of white breast meat with the wings to make them more equal in size to the others, veer wide. Trim off the wingtips and throw them into the stock bowl.

Turn the chicken onto its neck end and slice down through the ribs to free the back from the rib cage. Bend the lower back piece, the one that holds those two nice nuggets of meat behind the hip, backward until it breaks, and twist and cut it free. Slice downward through the rib cage to free the rest of the back, and throw it into the stock bowl. Lay the breast skin side down and trim away any stray rib bones and soft, dark tissue. Line up your knife up along the center line and pound it with your mallet, on the tang, to cut through the breastplate, dividing the breast into 2 pieces. Pound your knife again through each of these to divide them in half, to make 4 equal pieces of breast meat, each topped with a small cap of breastbone. That bone will protect the meat and make it less likely to overcook, but if it's too small or cracked, just get rid of it. Run your fingers along the cut ends of all the pieces to feel for bone shards. (People appreciate that.)

Cutting up a large chicken yields just enough trimmings to make a quick, concentrated brown stock. Heat a saucepot over medium heat, film the bottom with oil, and brown the pieces lightly on both sides. Add water to cover, along with any aromatics you might have lying around: a few onion peels, the trimmed tops and tails of carrots or celery, fresh thyme or rosemary sprigs or a bay leaf, a scattering of black peppercorns, the tiny center cloves of a head of garlic. (In fact, I save those irritating baby cloves—so hard to peel—for just this purpose.) Add some salt, bring to a simmer, and simmer the stock for just 45 minutes or so. It won't yield much, but even a cup is liquid gold.

coconut creamed corn with basil oil

A rusty chunk of fried chicken should always be so lucky as to sit in a puddle of creamed corn.

To my mind, creamed corn should have the texture of a swimming risotto, the kernels bound loosely by their own exuded starch. To achieve that nubbly creamed-corn effect, I cut two-thirds of the cobs clean and grate the rest of them on a box grater.

Because the butterfat in heavy cream can cling a little too thickly to the palate, I cut it with some coconut milk. I garnish the creamed corn with a few splashes of bright green basil oil, because basil and corn are partners for life—and also to make a dent in my ferocious basil patch.

If short on time, you could skip the oil, but both the basil oil and the creamed corn mixture can be made in advance and refrigerated. You may need to thin out the corn again with additional coconut milk and cream on the reheat.

Serves 8 to 10 (easily halved)

basil oil
1½ cups fresh basil leaves
¾ cup neutral oil, such as canola, chilled
A hefty pinch of fine sea salt, or to taste

creamed corn
12 ears corn, shucked and silks removed
4 tablespoons butter

1 large sweet onion, cut into small dice (2 cups)
½ teaspoon fine sea salt
¼ teaspoon freshly ground black pepper
¼ to ½ teaspoon minced Thai bird chile
3 garlic cloves, minced
¾ cup heavy cream
¾ cup coconut milk
⅓ cup thinly sliced fresh chives

For the basil oil, combine the basil leaves, cold oil, and the salt in a blender and process on high until smooth and bright green. Pour into a wide bowl set in a larger bowl of ice water to chill the oil and preserve its green color. Refrigerate; bring the oil back to room temperature before serving. (*The basil oil can be refrigerated for up to 3 days, or frozen shortly after making for up to 6 months.*)

For the corn, standing each one upright in the middle of your deepest mixing bowl, cut the kernels from 8 of the cobs with a knife. Then grate the remaining 4 ears on the large holes of a box grater. You should have 6 to 7 cups combined.

Heat the butter in a large frying pan over medium heat. Add the diced onion, salt, and pepper and cook until the onion turns soft, sweet, and golden at the edges, about 20 minutes. Make sure the onion doesn't brown, because you want it to melt invisibly into the corn.

Add the garlic and ¼ teaspoon minced chile and cook for another minute. Add the corn and cook until the kernels turn bright yellow, about 2 minutes. Add the cream and coconut milk, bring to a simmer, and cook at a slow pace until the liquid tightens into a creamy sauce. This will take just a few minutes if the corn is young and sweet, or as long as 8 to 10 if the kernels are more mature. Taste for seasoning and adjust with more chile and/or salt to taste.

Pour the corn into a shallow dish, decorate the top with a few tablespoons of basil oil, and serve, garnished with the fresh chives.

Addie's pepper cukes

When my Grandma Addie made these peppery marinated cucumbers, she cut them into wafer-thin slices with her saber of a knife, salted them liberally, and then squeezed them between her hands the way she would wring out a wet dishcloth. With force. Then she sharpened her knife on the leather strop that hung on the knob of her silverware drawer, ready for the next time. From start to finish, the process was rather intimidating, but the memory of the dish is even more formidable. Bludgeoned with black pepper and nearly shivering with vinegar it wasn't exactly a salad, but more like a refreshing pickle. We usually ate most of it before the main course hit the table, fished out of the cut-glass bowl slice by paper-thin slice.

When trying to re-create the taste of these cucumbers, I realized, after some frustration, that she probably made them with strong distilled white vinegar. It isn't used in the kitchen as often now as it was fifty years ago, but wine and cider vinegars just don't deliver quite the same painful tang.

Makes 2½ cups, enough for 8 to 10 as a side/condiment

6 medium knobby pickling or thin-skinned
    Persian cucumbers
¾ teaspoon fine sea salt, plus more to taste
½ teaspoon sugar

¾ teaspoon freshly ground black pepper
5 to 6 tablespoons distilled white vinegar
2 teaspoons finely chopped fresh dill fronds

Peel the cucumbers. Slice very thinly with a mandoline (or a sharp knife), transfer to a bowl, and mix with the salt, tossing with your hands. Let the cucumbers sit on the counter until they sweat their liquid, at least 15 minutes.

Drain and squeeze the cucumbers and then wring them out, as you might a delicate piece of handwashing: Do this over a bowl to catch the precious bright green cucumber water. You'll need just a tablespoon for the salad, to smooth out the vinegar, but you can save the rest to add to cocktails (it's great in a martini or a gin and tonic.)

Return the cucumbers to the bowl, add the sugar, black pepper, and 5 tablespoons vinegar, toss well, and give it a taste. The vinegar should already have a sharp presence but it will continue to penetrate the cukes, so the pickle may need that last tablespoon of vinegar in the end. Add the dill and 1 tablespoon of the reserved cucumber water and toss to combine. Hold the cucumbers at room temperature until you're ready for them. You could make this in advance and refrigerate it, but it's better when fresh.

braised collards with smoky tomato

There are very few menus that don't benefit from a soft heap of cooked greens. I braise these with big flavors, because with crowd favorites like fried chicken and creamed corn on the plate, the greens have some stiff competition. With smokiness coming at them from so many different directions—bacon, smoky piquillo peppers, and smoked paprika—these greens taste almost wood smoked. That said, you can omit the bacon to make this dish vegetarian, with no other adjustments needed.

Sometimes I'll add a minced serrano chile along with the garlic to make the greens ripping hot, because if there's a dish that spice-averse kids will never, ever touch, it's braised collard greens.

recipe continues

Serves 8 to 10 as a side

2 bunches collard greens
6 slices thick-cut bacon, diced
2 tablespoons butter
1½ large sweet onions, cut into small dice (3 cups)
½ teaspoon fine sea salt, plus more if needed
¼ teaspoon freshly ground black pepper
5 garlic cloves, sliced
3 jarred piquillo peppers, finely diced (or 1 small poblano, finely diced)

1 small serrano chile, minced (to taste)
1½ cups canned whole Roma tomatoes, preferably San Marzano, crushed
1 teaspoon smoked paprika
2 teaspoons minced fresh rosemary
Pinch of sugar if needed
2 tablespoons extra-virgin olive oil
Fresh lemon juice if needed

Strip the collard greens from their thick stems and wash in a large bowl of water to remove any grit; lift them out to drain in a colander and set aside.

Heat a large high-sided sauté pan over medium heat and add the bacon. Cook, stirring, just until it bronzes at the edges. Using a slotted spoon, remove the bacon, leaving the fat behind in the pan.

Add the butter, onions, salt, and pepper to the pan and cook, stirring, until the onions turn sweet and golden, about 20 minutes.

Add the garlic to the onions and cook for 3 minutes, then add the piquillo peppers and serrano, if using, and cook for 5 minutes, or until the peppers begin to melt into the onions. Add the paprika and rosemary, stir to bloom the paprika in the hot oil, and then add the tomatos. Cook until thickened, about 2 minutes, then remove the pan from the heat. If the canned tomatoes were a little less than sweet, add the sugar.

Bring a large pot of water to a boil and season with a handful of salt. Tear the greens into largish bite-sized pieces. Blanch the greens in two batches, until just tender, about 3 minutes. Scoop out with a spider and drain in a large colander set over a bowl to catch the water, turning the greens with a pair of tongs as they drain to remove excess moisture.

Add the greens to the sauté pan, along with the bacon. Then add the olive oil and enough of the greens' cooking water to loosen the mixture, giving the greens a sauce in which they can simmer. Cook gently, uncovered, stirring occasionally, until the greens are completely tender and the sauce has taken on a smoky flavor, 10 to 15 minutes.

Taste for seasoning and correct with salt and a squeeze of lemon juice if either are lacking. Serve warm.

green and yellow beans with garlic

In this menu, these very simply cooked green and yellow wax beans represent the rhythm section. This dish ensures that everyone will come away from the buffet with the correct well-balanced plate ratio—i.e., they'll have met their daily percentage of vegetables and not just loaded up on chicken.

Honestly, though, if you don't have access to spanking fresh green and/or yellow beans, I would choose to make something else, because it won't be special. If you do have beautiful beans, just be sure to blanch the two colors separately. Oddly enough, the skinnier green beans take longer to cook than the wider yellow wax beans.

Serves 8 to 10 as a side

12 ounces green beans
12 ounces yellow wax beans
2 tablespoons butter
2 tablespoons extra-virgin olive oil

3 garlic cloves, minced
Fine sea salt and freshly ground black pepper
Finely chopped fresh parsley, chives, or
    chervil, for garnish

Bring a large pot of water to a boil.

Keeping the green and yellow beans separate, line them up on your cutting board and slice off their blossom ends; if the beans are fresh, I leave their tails alone. Cut the beans on the bias into 2-inch-long pieces.

When the water boils, salt it heavily. Add the green beans and cook, uncovered, until they no longer resist at the bite, about 5 minutes. Scoop them out with a spider or a fine-mesh sieve and drain. Add the yellow beans to the boiling water and cook until they're tender, 4 minutes or so, depending on size and maturity; drain. Take extra care, because overcooked yellow beans are kind of fragile and can get mushy.

Heat a large saucepan over medium heat and add the butter and olive oil. When the butter foams, add the garlic and cook for 1 minute. Add the drained beans and cook until they feel hot to the touch, about 4 minutes. Taste a bean for seasoning, and add salt and pepper as needed.

Add the chopped herbs, stir to coat, and turn the beans out into a shallow serving dish. Good hot or tepid.

lemon nemesis

My sweet-seeking heart beats harder for lemon than for chocolate, for pie than for cake, and for meringue frosting over all others. This giant lemony ice cream cake—from its salted butter-cracker bottom to the racy lemon custard middle to the swirled toasted meringue on top—corrals all three of my personal temptations into a single dessert. It is my nemesis. My lemon nemesis.

It would have been easier to fill the cake with lemon ice cream and call it a day, but no, the ice cream froze too stiffly. My fork chased it around the plate. In my mind, the filling was smooth and custardy, like a frozen crème brûlée. I started again with a lemon semifreddo, or Italian no-churn ice cream. The eggy cooked lemon custard, lightened with swirls of softly whipped cream, was delicious, but it wasn't tart enough for my taste. When I bumped up the lemon juice, though, the frozen filling got icy and crumbled under my fork. So, throwing in all of my strategies at once, variables running wild, I added another egg,[*] a can of sweetened condensed milk, and some lemon-flavored vodka to keep the custard from icing up, and finally got what I was after: a dense, smooth, almost airless lemon silk pie filling. On its own, its lemon flavor is thrillingly tart, sour enough to bite back. But that's where the burnt marshmallowy meringue steps in, to temper the pain.

The best thing about this ice cream cake is that you can make it well ahead of time, store it in your freezer until opening night (we're talking a week or two), top it with the meringue, and brûlée it in front of the crowd. And for days afterward you can pop into the freezer to secretly carve off chunks if and when you need a bump.

You'll need a blowtorch for this recipe.

Serves 15 in healthy portions

cracker base
2 sleeves butter crackers, like Ritz (about 7 ounces)
6 tablespoons unsalted butter, melted
3 tablespoons maple syrup

lemon filling
3 large eggs
6 large egg yolks (save the whites for the meringue)
1¼ cups fresh lemon juice (from 9 to 10 lemons)
¾ cup sugar
2 tablespoons vodka, referably lemon vodka

4 tablespoons unsalted butter, cut into slices
One 14-ounce can sweetened condensed milk
2 to 3 drops lemon extract (optional if you used lemon vodka)
1¼ cups heavy cream

meringue topping
6 large egg whites (reserved from the filling)
1¼ cups sugar
½ teaspoon cream of tartar
2 teaspoons apple cider vinegar
A hefty pinch of fine sea salt
3 drops lemon extract (optional)

Preheat the oven to 325°F. Grease a 9 × 13-inch baking pan with a thin coating of neutral oil.

For the base, grind the crackers to a fine dust in a food processor, or put them in a heavy plastic bag and crush with a rolling pin. Combine the cracker crumbs, melted butter, and maple syrup in a medium

recipe continues

---

[*] The brighter the egg yolks, the more lemony this cake will look, and visuals are everything. Use farm-fresh eggs if you can.

bowl and mix quickly to moisten the crumbs. Scatter the crumbs across the bottom of the baking pan and gently press down, pushing them into the corners with the blade of your hand.

Bake the cracker base until you can smell it toasting and it has turned an even shade of almond brown, about 12 minutes. Remove from the oven.

Fill a large saucepot with a few inches of water for a double boiler and bring it to a simmer; make sure the bottom of the mixing bowl will hover above the water, not sit in it. Combine the eggs and yolks, lemon juice, sugar, and vodka in a large metal mixing bowl and whisk immediately to prevent the yolks from clumping with the sugar, then set the bowl over the simmering water. Cook, slowly stirring with a rubber spatula in a figure eight, until the mixture thickens into a custard that holds the trail of the whisk and measures 150°F on an instant-read thermometer, about 10 minutes. Immediately remove from the heat and whisk in the cold butter, then cool the mixture over a bowl of ice water, stirring occasionally, until cool. Stir in the condensed milk and lemon extract.

Meanwhile, whip the cream in a large bowl to soft peaks. For the creamiest custard texture, the whipped cream should be floppy, not stiff.

Before you get to the final assembly, clear a flat, level space in your freezer to hold the baking pan so that the custard will freeze evenly.

Fold half of the whipped cream into the lemon mixture to lighten it, then add the rest, folding it in until incorporated. Immediately pour the lemon filling into the cooled crust and spread it into the corners. Hustle the pan into the freezer to harden. After the top begins to freeze, press a sheet of plastic wrap or parchment paper against the surface of the filling to protect it from odors. (If planning to keep this in the freezer for any length of time, you may also want to double-wrap the pan in plastic wrap.) The lemon filling needs to freeze for at least 6 hours to be stiff enough to cut, but freezers vary. (*The lemon nemesis can be prepared to this point up to 2 weeks in advance.*)

Right before serving, make the meringue topping: Combine the egg whites, sugar, cream of tartar, vinegar, salt, and lemon extract, if using, in the bowl of a stand mixer or another large metal bowl and set over a pot of simmering water (the bottom of the bowl should not touch the water). Heat gently, whisking, until the egg white mixture feels uncomfortably hot to the touch, measuring about 150° F, about 5 minutes. Attach the mixer bowl to the stand, or use a hand mixer, and whip the egg whites on medium-high until the meringue looks glossy and thick and holds stiff peaks.

Spoon the meringue topping across the surface of the cake and smooth with an offset spatula or a pie server. If the cake has been frozen for days, transfer the cake to the refrigerator for about 15 minutes to gently thaw enough to slice.

Just before serving, brûleé the meringue with a blowtorch.

To serve, slice the cake into large squares. I generally divide it into 15 servings—rows of 5 divided by rows of 3—but you can serve any size you like. Lift out each piece with a pie server and transfer to serving plates. (If you have any difficulty prying the crust from the pan, pass the bottom of the pan over a hot stovetop burner to loosen the bottom crust.) If there happen to be leftovers, press a piece of plastic wrap against the cut surfaces and return to the freezer.

family brunch around the fire pit

FOR SIX TO EIGHT

— orange Julius with basil
— grilled garlic bread with bacon fat and smeared tomato
— potato tortilla
— smoked sausages with mustard-miso sauce and arugula
— muskmelon Caprese

Pulling my three cousins, Matt, Andy, and Joe, away from work at the meat market to come to my house for brunch happens about once every ten years, as rare as a blood moon. But when three butchers come to brunch, you can guess what they might bring: a box of meat. The last time it happened, my mom, Karen, immediately started unwrapping the white paper packages and threw a cast-iron pan on the stove, firing it up to make bacon snacks. (Because my family eats bacon like others eat chips.) An hour later, two pounds of bacon were gone, but I had a nice jar of bacon fat in my kitchen.

Everyone was sitting around the fire pit waiting for the sausages to cook, the little girls were starting to dance with hunger, and my mom began to cut up a loaf of bread to throw on the grill for garlic bread. The idea to mix some bacon fat into the soft butter came to us both simultaneously. It was just so obvious.

Because I was already making a Spanish tortilla, my mind went to pan con tomate, and I rubbed the sharp edges of the toast with a clove of sticky garlic. I passed the bread to my mom to brush with bacon-butter, because I knew she'd be more fearless with it, and then I dragged half of a ripe tomato across each piece and handed them around the fire. And that's how the kids took down two huge loaves of country bread before noon and completely spoiled their appetites, and garlic bread smeared with bacon fat and tomato became something of a house tradition.

After a rousing round of garlic bread, you may want to postpone brunch until lunch. Thankfully, everything else in this menu will hold. The tortilla should be made first thing in the morning, to give it time to settle. The mustard-miso sauce can be made ahead and rewarmed while you cook the sausages. And muskmelon Caprese is by nature a summer countertop lounger. The orbs of salted melon and marinated cherry tomatoes and ground cherries sink deeper into the mozzarella, and just get sweeter.

orange Julius with basil

Any Gen Xers who spent their early teen years cruising indoor malls in the Midwest will recognize this one. Even though it's shaken by hand instead of in a rotating drum, this big-batch tangy, creamsicle-like drink is my tribute to the Orange Julius stand.

It also tastes a lot like the milk-and-orange-juice afternoon pick-me-up that some of the cooks from Santo Domingo, D.R., used to make in the Bouley basement prep kitchen in New York, called *morir sonando*. They would shake this drink in quart container after quart container until every cook had been given their frothy, refreshing share. It's best when made with fresh orange juice, of course, but for a big batch, I add a little lemon juice for extra tartness—as well as some sweetened condensed milk to replicate the creamy mouthfeel of the industrialized American version.

You'll need a large 2-quart jar or lidded container. To keep the acidity from curdling the milk, make sure that all of the ingredients are cold, shake the jar vigorously, and pour it quickly before the frothy bubbles subside.

This is also delicious made with mango juice.

Makes 2 quarts, serving 8 in coffee mug portions, 10 in smaller glasses

3 cups cold whole milk
½ cup sweetened condensed milk, chilled
½ teaspoon pure vanilla extract
A large handful of torn and crushed basil
   leaves
Handful of ice cubes, plus more for serving

3 cups orange juice (freshly squeezed if
   you have a dozen or so oranges and the
   patience, but for this quantity I usually use
   top-shelf store-bought)
½ cup fresh lemon juice

Combine the milk, condensed milk, and vanilla in a 2-quart jar. Add the basil leaves to the jar, along with the handful of ice cubes. Cap the jar and shake to combine. Add the orange juice and lemon juice and shake heartily in the air until it's very frothy.

Line up your mugs or serving glasses, add a few ice cubes to each, and fill them with the orange Julius. You can strain out the basil, but I like to leave it in and just tell people to dodge it, as if it were loose-leaf tea. Serve immediately.

grilled garlic bread with bacon fat and smeared tomato

A simple starter like this one hinges on top-quality ingredients—smokehouse bacon, ripe in-season tomatoes, and, of course, a good country loaf of bread. Ciabatta works well, as does springy Italian American bread, or sourdough, or anything with a spongy, airy interior and open fretwork. My feeling is that the bread should be made from white flour rather than whole wheat, but that's just how I lean.

Serves 6 to 8

1 large loaf country bread
6 tablespoons bacon fat* (my mom would use more), at room temperature
6 tablespoons very soft butter (again, probably more)

2 garlic cloves, halved
2 large ripe beefsteak tomatoes
Extra-virgin olive oil for drizzling (optional)

Prepare a good, hot fire in a grill.

Cut the bread into thick slices (not too far ahead of time, or it will dry out). Mix the bacon fat and butter together in a small bowl.

Clean the grill grate. Grill the bread over the hot fire until the surface toasts evenly and the edges singe. As soon as the bread comes off the grill, brush each slice generously with the bacon-fat butter and

rub with the cut side of a garlic clove. I've heard some people say that the pressure should be light, the garlic flavor just suggestive, but the flavors coming from the grill marks and the bacon fat are already strong, so I say go bold. Rake the cloves across the ragged surface.

If the tomatoes aren't ripe and juicy, lightly pummel them to get their juices flowing. Cut the tomatoes in half. Rub the cut side of a tomato across each slice of toast, squeezing the tomato until their jelled seed sacs drop down onto the surface. I usually garnish these with a thin loop of extra-virgin olive oil, bringing the recipe's fat total to three, which is a little embarrassing, so let's call it optional.

Cut the bread in half on the board, or serve whole, passed hand to hand.

*A reminder that we should all be saving bacon fat. It keeps at room temperature for 2 days, and a really long time in the refrigerator.

239

potato tortilla

Having people over for brunch is generally not my first choice for entertaining. My inner odometer doesn't reach full cruising speed until at least 10:30. But making a Spanish tortilla is intuitive enough that anyone can do it through eyes drawn at half-mast. The ingredient list is short: 3 potatoes, 2 onions, a dozen eggs. You don't even need to count. Just wander into the kitchen, put on the water for coffee, and start peeling potatoes. By the time you've poured yourself a second cup of coffee and feel the urge to put on some real clothes, the tortilla will be steaming on the countertop.

It really needs to cool its heels there for at least 2 hours to settle, though you can serve it sooner if you need to. I've been told that in the pintxo bars in San Sebastián, the potato tortillas sit on the counters from noon until midnight, and they're not really considered prime until afternoon, when the gooey egg at the center has fused with the potatoes and onions into a sweet, solid cake.

This is one of those times when the pan can make or break the recipe. It should be nonstick, either seasoned carbon steel or cast-iron or Teflon, about 10 inches wide and not too shallow, with sloping sides that will help tip the tortilla from pan to plate.

Makes one 9-inch tortilla, serving 6 to 8

1½ pounds yellow potatoes (3 large)
⅔ cup extra-virgin olive oil, plus more for
   garnish
1 teaspoon smoked paprika, plus more for
   garnish

½ teaspoon plus ¼ teaspoon salt
2 large sweet onions, cut into large dice (about
   3½ cups)
3 garlic cloves, sliced
12 large eggs

Peel the potatoes and cut roughly into ¾-inch cubes. You want them to be two-bite– sized, large enough to slice through in the finished tortilla.

Heat the pan (see headnote) over medium heat and add the olive oil and ½ teaspoon of the smoked paprika. As soon as the paprika begins to sizzle, add the potatoes and ½ teaspoon of the salt and fry at a steady pace, occasionally turning them over. When the potatoes have browned lightly on all sides but aren't yet tender at the center, about 10 minutes, add the onions. Cook until the onions turn brown and sweet and the potatoes are just tender, about 10 minutes. During the last 2 minutes of cooking, add the garlic and cook until it sizzles.

Meanwhile, beat the eggs and the remaining ¼ teaspoon salt in a bowl with a fork until no threads of yolk remain. Pour the beaten eggs into the potato mixture. As soon as it begins to cook at the sides of the pan, push the cooked egg toward the center and shake the potato mixture flat. Repeat once or twice more, pushing the cooked egg at the edges toward the center, until the tortilla is curdy but still shiny with liquid on top. Pat the tortilla flat, reduce the heat to low, and cook slowly until the underside of the tortilla turns light golden brown and it looks mostly solidified, another 5 to 10 minutes; a thin surface pool of uncooked egg should remain.

To flip the tortilla, remove the pan from the heat and lay a large flat serving plate, upside down, over the top of the pan. With a thick pot holder in each hand, clamp the plate and the pan together and swiftly turn upside down.

Set the pan back over medium-low heat. Add a drizzle of olive oil and the remaining ½ teaspoon smoked paprika, then slide the tortilla back into the pan, patting it back into shape as necessary. Cook the tortilla for about a minute on the second side, just enough to set the bottom but not long enough to brown. The eggs should be cooked through but remain a bit custardy in the middle.

Remove the pan from the heat and slide the tortilla out onto the plate again. Drizzle with a bit more olive oil and brush it across the top of the tortilla to shine it up. Dust with a few sprinkles of smoked paprika and let cool at least until tepid, or, preferably, for a couple of hours, before slicing into wedges.

smoked sausages with mustard-miso sauce and arugula

Try to track down cold-smoked (not ready-to-eat) pork sausages for this recipe. High-end butcher shops and traditional smokehouses are more likely to make them. Heavily smoked over fruitwood but not fully cooked, these sausages still possess the potential to unleash juices on your plate.

Of course, I'm partial to the sausage made by my uncle, and now my three cousins, at Thielen Meats in Pierz, Minnesota. Our Great-Uncle Phil, who opened the meat market in the back of his furniture store in 1922, was a pretty shrewd scent marketer. Every couch and recliner he sold was infused with the aroma of smoked sausage—to the eternal frustration of every dog in town.

Bed the sausage onto a shallow pool of miso-spiked mustard sauce. Three kinds of mustard—Dijon, whole-grain, and spicy freshly ground yellow mustard seeds—suggest Eastern European tradition, but the spoonful of sweet yellow miso paste gives the sauce a curious depth.

Serves 6 to 8, with extra sauce

mustard-miso sauce
makes 1½ cups
1 tablespoon yellow mustard seeds
1 cup heavy cream
2 tablespoons whole-grain mustard
2 tablespoons Dijon mustard
1 tablespoon sugar
1 tablespoon sweet yellow miso
2 teaspoons fresh lemon juice
3 large egg yolks

Fine sea salt
Cayenne pepper

sausages and garnish
6 to 8 smoked pork sausages (1½ to 2 pounds)
3 cups peppery greens, like arugula or tatsoi,
   or even mizuna
Fine sea salt and freshly ground black pepper
Drizzle of extra-virgin olive oil
Juice of 1 lemon

For the sauce, grind the mustard seeds in a spice grinder until fine.

Combine the cream, ground mustard seeds, whole-grain mustard, Dijon mustard, and sugar in a small saucepan and bring to a boil. Reduce the heat and simmer gently until thickened and reduced by one quarter, about 3 minutes. Remove from the heat and let cool slightly.

Combine the miso paste and lemon juice in a small bowl and stir together until smooth.

Whisk the egg yolks in a small bowl, then add the hot mustard cream in a thin drizzle, whisking to combine. Scrape the sauce back into the saucepan, set over medium-low heat, and bring to a simmer. Cook gently, tracing the bottom of the pan with a silicone spatula in a figure-eight motion, until the sauce is slightly thickened, about 5 minutes. Add the miso-lemon mixture and heat, stirring, until it dissolves into the sauce. Season with salt and cayenne to taste. Cover to keep warm until needed.

Place the sausages in a large sauté pan or cast-iron skillet and add just enough water to cover the bottom by ¼ inch. Bring the water to a simmer, cover tightly, and reduce the heat to the lowest possible setting. Steam the sausages, watching for evaporation and adding water if necessary, until they are plump and firm—about 10 minutes for conventionally smoked sausages and 20 minutes for cold-smoked sausages. Uncover the pan and cook until the liquid clings thickly to the sausages.

Spoon the warm mustard sauce onto a serving platter and arrange the sausages on top, propping one against the other.

Toss the greens with a little salt and pepper in a bowl. Dress with the olive oil and then the lemon juice, and arrange in a large tuft next to the sausages.

muskmelon Caprese

Like so many height-of-summer dishes, this salad lives and dies on the quality of the melon, which should be soft and scoopable and highly aromatic. A vine-ripened melon will be heavy in the hand, full of juice. When you turn it over to sniff its bottom, it should smell sweet and faintly musky—heady like incense, not sour like fortified wine. In my experience, local farm stands sell the most consistently luscious melons, although you can get lucky at the grocery store, especially if you buy the melon a day or two in advance to give it time to soften on the counter. Here in the upper Midwest, we refer to all orange-fleshed melons as muskmelons, and they're fondly prized for their ability to immediately fug up your car with their musk.

Keeping things simple, I marinate a few handfuls of cherry tomatoes and ground-cherries* until they cough up their juices, then spoon them over the glistening hills of melon. To scoop the melon into egg-shaped "quenelles," drag a serving spoon through the soft flesh, rolling it into an oval: visualize ice cream.

When the salad is gone, save the juices to pour over tomorrow's summer salad. Although, actually, you'll usually find me in the kitchen after dinner, tipping the tart, olive oil–spotted melon juices from the platter into a shot glass to throw back while I load the dishwasher.

Serves 6 to 8 as a side

5 ounces yellow cherry tomatoes (about 1 cup), halved

¾ cup husked ground cherries (small gold tomatillos), halved

⅛ teaspoon fine sea salt, plus more for the melon

Freshly ground black pepper

Large pinch of sugar

1½ tablespoons fresh lemon juice

3 tablespoons extra-virgin olive oil, plus more for garnish

½ large ripe muskmelon (about 2½ pounds)

1 small ball (4 ounces) fresh mozzarella, preferably sold in brine

A handful of small fresh basil leaves for garnish

Combine the cherry tomatoes and ground cherries in a small bowl and season with the salt, pepper to taste, sugar, lemon juice, and olive oil. Toss and leave to macerate on the counter for at least 15 minutes.

Halve the muskmelon and scoop out the seed cavity. With a large oval serving spoon (I've found that a vintage spoon with thin edges and a pointed tip works best for this), scoop out the melon into oval quenelles: Tipping up the melon and pointing your spoon toward the center, scoop out the flesh, dragging it until it rolls into an egg shape.

Arrange the melon on a serving platter that's large enough to accommodate it in one layer. Season lightly with salt, to get its juices running. Tear the mozzarella into rough clods and tuck them in among the melon quenelles. Spoon the cherry tomato mixture over the melon and garnish with small basil leaves. Serve within 3 hours, at room temperature.

★ Ground cherries are small, golden tomatillos. The berries are marble-sized and taste fruity—dramatically fruity and sweet-sour balanced, like a childhood memory of canned pineapple juice—and they grow inside papery husks on arching tomato-like vines, anywhere that a tomato can be grown. Here in the northern Midwest, I've often heard them referred to as "grandkids' fruit." As if it were common knowledge that grandparents grow ground cherries for the younger generation to pick, hyper-attentively peel, eat, and discard. If picking or buying ground cherries, harvest them when their husks begin to turn from green to golden and start to dry out. Picked ground cherries stay fresh at room temperature for weeks if stored in their protective husks. (It's weird, actually, how insulating they are.) Peeled, they can also be frozen.

deer camp feast

FOR UP TO TEN

weekend drinks and snacks
— whiskey-sour gelatin shots with potted sour cherries
— chipotle-cashew salsa with bacon fat
— apricot snickerdoodles

post-hunt feast
— deer liver mousse with pickled grapes on the vine
— backstrap (venison loin) bordelaise
— cider-braised red cabbage wedges
— squash bake with goat cheese custard
— bitter lettuces with warm brown butter vinaigrette, fried shallots, and duck gizzards confit

Honestly, I considered cutting this menu to spare the tender-hearted and the squeamish, but I realized that it was in fact the centerpiece of this book, and of our year, and that deer-camp cooking (in my kitchen and in others) makes the best possible case for keeping this tradition alive. Without the celebratory post-hunt feast, hunting doesn't make much sense. The tradition of cooking has always given hunting its reason for being. And vice versa.

I've come to appreciate the art and solemnity of the preparation, both in the woods and in the kitchen. While the hunters head out to scout the trails for deer signs—trees rubbed raw by antlers, scuffed hoof marks in the snow, smooth salt licks—I start thinking about the menu. Like the hunters, I take the weekend as a challenge to distance myself from the safety of everyday life, to pay attention to my instincts, to look at my ingredients in finer detail. Modern American cooking has become so bloodless, so divorced from the source. This weekend serves as a correction.

The hunters get up in the dark, well before I do, to head to their stands. Deer are notoriously silent, and stealthy. To catch one off-guard, you have to be still, scentless, silent, and immune to the loud comings-and-goings of all the other animals: the squirrels chattering and bickering with each other, the voles racing through dry leaves, the occasional startled grouse breaking out of the brush, wings thumping bass. From my perch in the warm kitchen, I imagine that sitting and watching might feel like a meditation; reports come in that it's also pretty cold and boring.

Around 10:30 in the morning, the hunters start shuffling back into my kitchen, looking for snacks and coffee, announcing their plans to go out again a few hours before dusk while scouting around for a good place to nap before going back out just before dusk. There are men scrunched up on loveseats and men slung between two chairs, their snores calling and answering through the house like birdcall. This weekend, our sleeping, our eating, and our drinking all fall into a synchronous rhythm.

It's all very wait, wait, hurry up. Suddenly one of the hunters comes into my kitchen carrying a forked branch like a scepter—one fork holding a liver, and the other a heart—and I jump up, because now the feast has really begun.

The hardest thing about finding your way with wild game is that gulf of time between one year and the next. When ingredients arrive in your kitchen just once a year, you don't get the chance to practice. Consequently, the stakes are higher. But as I trim the heart, my knife clearing silverskin in wide arcs, I'm not squeamish, and not heartless, just sure: the liver and the heart should be cooked the night of the harvest, not only because that's when they have the best flavor, but because it's the honorable thing to do.

whiskey-sour gelatin shots with potted sour cherries

If I'm remembering correctly, the idea for this cocktail began as a challenge. "It's deer camp—where are the Jell-O® shots?"

As the campers sat around with their strong throwback drinks, the consensus was that cubes of lightly jelled whiskey-sour gelatin (you can substitute brandy, of course, as is the Midwestern way) melt and slink deliciously down the throat, and that all home bars should be stocked with these sugar-cured lemon slices. Entirely edible when made with thin-skinned Meyer lemons, they're also great in gin and tonics and homemade lemonade.

The potted cherries should be made in the summer, during cherry season, and stored in the fridge.

---

whiskey-sour gelatin shots
(makes enough for a dozen drinks)
8 ounces (1 cup) whiskey or brandy
¾ cup fresh lemon juice (from about 6 lemons)
½ cup Simple Syrup (page 204)
5½ teaspoons (2 packages) unflavored gelatin

sugar-cured Meyer lemons
2 Meyer lemons
3 tablespoons sugar

for 1 drink
6 cubes Whiskey-Sour Gelatin Shots
1 ounce whiskey
1 tablespoon Simple Syrup
4 Potted Sour Cherries (recipe follows), with some of their juice
1 slice Sugar-Cured Meyer Lemon
About ¼ cup tonic water for topping off

For the shots, combine the whiskey, lemon juice, and simple syrup in a large measuring cup.

Put the gelatin in a small bowl, add ¼ cup of the whiskey mixture, stir swiftly to combine, and let sit for 5 minutes to bloom the gelatin.

When the gelatin mixture looks sandy and has solidified, transfer it to a saucepan, add another ¼ cup of the whiskey mixture, and set over low heat. Cook, stirring, just until the gelatin melts. Pour the gelatin mixture into the remaining whiskey and whisk to combine.

Pour the gelatin mixture into an 8 × 8-inch baking pan and chill in the refrigerator until firmly set, at least 2 hours. When the gelatin has set, cut into ¾-inch cubes.

Meanwhile, for the sugar-cured lemons, wash the lemons and blot them dry. Generously lop off the tops and bottoms of both lemons and cut them crosswise into thin slices. (A mandoline makes nice uniform slices.) Transfer the lemon slices to a bowl, toss with the sugar, and leave them to sweat at room temperature, tossing occasionally, until their juices turn clear, about 30 minutes. (*These can be made well ahead of time and kept refrigerated.*)

To make each drink, drop the gelatin chunk by chunk into a small cocktail glass halfway. Add the whiskey, simple syrup, potted cherries with a small spoonful of the cherry liquid, the cured lemon slice, and the whiskey and top off with tonic water.

potted sour cherries When I first started making these pickled cherries years ago, I used Linda Ziedrich's recipe for Russian Sour Cherries from her excellent book, *The Joy of Pickling*. Over the years, the spicing has migrated a bit, but her sugar/vinegar/water ratio is perfect, and any recipe that doesn't ask me to pit cherries has my loyalty forever. This is a quick refrigerator pickle. It can be stored in the refrigerator for months, but it should not be preserved in a water bath.

Makes 3 pints

2 cups apple cider vinegar
1½ cups sugar
¼ cup water
1 cinnamon stick

4 cardamom pods, cracked
4 whole cloves
2 dried hot chiles
4 cups fresh sour cherries, not pitted

Combine the vinegar, sugar, water, all of the spices, and the dried chiles in a medium saucepan and bring to a boil. Simmer, whisking, until the sugar dissolves and the flavor of the spices leaches into the pickling liquid, about 15 minutes. Remove from the heat and let steep for 30 minutes.

Rinse the cherries and drain well in a colander, blotting them with a towel to remove surface moisture. Rewarm the pickling liquid until it steams, then add the cherries, remove from the heat, and let cool until the liquid is just warm to the touch.

Drain the cherries in a colander set over a bowl to catch the liquid. Return the liquid to the saucepan and simmer until slightly thickened and a drop of liquid feels sticky between your fingers, about 5 minutes. Remove from the heat and let cool to room temperature.

Drop the cherries into clean sterilized jars and pour the cool pickling liquid over them, making sure that the liquid rises above the cherries. Let cool, and cap the jars. Refrigerate for at least 3 days before using; the cherries can be refrigerated for as long as 6 months.

chipotle-cashew salsa with bacon fat

On deer-hunting mornings, I wake up to find the evidence of the campers' predawn breakfast: the hanging scent of black coffee in the air, burnt toast crumbs in the butter, and a bowl of cooling bacon fat. Someone always thinks to save the bacon fat for me. I pay them back by adding some to our salsa.

Loosely inspired by the smooth, nutty, hand-pounded salsas of Mexico—very loosely, given that you dump canned diced tomatoes, cashews, and chipotle chiles in adobo into a food processor and hit the buzz button—this salsa absorbs the bacon fat, leaving behind a scent trail of liquid smoke. You'll want to tell vegetarians to steer clear of this one, although chances are they'll already be keeping their distance from hunting camp.

I don't usually serve this as an appetizer at the big post-hunt dinner, instead setting it out in the afternoon, during the downtime between the morning and evening hunts. Serve with the thickest, snappiest tortilla chips you can find.

Makes about 2 cups

¼ teaspoon cumin seeds

1 large garlic clove

2 to 3 canned chipotle chiles in adobo (to taste)

2 tablespoons broken cashews

One 14.5 ounce can diced roasted tomatoes

¼ cup lime juice, plus more to taste

2 tablespoons bacon fat

Fine sea salt (optional)

½ cup finely chopped fresh cilantro, including tender stems

Add the cumin seeds to a dry food processor bowl and process until roughed up. Add the garlic and process until finely minced. Add the chipotles, cashews, canned tomatoes, and lime juice and pulse, mixing until well combined but not quite pureed.

Scrape the salsa into a medium serving bowl and stir in the bacon fat, and then the cilantro. (Blending either of these final additions in the processor dulls the color of the salsa.) Taste for seasoning. Canned diced tomatoes usually provide enough salt and acidity, but add a bit of salt or more lime, if you like. Serve with corn chips.

apricot snickerdoodles

This cookie is a hybridized cross between two small-town bakery classics, the snickerdoodle and the soft date-filled (here apricot-filled) cookie, for those of us who could never choose between them.

I tried to replace the artery-hardening Crisco of the snickerdoodle dough I remember with butter, but I've found that including a bit of hydrogenated vegetable fat in this dough is not only historically accurate, but also keeps the cookies soft.

The poached apricot filling, which can be made up to a week in advance, is a valuable side recipe. Poached slowly in water with a bit of white wine and sugar, standard-issue grocery-store dried apricots swell to twice their original size and become so fragile that they dent at the touch of a spoon. Here I mash the apricots for the cookie filling, but I also make them on their own for spooning over yogurt or draping across the tops of squares of gingerbread.

As always for cookies, the butter should be just slightly colder than room temperature. Cool enough to yield to finger pressure (like a ripe peach), but not soft and clammy.

recipe continues

Makes 22 large cookies

apricot filling
6 ounces dried apricots (a shy cup)
2 cups water
½ cup white wine
2 strips lemon peel
1 cinnamon stick or ½ teaspoon ground
    cinnamon
¼ cup sugar
2 teaspoons fresh lemon juice
1 tablespoon unsalted butter

dough
10 tablespoons (1¼ sticks) unsalted butter, at
    cool room temperature
⅓ cup vegetable shortening

1 cup sugar
1 large egg
1 large egg yolk
2 teaspoons spiced dark rum
2½ cups all-purpose flour
1 teaspoon fine sea salt
1 teaspoon baking soda
1 teaspoon cream of tartar
½ teaspoon grated nutmeg
½ teaspoon ground cinnamon

cinnamon sugar
⅓ cup sugar
2 teaspoons ground cinnamon

For the apricot filling, combine the apricots, water, white wine, lemon peel, and cinnamon stick, if using, in a small saucepan and bring to a simmer over medium heat. Cover tightly, lower the heat, and slowly poach the apricots for about 1½ hours, until they're so soft that they can be mashed with a spoon.

When the apricots are tender, uncover the pan, raise the heat slightly, and simmer until just a syrup clings to the apricots. Remove from the heat. Fish out the cinnamon stick and crush the apricots with a potato masher to a rough puree, then add the sugar, lemon juice, (the ground cinnamon, if using) and the butter. Simmer until the apricot puree thickens enough that a spoon swiped through it leaves a trail, about 3 minutes. Remove from the heat and let cool. (*The filling can be covered and refrigerated for up to a week.*)

For the cookie dough, combine the butter and shortening in the bowl of a stand mixer fitted with the paddle attachment (or combine in in a large bowl and use a hand mixer) and mix until smooth. Add the sugar and beat until the mixture has lightened, about 3 minutes. Scrape down the sides of the bowl, add the egg, the egg yolk, and the rum, and mix until soft and glossy, another 2 minutes.

Combine the flour, salt, baking soda, cream of tartar, nutmeg, and cinnamon in a bowl and whisk until no streaks of spice remain, about 20 strokes. Add the flour to the egg mixture and mix on low speed until the dough comes together.

Position a rack in the upper third of the oven and preheat the oven to 325°F.

Combine the sugar and cinnamon in a small bowl. Divide the dough into 24 roughly equal pieces and shape into balls, reserving 2 pieces for patching. Holding a ball of dough in your palm, press a deep pocket into it with your thumb, molding the sides up high like tulip petals. Fill the pocket with a scant 2 teaspoons apricot filling and fold over the edges to close the sphere. You may need to cover the top with a small circle of dough from your reserves. Pat the dough into a ball again, press to slightly flatten it, dip the top in the cinnamon sugar, and place on a double-stacked baking sheet. (Two sheet pans keep the bottoms light.) Repeat with the remaining dough.

Bake the cookies one sheet at a time until golden—lightly tan, not bronzed all over—and puffed, about 13 minutes. Remove from the oven and cool the cookies on a rack. Store in a tightly lidded container, where they will remain soft and delicious for about 5 days.

deer liver mousse with pickled grapes on the vine

I hesitated to include this mousse, because you can't exactly sidle up to a meat counter and buy a deer liver, but I know what it feels like to hold one in your hand and want to pay your respects in a luscious, crowd-pleasing way. So this is my master deer-liver–mousse recipe, tweaked over eight years of hunting festivities and honed to fit our particular camp tastes.

My recipe is based very loosely on Julia Child's chicken liver mousse, adjusted to amp up what I consider the three essential "Bs" of the season: bacon, butter, and booze. Julia used Cognac or Armagnac; I use the finest Midwestern brandy I can find.

An average deer liver weighs 2½ to 3 pounds, but to account for natural variations in size, here I call for half of one large liver. Fresh pork liver makes a good substitute.

You can serve the mousse alongside a platter of the pickled grapes on the vine—a particularly gorgeous sidekick (page 254). I devised the recipe to make use of my own homegrown grapes, and it was pure slacker's luck that clusters of grapes pickled whole, on the vine, were delicious, saving me the hand labor of picking off each and every grape. These grapes are a beautiful addition to any appetizer board, in fact, and they keep in the refrigerator for ages.

Makes 2½ cups; serves 10 or more

deer liver mousse
½ large deer liver (about 1 pound)
7 tablespoons Madeira
7 tablespoons brandy
¼ teaspoon pink curing salt (optional; see Pink Salt, page 166)
1 slice thick-cut bacon, cut into 5 pieces
4 tablespoons butter, plus 6 tablespoons butter at cool room temperature
⅓ cup small-diced sweet onion
¼ teaspoon plus ¼ teaspoon fine sea salt
3 fresh sage leaves, minced
½ teaspoon grated nutmeg or mace
¼ teaspoon ground allspice

¼ teaspoon ground cardamom
¼ teaspoon freshly ground black pepper
¾ cup heavy cream

Madeira jelly
2 teaspoons unflavored gelatin
2 tablespoons port
½ cup Madeira
1 teaspoon maple syrup

Pickled Grapes on the Vine (recipe follows; optional)
Baguette slices or crackers for serving

To prepare the liver, rinse it under cold running water and then soak in a bowl of cold water for 20 minutes.

Drain the liver, rinse, and lay on a cutting board. First, cut away all of the connective tissue and veins, and then remove all of the outside membrane: Slip the sharp point of your knife underneath the membrane and slice away from yourself. Dice the liver into 2-inch cubes. You should have about 1¾ cups, or 13 ounces.

Rinse the cubed liver under cold running water, drain, and pat dry. Put the liver in a bowl, add 6 tablespoons each of the Madeira and the brandy, and the pink salt, if using, and toss to coat. Cover and marinate in the refrigerator for a minimum of 1 hour, and a maximum of 12.

For the jelly, combine the gelatin and port in a small dish, stir, and set aside until the gelatin blooms, about 3 minutes; the mixture should stiffen to a sandy mass.

recipe continues

Heat the Madeira in a small saucepan over medium heat. When it begins to steam, remove it from the heat and whisk in the port-gelatin mixture, stirring until dissolved. Add the maple syrup. Remove from the heat and set aside. (*You can make this ahead of time and keep in the refrigerator, then gently remelt before using.*)

For the mousse, heat a large heavy skillet, preferably cast-iron, over medium heat. (Iron-rich liver tastes best when cooked in iron, that's just a law of nature.) Add the bacon and fry gently until it crisps at the edges and releases some of its fat. Remove the bacon, leaving the fat in the pan, and set aside in a bowl.

Add 2 tablespoons of the butter, the onion, and ¼ teaspoon of the salt to the pan. Cook over medium heat, stirring, until the onions are golden brown and sweet, about 10 minutes; add the sage during the last minute. Scrape the onions into the bowl with the bacon.

Drain the liver, reserving its marinade. Arrange the liver on a plate lined with paper towels and blot dry. Raise the heat under the pan to high and add another 2 tablespoons butter. Sauté the liver in two batches until darkened on both sides and the center begins to firm up when prodded—a bouncy medium/medium-rare, with a pink center. (If it's cooked past this point, the mousse will be gritty.) Drop the liver into a blender, then deglaze the pan with the reserved marinade. Boil until it reduces to a syrup, and add to the liver.

Add the remaining 1 tablespoon each Madeira and brandy, the onion/bacon mixture, the nutmeg, allspice, cardamom, the remaining ¼ teaspoon salt, the pepper, and cream to the blender. Process the mixture until smooth and thick, stopping once or twice to scrape the sides of the blender with a rubber spatula. Then, with the blender running on a low speed, feed the remaining 6 tablespoons butter into it, processing until the mousse absorbs it smoothly.

In theory, the liver mousse is now smooth enough, but pushing it through a fine-mesh sieve will make it even silkier and more lush-tasting. Set a sieve over a bowl and press the mousse through it with the back of a ladle. With a rubber spatula, scrape the mousse into a shallow decorative bowl, smooth the top flat, and refrigerate until cold to the touch.

Gently rewarm the jelly to a tepid liquid state and pour it over the top of the mousse. Chill again until the jelly sets, at least 45 minutes (or, if it's 10°F or lower outside, chilling it on the porch will take just 20 minutes).

Serve the mousse with the pickled grapes, alongside some baguette slices or crackers.

---

pickled grapes on the vine The laziest of all pickles (and possibly the prettiest). No stemming, no seeding, no canning required.

When the grape harvest overwhelms you and you cannot stand to pluck single grapes from the stems to make one more batch of jelly or jam or juice, throw whole on-the-vine clusters into your largest jar, cover them with a simple sweet-pickle brine, and store them in the refrigerator. The hot brine gently cooks the grapes enough to just soften them.

I use my own homegrown wine and juice grapes, Beta and King of the North varieties, but any Concord-type grape sold in clusters will work. Unlike table grapes, these wine or juice varieties have tart jelly-sac interiors and strong skins that pop seductively in the mouth. They do contain seeds, though, so you might want to set out a small pip bowl.

Makes 1 quart

A quart jar of tight grape clusters
4 cups distilled white or apple cider vinegar
1 cup water
2½ cups sugar

1 tablespoon black peppercorns
Two 1-inch chunks ginger, smacked with the
    side of a heavy knife
2 bay leaves

With scissors, trim the grape clusters to an inch of stem at the top and pull off any dried or stunted fruit. Swish the clumps through a large bowl of cold water to rinse them and lay on a clean towel to drain.

    Fill a clean quart jar with the grapes, arranging them to fill the space but taking care not to crush or crowd them. (Because this pickle will be refrigerated, there's technically no need to sterilize the jar, but I usually fill it with boiling water from the teakettle, cap it, and give it a shake, then pour out the water. Be sure to use a new, or freshly sterilized, lid and ring.

    Combine the vinegar, water, sugar, peppercorns, ginger, and bay leaves in a saucepan, bring to a simmer, and cook, whisking, until all the sugar has dissolved.

    Pour the hot brine over the grapes and let them cool to room temperature, now and then poking them with a sterilized butter knife to encourage air bubbles to rise.

    When the brine is cool, cap and store in the refrigerator. The grapes will be pickled through and ready to eat within 4 days. If you make sure that the brine covers the grapes, they will keep for about a year.

backstrap (venison loin) bordelaise

Old game cookery, especially the tradition in France, has always given me strong candlelit palace vibes. The recipes feel opulent, savage, and rarefied—all at the same time. Cooking game *is* rare. Hunters get just one shot to nail it, and, usually, cooks only get once chance to make it right. Little foie gras–stuffed songbirds (*becfigues*) roasted over a fire, roast woodcooks served on top of butter-crisped bread spread with their mashed innards, and even hare served in a sauce of its own blood all sound unbearably delicious—if a little macabre. In other words, recipes like these match my deer camp mood. Bordelaise, for example, one of the French master sauces, is made from a reduction of two bottles of Burgundy, demi-glace (a rich, sticky reduced veal stock), and thickened with the white fat gouged from marrowbones. Marrowbones aren't too hard to find, but veal bones are impossible, and I'm way too cheap to reduce good-quality French wine for a sauce. It's deer camp; we buy a few good bottles for dinner, and beyond that, we drink out of the box.

A bordelaise sauce made from the residue left in the pan after sautéing the venison loin (or backstrap) tastes nearly as royal, metallic, and deep as the all-day version, if you coddle it. (Using homemade chicken stock helps.) Thickening the sauce with fresh marrow fat at the last minute gives it that old French polished-leather sheen. You'll want to serve the bordelaise with some bread for sopping up every bit of sauce.

Serves 8 to 10 as part of a grand feast

2 marrowbones*
2½-pounds venison loin
½ teaspoon plus ¼ teaspoon fine sea salt
⅛ teaspoon freshly ground black pepper
1½ teaspoons dried thyme
¾ teaspoon ground ginger
⅛ teaspoon ground cloves
2 tablespoons canola oil
3 tablespoons butter

3 large shallots, halved and sliced
2 cups red wine (something deep and dry and inky)
2 tablespoons Cognac or good brandy
1 cup chicken stock, preferably homemade (recipe follows)**
1 bay leaf
1 cinnamon stick

To release the marrow, soak the bones in cold water for about an hour (longer if they've been frozen), until the marrow feels pliable, like clay.

Push the marrow out of the bones, prying it out with a butter knife if it's not a straight cylinder. Remove any veins or bits of blood from the marrow, roughly chop it, and reserve in a small dish in the refrigerator.

Cut the venison loin into 8-inch lengths (to fit inside your sauté pan) and season them with ½ teaspoon of the salt and the pepper. Combine the thyme, ginger, and cloves in a small dish and sprinkle evenly over the venison, rubbing it into the meat.

Warm the oven to 200°F.

Heat a very wide-bottomed sauté pan over medium-high heat and add the canola oil. Working in batches, sear the venison to a quick brown crust on all sides, taking care not to burn the bottom of the pan, and remove to a platter. The meat, when poked, should feel soft and rare.

Add the butter and shallots to the pan, along with the remaining ¼ teaspoon salt, and sauté over medium heat until the shallots darken at the edges and are tender, about 5 minutes. Add the wine and Cognac or brandy and bring to a simmer, scraping the bottom of the pan with a wooden spoon to incorporate the flavorful pan-stickings. Add the chicken stock, bay, and cinnamon and simmer the sauce until slightly reduced, about 5 minutes.

recipe continues

*Marrowbones can be found in many meat departments if you search the furthest reaches of the case, and certainly in butcher shops.

**Rich sauces like bordelaise get their voluptuous texture from stock made from gelatin-rich veal bones. For times like these, I go into my freezer to retrieve a roll of salted pig skin to add to my chicken stock, which adds a similar richness. I'm aware of how wildly unrelatable this sounds, but if you just so *happen* to be trimming away some excess pig skin from a pork belly—maybe you buy a fall pig for the freezer, for example—don't throw it away. Cut it into 6-inch squares, rub them with coarse salt and pepper, roll them up tightly and tie with string, and pop into the freezer for times like this.

Return the venison to the pan and simmer gently, turning it in the sauce, until it begins to feel firm, 3 to 5 minutes. You want to take it out when it measures 120°F, or rare, because the temperature will rise to the perfect 125°F as it rests (and on the reheat, if that's necessary). Remove the venison to a serving platter to rest while you finish the sauce.

Simmer the sauce until thickened and reduced to ¾ cup. If the venison needs reheating, warm it gently in the sauce, then transfer it to a cutting board. Pour any accumulated juices on the platter back into the sauce, then rinse and dry the platter and put it in the oven briefly to warm.

Add the bone marrow to the sauce and whisk to combine. The sauce should be thick and rich, but pourable. Strain the sauce through a fine-mesh sieve, pressing on the shallots with the back of a spoon to express their good liquid, then pour the sauce onto the warmed platter.

Slice the venison into thick medallions and set on the sauce, cut side up. Serve immediately, with a meat fork and a spoon for the sauce.

ABOUT THAT VENISON

Depending on where you live, venison is either really scarce or way too plentiful.

When I lived in a city, I rarely saw venison in butcher shops, even the high-end ones. If available at all, it was a special order. Much like specialty building materials, venison is sold mostly "to the trade." If you're friends with a chef, it might be time to exploit that friendship and ask them to slip your venison loin onto their next order. It will be farm-raised—plump, sweet, and perfectly aged. The same venison farms that cater to restaurants trade often accept mail orders, which is another good option.

In rural areas, though, and in hunting families everywhere, venison is often as common as beef. This reminds me of a story told by a friend who spent some time working in a small village on the coast of Guatemala in the 1970s. His hosts apologized profusely every night before dinner, because the only thing they had to offer him was lobster. Scarcity always sets value.

But even here in northern Minnesota, where each fall I open the door to a neighbor holding out packages of venison from last year's hunt—because his wife is just sick of cooking it and he needs to clear some freezer space—he's not offering up venison loins. The loins, or the backstraps as they're called, are always precious.

The haunch of venison has the most flavor, but the loin is the only cut that we serve medium-rare, like a beef tenderloin. If it comes from an animal that was well fed on acorns and field corn and spruce tips, carefully field-dressed, and properly aged, wild venison loin is the most luxurious of red-meat experiences. It has a depth of character, a natural spiciness, that farm-raised can't match.

But aging meat is nearly a lost art, and tough to pull off without a walk-in refrigerator or consistently cold 45°F days and above-freezing nights. Thankfully, wet-aging in vacuum-sealed bags works nearly as well. After we Cryovac the meat, I let it hang out for a day or two in the refrigerator before freezing it. And when I take it out months later, I leave it in the refrigerator for up to 8 days (still tightly sealed in its vacuum bag) before cooking it. Wet-aging tenderizes any roast, but it turns venison loin, in particular, into butter.

chicken stock The best chicken stock is made from a mixture of bones and meat. If you haven't saved up a large amount of raw chicken carcasses, buy chicken thighs (for flavor) and wings and backs (for body). And if you simmer it gently enough, the chicken thigh meat will still be perfectly edible. I usually chop it up for chicken salad, the finely chopped kind that's meant to be a sandwich filling. The meat's a little dry maybe, but it's nothing that an extra scoop of mayonnaise can't fix.

Save your thyme and rosemary stems and small inner garlic cloves and all vegetable trimmings for throwing into the stock.

Makes 2 quarts

3 pounds chicken bones and meat (a combination of thighs and wings)
Water just to cover (about 10 cups)
3 celery stalks
2 carrots, cut into thirds
1 small sweet onion, quartered, or the skins and tops and trimmings from 3 onions
1 head garlic, root end trimmed, top ½ inch sliced off to expose the cloves

Leek tops, if you have them
1½ teaspoons fine sea salt, plus more to taste
1 tablespoon black peppercorns
3 bay leaves
A handful of thyme sprigs (or sage or rosemary, or parsley stems whatever herbs you might have in excess)

Wash the chicken by putting it in the stockpot and running a few changes of cold water through it. Then fill the pot with enough fresh cold water to cover the chicken by 2 inches and bring to a simmer. When it boils, skim off the rising foam with a ladle and discard.

Add the celery, carrots, onion, garlic, leeks, salt, peppercorns, bay leaves, and herbs to the pot. Bring the liquid to a simmer and cook, uncovered, at a low speed, the liquid bubbling gently at the edges, until the chicken is fully tender when pierced with a fork and the stock tastes delicious, as flavorful as soup. It will take 2 to 3 hours.

Lift out the meat and bones and put into a bowl. Strain the stock through a fine-mesh sieve set over a large bowl and let cool on the counter. When the fat rises, skim it off by running a ladle in a circular motion from edge to center.

When the meat has cooled enough to handle, pick it from the bones and reserve. Cool the stock until tepid before storing in a covered container in the refrigerator. The more strongly it gels when cold, the longer it will keep. A bouncy-set stock will keep for a full week.

TURKEY STOCK VARIATION

Substitute turkey backs, drumsticks, wings, and/or necks, plus any trimmings from preparing your Thanksgiving turkey, in place of the chicken. Follow the recipe above, but add 3 whole cloves and 10 allspice berries.

Reserve 3 cups of picked meat for the Thanksgiving dressing; store it covered in stock, if making this in advance, to keep it fresh-tasting.

cider-braised red cabbage wedges

These gorgeous red cabbage wedges are braised in a deep slurry of dry cider and rich chicken stock until the wedges unfurl and collapse into their own tangy juices. Braised red cabbage is a reliable sidekick, but this one could also easily hold the center of a vegetarian menu.

I used to cook this dish until the cabbage was just tender, to the point at which its ribs began to droop, but one day I forgot about it. By the time I rescued it from the oven, the cabbage was limp, splayed flat against the pan bottom, and the color of an overripe plum. Every inch of it was caramelized and absolutely soused with flavor, and now I wouldn't have it any other way.

Serves 8 to 10 as a side

1 medium-large red cabbage (2½ pounds)*
Fine sea salt and freshly ground black pepper
1½ cups chicken stock, preferably homemade (page 259), or vegetable stock
2 tablespoons butter, plus more for finishing
2 tablespoons chicken or bacon fat (or more butter)

1 small sweet onion, quartered
½ bunch scallions, cut into 3-inch batons
1¼ cups dry cider (or fresh nonalcoholic cider)
2 tablespoons maple syrup
2 teaspoons brandy or whiskey
2 to 3 tablespoons fresh lemon juice, plus more to taste

Preheat the oven to 375°F.

Halve the cabbage, remove the wilty outer leaves, and cut into 1½-inch-thick wedges, hooked together at the stem end. Lay on a baking sheet and sprinkle on both sides with salt and pepper.

Put the stock in a small saucepan and boil to reduce by half, until it measures ¾ cup. Remove from the heat.

Heat your largest sauté pan over medium-high heat and add the butter and bacon or chicken fat. When it foams, working in batches to avoid crowding, sauté the cabbage wedges and onions and scallions until both sides turn golden brown; set aside.

Add the reduced stock, the cider, maple syrup, and brandy or whiskey to the pan and bring to a simmer. Return the cabbage (and onions and scallions) to the pan, cover, and pop into the oven to braise until the cabbage is just barely tender at the thickest part, about 15 minutes.

Uncover the pan, add the lemon juice, and turn the cabbage in its juices with a pair of tongs. Return to the oven, uncovered, and braise until the cabbage is tender and the juices have reduced to a glaze, 30 to 40 minutes.

Taste for seasoning, correcting the salt and adding more lemon juice if needed. Finish with a lump of butter and toss. Serve warm, straight from the pan.

*Cabbage weights vary a lot. A small cabbage that can be easily balanced in your palm will weigh about a pound. Large cabbages that span 10 inches across can weigh up to 4 pounds or more. No matter its size, cut your cabbage into wedges and use what you can pack into the pan, keeping in mind that it will shrink by nearly half during cooking.

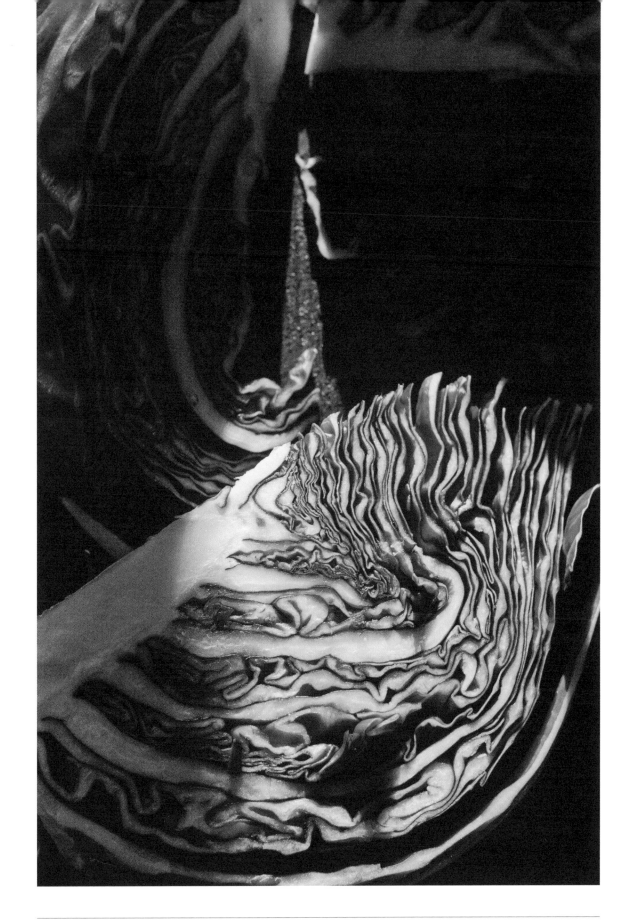

squash bake with goat cheese custard

When you're making a big complicated dinner, a squash is the lifeline you need.

It's hard to resist the temptation to make a baked squash dish that tastes like dessert. We all know the one, and love it, because marshmallows speak directly to the inner child in each of us. But since squash is naturally sweet, I'd rather top it with a soft pouf of savory, creamy custard, which achieves the same clouds-over-sweet-earth textural contrast. The flavor of the goat cheese is subtle, but it helps the surface of the custard blister and caramelize.

This dish would also make a winner of a Thanksgiving side.

Serves 8 to 10

squash layer
3 tablespoons butter, plus more for the baking dish
1 large buttercup or 3 small delicata squash (4 pounds)
¼ teaspoon fine sea salt, plus more to taste
Freshly ground black pepper
1 to 2 tablespoons maple syrup (to taste, depending on the sweetness of the squash)

custard layer
6 ounces fresh goat cheese, softened
2 large egg yolks
3 large eggs
1½ cups heavy cream
½ cup whole milk
½ teaspoon fine sea salt
¼ teaspoon freshly grated black pepper
½ teaspoon grated nutmeg

Preheat the oven to 325°F. Rub the interior of a wide shallow 2½- to 3-quart baking dish (I typically use a 13-inch-wide covered casserole) with butter.

When splitting a buttercup squash, use the heaviest knife you have, and cut straight down from the stem on either side to make a single lateral line. If the knife gets stuck, tap on its tang with a meat mallet to knock it through. Crack the squash line against the hard edge of the counter or cutting board to split it open. Delicata squash are easier to halve.

Scoop out the seeds and scrape the seed cavity clean with a serving spoon (see headnote). Season the interior of the squash with the salt and a little pepper.

Set the squash cut side down in a 9 × 13-inch baking pan. Bake until soft when poked and very tender all the way through, about 45 minutes or longer, depending on the thickness of the squash. (Delicata squash may require a little less baking time.) Better to overbake than underbake, as squash continues to gather sweetness after initially testing just-tender. Remove from the oven (but leave the oven on).

Scoop out the squash flesh—it should be a soft, spreadable puree—and transfer to a bowl; you should have 4 to 5 cups. Add the butter, more salt and pepper, and maple syrup to taste. Some squashes are naturally sweet, and some need help.*

Transfer the squash to the baking dish and smooth the top. (*At this point, you can refrigerate the squash if not ready to finish the dish. You can also make the custard topping ahead and refrigerate.*) Bake for 5 to 8 minutes, or until hot; remove from the oven and smooth again. You want a flat, almost impermeable bottom layer.

---

*If the squash isn't sweet, mix in a bit of maple syrup; if it's dry, mix in up to ½ cup warm water.

For the custard layer, put the goat cheese in a large bowl and beat until smooth. Add the egg yolks and whisk until combined, then whisk in the whole eggs, cream, milk, salt, pepper, and nutmeg.

Pour the custard on top of the squash and return it to the oven to bake for another 50 to 55 minutes, or until the custard no longer wiggles in the center and the top is is covered with abstract puddles of brown caramelization. Serve warm right from the dish.

This can be made up to an hour before dinner and gently rewarmed in a slow oven.

bitter lettuces with warm brown butter vinaigrette, fried shallots, and duck gizzards confit

If a salad could survive a week alone in the wilderness, it would come out looking like this one. The brown butter–poppy seed dressing, sweet fried shallots, and thin shavings of cured duck gizzards confit plot together to take over the healthy part, but the pale and peppery lettuces fight back pretty well.

Gizzards, which have the most unfortunate food name in the whole English language, live a glamorous double life in French as *gesiers confit.* When cured and then slowly bathed in fat and herbs, they taste no gamier than chicken thighs. After cold-aging for a few days under their preserving cap of fat, as the French farmhouse cooks who invented the technique intended, they taste something like aged Alpine cheese crossed with mushrooms crossed with wild game. I think of them as woodland truffles.

I once found a six-week-old pot of confited gizzards in the back of the fridge and set them on the counter with the intention of feeding them to my dog, but not before nibbling on one first to make sure they were still safe enough for her to eat. Safe! They were incredible. Even better than they'd been the first time. I sliced them into thin pink coins, fed a few to my girl, and shingled the rest across a piece of heavily buttered toast.

Serves 8 to 10

10 cups mixed pale, peppery, and bitter lettuces (lettuce hearts, watercress, and torn radicchio)
5 large shallots (about 10 ounces)
2 to 3 cups canola or peanut oil for frying
Fine sea salt

brown butter–poppy seed vinaigrette
1½ tablespoons poppy seeds
3 tablespoons butter
1 teaspoon maple syrup

3 tablespoons extra-virgin olive oil
1 teaspoon minced fresh thyme
1½ tablespoons sherry vinegar
¼ teaspoon fine sea salt, plus more for the lettuces
Freshly ground black pepper

8 to 10 Gizzards Confit (page 266), thinly sliced

recipe continues

Wash and spin-dry the mixed bitter lettuces and pale lettuce hearts and lay out on a large clean dish towel to dry. If prepping them more than 2 hours in advance, wrap the towel into a bundle and refrigerate in the crisper.

Slice the shallots crosswise with a mandoline into thin rings, the thickness of a nickel (or use a very sharp chef's knife).

Line a baking sheet with paper towels. Add oil to a medium saucepan to come to a depth of 3 inches, then add the sliced shallots and slowly bring to a simmer over medium heat. Cook, stirring occasionally, as the shallots pop and sizzle and burn off moisture. Once they quiet down, monitor the heat to maintain a gentle simmer and stand by, stirring, as the shallots begin to slowly brown, about 8 minutes. When they have turned evenly light brown—don't let them go past amber, as they will continue to darken as they cool—scoop out the shallots with a spider to the lined baking sheet. Spread them out and sprinkle lightly with salt. (*This recipe makes more than you will need for the salad, to account for snitching—inevitable—but any remaining shallots will keep for days in a tightly covered storage container, lined with a fresh paper towel to absorb oil, at room temperature.*)

For the vinaigrette, grind the poppy seeds in a spice mill until they begin to clump up on the sides.

Heat a small sauté pan over medium heat and add the butter. Cook, undisturbed, until the butter rises into a foam and starts to brown. Whisk to incorporate all the stuck bits on the sides and bottom of the pan, remove from the heat and let cool for a minute, and then add the poppy seeds, maple syrup, olive oil, thyme, sherry vinegar, salt, and freshly ground pepper to taste. If you're making this in advance, the brown butter will solidify, so melt it quickly with a few brief pulses in the microwave until pourable again before using.

Toss the mixed greens with a bit more salt and pepper in a wide salad bowl, and toss with enough of the vinaigrette to lightly coat. Top with a large handful of fried shallots and the gizzards confit and serve.

recipe continues

gizzards confit This old French technique for poaching salt-cured chicken gizzards in a hot bath of fat feels at once ancient and avant-garde, and it rescues a perfectly good but often discarded part of the chicken. Slow-cooked cured gizzards are meaty, not gamy at all, and have a dense, almost waxen texture. In many cafés in rural France, you'll find *salade de gésiers* on the menu, and you should definitely order it. Just before serving, they'll shower your mustardy greens with thin slices of ruby gizzards.

All gizzards must be properly cleaned before cooking. Once you open them up and lay the two lobes flat, it's very easy to see the thick membrane, the part that needs to go. Trimmed farm-raised duck and chicken gizzards will yield spheres of meat that vary in size from golf ball to mothball. Wild duck gizzards are nearly too small to be worth the time to clean them, but if you find yourself with plenty of spare time in the evenings to pare gizzards, these have a particularly deep, spicy flavor.

Stored in their cooking fat, where no oxygen can reach them, refrigerated gizzards confit keep for 6 weeks.

Makes two to three times what you need for the salad but keeps well in the refrigerator

1 pound duck or chicken gizzards
2 teaspoons kosher salt or 1½ teaspoons fine
    sea salt
4 garlic cloves, smashed and peeled
4 sprigs thyme

2 bay leaves
1 teaspoon black peppercorns
Melted duck fat, lard, or bacon fat to cover the
    gizzards (2 cups, more or less, depending
    on the size of your pan)*

With a sharp paring knife, separate each gizzard into 2 lobes, then trim off the thick, pale outer membrane, starting with the connective tissue. Run your paring knife around each lobe, removing as much of the thick skin as you can by slipping the thin tip of the knife beneath its surface and shearing outward and upward.

Toss the gizzards with the salt and 2 of the smashed garlic cloves in a bowl. Cover and cure in the refrigerator for at least 12 hours, and as long as 24.

Preheat the oven to 225°F.

Quickly rinse the gizzards and pat dry. Combine the gizzards, the remaining 2 garlic cloves, the thyme, bay leaves, and peppercorns in a small heavy frying pan or baking dish. Add enough melted fat to cover and bake the gizzards, uncovered, until very tender when poked with a thin fork, about 3 hours. The fat should bubble casually the entire time. If you see it boil, reduce the oven temperature to 200°F. Remove the gizzards from the oven and let cool to room temperature in the pan.

Pick out the gizzards and transfer them to a clean glass storage container. Rewarm the fat briefly if it has solidified, and strain it through a fine-mesh sieve into a bowl, stopping before you get to the dark, flavorful stock at the bottom. Pour the fat over the gizzards. You want to cover the gizzards with fat, and only fat, but do save that delicious cooking stock for throwing into something else you might have going: soup, beans, risotto, etc.

Press a square of plastic wrap against the surface to prevent oxidation, cover the container, and store the gizzards in the refrigerator until needed (for up to 6 weeks). To use, pluck out the gizzards one by one and wipe off excess fat. They're wonderful on salad, but also pretty slamming on a cheese plate, thinly sliced and carefully shingled.

---

*Any combination of these fats will work fine, and in a pinch, you can top it off with canola oil as necessary.

annual birthday blowout for my brother

FOR SIX TO EIGHT

— raw oyster bar
— corn soup with coconut and littleneck clams
— pork-stuffed barbecued chicken thighs
— sticky rice
— stir-fried greens and leeks
— honeydew and cucumber salad with cilantro-lime dressing
— single-origin chocolate cake

Raw oysters on the half-shell are merely the decadent preamble to the dinner I cook for my brother Marc's birthday. We can't source fresh oysters locally, which is why we spend two days debating what varieties we're going to order, and from which coast. Creamy or briny, East or West? There's so much weight to this decision. And ever since Marc taught Hank how to throw them back, slamming each empty shell upside down on the counter like a shot glass on a bar, we've needed to add at least another dozen.

Marc also likes clams (might as well tack on a bag of littlenecks), and Southeast Asian flavors, and greens from the garden, and while I'm at it, maybe just a small wedge of dense, not-too-sweet chocolate cake. Obviously, I spoil my youngest brother. But I need to cook for a discerning crowd—it makes me better—so for this dinner, I usually invite my whole family, bring out my good Japanese knives, strap back my hair, and start cooking the night before. My family's pickiness gives me purpose, and an excuse to mail-order faraway seafood. If this menu has a roaming helter-skelter feel to it, starting in Duxbury Bay, MA, before hopping willy-nilly all over Southeast Asia, that's because it follows Marc's cravings.

The barbecued pork-stuffed chicken, a dish I've been refining (or, rather, inauthenticating) for years, borrows its spiced marinade from Indonesian cooking but owes most everything else to my favorite Hmong-style pork-stuffed chicken wings—the filling flush with cilantro. The stir-fried greens satisfy our collective need for something simple and straight from the garden, and the sour and spicy honeydew and cucumber salad balances out the richness of the meat. But the corn soup is the dish that brings this collection of desires together, the makrut lime leaf–scented corn and coconut base is as sleek and fancy as the clams are rustic. I don't shuck the clams, because the little purple shells protect the clam bellies from overcooking, and plucking them out as you eat just adds to the all-hands-on deck gourmet experience.

raw oyster bar

Ordering oysters by mail feels like a staycation. I've never physically visited the sources, but I *feel* like I've been there via the oysters. For example, I like briny, classic oysters from the East Coast, especially the ringing salinity of those from Duxbury Bay, Massachusetts. But I also like the creamier, melon-bellied Totten Inlets and the toasted-nori aromas of the Shingoku, both from the West Coast. The flavors of oysters are subtle. Some taste like the surf, others more like a gravelly cold beach. Some are firm, almost crispy; others soft and custardy. Appreciating oysters is an exercise in dialing in our palates, because they don't broadcast loudly.

It's impossible to gauge the freshness of an oyster just by looking at it, so you want to buy them from a trusted place. And check the fish tag for the harvest date; they shouldn't be any more than five days away from the water.

Serves 8

3 dozen fresh oysters (4 to 5 per person) or more if your guests are big oyster-eaters

if the oysters are fresh, I'll take them neat, but it's always nice to assemble a few condiment options
2 lemons, cut into wedges
Your preferred hot sauce
Basil Oil (page 227)
Spicy Black Vinegar Dipping Sauce (page 119)
Homemade Chile Oil (page 60)

you will also need
3 cups ice cubes, crushed to fine shards and refrozen until needed, for chilling and stabilizing the oysters on the serving platter
An oyster knife (or two, to shuck them faster)
An oyster shucking glove, reinforced to protect your palm in case the knife slips, or a thick dishcloth

Scrub the oysters to remove any grit and mud, lay them in a large container, drape a clean wet towel over them, and refrigerate. If time is short, you can chill them on ice, but don't let them swim in it as it melts.

Set up your little oyster shucking station with a clean folded towel to protect your hands, a sharp oyster knife, a bowl for the shells, and a plate filled with a hill of coarse salt or cracked ice for holding the shucked oysters (and your beverage of choice). Pull out some small plates and forks for those who might need them, and have some lemon wedges and your favorite hot sauce for garnishing ready.

Point the tip of the shucking knife into the oyster's back hinge, wiggling it in until the tip pushes through the muscle into the cavity. Twist the knife and pop off the top shell. Being careful not to spill the overflowing oyster liquor, wipe away any loose shell fragments and gently slip your knife underneath the oyster to sever the fleshy button (aductor muscle) that secures it to the shell. Then flip the oyster over to serve belly side up (this is optional, but prettier) and set the shucked oyster on the platter of ice.

At some point, the ice, if that's what you are using, will probably melt and capsize the oysters and it will make more sense to start handing them directly across the counter, like sushi. Once you get into the groove of shucking oysters, you'll crack one open and know right away to whom it should belong. The young, translucent oyster that's brimming with brine goes to the teenager trying them for the first time. That's a teaching oyster. The little one with the creamy belly and the fat aductor pad is for me. The large shiny oyster with the almost-bluish ivory belly and the softly gathered edges swimming in a saucer of juice—that one's for my Marc (if I can get it past Hank). There you go, that's your gift.

corn soup with coconut and littleneck clams

Sweet corn, coconut milk, and briny clams mesh together so naturally that they feel like one of the world's great culinary threesomes. This isn't one of those recipes that can handle a lot of ingredient downgrading, though. You'll need really fresh corn, and fresh makrut lime leaves—because their strong floral presence brings it all together—and spanking-fresh clams. I prefer small clams, like littlenecks, that roll around daintily in the bowl. The kind with pink bellies and ruffled edges that look like they're winking at you.

If time is an issue, make the corn base ahead of time and chill it—even the day before you'll need it—but cook the clams at the very last minute.

recipe continues

Serves 8

corn soup base

6 ears corn, shucked and kernels cut off (about 5 cups kernels), cobs reserved

½ teaspoon fine sea salt, plus a pinch

4 tablespoons butter

½ sweet onion, diced

2 tablespoons minced ginger

3 garlic cloves, sliced

1 cup chicken stock, preferably homemade (page 259)

1¼ cups coconut milk

2 makrut lime leaves

1 small Thai chile, slit down one side

2 tablespoons fish sauce, preferably Red Boat brand

1 tablespoon maple syrup

littlenecks

3 tablespoons butter

2 shallots, diced

Pinch of fine sea salt, plus more to taste

2½ pounds littleneck clams

2 makrut lime leaves

1 small Thai chile, slit down one side

2/3 cup white wine

1 large sprig basil

Fresh baby basil leaves, green or purple or Thai, for garnish

For the soup base, break the corncobs in half and put in a large saucepot. Add just enough water to come level with the top of the corn and bring to a boil. Add a pinch of salt, bring to a simmer, and cook, uncovered, for 1 hour, or until you have about 6 cups of concentrated corn stock. Strain and reserve.

Heat the butter in a large high-sided sauté pan over medium heat. Add the onion and the ½ teaspoon salt and cook until the onion turns golden brown at the edges and tastes sweet, about 15 minutes.

Add the ginger and garlic and cook for another 3 minutes. Add the corn kernels and cook briefly, just until they turn shiny and a deeper shade of yellow, about 2 minutes or so.

Add the chicken stock, coconut milk, lime leaves, chile, fish sauce, maple syrup, and 5 cups of the corn stock and bring to a simmer. Cook until the corn loses its raw, starchy taste and the aromatics have infused into the broth, about 10 minutes.

Remove from the heat and let the broth sit for a few minutes to cool off, then puree in a blender, in two batches, until completely smooth. Depending on the age of the corn, you may need to add more of the corn stock to achieve a pourable consistency. Strain each batch into a bowl as it comes out of the blender, pressing on the solids with the back of a ladle to express all of the liquid. (*This corn soup base can be made ahead, cooled, covered, and refrigerated for up to 2 days.*)

When you're ready to serve, pour the corn soup into a large saucepan and reheat gently.

Just before serving, cook the clams: Heat a large skillet over medium heat and add the butter. When it sizzles, add the shallots with the salt and sauté gently until golden and sweet, about 10 minutes. Add the white wine and simmer for 1 minute.

Add the clams, lime leaves, hot chile, and basil. Turn the heat to medium-high, cover tightly, and steam until the clams open, 5 to 7 minutes. As the first clams pop open, remove them with a pair of tongs to a bowl and then keep cooking the others; discard any clams that haven't opened;

Set a large strainer over the corn soup and pour the clam mixture through it, including the juices that have collected in the clam bowl. Pick out the clams and discard the aromatics. Whisk to incorporate the broth and taste for seasoning, adding more salt if necessary; thin with water to make a thin but pourable cream.

Ladle the soup into bowls, top with the clams (still in their shells), and garnish with basil.

pork-stuffed barbecued chicken thighs

Whenever I'm in Minneapolis-St. Paul, I'm game for eating in the food court at the HmongTown Marketplace. I zero in on the stuffed chicken wing stand in the far corner, where deboned chicken wings stuffed with cilantro-rich Hmong pork sausage (kooj tis qaib) are deep-fried to a golden crisp.

My take on this dish has strayed some from the original, given that I no longer have the patience to surgically remove the bones from a dozen chicken wings and I can't source that delicious fresh Hmong chicken. (Hmong cooks treat chicken the way some people treat fish. Never frozen, and often sold in need of a manicure, it is *fresh*.)

For parties, I buy packs of chicken thighs, bone them, and marinate them in a syrup of honey, freshly ground spices, fish sauce, and soy—which is actually more Indonesian—and then stuff them with peppery kooj tis qaib–style pork filling. When stacked on a baking sheet and roasted in the oven, the tops caramelize daringly, and the pork stuffing keeps the surrounding meat moist. After many years of toothpicking the slippery flaps of each boned thigh together to keep the filling from oozing out, I realized that if I just huddle the chicken bundles together in the center of the pan, the stuffed thighs will naturally fuse together in the heat of the oven.

This recipe scales up easily and can be made in mass quantities to feed a crowd.

Serves 6 to 8

chicken thighs
4 teaspoons coriander seeds
1 teaspoon black peppercorns
½ teaspoon anise or fennel seeds
½ teaspoon cardamom seeds
1 teaspoon hot pepper flakes
3 pounds skin-on chicken thighs (10 to 11)
½ cup honey
¼ cup soy sauce
2 tablespoons fish sauce, preferably Red Boat brand
½ teaspoon fine sea salt
5 makrut lime leaves

ground pork filling
One 1-ounce block mung bean noodles (sai-fun)
12 ounces ground pork
1 teaspoon sugar
1 heaping cup minced fresh cilantro (stems included)
⅔ cup minced scallions (both white and green parts)
1½ tablespoons grated ginger
2 teaspoons toasted sesame oil
½ teaspoon fine sea salt
½ teaspoon freshly ground black pepper

Toast the coriander, peppercorns, anise or fennel seeds, and cardamom in a dry pan over medium heat until fragrant, about 2 minutes. Remove from the heat and let cool slightly, then add the pepper flakes and finely grind in a spice mill (or clean coffee grinder).

Remove the bones from the chicken thighs: A serrated steak knife seems to work best. Cut down along both sides of each thigh bone to expose it, then slide your knife under the bone, up toward the ball joint, angling it up, to free it. Scrape down all meat with your knife until you get to the joint, then slip your knife around it and cut out the bone. Run your fingers over the meat, feeling for knobs of bone or cartilage, and remove them if you find any. If you're new to deboning, just do it as quickly as you can and don't worry about leaving a little meat on the bone, because that's the nature of it. Transfer the deboned thighs to a wide bowl. If you have the time, drop the bones, along with any trim pieces, into a saucepot to make a quick stock. (Or freeze the bones for a future stock-making session.)

recipe continues

Add the honey, soy sauce, fish sauce, salt, makrut leaves, and ground spice mixture to the thighs, toss to coat, and leave to marinate—at least 1 hour at room temperature, and as long as 8 in the refrigerator.

Preheat the oven to 375°F.

For the filling, cook the mung bean noodles in boiling water for just 2 minutes and drain them in a sieve. Run a little cold water over them—not too much, you want them to remain sticky—and put the sieve on top of the dry pot to steam dry.

Using scissors, cut the noodles into 2-inch lengths. Combine the ground pork, sugar, cilantro, scallions, ginger, sesame oil, salt, and pepper in a bowl, add the noodles, and mix together with your hands.

Drain the chicken and pour the the liquid into a small frying pan to reheat later for glazing. Lay a few thighs skin side down on a baking sheet, and fill the cavities with about 2 to 3 tablespoons of pork filling each—as much stuffing as the thighs will hold. Roll each thigh closed and arrange them, huddled snugly together, in the center of a large baking sheet. Repeat with the remaining thighs and pork filling.

Bring the marinade to a boil and cook for a minute to thicken it. Brush the tops of the thighs with a generous coating of marinade and roast for 10 minutes.

At this point, juices will have begun to seep from the chicken; carefully tip up the pan and spoon the collected juices back into the marinade. Bring the marinade back to a boil, then brush the chicken with another thick coat of it and roast for another 10 minutes. Brush the thighs one more time with the marinade, using all of it, and continue to roast until the skin is deeply caramelized and the pork filling inside the chicken runs hot and clear when pierced with a fork, another 10 to 15 minutes (for a total of 35 minutes in the oven).

Transfer the stuffed thighs to a platter and serve.

sticky rice

There is no substitute for it. When steamed, sticky rice clings together uncontrollably and has a chewy, addictive bounce-back in the mouth. In stores, it may go by a couple of aliases—sweet rice or glutinous rice—but it will be the only opaque, chalk-white round rice on the shelf.

Sticky rice should be cooked over open, rolling steam. Some home cooks line their bamboo steamer baskets with a few layers of cheesecloth, but if you cook sticky rice regularly, I recommend picking up a traditional sticky rice steamer, with an uncovered woven conical basket that fits into the top of a lightweight metal drum, sending plumes of steam up through the rice and out the top. Mai Ly, the woman who taught me to make sticky rice in her kitchen in suburban St. Paul, sent me to a vendor at the HmongTown Marketplace, where I bought one for about 20 dollars.

For a party of 6 to 8 people, cook at least 4 cups of sticky rice. Unlike most other rices, sticky rice doesn't swell much after cooking. What you see raw is pretty much what you'll get.

Presoak the rice for at least 4 hours, and as long as overnight, refrigerated.

Drain the rice in a sieve and rinse it just to freshen it, then pour it into the conical basket and shake it level. Fill the metal drum with water to come just below the bottom tip of the basket and bring it to a boil on the stovetop; then fit the conical basket into the drum. (If using a bamboo steamer, line the basket with three layers of damp cheesecloth, leaving a bit of overhang, and set it over a water-filled wok or a wide saucepot; the cooking time is the same as for the rice cooked in the basket steamer. You'll want to keep an eye on the water level as it steams, and refill as needed; my wok often runs dry halfway through.) Count 20 minutes from when the rice begins to steam. When it is translucent and starting to detach from the basket, it's time to flip it. Hold the basket out in front of you with both hands and, with a

recipe continues

good strong jerk of the wrist, throw the rice up into the air in a single cascading motion. Hopefully it will catch enough air-time to turn over. Anyone who grew up watching someone flip sticky rice can turn a perfect somersault right away, but it generally takes me a few tries. Set the basket back into the drum and continue to steam the rice until the kernels are chewy and perfectly tender, about 10 more minutes. If not serving immediately, cover the rice with a pot lid to keep warm.

Sticky rice should always be served steaming hot, so reheat before serving if necessary. To hold the rice for any length of time at the table, cover it with tight-fitting plastic wrap.

stir-fried greens and leeks

A menu that has two loud talkers like barbecued chicken and spicy cucumber/honeydew salad needs something that whispers, such as this simple, no-nonsense dish of stir-fried greens and leeks. Buy the freshest, most lively looking greens at the market—I've included cooking time variations below—and make this right before serving.

Serves 6 to 8 as a side

2 bunches (close to 2 pounds) greens such as yu choy, water spinach, gai lan (Chinese broccoli), turnip greens, mature Swiss chard, or tender kale
1 medium leek
1 teaspoon light soy sauce
1 teaspoon oyster sauce

1 teaspoon water
3 tablespoons coconut oil
2 tablespoons minced ginger
5 garlic cloves, minced
¼ teaspoon fine sea salt, plus more to taste
Pinch of sugar, plus more to taste

Bring a large pot of water to a boil for blanching the greens.

Dunk the greens in a large bowl of cold water to wash them, twice if they're gritty, then lift out and drain in a colander. Slice tender-stemmed greens like yu choy, water spinach, or gai lan (stems peeled on this one) into 2-inch lengths; strip turnip greens, Swiss chard, or kale leaves from their stems and tear into large two-bite pieces. You should have 12 to 14 cups.

Remove the soft, wilty outer layer of the leek. Trim the stem end, but leave it attached, then cut off the dark green tops where they start to droop, leaving as much tender green as you can. Slice the leek lengthwise in half and run the leek halves under running water, parting the layers to flush out any dirt. Drain, pat dry, and slice on the bias, ½ inch thick.

When the water boils, add salt until it tastes as seasoned as soup. Blanch the greens in two batches, uncovered, over the highest heat, until fully tender: 1 minute for tender Asian greens, closer to 3 minutes for turnip greens, chard, or kale. Scoop out the first batch of greens with a spider and drain in a colander set over a bowl. Toss the greens with a pair of tongs and squeeze gently to express excess water, but don't wring them out; a little internal moisture keeps them looking alive. Transfer the greens to a large plate to cool off, and unwind them from the lump to keep them from turning olive-green. Repeat with the second batch.

Combine the soy sauce and oyster sauce, along with the 1 teaspoon water to lighten, in a small dish; set aside.

recipe continues

For stir-frying, use either a wok or a large cast-iron skillet, whichever is larger and heavier. With a typical stove (or if you only have a light wok), the cast-iron skillet may be the better option. Preheat the pan or wok over high heat. Add the coconut oil, immediately add the leeks, and sprinkle lightly with salt. Cook, stirring every 30 seconds, until the leeks are tender and lightly charred; remove from the pan. Return the pan to a smoking-hot condition, add the garlic and ginger, and stir. Immediately follow with the blanched greens and leeks and cook, tossing and mixing with tongs for a minute to put all the greens into contact with the hot pan, adding the ¼ teaspoon salt and the sugar. Add the soy sauce mixture, toss to combine, and taste for seasoning; add more salt or sugar as needed.

Lift the greens onto a wide platter, keeping them airy, and serve.

honeydew and cucumber salad with cilantro-lime dressing

Sticky Southeast Asian barbecued meat and sticky rice need a juicy sweet/hot/sour/fishy/herby salad to round out the trifecta. Like papaya salad, this cucumber and honeydew salad should be dressed heavily, so that its spicy cilantro-lime dressing seeps into the sticky rice. What at first glance looks like a strange marriage of fruit and vegetable really isn't when you consider that melons and cucumbers actually belong to the same botanical family, the Cucurbits. Look for a ripe but firm summer melon, preferably honeydew, but a white-fleshed or orange cantaloupe would also be fine.

The cucumbers, melon, and dressing can all be prepped in advance, but wait to dress the salad until you're nearly ready to sit down at the table. Serve it on a deep, wide platter or in a bowl with a wide spoon for scooping some of the spicy/sweet juices onto the sticky rice.

Serves 6 to 8 as a side

salad
Half a large ripe but firm honeydew melon (2 pounds)
1¼ pounds thin-skinned Persian cucumbers (about 8), peeled
1½ teaspoons fine sea salt
1½ loosely packed cups fresh herb leaves, preferably a mixture of mint, cilantro, and Thai basil
5 thin feathery arcs of sliced red onion
⅓ cup fried shallots (page 263) or store-bought Thai fried shallots, or ⅓ cup roasted salted peanuts, crushed

cilantro-lime dressing
2 to 3 Thai chiles, finely minced, to taste
2 makrut lime leaves, finely minced, or 1 teaspoon finely grated lime zest
2 tablespoons finely minced fresh cilantro
2 tablespoons sugar
5 tablespoons fresh lime juice
2½ teaspoons fish sauce, preferably Red Boat brand
1 tablespoon canola or peanut oil

Scoop the seeds from the melon and slice off the rind. Set the melon cut side down on your cutting board and cut into 1-inch cubes; you should have 3½ cups. Pile into a mixing bowl.

Peel the cucumbers, trim the ends, and cut on the bias into 1-inch chunks. (If the cucumbers are fat and have large seeds, first halve them and scrape out most of the seed pockets.) You should have 3½ cups of cucumbers as well. Add them to the mixing bowl, and if not finishing the salad immediately, cover and refrigerate.

For the dressing, combine most of the minced chile, the lime leaf, and the cilantro in a small bowl. Stir in the sugar, lime juice, fish sauce, salt, and oil, and taste. It should be boldly spicy, so if not, add some of the remaining minced chile. (*The dressing can be made in advance and refrigerated.*)

If the herb leaves are large, pile them on the board and run your knife through them just once.

Sprinkle the thin arcs of sliced red onions over the melon and cucumber mixture, then add all of the dressing and the herbs and toss. The salad will be aggressively dressed, and it will begin to weep immediately. Shuttle onto a wide platter, sprinkle the fried shallots (or peanuts) over the top, and serve.

single-origin chocolate cake

I wanted to make a chocolate cake that tasted like a twelve-dollar bar of dark chocolate—you know, one of those single-origin bars that comes with coffee-tasting notes: *burnt caramel, citrus, toasted almonds, sweet spices*. So as not to break the bank, I used regular semisweet baking chocolate from the grocery store and then tarted it up with a splash of whiskey, some sour orange juice, and dark spices. This cake isn't flourless, but it's nearly flourless, with just enough flour to give it the structure to rise high in the oven and then exhale slowly on the countertop. To make it denser and even more (sickeningly) rich, I press it with a heavily weighted plate, and then pour a puddle of shiny chocolate ganache into the center to fill in the concave top.

This cake is gluten-free if made with buckwheat flour instead of all-purpose. I actually prefer the nuttiness that the buckwheat brings to this cake, but then I miss the texture of the original, which has a slightly heavier chew.

Bake this well in advance to give it time to cure (I hide it) and because, I'll just tell you now, it takes a while to get this cake into the oven. A cup of sugar here, half a cup of sugar there, three tablespoons of *tangerine juice* . . . even I'm rolling my eyes. But it's worth it.

Makes one 9-inch cake, rich enough to serve 12 in small slices

cake

½ pound (2 sticks) unsalted butter, sliced into pats, plus softened butter for the pan

¾ cup (2 ounces) sliced almonds

⅓ cup all-purpose flour or buckwheat flour (to make it lighter)

3 tablespoons Dutch-process cocoa, preferably dark

8 ounces dark chocolate (60 to 80% cacao), chopped

½ teaspoon grated nutmeg

½ teaspoon ground ginger

¼ teaspoon ground cinnamon

½ teaspoon plus ½ teaspoon fine sea salt

3 tablespoons fresh tangerine juice (clementine, tangelo, or a mixture of sweet orange and lime juice are all fine)

2 tablespoons whiskey (Jack Daniels or Jim Beam, or basically anything brown)

5 large eggs, separated

1½ cups sugar

½ teaspoon cream of tartar

chocolate ganache icing

4 ounces dark chocolate, finely chopped

⅔ cup heavy cream

Whipped Cream (recipe follows) for serving

recipe continues

Preheat the oven to 350°F. Butter a 9 × 3 inch springform pan, dust it with flour (or buckwheat flour for gluten-free), and set on a rimmed baking sheet (in case the cake leaks butterfat).

Pour the almonds into a small baking dish or sauté pan and toast in the rising heat of the oven until golden brown, about 20 minutes.

Transfer the almonds to the bowl of a food processor, add the flour and cocoa, and process in bursts until the nuts are very finely ground.

Melt the chocolate and butter in a double-boiler setup: Put the butter in wide heatproof bowl, cover with the chopped chocolate, and set the bowl over a wide saucepot of simmering water (the bottom of the bowl shouldn't sit in the water). Lower the heat and let the mixture sit, without stirring, until both the chocolate and the butter have melted. Whisk until smooth and remove from the heat. Add the spices, ½ teaspoon of the salt, the tangerine juice, and whiskey to the chocolate mixture and whisk until combined; set aside to cool to tepid.

Separate the eggs, dropping the yolks into a wide bowl and the whites into the bowl of a stand mixer fitted with the whisk attachment (or use a large mixing bowl and a hand mixer). Add 1 cup of the sugar to the yolks and whisk by hand until they thicken and lighten like soft summer butter, about 2 minutes. Add the chocolate mixture in a slow stream, whisking to emulsify. Add the almond-cocoa mixture and mix until just incorporated.

For the meringue, add the remaining ½ teaspoon salt and the cream of tartar to the egg whites and whip at medium speed until the egg whites thicken and you can no longer see any yellowish liquid white. Add the remaining ½ cup sugar very slowly, over the course of 5 minutes, beating until the whites hold a soft peak and look glossy and iridescent, which tells you that the sugar has melted.

Add a large spoonful of the meringue to the chocolate mixture to lighten it and mix to combine, then carefully fold in the rest of the meringue, dragging the chocolate mixture up from the bottom in wide swaths over the meringue, rotating the bowl, and folding until no wisps of egg white remain. Pour the batter into the prepared pan.

Bake the cake for 50 to 55 minutes, or until a toothpick comes out clean. Remove from the oven.

As it cools, the cake will deflate slightly. While it's still warm, gently nudge the edges back from the rim and tuck inside the cake pan. Unlock the springform and cover the cake with a plate that just fits inside the perimeter of the springform. Set a weight on top of the plate to press the cake to make it denser and more evenly level. Let the cake cool to room temperature, then remove the springform sides, lift off the plate and weight, and transfer to a cake plate.

For the icing, put the chopped chocolate in a small bowl. Heat the cream to just short of a simmer (on the stovetop or in the microwave) and pour over the chocolate. Let steep for 5 minutes, or until the chocolate has melted. Starting from the center, whisk until the ganache is smooth.

Pour the ganache on top of the cake, tilting the pan to widen its puddle a bit but letting most of it fill the shallow well in the center of the cake. Let the ganache cool and firm up before slicing.

This cake goes down fine served with vanilla ice cream, but I much prefer it with lightly sweetened whipped cream, in an equal ratio of cream to cake.

whipped cream Use this lightly sweetened whipped cream for rich or very sweet cakes.

Makes 3½ cups

2 cups heavy cream
3 tablespoons sugar
½ teaspoon pure vanilla extract
Pinch of fine sea salt

You can use a stand mixer or a hand mixer to make this, or you can whip the cream by hand with a whisk. A chilled bowl and a large balloon whisk make short work of it, and I think that hand-whipped cream is denser and more luscious. Combine the cream and sugar in a large bowl and whip until the mixture thickens. Add the vanilla and salt and continue to whip until the cream starts to mound softly on the whisk.

Casual Walk

buffets for fifteen to twenty, or more

abouts

Menus

Argentinian-style asado

FOR TWENTY OR MORE (WITH POTLUCK) 287

open-air barbecue with salmuera and
    chimichurri   294

marinated chickpea salad with lemon and
    Swiss chard   298

zucchini carpaccio   300

spicy cinnamon flan   303

secretly thrifty Brazilian-inspired buffet

FOR FIFTEEN   306

rhubarb lemonade   308

feijoada for a crowd   309

grilled leek salad with hard-boiled eggs
    and smoky anchovy dressing   311

sour orange platter salad with parsley and
    pistachios   314

I call this chapter Casual Walkabouts because these are the parties where people outnumber the dining table chairs by two to one.

Both of these menus are designed to serve a wandering, plate-holding throng, but without a doubt, these are the hardest kinds of parties to pull off. When you need to gently shoo away chatting people so you can pull the potatoes from the oven, and the nuts are threatening to burn on the stovetop, and the newfound friend needs a drink but doesn't know where to find the glasses, there will be a moment when you feel like the center will not hold, that you've lost control.

The great irony is that we think being in control is reassuring, when the fact is that cooking is an unpredictable, sensory business. I can't think of another craft that uses materials that are quite as unreliable as edible ingredients. At some point, you have to just accept that cooking— savory cooking more than baking—contains a certain amount of volatility. A platter of marinated tomatoes isn't luscious because it's orderly. It speaks to us when it brims with juice and gleams with a little too much olive oil. Sautéed eggplant is good, but charred eggplant cooked to the brink of burnt is the stuff of dreams. Great cooking depends on close shaves with disaster; without them, there would be no brilliant saves. And this is when you take a deep breath and embrace the great vibrating instability. Keep building flavors and licking your spoon and talking to the people standing right in front of you, because cooking thrives on chaos. Feeding all these people is the goal, and this may get messy.

That said, when cooking for large groups, I try to be strategic about three things: time, serving sizes, and money. Do as I say and not as I do, and don't worry about seating. People perch like birds on anything. Don't worry about matching plates or napkin rings. Don't worry about cleaning the bedrooms. Your only concern is making the food, and enough of it.

For big groups, I almost always circle back to the same solution: rice and beans. Cheap, filling, delicious, and easy to make on a jumbo scale, rice is a savior for large groups. This leads me away from my own long-ago French and German roots, where potatoes and spaetzle reigned. It is possible to make potatoes for a large group (see Fun-House Baked Potatoes, page 339, a wedding-hall standard), but it requires more handiwork.

Keep in mind that mine is not the last—or even the first—word on any of these cultures beyond my own, and that both the asado and the Brazilian feijoada menu are nothing more than the wanderlust fantasies of a cooped-up isolated northern cook at work. They're as faithful a representation of a faraway culture as I can muster, and to my friends, sick of burgers, that's enough. So feel free to view these recipes with what my mom used to call "a jaundiced eye," i.e., a particularly critical sort of skepticism. She often used it in reference to my worldview, and she wasn't exactly wrong. I identify with critical skepticism. It's one of my love languages.

When trying to dig into a new-to-you food culture, I think the best way in is through its vessels, its equipment. An Argentinian-style asado cannot faithfully be replicated on any other sort of grill or smoking rig. But a full day spent tying meat to metal crosses, basting it with a garlicky saline brine, and occasionally rotating the crosses over the smoky fire brings us into communion with the culture: its choreography, its sense of moving time, the way it prioritizes flavor. Unfamiliar equipment also dispels rigid thinking and shows us a new side to familiar ingredients. The wok teaches us that vegetables can absorb smokiness quicker than lightning, without a deep penetrating sear. The mortar and pestle shows us how pesto was meant to be made—crushed until the kitchen fills with the aroma of basil. Asado-style barbecue teaches us that we've been overthinking and oversaucing all these years, and that meat needs nothing but salt, smoke, and time.

Argentinian-style asado

FOR TWENTY OR MORE
(WITH POTLUCK)

— open-air barbecue with salmuera and
   chimichurri
— marinated chickpea salad with lemon and
   Swiss chard
— zucchini carpaccio
— spicy cinnamon flan

I can sum up this asado party in three words: Heavy. Metal. Meat. It sounds like a metal concert crossed with a ranchers' convention, and that's not far off. There's enough meat here to make a tenderhearted vegetarian stage a protest, tons of black metal rebar crosses, and Judas Priest blaring from the outdoor speakers. Until I change the music.

Unlike pit-smoking or pellet-smoking, this open-air style of barbecue doesn't require an elaborate smoker. (Of course, this means that if the meat doesn't turn out well, there's no rig to blame. Although you could literally blame it on the wind, blowing the smoke in the wrong direction; I know I have.) The rig is you, your hands, some metal crosses, the fire—and a crowd. This is a party you "put on" like an event, not one you dare go alone. Between digging the pit, butterflying the meat, wiring it to the crosses, basting it with brine every fifteen minutes, fiddling with the coals, and sitting watch, an asado will keep half a dozen people entertained for the day.

For all of its macho intensity, though, asado is the most subtle form of barbecue I've ever known. It doesn't bean you over the head with rubs and sauces and defined smoke rings. The flames breathe in and out of the logs, the orange coals seethe and crackle, the blue smoke drifts lazily around the meat for hours. At some point while sitting in lawn chairs around the pit, my friends and I start to hallucinate from the combination of fire, heat, day-drinking, and smoke inhalation and we stare into the flames as if we're all watching the same show on TV.

With that many cooks in the kitchen, I've been surprised that we've never disagreed about an asado. This may be because the sight of meat roasting over the pit teases us all mercilessly, but equally, and by the end of the day, we're pretty single-minded about our end goal: slicing into that meat.

You may notice that this menu is pretty short, and that the title includes "potluck." It may seem odd that a cookbook would suggest bringing in outside food, but think of it this way: An asado is by its very nature a community-building meal, a celebration of meat and fire. To also singlehandedly cook all of the side dishes for this meal would contradict its ethic. I've hosted seven of these asados, and cannot, in good conscience, fill this menu with the additional recipes needed to feed 20 or more people. In my experience, this menu as it stands constitutes the limits of what is humanly possible for one cook to make without pulling an all-nighter, hiring help, or going insane.

So go big on the meat, cook up a giant pot of chickpeas (that salad will be your main starch and serves 20), make enough chimichurri for all, and a more reasonably-sized platter of zucchini carpaccio, and enough flan for twenty—but then call potluck for the rest. If anyone asks what would go well with this menu, tell them, "Vegetables."

If a signature dish doesn't automatically spring to guests' minds, curate the side dishes. Assign dishes that play to each person's particular strengths, and don't worry about being bossy. Some people take on a lot of pressure at the mention of a potluck; a little firm governance is often the kindest approach. If suggesting side dishes from this book, I'd point people toward:

Braised Collards with Smoky Tomato (page 229)

Green Salad with Invisible Vinaigrette (page 187)

Sweet-and-Sour Marinated Peppers with Swiss Chard (page 110)

Creamed Poblano Spinach (page 158)

equipment you'll need, in order of importance

A hose, for fire control

A staging table set up near the fire, to use when loading and unloading the crosses

A shovel or rake, for moving coals around

Heavy bendable wire, for securing the meat to the metal

A pair of pliers, for cranking or loosening the twisted wire when it's hot

Heavy leather grill gloves or thick hot pads for turning the crosses

Large baking sheets and/or plastic tubs for transporting the meat

Squirt bottles for applying the salmuera (or a bowl and a brush for mopping)

Paper towels

Lawn chairs, for sitting around the pit

Water for hydrating during most of the cooking and beer, or a big-boned leathery red wine, for drinking toward the end of the asado

the meat

Let's be honest, an asado is an excessive, dramatic declaration of one's love for meat. So there should be a shocking lot of it. Budget between 1½ to 2 pounds of meat per person, leaning to the heavy side if you choose a whole lamb or pig, because so much of their weight is bone. When ordering from a butcher shop, make sure to specify full, untrimmed racks of short ribs and spareribs, and long, tied strings of sausages to loop over the armatures.

Obviously, this is not a cheap party. A whole young animal is always a dramatic sight, but it's just a fantasy without an affordable way to source it. Local butchers and meat lockers can usually order directly from the animal auction barn for the wholesale price plus processing, or even hook you up directly with a farmer. If the seasonal timing is right—if, say, it's July and the spring lambs are reaching forty pounds but still too young to sell—you might get a deal that makes all of this extravagance secretly doable.

I usually cook three kinds of meat, maybe four. Generally I aim for one that's visually dramatic and traditional (like a young lamb or pig), some full racks of beef or pork ribs, and a bunch of cheaper chickens or smoked sausages to bulk it out. The best of all possible choices, in my opinion, are the whole beef short ribs. (Not coincidentally, they're the most expensive.) The slow, gentle heat cooks them to tenderness but doesn't cause them to collapse like a braised short rib; they come out tasting like long-smoked Texas brisket.

To serve 20 people, you might pick any three of the following options:

Two full racks of beef short ribs (each 4-bone rack weighing 4 to 5 pounds)

Two full racks of pork spareribs (5 pounds each)

Two 4- to 5-pound chickens, butterflied

One 30- to 40-pound young pig, split and butterflied (preferably scalded)

One 30- to 40-pound teenaged lamb, split and butterflied

Two long strings of smoked pork sausages (4 pounds, or about 12 sausages)

asado timeline

about a week before the party

— Start thinking about the meat, because some cuts might require a phone call or a special order.

— Buy (or make) three or four metal asado crosses. Aaron and many of our friends who typically help with the asado party are sculptors, so they can weld. Our set of rebar metal crosses leans against the shed, through summer and snow, waiting for the next time. But Argentinian asado crosses are available for purchase on the internet. Depending on your comfort level with an MIG welder, that might be easier. (Although if you were looking for a reason to learn, this is it.) Or contact a metal fabrication shop and ask if they do small jobs like this one (maybe in exchange for an invite). One 7 × 3-foot metal cross will hold a full rack of pork spareribs, two chickens, four full racks of beef short ribs, or one butterflied baby pig or lamb. Uncut strings of sausages can be looped up and woven around the meat.

— Bring in or collect the wood you'll need for the fire. You'll need an abundance of dry oak, or any other hardwood, split down into small, almost kindling-sized pieces. Start the fire with just about anything you have—we feed it pine at first, because it's easier to come by here—but when it comes time to start cooking, you want a big bed of hardwood coals. Compared to pine or birch, small pieces of split oak will make longer-lasting coals, with higher BTUs.

the day before the party

— Soak the chickpeas.

— Make the flans and chill.

— Pick up the meat and refrigerate. Unless you have access to a large walk-in refrigerator, leave the young pig or lamb at the butcher shop and collect them the morning of the party.

— Make the salmuera and pour it into squirt bottles.

— Make the chimichurri

the morning of

— Dig the pit: Look for a spot in an open area, free of any trees looming overhead. Dig a 3-foot-wide by 8-foot-long trench, about a foot and a half deep, one side for fire-making and the other for cooking. You'll build a large fire to produce coals on one side and cook the meat on the other. Feeding the fire throughout the day will ensure a constant supply of fresh hot coals for cooking.

— Figure out how to secure the metal crosses in the ground at a roughly 75-degree angle that gently tilts the meat toward the fire. If the ground around the fire pit is firm, you may be able to just pound them in, but keep in mind that that they may be holding as much as 40 pounds of meat; if they fall into the fire, the meat will burn faster than you can retrieve it. Our soil is sandy, so we secure our crosses in sheaths, 1-inch-diameter metal pipes buried in the ground. Pound in the pipes at a slight (75-degree) angle at 2-foot intervals around the cooking end of the pit, about a foot away from the edge. There is, however, another slightly less traditional method. During our sixth asado, we discovered that if we set tall logs on either side of the cooking pit, we could prop the crosses between them to span the fire, leaving the meat to hang a couple of feet above the coals. This method cooks the meat little more quickly than the traditional setup, and with less drifting smoke influence, but it's a lot easier.

— Once the meat has begun to cook, make the chickpea salad and zucchini carpaccio.

I HEAR, "CAN YOU MAKE THIS VEGETARIAN?"

That is a great question. Yes, you can. Start by raking a mixture of bluish ash and orange glowing coals into a mound and burying a whole buttercup squash. After it's been cooking a while—we measure asado time in intervals of drinks, so, after "one beer"—wrap some beets, potatoes, and onions in aluminum foil and bury them in the coals as well. Remember where you hid them, because you'll need to unearth them from time to time to check for doneness. When they're starting to get tender, after an hour or two, strap some large eggplant, leeks, sweet bell peppers, and a few of those extra-large garden zucchini that got away from you onto the crosses, tying them tightly with wire, because they will shrink. Tilt the vegetables toward the fire, spray them with the salmuera, and cook until blackened on the exterior and soft within, about an hour. Continue to move coals from the hotter end of the fire to cover the buried roots and onions to keep them going. The squash and the large roots can take a surprisingly long time to cook in the coals, depending on the heat of the fire and the thickness of the squash skin. Slide a knife in each to test. When they're extremely tender, the knife just slipping right out, dig them out and wipe off the ash with a towel. Split the squash, remove the seeds, sprinkle it with salt and pepper, butter it or drizzle with olive oil, and set on a large platter. Peel the vegetables that need peeling—the peppers, onions, beets—and cut into slabs, sprinkle with fine sea salt, and arrange next to the squash. Serve the vegetables with the chimichurri.

open-air barbecue with salmuera and chimichurri

I like to rub the meat with a marinade of olive oil, black pepper, thyme, and minced garlic to boost the flavor, but it's optional. In traditional asados, all the seasoning comes from just two sources: the smoke and the salmuera (salt-garlic basting brine). Make the salmuera well in advance to give the garlic a chance to permeate the brine. The smashed garlic cloves will clog your squirt bottles, but they can be fished out; minced garlic would be worse. The chimichurri sauce can be made a day in advance. Refrigerate if holding at room temperature longer than 6 hours.

marinade

Makes enough for 30 to 40 pounds of meat

1 bunch thyme, leaves stripped from the stems

3 large heads garlic, cloves separated and peeled (about 30 cloves)

About ⅓ cup black peppercorns

Extra-virgin olive oil

Add the thyme to the bowl of a food processor and pulse to a fine chop, then add the garlic and process until finely minced. Scrape the garlic and thyme into a bowl.

Working in batches if necessary, buzz the peppercorns in a spice mill (or a dry blender) until medium-fine. Pluck out any large, stubborn peppercorns to add to the next batch, and repeat until the peppercorns are evenly cracked.

Lay the meat on large baking sheets. Coat with a thin layer of olive oil and an even sprinkling of black pepper, then rub the garlic-thyme mixture all over the meat, working it in with your fingertips.

salmuera (salt-garlic brine)

This salt-garlic brine can be made well in advance, poured into large squirt bottles, and stored in the refrigerator. As much as this makes—9 quarts—sometimes volunteer basters will really go through it, and I've had to run into the kitchen halfway through the day to make more.

makes about 2½ quarts

9 cups water

⅔ cup kosher salt

9 garlic cloves, crushed and peeled

¾ cup extra-virgin olive oil

Combine the water, salt, garlic, and olive oil in a saucepan and bring to a simmer. Cook until the salt dissolves, whisking, then remove from the heat and let cool.

Pour the salmuera into two large squirt bottles, or into a storage container for mopping on with a brush. Basting the meat with a squirt bottle rather than applying it with a brush will make your life easier.

chimichurri   Chimichurri should be sharp and fresh, and thick with fresh parsley and oregano. When the sauce hits the hot meat, the oregano blooms and dominates. Compared to the damp earthiness of thyme and rosemary, fresh oregano smells drier and more floral, like the high desert.

This sauce should be made either the night before or early on the day of the party, to give it time to get its bearings and calm down. Sauces that contain vinegar usually need that.

Makes 3 cups, enough for 20 guests who splash liberally (but easily halved)

8 garlic cloves

1 scant cup fresh oregano (leaves and soft
   stems only)

2 tablespoons chopped fresh marjoram
   (optional)

1¾ teaspoons fine sea salt

1 tablespoon hot pepper flakes

1½ tablespoons toasted and ground coriander
   seeds

½ teaspoon toasted and ground cumin seeds

2 lightly packed cups fresh parsley leaves

2 lightly packed cups roughly chopped fresh
   cilantro, including tender stems

6 tablespoons sherry vinegar or red wine
   vinegar

⅓ cup water

1¼ cups extra-virgin olive oil

Combine the garlic, oregano, marjoram, if using, salt, hot pepper flakes, coriander, and cumin in a food processor and process until smoothly ground. Add the parsley and cilantro and process until minced but not pureed. Add the vinegar and pulse until just combined.

Scrape the herb mixture into a bowl. Add the water to the bowl of the food processor and process to capture all the remaining bits of garlic and herbs, then pour into the chimichurri. Using a fork, stir in the olive oil.

The water has a mellowing effect on the sauce, as does time. Let the chimichurri sit at room temperature for at least 3 hours, and preferably 6. In Argentinian restaurants, chimichurri sits on the table all day. You can make the sauce up to 2 days before the event and store it in the refrigerator.

method for cooking the meat

Digging an 8-foot-long trench in your yard on the morning of a party broadcasts a certain signal, illustrating to all precisely the lengths to which you're willing to go in pursuit of deliciousness. So do that first. Then build a large fire with hardwood on one side of the pit.

As the fire burns, secure the meat to the metal crosses with thin, bendable wire: Loop it around the meat and then around the crosses, pulling it tight, and, using a pair of pliers, twist the ends of the wire to secure them. Keep the pliers close by, as the meat will shrink as it cooks and the wires will need to be retightened.

When the logs have burned down quite a bit, rake a mixture of black, white, and red-hot coals to the cooking side of the pit. Set the asado crosses into the buried pipes, tilting the meat at a 75-degree angle toward the fire, with smoke trailing up and around it. Ideally the meat should start to gently cook after about 15 minutes, so if it's a windy day, you may need more coals. Baste the meat with the salmuera, and then again every 20 minutes or so thereafter, at which time it might also be a good idea to turn the crosses. To maintain a steady heat, keep adding new coals to the pile underneath the meat, and keep feeding fresh logs into the fire.

Each cut of meat will reach doneness at a different time, so stagger the start times accordingly. Budgeting about 8 hours for the entire process, start cooking the whole animals and beef short ribs first, then follow with the spareribs after an hour or two, then the chickens, and, finally, the sausages. As for doneness cues, asado-style beef short ribs are done when the skinny tines of a fork slip easily into the meatiest ends and juice spurts from the holes. The ribs will be positively melting when cut across the grain into thin slices, with a faint pink line of smoke around the edges. They will cook to near tenderness early on, and then will plateau for awhile, but keep going, as they can take up to 8 hours.

You might assume that a barbecued young pig will take a long time to cook and should be as collapsing-tender as pulled pork, but a baby pig will dry out by that logic. A 30-pound pig is actually pretty thin, with tender, pale meat, and reaches smoke-touched juicy doneness at about 165°F on an instant-read thermometer. A lamb can take a little more heat and can be brought nearer to the fall-apart zone you've come expect. Because of that, an asado-cooked lamb will absorb more of the flavor of the fire.

Pork spareribs should be tender but not falling off the cross. Like competition barbecued pork ribs, a perfect asado-style sparerib will be juicy but retain some bounce. Whole racks of spareribs can be done is as few as 4 hours, but they can handle another 2 hours over a lower heat. An ideal asado-smoked chicken resembles a roast chicken: tender, with burnished skin, and wings that wiggle loosely in the pocket. Large 5-pound chickens take about 4 hours, and small 3½-pounders just 3. Sausages will cook in just an hour.

Of course, these cooking times are approximations, and they will vary with the distance between the meat and the fire, the pitch of the crosses, the BTUs of the coals, and the mph-speed of the wind. I'm not being facetious about the wind speed, either. If it's really windy, or blowing the wrong way, tack on another 2 hours. And lean on your good sense to assess doneness. Carve off small pieces to test—often.

marinated chickpea salad with lemon and Swiss chard

I saw this chickpea and Swiss chard salad recipe years ago in a cookbook from the River Cafe in London and knew from the ingredient list alone that it would ring all my bells. I've since tampered with it plenty, making it spicier, trying it with fresh shell beans, adding smoked paprika, but the simple genius of the method remains. The white wine, tomato paste, and all of that olive oil reduce down to a softly acidic syrup that wraps the tender chickpeas in a tight but slippery sauce. Less well-protected beans sitting in a bath of watery vinaigrette will eventually soften and start to dissolve, but these hold their shape.

Make the salad up to 2 hours ahead and let it hang out on the stovetop, or up to a full day ahead (in that case, refrigerate it). Before serving, spoon the vinaigrette from the bottom up to the top to refresh. This salad is one of my most beloved leftovers.

Makes a generous 3 quarts, serving 20 (easily halved)

1½ pounds (3½ cups) dried chickpeas, soaked overnight in water to cover generously

1 whole head garlic, plus 6 garlic cloves, sliced

3 bay leaves

4 dried hot chiles

1 teaspoon plus ¾ teaspoon fine sea salt, plus more to taste

½ teaspoon baking soda (optional)

¾ cup extra-virgin olive oil

2 medium sweet onions, cut into large dice (3 cups)

5 carrots, cut into large dice (2½ cups)

1 tablespoon hot pepper flakes

1½ tablespoons tomato paste

1½ teaspoons sweet paprika

1 teaspoon smoked paprika

2 teaspoons minced fresh rosemary

1 cup white wine

1½ teaspoons honey

5 tablespoons fresh lemon juice

2 small bunches Swiss chard, washed, trimmed, and plucked into large bite-sized pieces

Drain the soaked chickpeas and put in a pot with water to cover by 3 inches.

Rub the excess paper from the head of garlic, trim its root end to remove any dirt, and lop off the top ½ inch to expose the cloves. Add the garlic to the pot, along with the bay leaves, chiles, and 1 teaspoon of the salt, bring the water to a boil, and boil for a few minutes, skimming off the rising foam. Reduce the heat to hold a consistent simmer, partially cover the pot, and cook until the chickpeas are tender to the bite but still holding tight in their skins, 1½ to 2 hours. If they're not beginning to soften after 1½ hours, add the baking soda. When the chickpeas are tender, remove them from the heat. They can sit in their cooking liquid for up to 2 hours at the back of the stovetop.

Meanwhile, heat a large high-sided sauté pan over medium-high heat and add ½ cup of the olive oil and the onions. Cook until the onions turn light golden brown at the edges, about 10 minutes. Add the carrots and the remaining ¾ teaspoon salt, raise the heat, and cook until the corners of the carrots bronze and take on a rounded-shoulder look, about 8 minutes; they should be crisp-tender and slightly resistant to the bite at the center. (This dish will be served warm, or more likely at room temperature, and no one wants to confront mushy leftover-from-dinner carrots in a lemony vinaigrette; what you want are cooked, sprightly "salad carrots.")

By this time you should have a coppery, oily base at the bottom of the pan. Add the hot pepper flakes and sliced garlic, reduce the heat to medium, and cook for about 1 minute, stirring, until the garlic is tender. Add the tomato paste, both paprikas, and the rosemary, raise the heat to medium-high, and stir until the tomato paste begins to stick to the bottom of the pan, 3 to 4 minutes.

recipe continues

Add the white wine to deglaze, and bring everything to a simmer, scraping the bottom of the pan with a wooden spoon to release its flavor cache. Add the lemon juice, honey, and the remaining ¼ cup olive oil and simmer for a few minutes to thicken the liquid, then taste for seasoning. The sauce should hang in the balance between sweet and sour, offset by the round fattiness of the olive oil. Add salt as needed.

Drain the chickpeas in a colander (discard the aromatics) and shake to rid them of excess moisture. Add them to the sauté pan and bring to a simmer over medium heat. Cook until the vinaigrette clings saucily to the chickpeas and they taste infused with the sauce, about 15 minutes. If the sauce is too tight, add a bit of water; if it's too loose, reduce it further. (This is where if you've got something more pressing to do, you can step away and leave the chickpeas to marinate.)

When you're ready to plate the salad, return the pan to medium heat, add the Swiss chard, and fold it in. Cook very briefly, just long enough for the chard to buckle and start to wilt.

Immediately spoon the chickpea mixture onto a wide platter, scraping all of the flavorful sauce over the top. It should seep around the salad in a shiny, rusty pool. This salad is as delicious warm as it is at room temperature. You can plate it up to an hour ahead; to refresh, spoon the pooling juices over the chickpeas.

SHELL BEAN VARIATION

When fresh shell beans (mature beans picked before they've dried out, sold in their pods) start to show up in the market in the late summer, use them in place of the chickpeas. Their texture is like velour. Substitute 8 cups cups raw shell beans for the chickpeas and cook them to tenderness in the same way, but for much less time—just 30 to 40 minutes.

zucchini carpaccio

Raw zucchini has a mild, nutty flavor and a talent for soaking up anything we throw at it—in this case, a few shards of Parmesan, some buttery roasted pine nuts, and a slippery bath of lemon vinaigrette. I've made this salad for years and have zeroed in on what makes it sing: pre-salting the zucchini until it exudes liquid, then squeezing it between two platters to drain off the excess brine. If you don't remove that zucchini water, the lemon's bite will be lost.

Try to use firm ridged heirloom zucchini for this one. I grow Costata Romanesco, a restless, sprawling, atypically unproductive Italian variety. It takes up too much room in the garden but is so sweet and so firm, almost crunchy, that I give it a pass.

This dish is just not worth making with out-of-season zucchini from the store.

Fills an oversized platter, serving a large group as part of a buffet

A 2½-ounce chunk Parmesan, grana padano, or Sartori Bellavitano cheese

2 pounds zucchini (4 medium-large), preferably a firm, nutty heirloom variety like Costata Romanesco

Rounded ¾ teaspoon fine sea salt, plus a little for the pine nuts

Freshly cracked black pepper

A small handful of young basil leaves, torn

½ cup extra-virgin olive oil

2 garlic cloves, smashed and peeled

3 tablespoons pine nuts

1 sprig rosemary

¾ teaspoon hot pepper flakes

7 tablespoons fresh lemon juice

Locate two large serving platters of the same size, which you'll need to press the zucchini to drain off the excess brine. Thinly slice the cheese while it's still cold so that it flakes off in shards.

Thinly slice the zucchini on a mandoline—the width of a nickel, not a dime (or use a sharp knife). Each slice should bend with a little resistance. Arrange a layer of slightly overlapping zucchini slices on one of the serving platters and evenly, lightly season it with a large pinch of the salt, a few crackings of black pepper, a scarce scattering of the torn basil, and just a few shards of cheese. (You want to reserve most of the basil and cheese for garnish.) Continue making layers until you've used up all of the zucchini (and all of the salt). Depending on the size of your platter, you'll have three or four layers. Gently press the zucchini against the platter to force it all into contact with the salt, then set the second platter on top. Give it least 20 minutes to sweat its liquid.

Squeeze the platters together and hold them up sideways over the sink to drain off the excess liquid. Remove the top platter and blot the surface of the zucchini dry with a clean towel.

Heat 3 tablespoons of the olive oil in a small frying pan over low heat and add the garlic, pine nuts, and rosemary. Season with a little salt and fry gently until the pine nuts turn golden brown, about 5 minutes. Add the pepper flakes and cook for just a few seconds, then add the remaining 5 tablespoons olive oil. Remove from the heat and remove the garlic and rosemary.

Spoon the lemon juice over the zucchini, lifting it up at the edges to encourage the lemon to flow underneath. Then spoon on the olive oil and pine nut mixture. Scatter the reserved cheese and torn leaves of basil over the top of the salad. You can serve this right away, but the flavors fuse together better when left to sit at room temperature for an hour or two.

spicy cinnamon flan

Nothing could be more predictable than a flan ending to an Argentinian asado. But after standing watch around a smoky fire all day and consuming untold pounds of meat, if anyone can manage to raise a feeble hand at the mention of dessert, they deserve a Good Eater award and a dish of cold, caramelized custard with a sizable tuft of whipped cream. It's the height of creamy, grandmotherly comfort.

When you're cooking the dry caramel in the pan, watching the sugar melt and turn dangerously brown, make sure to have your cinnamon close by, because you'll need a lot of it. I owe this excessive amount of cinnamon to a European pastry chef's book that I found in a restaurant office years ago. On the cover, Chef Frederic Bau struck a magician's pose against a black velvet backdrop (it was the '90s), and the caramel layer in his crème renversé called for so much cinnamon I thought it might be an error of translation. It proved to be wizardly. Pushing the cinnamon to its absolute limit makes the caramel taste actually *spicy*. Even more so when you use fresh high-quality cinnamon; my favorite is the Vietnamese cinnamon from Penzey's.

I always mix my custards with a whisk in a large bowl, because machines incorporate too much air. A flan should be thick and lush and creamy, like the heavy hand of sleep.

The custard needs to chill deeply before serving, and it keeps well in the refrigerator, so make the flan ahead—up to 2 days in advance.

Makes 2 large flans, serving 15 to 20 (the half-batch recipe follows)

cinnamon caramel
1 cup sugar
2 tablespoons ground cinnamon (see headnote)

flan
4 ounces cream cheese, softened
½ cup sugar
¼ cup maple syrup
10 large eggs

2 large egg yolks
3 cups heavy cream
3 cups whole milk
1 teaspoon fine sea salt
2 teaspoons pure vanilla extract

A double batch of Whipped Cream (page 281)
 for serving

First make the cinnamon caramel: Have two 9-inch pie plates ready. Preheat a large frying pan over medium-high heat for a few minutes. When it's hot, sprinkle the sugar evenly across the surface of the pan and let it cook undisturbed, standing by with silicone spatula in hand. The sugar will melt at the edges first; when it turns amber brown, take the pan off the heat and stir with your spatula until smooth. Add the cinnamon and press out any lumps with your spatula, stirring until the caramel is smooth and dark mahogany brown, returning it to the heat as needed.

Divide the caramel between the two pie plates and immediately tip them this way and that, sliding the caramel until it covers the bottoms completely. (Pour water into the caramel-cooking pan to loosen it for later dishwashing.) Let the caramel sit until it hardens and feels cool to the touch.

Preheat the oven to 325°F.

For the custard, put the cream cheese in a large mixing bowl and mix it with a rubber spatula to beat out the lumps. Add the sugar and mix until smooth, then add the maple syrup and one egg and beat until just combined—not too vigorously, because you want to avoid aerating the custard. Switch to a sturdy whisk, add the rest of the eggs and the yolks and whisk until smooth. Then whisk in the cream, milk, salt,

recipe continues

and vanilla. Let the custard sit a few minutes to ensure that the sugar has dissolved, then strain it through a fine-mesh sieve into a bowl. (*The custard can be made in advance and refrigerated overnight.*)

Set the two caramel-lined pie plates in a large baking or roasting pan and pour enough hot water into the pan to reach halfway up the sides of the pie plates. Divide the custard between the pie plates and transfer to the oven.

Bake for about 55 minutes, until the custard sets up firmly and wiggles tightly when shaken. Remove from the oven and let cool in the water bath. Press a sheet of plastic wrap against the surface of each flan and refrigerate until thoroughly chilled, at least 6 hours and up to 2 days.

To unmold the flans, run a thin knife around the perimeter of each one. Set a round serving platter upside down on top of the pie plate and, holding the platter and pie plate tightly together with both hands, flip over swiftly. Tap the platter on the countertop to release the custard. Scrape any loose caramel still clinging to the pie plate onto the top of the flan.

Serve the flans with the whipped cream.

---

a more reasonable half-batch

Serves 8 to 10

cinnamon caramel
½ cup sugar
1 tablespoon ground cinnamon

flan
2 ounces cream cheese, softened
¼ cup sugar
2 tablespoons maple syrup
5 large eggs
1 large egg yolk
1½ cups heavy cream
1½ cups whole milk
½ teaspoon fine sea salt
1 teaspoon pure vanilla extract

Follow the instructions above, using one 9-inch pie plate.

secretly thrifty Brazilian-inspired buffet

FOR FIFTEEN

— rhubarb lemonade
— feijoada (black beans with smoked pork and spareribs)
— a double batch of garlic and coconut–scented rice (page 89)
— grilled leek and hard-boiled egg salad
— steamed and glazed white sweet potatoes (page 88)
— sour orange platter salad with parsley and pistachios

This is a party that hides your thrift behind a deep, velvety black curtain of black beans. Feijoada, black beans stewed with up to four different kinds of pork, some orange peel, garlic, and bay leaves, is the national dish of Brazil, where it is pretty much synonymous with a party. In theory, you could make a small batch of feijoada. But given that it tastes best when cooked low and slow for many hours, until the black beans throw out their ink, the pork fat melts into the sauce, and the whole house fills with its earthy, smoky perfume, I think this is a recipe that begs to be stretched, not contracted.

Not only is the grocery bill surprisingly doable, but for a party of this size, these dishes make few demands on your time. The feijoada and sweet potatoes can be made in advance, as can the leeks and the hard-boiled eggs for the salad. You can peel the oranges and leave them whole for slicing at the last minute. But do boil the kale and steam the rice right before serving. These tasks are easy, and they'll light up the room with fragrance, sound, and energy.

rhubarb lemonade

Rhubarb lemonade is thrillingly tart, it's cheap to make, and it glows a tempting pink in a "cut-crystal" plastic cup. To dress it up, slip a shiny sugar-cured Meyer lemon slice in among the ice cubes, which isn't just decorative, but edible.

Make the rhubarb syrup concentrate base well ahead of time to give it time to chill. Better yet, make it when rhubarb peaks in early summer and freeze it. The citric acid in the rhubarb syrup stabilizes the juice, keeping it bright and fresh-tasting through both freezing and thawing. Without it, even day-old rhubarb juice will start to taste a little vegetal.

If you grow rhubarb or know someone who does, you can fill your freezer with rows of jars of rhubarb concentrate. It also makes a great snow cone, and a killer rhubarb whiskey sour.

Makes 4 quarts rhubarb lemonade, enough to serve 15

rhubarb concentrate (makes 4½ cups)
3 pounds rhubarb, trimmed and cut into 1-inch lengths (about 11 cups)
4 cups water
2 cups sugar
6 tablespoons fresh lemon juice
2 teaspoons citric acid (see page 331)

rhubarb lemonade (makes 4 batches)
Juice of 4 lemons
Rhubarb Concentrate
14 cups water (3½ cups per batch)
A double batch of Sugar-Cured Meyer Lemons (page 248) for garnish

For the rhubarb concentrate, put the rhubarb in your largest wide-bottomed saucepot and add the water. (A wide-bottomed pot will keep the rhubarb from stacking up and overcooking and also keep its color bright, so if you don't have a large pot, such as a jam pot, you may want to divide the rhubarb between two pans.) Bring to a quick boil over high heat, stirring to drive the heat to the center, then reduce the heat to the lowest setting. Cook until the rhubarb swells and glows and feels soft when pressed, about 15 minutes. Maintain a bare simmer to ensure that the rhubarb keeps its shape and doesn't disintegrate; if it turns to mushy pulp, the syrup will be cloudy. Remove from the heat and let the rhubarb sit in its bright pink liquid for a few minutes while you pull together the straining setup.

Set a large, very fine-mesh sieve over a large bowl. (A fine conical chinois—see page 324—or a jelly bag would be ideal, but you can also line whatever sieve you have with multiple layers of damp cheesecloth.) Pour the rhubarb and its juices into the sieve to drain, without pressing on the pulp. Let it drip until it seems to have finished, at least 30 minutes. You'll have about 3¾ cups.

Pour the rhubarb juice into the clean wide-bottomed pot. Add the sugar and bring to a slow simmer over medium-low heat, stirring until the sugar dissolves, about 2 minutes. Add the the lemon juice and citric acid, whisk, and cook until just incorporated, another minute. Taste the syrup. It should be sweet, tart, and intense.

For the sake of clarity, strain the syrup. You should have 4½ cups rhubarb syrup concentrate (a little over 2 pints). Let cool.

Pour the rhubarb syrup into glass or plastic canning jars, making sure to leave at least ¾-inch headspace. Cap the jars and refrigerate the rhubarb syrup for up to 1 week, or freeze for up to 1 year. Before using, thaw the container in a bowl of lukewarm water, or overnight in the refrigerator.

For the rhubarb lemonade, I'm just going to assume you won't mix the whole batch of lemonade in a commercial-sized 6-quart container (though by all means do so, if you have one) but will make it quart by quart, as I usually do. Squeeze the juice of 1 lemon (2 to 3 tablespoons) into a clean quart jar and add 1 cup plus 2 tablespoons of the rhubarb concentrate. Add 3½ cups cold water to the jar, nearly filling it up, to make an insistent but not cloyingly sweet lemonade, one that can handle a little dilution from the ice. To serve, fill each glass with some ice cubes, add a sugar-cured lemon slice, and top off with the rhubarb lemonade.

Refrigerate any leftover lemonade or syrup. The lemonade will stay fresh-tasting for a couple of days, the syrup for about week.

feijoada for a crowd

After a long day of cooking with pork, fresh and smoked, it's a revelation to discover that the beans and their smoky liquor actually upstage the meat.

You'll want to cook the beans with the best local materials you can find: I use pork and beef ribs, smoked pork sausage, and sometimes cubes of fresh pork belly or bacon. I'm going to skip the iconic toasted farofa (manioc) topping (and, sadly, the traditional pigs' ears) this time because both can be difficult to source.

Next, think about which vessel you'll be using to cook this monstrous feast. I use an electric countertop cooker, the rural woman's workhorse. My childhood friends and I call them "church lady roasters," in reference to the women volunteers who lined up their trusty electric roasters in the church kitchen for funeral lunches, each filled with a different kind of hotdish. Some call these Nescos, in tribute to the most popular brand. Electric roasters are cheap to buy, or easy to borrow, and they're nice to have. For example, you can plug in an electric roaster outside, or on the porch, during the summer to move the heat of cooking out of the kitchen. Designed to handle a 20-pound turkey, an electric roaster has no problem with beans to serve 15. Otherwise, cook the feijoada in a large two-handled roaster in the oven. In fact, any pan capacious enough for a large Thanksgiving turkey will be big enough to cook this feijoada.

Makes about 4 quarts, serving 15

1½ to 2 pounds bone-in pork country ribs or 1 rack baby back ribs

½ teaspoon plus 1 teaspoon plus ¾ teaspoon fine sea salt

1 teaspoon ground cumin, preferably toasted and freshly ground

1 large smoked ham hock or 1 pound smoked slab bacon

2 tablespoons extra-virgin olive oil

1 tablespoon butter

2 extra-large sweet onions, roughly chopped

4 ounces hard chorizo, thinly sliced (or substitute 2 teaspoons smoked paprika)

8 garlic cloves, minced, plus 2 heads garlic

5 dried red chiles

2 wide strips orange peel

3 pounds dried black beans, soaked overnight in water to cover generously

5 bay leaves

1¾ pounds beef short ribs or brisket

1 pound smoked pork sausages, cut into 2-inch lengths

A double batch of Garlic and Coconut–Scented Rice (page 89) for serving

recipe continues

If using baby back ribs, cut the ribs between the bones to separate them. Put the ribs (country or baby back) into a bowl and toss with ½ teaspoon of the salt and the cumin.

If using slab bacon, cut it into 2-inch cubes. Heat a large frying pan over medium-low heat and add the bacon cubes. Cook until the edges brown and the fat begins to render, about 10 minutes, then remove from the pan.

Add the olive oil, butter, onions, and 1 teaspoon of the salt to the same pan (or to a new pan if you're not using the bacon) and raise the heat to medium-high. When the onions start to darken at the edges, reduce the heat to medium and add the chorizo (or smoked paprika), and garlic. Continue to cook the onions slowly until they're soft and brown, another 20 minutes or so.

Meanwhile, if cooking the feijoada in a large (nonelectric) roaster, preheat the oven to 325°F.

To make the sachet, rub off the loose papery skin from the heads of garlic, scrape the root ends with a paring knife to remove any grit, and lop off the top ½ inch of each one to expose the cloves. Put the garlic, chiles, and orange peel on a square of cheesecloth and tie the four corners into a tight bundle. (If you don't have cheesecloth, just add the aromatics to the beans, loose, and be sure to remove them before serving. The orange peel might be hard to find, but since it's a particularly unpleasant accidental bite, do make the search.)

Scrape the onions into your chosen cooking vehicle: the insert of an electric countertop roaster or a large two-handled turkey roaster. Add the drained beans and add enough water to cover the beans by 3 inches. Set the pan of beans on the stovetop, across two burners, and bring to a simmer. (I know that it may sound a bit unconventional to heat the pan from an electric roaster on the stovetop, but I do it all the time without any trouble. Slow cookers always need a kick start.) When the foam rises, skim it off and discard. Add the remaining ¾ teaspoon salt, the bay leaves, the sachet, short ribs or brisket, and browned chunks of bacon or the ham hoc. and bring the liquid to a simmer.

Transfer the roaster insert to the electric roaster, cover, and set the heat to 325°F; adjust the heat as needed to maintain a slow, continuous burble. Or cover the roasting pan with foil and put it in the oven. Cook the feijoada, stirring occasionally and checking to make sure the liquid remains just above the level of the beans, until both the meat and the beans begin to soften, about 2 hours.

Add the sausages and continue to simmer until the beans and the meat are very tender and the thickened sauce covers the meat in a thick purplish-black blanket, 1½ to 2 hours longer. (The total cooking time runs between 3½ and 4 hours, but feijoada can be kept warm on a very low setting or in a low oven for up to 2 hours. If shooting for a 7:00 p.m. dinner, start making the beans by 1:00, and start cooking them by 2:00.)

Before serving, remove the sachet (or aromatics) and bay leaves. Serve the feijoada ladled over the garlic rice.

grilled leek salad with hard-boiled eggs and smoky anchovy dressing

Leeks are one of my favorite vegetables to grill. They char easily and quickly, their thin layers picking up blackness and popping dramatically against the lime-green background like tree rings. Even when blackened, leeks never taste burnt. They can be charred on a grill or, in deep winter (subzero does stop me from grilling, occasionally), in a hot cast-iron pan on the stovetop.

The leeks need to be parboiled first, because they won't become tender on the grill alone. But I enjoy the time I spend with them, peeling back their wet outer leaves and arranging the bright green hearts on the tray that I take to the grill. The light green heart of a leek, harvested from the point where the stem begins to taper, is always the most succulent part, and the dark green leaves are tender too. I have no idea who first started this practice of lopping off and discarding all of the the green parts, but I can tell you who made me stop that wasteful madness: the famed Southern cook and writer Edna Lewis. Her recipe for Steamed Leek Greens taught me that the green parts of the leek are a juicy vegetable in their own right.

You'll need kitchen string to tie the leeks together.

Fills an extra-large platter, serving 15 as a side

anchovy dressing
3 anchovy fillets
2 rounded tablespoons capers, preferably
    salt-packed
2 large garlic cloves
Leaves from 1 sprig rosemary
2 cups fresh parsley leaves
3½ tablespoons fresh lemon juice
6 tablespoons olive oil (plus an additional
    tablespoon if using store-bought chile oil)
2 tablespoons Homemade Chile Oil (page 60)
    or store-bought hot chile oil (to taste; it's
    spicier)

1 tablespoon water
Fine sea salt

5 large eggs

leeks and scallions
2½ pounds leeks (4 large, not jumbo)
Extra-virgin olive oil
Fine sea salt and freshly ground black pepper
1 bunch scallions, trimmed

For the dressing, rinse the capers, and if they are salt-packed, soak them in water for at least 20 minutes. Unless the anchovies are really beautiful, I often rinse those too—very briefly under running water. The Italian grandmothers will not be pleased, but sometimes the oil surrounding grocery-store anchovies tastes a little funky.

Chop the anchovies to a fine paste and place in a small bowl. Roughly chop the capers, grate the garlic finely, and finely mince the rosemary, and add them to the bowl with the anchovies. Take ½ cup of parsley leaves to mince finely, reducing them to a paste, and add them to the bowl. Reserve the remaining parsley leaves to rough-chop for garnish; you want the parsley to be dry and loose for the garnish, so if they're moist from washing, rake the leaves across a plate in one layer to air-dry. Stir in the lemon juice, olive oil, chile oil, water, and a pinch of sea salt. Taste, and adjust salt and level of chile heat to your liking. Let the dressing sit out at room temperature for up to 3 hours to mellow. It should taste frankly lemony,

recipe continues

with a buttery backbone of olive oil. (*The dressing can be made the day before, covered, and refrigerated; bring to room temperature before using.*)

To cook the eggs, put them in a large saucepan, cover with 2 inches of cold water, and bring to a gentle boil over medium-high heat. Simmer for 2 minutes, then cut the heat, cover the pan, and let the eggs steep in the hot water for 10 minutes. (I like this salad best when the yolks are fully set but still slightly moist and fudgy in the center. Let them steep for 12 minutes for a crumblier yolk.)

Drain the eggs, crack the shells, and cover with cold water. Peel immediately.

Fill your largest pot with water for poaching the leeks and bring to a boil. To clean the leeks, strip off any wilty outer leaves and carefully trim the root ends, slicing off just the dirty parts but keeping the leeks attached at the stem. Cut off the dark green tops at the point where they start to flop over and branch widely, keeping most of the green parts. Slice the leeks lengthwise in half and clean them carefully under running water, gently parting the layers to flush out any dirt. Put the leek halves back together with their partners. If they're too long to fit in the pot, cut them in half. Bind the leek halves together with kitchen string, looped around in a crisscross fashion from one end to the other, and tie it tightly.

When the water comes to a rolling bowl, salt it generously (aggressively, I mean, because this is their only chance for internal seasoning) and add the leeks. Poach at an energetic simmer until the tip of a knife pierces them easily but doesn't quite slide in and out, about 3 minutes. Drop the leeks into a bowl of ice water to stop the cooking and then drain them on a baking sheet lined with paper towels, rolling the leeks around to shed excess water.

Cut the strings and remove the outer leek layers if they feel mushy. Slice them neatly on the bias into 3-inch lengths, two or three bites each, and line them up on a small baking sheet or platter. If not grilling them right away, cover with plastic wrap and refrigerate. (*The leeks can be poached and cut the day before you need them.*)

Prepare a hot fire in a grill. Rub the leeks with a thin film of olive oil, season both sides lightly with salt and pepper, and grill until pleasantly—edibly—charred on the outsides and hot and tender within, about 5 minutes. Remove from the grill, toss the scallions with a bit of oil and salt and pepper, and grill over high heat until wilted and tender at the white end.

Cut the eggs into quarters. Arrange the leeks and scallions on a platter, tuck in the quartered eggs, and douse everything with spoonfuls of the anchovy-chili vinaigrette, drizzling a little extra onto the platter. Roughly chop the reserved parsley and scatter it across the salad.

This salad can be served right away but it does not suffer at all if left to wait on the countertop and, in fact, probably improves. It takes time for the dressing to work its way into the leek layers. Before serving, tip the platter and baste everything again with the vinaigrette, to regloss and refresh.

sour orange platter salad with parsley and pistachios

A platter of freshly sliced oranges is a classic accompaniment to feijoada. Refreshing. Perfect. It needs no tinkering. But if you haven't already picked up on it, I have a pretty big three-way crush on oranges, salt, and olive oil, especially when the oranges are tart and the olive oil is strong and green. The salt is key. A fine mist of sea salt makes the oranges break out in a sweat, which gets all the juices going. Parsley and pistachios push this situation further along into salad territory, until it's skating the edge between savory and sweet, dinner and dessert.

Since this recipe requires such a small amount of ground coriander, you can use preground, but its fragrance pales in comparison to the freshly toasted and ground. Toasted coriander seed has a strong floral aroma that intensifies when first crushed but fades fast. It's gone within a week. If you toast more than you need, just promise yourself to remember use it.

Makes an extra-large platter, serving 15 as part of a big menu

5 oranges (any kind, but I like a mixture of Cara Cara, Minneola tangerines, and blood oranges)
Rounded ¼ teaspoon fine sea salt
Freshly ground black pepper
Juice of 1 lemon
½ teaspoon ground coriander, preferably toasted and freshly ground

½ teaspoon Aleppo pepper or ¼ teaspoon hot pepper flakes
6 tablespoons strong, fresh-tasting extra-virgin olive oil
A small handful fresh parsley leaves, roughly chopped (it looks and tastes better if the parsley is chopped when dry, so that it's loose and fresh, like grass clippings)
3 tablespoons crushed shelled pistachios

Lop off the tops and bottoms of the oranges so they can sit flat on your cutting board. With a sharp knife, cut off the peel and white pith in curving swoops, and trim off any remaining pith with a paring knife. Turn the oranges on their sides and thinly slice.

Lay the orange slices on a large platter, slightly overlapping, and sprinkle the salt evenly over them. (If the serving platter is small and you need to make two layers of oranges, salt each layer.) Squeeze the juice from the orange carcasses over the oranges and add the lemon juice.

Sprinkle the coriander, Aleppo pepper, and some freshly ground black pepper over the oranges and drizzle with the olive oil. Scatter the chopped parsley and crushed pistachios over the top.

This salad can be served right away or held for up to an hour or two at room temperature. Give it a quick baste with its juices before serving to refresh.

A Note on Cleaning Up

I am what you might call a classical dishwasher, a stubborn elder who doesn't understand this trend toward the single-basin farmhouse sink. My sink has three basins—one for hot soapy water, one for rinsing, and one for stacking clean pots or pans to dry out of sight. On any given night, you'll find me with my hands sunk into smoking-hot water, feeling around in the dark water for the coiled metal scrubber, my face staring back at me in the black mirror of the window above the sink. I'm most likely thinking about how much time I spend doing dishes (too much), and how much worse it would have been one hundred years ago, before hot water ran nearly boiling out of the tap. I'm thinking about how I actually sort of enjoy wiping down the counters with wide strokes of the dishcloth, returning again and again to the sink to rinse, wring, repeat—and how I should probably keep this to myself and never confess it, ever. But I do think it's hard to love cooking on a regular, daily basis if some part of you, even a small grumbling part, doesn't feel some satisfaction in cleaning up.

We cookbook people rarely talk about cleaning, preferring to skip over the ugly parts, but old cookbooks would not shut up about it. It seems that cooking, cleaning, and food safety were once indivisible; three pillars of the same art. Of course, before the age of refrigeration, ignorance about food safety was actually dangerous. Unpasteurized milk infected with Listeria sickened, and sometimes killed, children, and one bad custard pie could lay out a whole household for days. In the war against invisible, little-understood enemies—what we now understand as unsafe microbes and bacteria and viruses— information about sanitation kept people healthy and, in some cases, alive.

As the only girl born to my generation in a long line of women who were traumatized by post–World War II hygiene hysterics, I was subjected to endless demonstrations on how one runs a tight, sanitary household ship. My mom's dishwater wasn't just hot enough to dissolve grease; I remember my hands cooking in it, turning red like boiled lobster shells. Every day brought a fresh clean dishcloth, thin and nimble enough to wrap around a fingertip and get into tight, filthy corners. Yellow sponges were for bathing babies; kitchen sponges were petri dishes of bacteria. Not doing dishes within an hour after dinner was "inviting mice to the table," and to leave crumbs on the counter . . . are you kidding? Crumbs are left by people who don't see crumbs. I was taught to not only see them, but to *feel* them, like an oyster feels the sand in its belly, as a foreign irritant.

As a young feminist, I found this housewife training initiative offensive. In rebellion, I did a bad job, perfecting the art of lackadaisical counter wiping. But I had absorbed my mom's sanitation program by osmosis, enough to grow up to be one of those annoying people who doesn't believe in soaking pans overnight. (What doesn't loosen up within an hour probably never will.)

The transformation was very gradual. Back when Aaron and I were twenty years younger and throwing enormous parties in tight Brooklyn apartments, the transactional agreement was clear: The host provided the space and a bunch of snacks that in theory constituted dinner; the partygoers arrived with six-packs of beer. At the end of the night, friends and inevitable strangers alike dug through the coat pile to find their stuff and descended our steep stairway in huddled packs to prop up the stumblers. No one stayed to help us clean up, and I didn't expect them to, because they were already facing a buzzkill: the bright, sobering lights of the subway system. Aaron and I viewed the party's remains—the endless beer bottles, the plastic cups of wine with cigarette butts floating in them, the gored-out rinds of cheese— as evidence of a successful evening and got to work, each with our own garbage bag.

Thankfully, we're past the era of such howlers. At dinner parties today, the collected kids swarm the tables like bugs before a rainstorm, descending ravenously and then flying away en masse, leaving a cool breeze of relief (and a bunch of plastic cups) in their wake. Our drinking has either lessened or become more methodical or ceased altogether—but whatever the case, we use real glassware. Most of us possess a medium level of household competence and a full, bone-deep understanding of household guilt. We're perhaps even more sensitive to our friends' domestic workloads than we are to our own family members', and can't wait to prove our usefulness by scrubbing pans at someone else's house. I love the help, but on principle, I think this impulse should be thwarted. The new transactional party agreement is this: I give you a day-pass from kitchen chores, and someday you'll give me one in return.

But there's no question that a large pile of dirty dishes makes us all nervous. To minimize this anxiety, I try to wash most of the heavy-equipment mess before people even start to arrive, and I nest the dirty pots and pans from the last-minute cooking in neat stacks. But after the main course has been cleared—after the angel who makes it their mission to track down matching lids to my storage containers helps me put away the leftover food—I put an end to the post-game stadium cleanup and usher everyone back to the candlelit table. Putting the food away and stacking the dirty plates restores a welcome sense of order, but nothing kills a party faster than a host bent on cleaning up the aftermath. Bringing out the broom is equivalent to a bartender's last call, and taking out the garbage instantly breaks the fourth wall of entertaining.

There are exceptions to this, of course. At the end of last year's New Year's Eve party, after the room had cleared out on the dot of 12:30, two of my closest friends stayed behind to clean up. We talked and talked and washed and dried and put away every last dish. But I still kicked them out before I got out the broom. I find something very satisfying in giving my counters that final wipe-down, in recorking open bottles of wine and buttoning down my kitchen for the night. I find comfort in ending the night how I began, alone in the kitchen. There's peace and solitude in it.

At some point, after so many years of cooking and cleaning up, the two fuse and eventually settle into a daily practice. They feed off each other. Cooking is a creative outlet for letting off steam; cleaning up restores order to the fragile kitchen ecosystem. For some, cooking might remain an occasional dalliance, and deep kitchen cleaning a tolerated chore, and that's okay. But when cooking deepens into a pleasure-seeking, restorative daily practice, a certain fondness for cleaning the kitchen usually follows.

When times are bad, we can lean on our kitchen practice, and count on it to give our hands something to do. We can feed a sourdough starter. Or put a pot of rice on to cook, its perfume filling the room like a vase of fresh cut flowers. Or we can wipe down the countertops, erasing the whole day's blackboard of negativity. In this way, cooking ends with a fresh start, every single night. After dinner, we clean the stovetop so that we can wake up and look forward to making breakfast. The next morning, we turn on a burner, and when its sparking click-click-click sound stops, it's hard not to feel this hopeful thing all over again.

A Well-Battered Batterie de Cuisine: Tools and Equipment

I've always loved that the French refer to one's collection of cooking equipment as a batterie de cuisine.

My own battalion is indeed battered. The exteriors of my stainless steel pots look like charcoal-washed sunsets. The bottoms of my cast-irons are crusty with the memories of old flames. My heavy-gauge aluminum baking sheets are stained with grease burns, but they still lie flat on the counter, dead serious, ready to make cookies.

This is not the place where I will tell you that despite my outsized cooking habit, I work with just a lean collection of basic hand tools. I love the romance of that idea, but it's not the truth.

It is true that anyone can make a great dinner with nothing but a knife, a cutting board, and a simple pot. And on certain summer days, I enjoy cooking without any equipment at all, just throwing whole baby peppers, spring onions, and a long unfurled scarf of skirt steak onto the grill, and tearing basil leaves and drizzling olive oil over the top of my one-platter dinner. That's very satisfying, but it feels a bit like camp-cooking—a nice break from my everyday creature comforts, only because I know it'll be temporary. Cooking is a craft, and, like any other, it requires some tools of the trade.

I'm not saying we should outfit our kitchens with needless tech—wireless thermometers or handheld blenders—but only that at this point there are some pieces of cooking equipment I would be really peeved to live without. A funnel, for refilling my oil bottles and spice jars. A metal spider, for fishing things out of boiling water

without having to drain the whole pot. Metal sieves and colanders of varying fineness and size. A large high-sided pan big enough to hold braised chicken to serve eight. And that's not even getting into the baking section—the cake pans and ceramic dishes, the cookie sheets and wire racks crammed into every available space. If you're in the habit of cooking for others, you will need large pots and pans, there are no two ways about it. If I could get rid of some of this stuff, believe me, I would.

What you don't need to do is spend a lot of money on brand-new equipment. In fact, some things are actually better secondhand. My thin-edged spatulas and heavy enameled roasters are the beloved rescue-dogs of my kitchen. I've rarely plonked down my own hard-earned money for fancy equipment, save my copper jam pot (which I've never regretted) and a few intricate Bundt pans. Most everything else I use I've either been gifted or bought cheap in thrift stores or restaurant supply stores, at estate sales, and online. That brand-new rubber-handled metal spatula with the awkwardly thick rolled edges has nothing on my sharp-edged metal spatula from the '60s, which slips, thin and clever, underneath a panfried fish fillet. (My mom would like me to say here that there are two things you should never buy used: wooden utensils and vintage shoes. I've defied her many times on the shoes but agree with her about the wooden spoons and paddles.) I admire my pre-owned tools for their usefulness, but I treasure them because they are storied. Even if they're new to me, someone else loved them first.

So here's a list of things I consider essential—selected, condensed, and stacked in order from biggest to smallest.

Stainless Steel Pots and Pans

Stainless steel pans are a mainstay for a reason. They're thick, conduct heat well, and last pretty much forever. They'll never be as nonstick as chemically slick DuPont Teflon, but that's actually why we love them: because they're thankfully, reliably, semistick. And those "pan stickings" are pure flavor. For instance, I can predict that when I sauté chicken in a preheated stainless steel pan, the golden brown skin will release from the bottom of the pan about 90 percent freely, leaving 10 percent of its dark side behind. On that residue, atop the caramelized shards of skin and resinous puddles of reduced chicken juices, we will build our sauce. With a nonstick pan, all of the flavorful bits exit the pan with the chicken. And you can't make something delicious out of nothing.

You'll want a 10-inch stainless steel frying pan (or skillet) with sloped sides for sautéing vegetables, and a tall 4-quart stockpot for making stocks and soups, and then something larger and lidded for making braises and stews, or anything at all that will serve 6 people or more. The hardest-working pan in my kitchen is a 3-quart stainless steel sautoir, a high-sided 12-inch sauté pan. Judging by its thick blackened exterior, I can carbon-date it to the late 1990s, as I know I didn't start scrubbing the bottoms of my pots and pans until at least 2005. A few years ago, my mom tried to scrub it clean, giving the pan everything short of a chemical peel to remove those exterior stains—but no dice. At the end of the day, we had to declare its stained exterior situation irreversible. But its silver interior, the part that really matters, remains as shiny as the day it was born. I use this pan daily and grow ever more attached to it. (You can see its beautiful damage in the photo on page 320.)

Cast-Iron Pans

Cast-iron skillets are lifetime pans. They will outlive us all.

My favorite cast-iron pieces are the vintage ones I've pulled out of precarious piles in thrift stores. They weigh less than the new pans, which is easier on one's elbow joints over the long term.

The myths surrounding seasoning deter a lot of people from using cast-iron, the world's most forgiving, indestructible cookware. To season a new pan, heat it on the stovetop or in the oven until it smokes and then rub oil all over it, inside and out, until it gleams. It's like a quick facial: open the pores, seal them shut with moisturizer. I re-season my pans like this about every five years at best. In the meantime, I break every rule in the cast-iron handbook, and they work fine for me—I think because I follow two main laws of cast-iron cooking: One, preheat the pan. And two, preheat the fat. If you heat the dry pan for a few minutes until it's too hot to touch, then add the cooking fat and let *that* get good and hot before you add the ingredients, you'll essentially be re-seasoning the pan every time you use it. If you're generous with the cooking fat, nothing will ever stick. An egg fried in a dime-spot of butter might stick and resist the flip, but one fried in a proper tablespoon will reward you with lacy edges that lift easily from the bottom, leaving the excess butter behind.

After frying chicken or making hash, I scour the scabby pan bottom with soap and a coarse metal scrubber and then turn it upside down in my dish sink to air-dry. Sometimes after light-duty tasks, like frying bread, I can get away with rubbing in the leftover oil with a paper towel, but I've learned the hard way that if I don't use soap on a sticky pan, the scents will linger. The next time I heat it up, the ghosts of dinners-past will rise up to haunt me.

I do follow one rule—never letting my cast-iron pans soak in water, because that *will* invite rust—but in general, I think that maintaining a nonstick cast-iron surface has more to do with proper cooking and maintenance than with aftercare.

Woks

I dug my wok out of a pile of stacked junk at a thrift store in St. Paul in the mid '90s. It was large, 16 inches across, with a black steel bowl and a smooth round wooden handle toasted brown at the neck from years of licking flames. It cost $15, a not-insignificant amount of money to me at the time, but I bought it without hesitation, because it was large enough to stir-fry in and light enough to attempt a proper cascading flip. (There's a good chance it's older than I am.)

Since then, I've flirted with other woks in upscale cookware shops, but none can compare. Most Western-manufactured woks are too heavy to execute a flip, and most seem a little expensive. After spending a year cooking in a Chinese restaurant in New York City, I learned that an "expensive wok" is almost a misnomer. For my Chinese coworkers, inexpensive but high-quality cookware wasn't just their preference, but an ethic. When I asked them where to buy a wok, they sent me to a shop in Chinatown where their preferred woks were made of thin black steel and at the time didn't cost more than $20. I bought a jumbo wok there, which I pull out when cooking for groups of 6 or more. If I had to replace my small everyday wok, I'd get a Tawianese-style one: flat-bottomed, with a sturdy round handle, it's the type that works best on modern stovetops. (If cooking on an electric stovetop, a 14-inch or larger cast-iron skillet is the best way to approximate the necessary high heat of a hot wok.)

To season a new wok, heat it dry over high heat until the light silver coating burns off, then rub it all over with a thin layer of oil. Before cooking on a regulation home gas stovetop, a black steel wok requires a few minutes of preheating in order to get hot enough to stir-fry—but do not attempt that with a thin silvery aluminum wok. Thin woks are too thin to preheat and may set the oil on fire. I speak from experience when I say that pouring at least half a box of kosher salt onto a small kitchen grease fire will extinguish it immediately—so it's never a bad idea to keep a box of salt within reach.

Carbon-Steel Pans

Carbon steel is lighter than cast iron and equally nonstick. A few years ago, I inherited a pan I'd never seen anyone use, my Great-grandma Mary Hesch's carbon-steel skillet. It looks and feels like an antique badminton racket: a super-long handle on a dented-up round basin. It's so light in the hand it almost feels flimsy. But carbon steel is an immediate, reliable conductor. A quick study. It heats up quickly over a flame, though that heat peters out nearly instantly once removed from it.

Once my eyes were opened to carbon-steel pans, I began seeing them everywhere and have since added a campfire pan from the farm-and-fleet store that can hold paella for 12 and a low-sided French crepe skillet that turns out one perfect light brown doily after another.

Baking Sheets

After finally getting rid of a cluttered old cabinet of mismatched, warped cookie sheets, I replaced them with a fleet of basic stackable, heavy aluminum baking sheets. The ones made by Nordic Ware or Chicago Metallic are thick and sturdy, warp-resistant, and affordable. I'm not a fan of the nonstick versions; they're easier to clean, but the dark finish always burns the bottoms of my cookies. The stainless steel pans will take on a stain, but that can be avoided if you line them with silicone liners or parchment paper. (And if you bake regularly, I highly recommend the pre-cut 16 × 11-inch sheets of baking parchment that come in a flat box. You will never have to fight with a stubborn coil of rolled-up paper again.)

I've recently been turned on to quarter-sheet pans and use them for everything: to hold marinated meat, bake squash, and toast nuts. They're cute, cheap, and, at 9 × 13 inches, even fit in tiny ovens.

Pâté/Terrine Mold

Traditional pâté or terrine molds are narrower, longer, and heavier than a standard American loaf pan. The skinnier width ensures that a pâté mixture cooks evenly from edge to center, and it makes for a smaller, more petite slice. Terrine molds are strictly unnecessary, but nice to have if you enjoy making pâté or molded salads or desserts. Le Creuset sells brand-new enameled cast-iron terrine pans, but you can find vintage ones on the internet.

Wooden Spoons versus Rubber Spatulas

My collection of old wooden spoons has slid to the back of my drawer and been replaced by high-heat-tolerant rubber (technically, silicone) spatulas. Rubber spatulas efficiently sweep the pans, getting way into the corners. They can go into the dishwasher. They don't age as well as wooden spoons, and they will never earn that lusciously soft dogs'-ears texture that comes from soaking up generations of soup. But where some people might see nostalgia, I was taught instead to see years of compound bacteria. If you, too, were raised by a mother with 1950s sanitation standards, you probably replaced your wooden spoons with rubber spatulas long ago. But if you think germaphobia is more of a myth, and you like to leave a stir spoon perched on the edge of the pot, then wooden spoons—which never get too hot to touch—are for you.

Whisks

Whisks are my favorite smallwares purchase in cooking gift shops. I have a small one for whisking up flour, a medium one for whisking whole eggs, and—a splurge—a very large, voluminous balloon whisk for whipping cream or egg whites. With a balloon whisk, cream whipped by hand stiffens magically, more quickly than you might think. Hand-whipped cream is also denser and richer tasting than machine-frothed.

Sieves and Colanders

Draining and sifting are arguably the most important of all maneuvers in the kitchen. Because the correct gauge of sieve makes the difference between a velvety soup and a gritty one, I have a half-dozen sieves of varying grades and sizes, from the fine teacup-sized (perfect for dusting confectioners' sugar over cakes) to the large and wide-meshed, for straining thick purees. You'll also need at least one colander, for draining pasta and rinsing fruit. I also have a beloved restaurant-grade conical fine sieve, called a chinois, indispensable for straining fruit purees for a clear, limpid jelly.

Graters

A single four-sided box grater will do you just fine, but I prefer to have a whole selection of flat graters, because they're easier to wash. Microplanes—the brand name, and also the common name—are god-sent. I have one with big holes for coarsely grating soft cheeses, another with tinier holes for grating carrots to a fine slush, and then a couple of superfine ones for grating garlic, Parmesan cheese, nutmeg, ginger, and just about anything else you need to turn to fluffy, fine snow.

Pot Holders (aka Hot Pads)

Maybe it's because I cooked professionally for a while and picked up the line cook's habit of lifting hot pots with folded kitchen towels, but I have never taken a shine to puffy pot holders. To me, it feels like trying to move a pan out of the oven with two overstuffed cushions. My grip is more stable when I can feel the pot handles or edges of a pan beneath it. I much prefer the old-fashioned quilted pot holders that were popular a few generations back, and I've made it one of my life's side-hustles to seek them out. They're thin enough so you can feel the pot, and if the heat threatens to burn through, you can simply double them up. A few years ago, I ran across the motherlode at a small-town craft store, made by senior citizens from old workwear and heavy curtain fabric. The sign said "Hot Pads," which is what I've always called them, "$2/pair." I bought thirty pairs, which I hope will be a ten-year supply.

Offset Spatulas

The 90-degree-angle tilt of an offset spatula makes spreading icing on a cake or tomato sauce across the top of a pan of lasagna easier and much more pleasurable. A pie or cake server, which has a relatively similar bend to it, works nearly as well.

Scales

When I'm testing recipes, I weigh almost everything, but for everyday off-the-cuff cooking, there are only a few things worth pulling the scale down from the shelf: nuts, fruit, meat, and flour. For most other ingredients, you can get close enough with an educated guess. Conventional grocery store produce has gotten pretty standardized—a regular-sized carrot from a bag weighs about 4 ounces, and a medium zucchini 8 ounces—and you can mete out precise ounces of butter and cream cheese if the paper wrapping is set on straight, but a scale is really a must for consistent baking, because flour compresses in the bag. Scoop-and-level measuring is fine for quickbreads and snacking cakes, but if you want to dial in the more delicately balanced pastries and cakes (like the Pastis du Quercy on page 75), it's best to weigh the flour.

I used to use a small portable digital scale that toggled between ounces and grams with ease, but eventually I realized that I don't have the attention span for digital. Take one distracting phone call, and the scale tares back to zero and you have to pour the berries out of the bowl and begin all over again. So I bought an old-fashioned looking analog scale a few years ago, and I've never looked back. I can start weighing strawberries when making jam, run outside to sign for a package, and come back to it without missing a beat.

To keep the scaling bowl clean, line it with a piece of plastic wrap or a butter wrapper.

Mandoline

Using a mandoline (a flat slicer with a stationary blade) to slice potatoes for gratins and vegetables for salads will make your dishes look stunningly professional and shave hours off your lifetime prep clock. I like the Japanese Benriner brand. They're cheap—about $30—lightweight, and easy to clean and store, and the blades stay sharp for years. I don't use the guard, because it's awkward and round vegetables never stay put beneath it, but I'm really careful. I hold the vegetables with a light touch as I slice, and I switch my grip from clenched to open-palmed as I near the stem end and always leave a good ½-inch buffer margin at the end. I'll sacrifice a little vegetable matter if it means I get to keep my fingertips.

Cutting Boards

Wooden butcher blocks are my cutting boards of choice. They have a comforting, human touch, and I've found that man-made materials dull my knives. My favorite board is made of thick walnut and large—extra-large, the size of a pillow, but twenty times as heavy. Heavy to lug around and awkwardly large to wash, it's big enough to hold three separate hills of chopped onions and carrots and celery at once. Its size makes the idea of whipping up a quick soup for dinner a lot more doable.

To clean wooden cutting boards, scrub them hard with a soapy wire scrubber and leave them to air-dry. Once in a while, you'll want to sanitize them properly: Cover the surface with a thin layer of kosher salt and leave it overnight. Scrub it off in the morning and run the cut side of a lemon over the surface; after it dries, apply a fresh coat of butcher block oil. More occasionally, sand down the board, top and bottom, until you reach smooth new wood, and then re-oil it.

I do keep one plastic cutting board for cutting raw meat or fish, because I can sterilize it in the dishwasher, and another one dedicated to cutting fruit—especially pineapple, which picks up any lingering cutting-board odors very easily.

Funnels

I never used to care much about the occasional spill, but as I get older, I find funnels to be incredibly reassuring. I have a skinny one for refilling oil bottles and a wider one for ferrying dry ingredients from store sacks to storage jars. The wider one, 2 inches across, which is actually a canning funnel, also comes in handy when I need to ladle out soup into bowls for a group. The soup passes neatly through the funnel and never spatters.

Stovetop Heat Diffuser

Most stovetop burners do not go low enough to maintain a gentle simmer, and that's where diffusers come in. I inherited mine, a circular perforated metal disk with a wooden handle long burnt off from use, from my grandma. This two-sided metal contraption with a slim air pocket sits on the burner, where it elevates my stockpot by an inch, both distancing it from the flames and diffusing the heat. A diffuser will hold a large pot of chicken stock to a steady, lazy simmer. When you're reducing thick, sugary mixtures like poppy seed filling, or applesauce, a diffuser is a must.

Mixing/Prep Bowls

My twenty-some metal mixing bowls range in size from petite to gigantic, are easy to lug around and to wash, and nest perfectly in a single cupboard drawer—and sometimes I think I might even need more of them. Which isn't a problem, since restaurant supply stores and Asian markets sell them at a very affordable price. (Don't forget to get a couple of giant bowls for mixing and holding large quantities.) Small glass nesting bowls or ceramic ramekins for holding chopped garlic or herbs and the like are also essential, because they free up space on your cutting board.

Plastic Wrap

It's been more than twelve years since I left my last professional cooking job to become a proud home-cooking civilian, and in that time, I've dropped nearly all of my professional allegiances except one: my slavish devotion to commercial plastic wrap.

You can stretch commercial wrap, which is three times as strong and twice as resilient as grocery store plastic, around a bowl so tautly that a dried bean could bounce on its surface. Tip the bowl upside down, and its seal remains tight and leakproof. You'd think that a large box of plastic wrap would encourage waste and be hell on the landfill, but in fact the strong cutting blades give you the precision needed to cut a perfect 3-inch square to cover a small ramekin.

Commercial wrap is good for other things too. When I worked in professional kitchens, most of us lady line cooks hitched up our too-big, man-sized work pants with makeshift belts made from a stretched-out arm's-length of plastic wrap. During first aid crises, we all wrapped plastic wrap around our cut fingers for tourniquets. These days, I use it more often to seal leaking bags of rice or to wrap my shoes before packing them in my suitcase.

After leaving professional kitchens, I gave the grocery store plastic wrap a solid go. I found myself scratching at the roll to find its end and struggling to spread a sheet of it out flat on the counter to wrap up a large potluck dish, as the stuff doubled back on itself like demonic double-sided tape. When I laid a sheet of it over the top of a pan, it didn't stick. I'd wad up balls of it, sick with the waste. Once you've had a taste of military-grade plastic wrap, there's no going back. So I picked up the phone, dialed a restaurant on Main Street, and asked them to order a 12-inch-wide roll for me from their supplier. When it came, I parked the ugly white box on my counter. Aaron, seeing that the box wasn't going anywhere, eventually built a wooden box to house it—similar to the way that people cover unsightly tissue boxes with crocheted cozies.

I hear that some big-box stores sell commercial wrap now, but ordering a box through your favorite restaurant is a surefire way to become one of their most valued regulars. They get it.

Spider

How do you remove potatoes from boiling water without having to drain the whole pot? A slotted spoon is too small. A fine-mesh strainer is too large. This job, and countless others, requires a long-handled metal spider. You can find an Asian-style wire scooper in any cooking supply store, but if you want to go all in, look for a sturdier metal German "noodle scooper." Whichever kind you get, a spider is invaluable for pulling multiple batches of vegetables, noodles, dumplings, or anything else you might want to boil from the same pot of frothing water.

Knives

To my mind, the three essential knives are a sharp paring knife, a decent serrated bread knife, and an 8- to 10-inch chef's knife, which is probably the most-used tool in my kitchen. I don't want to give too much advice about chefs' knives, though, because they're very personal. A knife should feel right in the hand, so comfortable that it becomes an extension of yourself, instantly responsive to your intentions.

I like a Japanese carbon-steel chef's knife, shorter than average (just 8 inches from tang to tip) and so lightweight that I can forget I'm holding it, often wielding it with threatening abandon as I gesture in the air. Carbon steel rusts (nothing that a little steel wool can't handle), but it keeps a sharp edge longer than any stainless steel chef's knife. No matter how long it's been since I last honed my knife on the sharpening stone (lately, biannually), my carbon-steel chef's knife remains the only one in the drawer that can reliably fillet any fish, butcher any roast, and slice even the ripest of summer tomatoes.

Food Processor versus Mortar and Pestle

I think of both of these tools as essential, because they puree very differently.

The whirring blade of a food processor blitzes things to bits, or to a sleek puree, depending on how long you press the button. It incorporates air into whatever it blends, which is a positive thing when I'm going for a fluffy, voluptuous texture or making a whippy dip.

But motorization isn't ideal for everything, especially when it comes to sauces. Where a food processor cuts the ingredients' fibers, a mortar and pestle pulls at them longitudinally, coaxing them into a relationship. When I want to make a rustic, textured sauce, like romesco or salsa verde, I lug out my old granite mortar and pestle. It holds about 2 cups, an amount too small for the processor, but just right for a party of 6 to 8. And sauces made in a mortar and pestle will have more flavor, as well as more texture. When making salsa verde, for example, the pestle mashes the garlic, salt, capers, and herbs together into a single perfumed unit. Herb sauces made in a mortar will take on a downy texture and will bloom on hot meat or vegetables on contact, releasing their aromatics.

Mostly, though, making a sauce in a mortar and pestle is good dinner theater. When guests are milling around but you still need to make the sauce, a mortar and pestle has an appealing, timeless knocking sound that only adds to the orchestral din of the party. It makes a last-minute rush look improvisational and in charge instead of electrically frantic.

Food Bunker Basics: Ingredients

Half of cooking is shopping, one quarter is proper ingredient storage, and the rest is just recipes.

So much of the success of dinner hinges on smart management of the whole kitchen ship.

If you're buying for just that day and laying all of your ingredients out on the counter, that's one thing. It's idyllic. In the summer, I pick vegetables from the garden every day, throwing dirt-caked carrots into a wicker basket just like they do in food documentaries—for two months of the year. Here in the north, the idea of producing what I need all year round is totally unsustainable. My winter table would get austere pretty quickly.

Most of the time I shop at the grocery store, prowling the aisles like a crabby mountain lion. If, like me, you take a pleasure in the hunt, though, you will find deals and disappointments and happy surprises every time. It will be anything but boring.

When you go to the store, don't settle for just anything. Ingredients matter so much. Pinch the peaches, squeeze the avocados, turn the melons over and sniff their bottoms like you're checking a baby's diaper. You have to. A lot of commercial produce is engineered to look better than it tastes. If you narrow your eyes and look for subtler clues, you'll see the smoother skins on the limes that indicate they'll be juicier, or the opalescent gleam on a fillet of fresh fish. And if you get home and find that the yogurt is curdled (meaning it was frozen in transit) or the ground pork smells like a barnyard, march it right back to the store. At my local grocery store, the manager can see me coming by the way I walk in the front door, and he no longer asks me for the receipt.

My pantry is so well stocked I could probably open a country store. I'm not sure if this is because I live twenty-five miles from the nearest grocery store or because I'm a hoarder, but I suspect it's a little of both. We're talking three packs of tamarind paste, four kinds of lentils, six kinds of rice. Jugs of peanut oil, big bottles of olive oil, three open jars of walnut oil. A collection of ramen from the whole Asian diaspora. I tell myself that remembering where the pantry ingredients live keeps my brain active, like memorizing phone numbers or playing bridge, but the truth is, every day is only as good as my last game of memory match. If I were hospitalized tomorrow, Aaron would never be able to find the ingredients to cook dinner. The pantry, colorful and overstocked and slightly deranged-looking, is obviously my private domain.

I suspect that it has some deeper psychological roots. When I feel down, I buy food. When I feel up, I buy food. When the bank account dips low, the first thing I do is go to the grocery store and buy polenta, beans, Arborio rice, popcorn—anything to sandbag the pantry and make me feel safe. Some people keep three-months' income in the bank at all times; I have at least three months' worth of ingredients. Every day I cook from it and whittle it down a bit. Every other day, I add more to it with my incessant grocery shopping, bringing it back to par. I've come to accept that my food bunker represents an existential battle that cannot be won.

All that said, let's comb through it, in a selected fashion, because I have some thoughts.

Dry Storage

Flour

Most of the recipes in this book call for all-purpose flour, but it's important to keep in mind that brands do vary. Some have a higher protein content—more gluten, good for producing the chew you need in a loaf of bread—and some have a lower protein content—less gluten, good for making cakes and biscuits. Back in the day, protein content varied from region to region. The South grew soft wheat with a low protein content, which is why Southerners have a well-deserved reputation for making biscuits lofty and light as clouds. The Midwest grew hard spring wheat with a high protein content that was valued for its strength, the reason the region became known for its bread and, notably, one signature dessert: the double-crust pie. Midwestern pie crust recipes trick the hard wheat flour into tenderness. Their high ratio of fat to flour disrupts the flour's natural inclination to form chewy, glutinous strings. That is why vintage cookbooks call it "short pastry," because all that fat breaks the gluten down into frustrated, short-tempered pieces that can't help but be tender.

These days, most flour mills mix their wheats and sell their products around the world, so regionality isn't as much of a factor. But some mills grind their flour finer than others, which affects water absorption, and that will throw off baking recipes more than you might think.

If I'm just fooling around, I'll use locally ground wheat and rye and spelt flours, because freshly ground flour is kind of a revelation. But for the sake of consistency here, I used the standard and widely available Gold Medal all-purpose flour, which has a protein content of 10.5 percent. I always get the bleached. Its pH differs slightly from the unbleached, and in my experience, baked goods made with it rise higher and more reliably.

Oil

Peanut oil is really the best choice for both deep- and shallow-frying. It burns the cleanest and has the most pleasing flavor should some oil cling to the surface of your crust. Given the rise of peanut allergies, though, I usually fry in canola oil. Avoid generic vegetable oils, because some of the off-brands foam up dangerously in the frying pot.

The only kind of olive oil to buy is extra-virgin. My mainstay is a rich, buttery, decent but not exorbitant Spanish oil, which I buy by the liter, though I also keep a smaller bottle of greener, more peppery Italian extra-virgin on hand for drizzling on fresh vegetables and salads.

Sesame oil should be "toasted" sesame oil, dark in color and, preferably, Korean. Pressed from toasted sesame seeds, fresh sesame oil smells like roasted peanuts. Light sesame oil tastes nothing like the dark and can't be substituted. (I'm not quite sure of its best use. Tanning leather? Deep-frying? Feed me your tips.) Store sesame oil in the refrigerator after opening it.

Dried Legumes

Dried beans rarely go bad, but they do age. The packages are never dated, so your only clue is a pot of beans that refuses to soften. When I can, I buy beans from the bulk bins in natural foods markets, where I can be reasonably sure that the clientele keeps the beans on heavy rotation. Or I order from online sites that specialize in new-crop beans (like Rancho Gordo).

Chickpeas are especially susceptible to old age, and they can sometimes take hours to cook. When cooking chickpeas, I almost always add a scant teaspoon of baking soda. It lowers the pH and speeds up the process. A pinch of baking soda also works like a charm when you're cooking any kind of bean in hard, minerally water.

I like to buy the small, firm lentils that hold their shape when cooked, like the French slate-colored lentilles du Puy (often labeled French green lentils) or black Beluga lentils, or, when I can find them, Italian Casteluccio lentils. As with all dried legumes, rinse well before cooking, and presoak if you have time.

Rice

When possible, buy rice at smaller ethnic markets rather than supermarkets or big-box stores. The selection is better and tied to a specific region (e.g., basmati rice from southern India or Pakistan, rather than just "basmati"), and the bags often specify the harvest year. New-crop rice is always more delicate and fragrant. When I go to one of these markets, I try to limit my focus to just four types of rice: **Basmati** is light and loose on the plate and makes your whole house smell like freshly baked buttered bread. Round **sushi rice** cooks into pearly, elegant, distinct grains. (And sushi rice can also be substituted for Spanish Bomba paella rice.) Opaque white **sticky rice** from Southeast Asia (also known as glutinous rice) is chewy and translucent, and the cooked rice will hold together in a round ball but fall apart into springy grains when sauced. There is no substitute. **Jasmine rice**, semi-sticky, fragrant, and neutral, is my gold standard. I buy a Chinese brand new-crop rice in 25-pound bags. Although I don't particularly care for the brown versions of rice varieties that are more delicate when polished, like brown basmati, I can appreciate a nice nutty, brown round rice. But, I think it behaves and tastes more like a grain.

Vinegar

Apple cider vinegar does the heavy lifting around here, because it's both affordable and ubiquitous in the Midwest. (The natural version, with a floating "mother," tastes the most nuanced.) I also use both **red** and **white wine vinegars** regularly, and I love the caramel-like flavor of **sherry vinegar** for vinaigrettes. (Softer, more expensive wine vinegars should always be refrigerated after opening; because they're so natural, they'll eventually get funky and separate.) I appreciate the clean neutrality of **rice wine vinegar**—always unseasoned. A high-end imported **balsamic vinegar** can be explosively delicious drizzled over summer lettuces, but you'll pay for it, and cheaper balsamics are a pale version of the real thing. Although if you reduce ordinary balsamic vinegar by half in a saucepan, it makes a pretty decent substitute.

I keep a big jug of **distilled white vinegar** on hand for pickling. (You can make pickles with apple cider vinegar, if you don't mind the sepia-toned cast.) Distilled white vinegar gives pickles the jolt of spine-sparking tartness that many recipes require—and it's the only one that works to re-create my Grandma Addie's pepper cukes (page 229). Nothing else has quite the same bite.

Citric Acid

The word *acid* may sound a little alarming, but citric acid is nothing to fear; it's found naturally in citrus fruits. Powdered citric acid is used commercially to preserve canned or jarred foods, and at home to add a surprise jolt of tartness (see Black Currant Finger Jell-O, page 44, and Rhubarb Lemonade, page 308). And on the household-hint front, if you have hard water (as I do), lob a tablespoon of citric acid into your dishwasher. Acid eats base, and it cuts right through caked-on calcium.

Vanilla

I like to keep a few **vanilla beans** on hand for holiday baking and for making custards. Vanilla seeds have a more subtle presence than the extract but are more haunting. Fresh vanilla beans are flexible and feel like leather. To keep them that way, store them in a tightly sealed plastic bag.

Real, unadulterated **vanilla extract** has become outrageously expensive. Given the skilled handwork needed to pollinate and harvest vanilla, I don't begrudge producers their price, but still: the stuff will break the bank. I'm not tempted to save money by using lower-quality vanilla extract, the kind that many of us knew growing up, because the real thing has ruined it for me.

But when I run out of good vanilla extract, or feel like the expense doesn't justify the use, I swap in the same measurement of dark spiced rum. It's just as flavorful and potent but costs less per tablespoon. (I like Myer's dark rum, or ideally, Minnesota-based Far North Distillery's spiced rum, a perfectly balanced and subtle take on a classic.)

Asian Condiments

When **fish sauce** is good, it's very, very good. It will have a sharp sea funk on the nose but taste round and almost sweet in the mouth. When fish sauce tastes bad, it's probably rotten and been sitting open on the shelf too long. Red Boat brand has a well-deserved cult following and is gaining distribution in mainstream supermarkets, but 3 Crabs brand is a decent runner-up. If you'll be keeping an opened bottle of fish sauce for a while, store it in the refrigerator.

Toban djan (or doubanjiang) is a spicy, earthy, fermented Chinese chile bean paste, and it can be found in many markets large and small. Lee Kum Kee markets their toban djan for the American market, but if you're shopping in an Asian market, look for jars labeled doubanjiang or Sichuan (Szechuan) spicy bean paste. I add toban djan to all kinds of things. (For example, if you're making a soup that's mysteriously lacking in flavor, a teaspoon of toban djan will add the necessary depth.) When using it, mind the salt content of the rest of your recipe, because some brands are saltier than others.

My mainstay **soy sauce** is light (sometimes called "thin") Chinese soy sauce, more delicate and refined than the cheaper dark soy sauce. For everyday cooking, I buy Kimlan, Wan Ja Shan, and Pearl River Bridge brands or, in a pinch, Kikkoman, all of which are made from a combination of soybeans and wheat. Avoid artificial soy sauces with ingredient lists that include hydrolyzed soy protein, caramel color, and/or corn syrup. (Sweet dark soy sauces can be delicious too, but they can't be substituted for light soy sauce.) Japanese soy sauce (*shoyu*) is usually made from both wheat and soy, and I especially like *usikuchi,* which has a light color and high-ringing salinity to it that works well in vinaigrettes and sauces. **Tamari**, a naturally gluten-free Japanese-style soy sauce made from fermented soybeans, has a rich bottomless flavor and is thicker and darker than light soy. It tints sauces like a drop of black paint.

Maple Syrup

Maple syrup is my alt-sweetener of choice. I generally avoid buying it at the grocery store and instead try to get it at farmers' markets from local producers. (Some producers also sell granulated maple sugar, which is made by cooking maple syrup past the syrup stage until it turns granular. Dry and highly aromatic, maple sugar turns buttered toast into dessert.) I never refrigerate my maple syrup, and I always keep a small jar out on the counter, where it's always at the liquid ready for pouring into a recipe, for everything from desserts to marinades to sauces.

Bay Leaves

One aged khaki-colored bay leaf won't influence a pot of soup one iota, but two or three nice olive-green bay leaves will give it flavor for days. If you plan to cook from this book in any kind of depth, you'll want to stock up, because I have a thing for bay leaves. I buy bags of dried Turkish bay leaves from Penzey's, on a subscription. California bay leaves, whether fresh or dried, have a bold, floral—almost citrusy—fragrance. They're nice too, but they don't taste like the Turkish bay leaves I know and love.

Dried Red Chinese Chiles

I use a lot of semi-hot dried red Chinese chiles. They're spicy when used en masse (not fearfully so), but two or three added to a soup or broth bring a latent, smoldering heat. I use them a lot in the recipes in this book, and when you see them called for, I'm always referring to the thin, flat, mildly spicy 2-inch-long red chiles I buy at Asian markets. On the chile heat index, they score somewhere in the medium-hot zone. They may go by names such as Japones or Tien-Tsin or Sichuan chile, but the bags I buy are labeled more generically.

Perishables

Herbs

There are two kinds of herbs: hardy and soft. Hardier herbs—sage, thyme, rosemary, marjoram—have woodier stems and a more resinous flavor, and they will last longer in the refrigerator. I use them fresh all year round, but more often in my winter cooking. The hardy herbs retain a lot of flavor when dried, so stock the spice drawer with dried thyme, rosemary, sage, and oregano, the rare soft herb that tastes better dried than fresh. A bundle of fresh sage wrapped with kitchen string and hung from a cabinet handle will dry out within a week (and is also a great emergency hostess gift).

Softer herbs—basil, chives, parsley, tarragon, savory, mint, cilantro, and oregano—are more fragile and expire more quickly, so I tend to use them more often in the summer, picked fresh from my herb bed. But there are times in the middle of February when I'd kill for a taste of summer and so I buy that fresh basil in the plastic clamshell pack. Its flavor will be a mere ghost of its summer self, but it meets a certain need. Cilantro is a better year-round bet, and I rarely leave the store without buying a bunch or two. Still, winter cilantro doesn't hold a candle to summer-market cilantro, which tastes so much bossier. I always find the best cilantro in Asian or Latin markets, where it's sold with the root ends still attached.

Both cilantro and parsley will keep better if you wash them soon after bringing them home. Chop off the tail ends of the stems, dunk the bouquet in a bowl of cold water, swishing to remove grit—the leaves can be sandy—and pick off any yellow leaves that float to the surface, then shake it over the sink and roll up in two layers of paper towels. Packed in a plastic bag and stored in the fridge, cilantro will last a week and parsley up to 2 weeks. The same method works really well for dill, somewhat for thyme and sage and rosemary, and hardly at all for basil. Basil is happiest when stored roots down in a tall glass of water in the fridge, like a bouquet of flowers.

Lemons

I must confess a weakness for **Meyer lemons**. Conventional lemons are picked and shipped in a green state and then ripened in storage, and every so often I'll get one that looks faithfully yellow but whose juice tastes green and astringent—evidence that it was picked too early. Meyers are picked ripe. They're more fragrant and sweeter, and they have a softer acidity. (They're also more perishable, so be sure to store them in the refrigerator.) I buy them at my local grocery store, and if they're available even here in small-town northern Minnesota, their range must be wide. They're a bit pricier than conventional lemons, but they also yield more juice, so pennywise, it's a wash. If a sauce or vinaigrette made with conventional lemon juice tastes slightly too sharp and green, you can just add a small pinch of sugar to bring it back into balance.

Onions and Shallots

Yellow storage onions, the ones with tight skins, are grown specifically to be cured (or dried) and stored before shipping. Most of them have a pleasant, peppery bite, but they can easily turn the corner from well-aged to sharp and musty. So I stick to sweet onions—Vidalia, Walla Walla, and their branded look-alikes. Their skins are thin and wispy, easy to peel, and dicing them doesn't make you cry. They're higher in moisture and sugar content, which makes them quicker to melt down into sweet, caramelized slush. Note that 1 large regulation-size Vidalia yields 1¾ to 2 cups when cut into medium dice; the jumbos yield just over 2 cups.

When you can get fresh shallots, shiny and heavy and tight in their skins, they're sweet enough to use raw in salads. The long-storage thick-skinned shallots I usually see at the grocery store aren't always so nice, so I generally use them for cooking.

Garlic

Garlic is one of the few things I don't grow in my garden, because, frankly, it's a space hog. It takes a full two seasons to ripen, all the while sitting on precious garden-bed real estate. Instead I buy a few heads of garlic nearly every time I go to the grocery store—they're cheap and oddly perishable. After you've peeled back the papery skin and begun to pluck out cloves, the rest of the head will dry out pretty quickly. And nothing ruins a dish more effectively or mysteriously than a few cloves of stanky old garlic. After harvesting the large, easy-to-peel cloves all the way around the head, toss the skinny inside cloves aside and save them for throwing into stock or into the cavity of a roast chicken.

In the spring and fall, when fresh garlic comes into the markets, I buy as much as I can get, but I use it differently from regular garlic. Fresh garlic is sticky and mild, and it can be sautéed in mass quantities. It functions more like a vegetable than an aromatic.

Potatoes

Speaking from the town home to the largest French fry factory in America, surrounded by fields upon fields of giant russet potatoes, I want to say that it's really important to buy organic potatoes. The chemicals added to conventional potatoes are a real horror show. Potatoes naturally grow well in light, sandy soil, but super-sized potatoes require a lot of added nitrogen. Like sponges, potatoes absorb everything around them, from fertilizer to anti-sprouting agents, and their skins are too thin to protect them from any of it. In the fall, I buy potatoes by the bushel from a local Amish farmer, store them in the refrigerator, and try to use them before they begin to sprout—which is usually around the first of the year.

Bacon

Long story short, I'm descended from a family of German American butchers—something of a Minnesota bacon dynasty—and am a bit of a zealot about bacon. Here's what you're looking for in good bacon: fat that feels rock solid when cold. When properly cured (without too much sugary, dextrose-pumped brine) and slowly cold-smoked over wood, bacon will feel firm. It will cube up neatly. Its fat will be thick and opaque and will never smear on your board.

Always save surplus bacon fat! Roast vegetables in it, or add it to popcorn or scrambled eggs. I even add it to salsa (see page 250).

Cream

The best cream is the thickest, heaviest kind you can find. Not whipping cream, which is actually a lighter-weight cream fortified with carrageenan to help it whip to a light froth. Some brands confuse things by promising "heavy whipping cream," but I've found that the word that really matters most is *heavy*. The best heavy cream will be pasteurized, not ultra-pasteurized, and thickly clotted at the top. It will pour slowly, like motor oil, and whip to a nice heavy drift.

I'm all about having just two types of dairy (heavy cream and whole-fat milk) on the grocery list rather than three, so I rarely buy half-n-half (which spoils more quickly than heavy cream). Besides, half-n-half can always be made by literally measuring half-milk and half-cream.

Butter

I used salted butter for the recipes in my first cookbook, because that was what my mom and many Midwestern cooks before her had always used. They were loyal to it, and so was I. But I've actually always preferred the flavor of unsalted butter. When I chip off a bit to melt on my tongue, it tastes creamy, not fatty. Sitting out on the counter on a hot summer day, it seems to melt more slowly than the salted. And because it can't rely on salt as a preservative, I assume it must be fresher. Land O'Lakes is a solid choice for everyday cooking, and it has the perfect water content for baking high, lofty cakes. Higher-butterfat butters, like creamy Kerrygold, work wonders in cookies and pastries.

Eggs

All the eggs in this book are large.

When we had laying hens, I used their eggs, and what they say is true: freshly laid eggs taste better, and the yolks are orange, as thick as paint. They were fun to bring home, and fascinating for a while, but if I were to say I missed the hens, I'd be lying. They fouled the yard and ate my flowers, always seemed frazzled, and couldn't make eye contact. Throughout the long, cold subzero winter when we heated their pen to keep their beady little toes from freezing, I constantly worried about them. It's just so hard to tell if a chicken is truly happy.

Now I buy farm-fresh eggs from other people, but even when we had our own hens, I always kept some store-bought eggs in my refrigerator. One day as I was waiting for a hen to lay an egg so I could finish making a cake I thought, "I'm into slow food, but this is ridiculous." Even if you buy farm eggs for your morning scramble, keep an extra dozen store-bought eggs for baking. They cost less than two bucks and last a suspiciously long time.

Frozen

The freezer is the place where good intentions get postponed or, sometimes, where they go to die. It's tempting to think of frozen ingredients as perpetually preserved, but all freezers are not created equal. Some, like the freezer compartments in refrigerators, are supposed to hold a temperature of 0°F. But if the ice cream is more scoopable than rock-hard, the temperature is probably closer to 10°F—cold enough to keep a pound of hamburger stiff, but not enough to keep it from marching slowly toward spoilage. I think of my refrigerator freezer as a short-term holding tank where I can store the small items that I use on an almost daily basis, like fresh Thai chiles, and poppy seeds, and makrut lime leaves, fresh bread crumbs, and lemongrass, twisted into knots, for throwing into soup. And, of course, ice cream. If I store meat in this freezer, I use it up within a few months.

Dedicated deep freezers, like the cheap white top-loaders that many a Midwesterner keeps in their basement or garage, are designed for longer storage. They have an adjustable temperature dial, which I turn to -10°F or lower. The difference between 0°F and -15°F means the world to a frozen pork chop. So if you plan on freezing a lot of locally raised meat, you might want to think about getting a dedicated deep freezer. Or two, if you want to keep your protein options open.

Ironically, the only drawback to a big top-loading deep freezer is its size. Once it gets full, those "I'll use it someday" parcels have a way of burrowing their way down to the frosty freezer-burnt land of, "What the heck was this?" My two deep freezers hold a lot of meat, fillets of walleye, bags of berries I plan to make into jam someday, egg roll and pot sticker wrappers, loaves of bread, and the kidneys from every pig I've butchered since 2011. (If you like pork kidneys, come and get 'em.) The name of the game here is rotation, rotation, rotation. Every winter I set a goal: to cook from my deep freezers all winter long so that by the time spring comes, I can see the bare white plastic bottom of at least one of them. Then it's time to knock off the ice rafts with a hammer, defrost the freezer, and start all over again.

Individual Recipe Index

When composing a menu, take the most brilliant, flavorful ingredient you have—it could be shiny fresh eggplant, or beautiful summer tomatoes, or a hunk of marbled pastured pork—and then build the meal around it.

I love a meatless meal, but for crowd-pleasing impact and sheer caloric density, animal protein is still the sun around which my vegetable planets revolve. (The key to balance lies in multiple vegetable planets.) Imagine its best starch buddy, whether crispy or mashed or creamy, and build out the rest of the plate with a mind to the flowing juices. Maybe you need a light potato and cabbage pancake to soak up panfried chicken's natural golden jus. Or caramelized sweet potatoes to mash into coconut rice. Or something simple, crunchy, and raw. If one side is punchy and bold, the other can be calming, even plain. Not everything should be a crescendo. Meals need their rhythm section too.

Appetizers are the most expendable part of any dinner party. My menu sketches often include an elegant starter, but when pressed for time I will red-line it and just set out something quick and scrappy (see page 80 for ideas). In my ideal world, the dessert has been made in advance.

Cooking for multiple dietary restrictions is an unavoidable issue, and there are times when making such a menu feels like working on an unsolvable math problem. 1 GF (gluten-free) plus 2 VEG (vegetarian) plus 1 PSK (picky, starch-only kid) multiplied by 4 CAR (carnivores) equals exactly zero. When faced with math like that, again, just add another vegetable side.

* a make-way-ahead recipe (can be made up to 24 hours in advance or more)

** a make-somewhat-ahead recipe (can be made up to 3 hours in advance or fully prepped before last-minute assembly)

Dips and Spreads

250 chipotle-cashew salsa with bacon fat**

204 reformed dill dip with iced garden vegetables*

38 homemade Boursin with grilled bread*

253 deer liver mousse with pickled grapes on the vine*

102 deviled egg dip*

Fish or Shellfish Starters

270 raw oyster bar

152 cast-iron garlic shrimp with chorizo and green olives*

119 crab legs with spicy black vinegar dipping sauce**

93 sardines with lardo and Parmesan on bran crispbread

Appetizers

239   grilled garlic bread with bacon fat and smeared tomato

26   grilled pickled half-hots★★

59   steamed eggplant with chile oil, lemon, and 'nduja★★

164   baked spiced quince with soft cheese★

165   sylta★

149   pâté grandmère★

190   deviled eggs with Roman Jewish fried artichokes★★

Soups

96   yellow split pea soup with spareribs★

271   corn soup with coconut and littleneck clams★★

177   green cabbage sipping soup★

259   chicken or turkey stock

Leafy Salads

53   bok choy salad with ramen-almond brittle

131   baby greens with glassy pecans and Pecorino★★

161   watercress and Bibb with smoky blue cheese dressing★★

187   green salad with invisible vinaigrette★★

263   bitter lettuces with warm brown butter vinaigrette, fried shallots, and duck gizzards confit★★

Creamy Salads

86   iceberg plate salad with green chile dressing★★

64   winter white salad★★

196   creamy baby turnip salad with dill

Marinated Room-Temperature Vegetables or Beans

300   zucchini carpaccio★★

184   marinated roasted beets and grapes with radicchio and hazelnuts★

97   warm wilted spinach with caramelized celery root and crispy shiitakes

31   boiled zucchini with herb oil★★

110   sweet-and-sour marinated peppers with Swiss chard★★

311   grilled leek salad with hard-boiled eggs and smoky anchovy dressing★★

208   three-bean salad with salumi, celery hearts, and smoked provolone★

298   marinated chickpea salad with lemon and Swiss chard★

Juicy or Fruity Salads

314   sour orange platter salad with parsley and pistachios★★

213   tomato-on-tomato salad

244   muskmelon Caprese

278   honeydew and cucumber salad with cilantro-lime dressing

34   smoky tomato terrine★

49   smashed garlic cucumbers★

127   sour orange cranberry jelly

229   Addie's peppered cukes

Hot Cooked Vegetables

43   sopped greens with butter-roasted walnuts

229   braised collards with smoky tomato★

231   green and yellow beans with garlic

54   stir-fried peas and their greens

158   creamed poblano spinach★

195   wok-fried black pepper asparagus

276   stir-fried greens and leeks

74 bacon-fat roasted cauliflower with herb salad

159 caramelized carrots★★

170 citrusy braised red cabbage★

173 crispy curried cauliflower with mustard seeds

184 creamed carrot coins

260 cider-braised red cabbage wedges★★

210 milk corn

Creamy or Mashed Starches

227 coconut creamed corn with basil oil★

88 steamed and glazed white sweet potatoes★★

130 turnip-date gratin★★

30 salt potatoes

156 aligot (stretchy mashed potatoes with cheese)★★

169 mascarpone whipped potatoes

Crispy or Browned-Edge Starches

183 yuca fries persillade

126 classic buttery dressing★

129 spiralized roast potatoes

72 matafans: raised potato and cabbage pancake

109 Fun House baked potatoes★★

197 hot water rolls★

Rice

50 jasmine rice★★

89 garlic and coconut–scented rice★★

275 sticky rice★★

Slow-Cooked Meat

46 Mei's ginger-glazed baby back ribs★★

105 Bundt pan chicken with bagna cauda butter

124 lardo-crisped roasted turkey with mushroom gravy

179 slow-smoked brisket pastrami with creamy zhug

182 quick-steamed pastrami

193 ham cooked in milk, honey, and sage

154 smoked prime rib with celery-leaf salsa verde

294 open-air barbecue with salmuera and chimichurri

309 feijoada for a crowd (black beans with smoked pork and spareribs)★

Quick-Cooked Meat

242 smoked sausages with mustard-miso sauce and arugula

207 homeground burgers with hot-and-sauer pub cheese★★

27 wood-fired rib eyes with fava butter★★

70 crispy smashed chicken breasts with gin-and-sage jus

168 spiced meatballs with cream gravy★★

256 backstrap (venison loin) bordelaise

222 double-dipped fried chicken★★

273 pork-stuffed barbecued chicken thighs★★

Vegetarian Centerpieces

39 nightshade confit★★

61 chitarra pasta with roasted cherry tomatoes★★

72 matafans: raised potato and cabbage pancake

262 squash bake with goat cheese custard★★

240 potato tortilla★★

Fish and Shellfish

152 cast-iron garlic shrimp with chorizo and green olives★★

83 deep-fried sour cream walleye

119 crab legs with spicy black vinegar dipping sauce★★

Drinks

238 orange Julius with basil

202 cilantro lime juleps★★

248 whiskey-sour gelatin shots with potted sour cherries★

308 rhubarb lemonade★

45 black currant juice★

99 coffee with Chartreuse and smoked almond praline★★

Fruit Desserts

233 lemon nemesis★

44 black currant finger Jell-O®★

68 apple fritto misto with peels, lemons, and sage

75 pastis du Quercy★★

90 Pavlova with winter citrus, good olive oil, and sea salt★

174 cranberry cookie tart★★

214 rhubarb-raspberry pie★★

199 rhubarb-almond envelope tart★★

Cakes, Cookies, Custards

279 single-origin chocolate cake★

138 Bohemian poppy seed coffee cake★

188 sticky date olive oil cake★★

140 mincemeat baklava★

144 olive oil thumbprints with lemon curd★

143 sesame pralines★

145 lacquered walnuts★

251 apricot snickerdoodles★

303 spicy cinnamon flan★

133 buttercup bourbon pie★★

Acknowledgments

I've put some very good people through the wringer while writing this book. I was slow, I was indecisive, I frayed nerves and concerned my agent; this book took an absurdly long time. Slow-rowing a book into being isn't in itself a bad thing, until you realize that you're not the only passenger in the boat, and that there are some very fine people riding alongside you. This book owes its life to this incredibly talented, patient, and well-regulated village.

A mere thank you feels too cheap to describe the everlasting gratitude I feel for my editor, Melanie Tortoroli. Thank you for your faith, encouragement, and seemingly endless supply of patience when my Fridays became Mondays— and then Wednesdays. Through it all, you managed to always bring fresh ideas, and a sharp, wise, compassionate eye to these pages. Every Thanksgiving, I will give thanks for you.

Thank you Janis Donnaud—for so much; everything, really—but specifically with this book, thank you for knowing exactly when to push and when to pull, and for being a truly compassionate listener.

To Holly Coulis, one of my favorite artists, thank you for so generously lending your painting to this cover. This body of work was my first, my only, inspiration for the jacket, and I'm honored you agreed to contribute to this project.

Kristin Teig, I truly don't know how you stay so humble. I love these photos. They remind me how thrilling it was to make this book with you. I remain in awe of your talent, your endless creative curiosity, your ability to shift with the rolling tides and to always find the center of delicious. Thank you also to Rick Holbrook, Kristin's assistant, for the good taste and sharp wit you brought to the shoot. Thank you Alison Hoekstra, my longtime prop stylist, my friend, my hoarder-in-arms; you have an unfailingly good eye, a covetable work ethic, and a true gift for persuasion. Thank you, Catrine Kelty, my incredible food stylist, for putting up with me. I am grateful for your deep skill set and your talent. Thank you to the photoshoot kitchen crew, my longtime friends Christina Montouri and Luisa Fernanda Garcia-Gomez—I couldn't have done it without either of you—and to Evelyn Staats, my hardworking intern. Thank you also to my unflappable assistant, Faith Kern.

Thank you to Steve Attardo, art director, for designing an absolutely stunning cover package. Thank you to Meredith McGinnis for your patience and willingness to pivot. Will Scarlett, I so appreciate your creativity, kindness, and doggedness. Also at Norton, thanks to Lucy Thompson for designing a book that met, and exceeded, the one I had in my mind's eye; to Susan Sanfrey for the marathon-like endurance you brought to our editing sessions; and to Julia Druskin for deftly shaping these challenging rolling-recipe pages. Special thanks, topped off with extra apologies and whipped cream, go to Judith Sutton, my copyeditor, who basically spun straw into gold.

Thank you to my trusted friends and early readers Chelsey Johnson and Ted Lee, both of whom read multiple early versions of this book, some of them just shards of thoughts, and who always encouraged me to see the bits as valuable kindling.

Thank you Cameron Gainer for letting me borrow the name of your project space— Company—and for your, and Olga's, consistently radical hospitality.

I want to thank my friends and family who braved the eye of the camera to come to these parties. I love seeing all of you in these pages:

Joe Allen, Sadie Allen, Zoe Allen, Claire Arnold, Drew Arnold, Jen Arnold, Vivian Arnold, Mike Berre, Bruce Brummitt, Kerrie Coborn, Matt D'Incau, Rebecca Dallinger, Ranae Doll, Bruce Engebretsen, Dan Haataja, Erin Haefele, Ryan Haefele, Megan Handke, Katie Kueber, Ginny McClure, Kyle McClure, Nick Muller, Jill Odegaard, Grace Officer, Todd Officer, Tyler Officer, Budd Parker, Elise Rice, Melanie Rice, Robert Saxton, Jim Schell, Vern Scholz, Deborah Solien, T. L. Solien, Franny Stewart, Veritas Stewart, Eleanor Strand, Gretchen Strand,

Alex Thielen, Heidi Thielen, Henry Thielen, Jackson Thielen, Jenny Thielen, Olivia Thielen, Presley Thielen, Cheryl Valois, Beth Walker, Natalya Walker, David Welle, Brian Wiggins, Sally Wiggins, and Sawyer Wiggins. Special thanks to Nicolle LaFleur, Didi Ning LaFleur, and Tea Renee Ning LaFleur for letting us invade Walden, their cabin on Linbom Lake.

Thank you Deer Campers for so gamely taking up screw guns and helping us assemble the new kitchen cabinets at the eleventh hour before one of these photo shoots: Chris Bailey, Matson Bailey, Brian Bruse, Darin Bruse, Todd Bruse, Chris Hand, Woody Hartman, Rob Fischer, John Friedrichson, and Chad Scott—and Beth "Friedski" Friedrichson, especially.

Thank you to Sara Woster for the use of her painting in the deer hunting party spread, and for letting us use her and Rob's house next door during times of production.

Thanks to my family, my parents Karen and Ted, their spouses Bob and Mary, my brothers Marc and Bob, and Jill, George, Maria, and Carolyn Thielen, and my Spangler family, Carolyn and Maurice, Sarah and Paul and kids, for your sustaining support.

Thank you Hilly, for your attentive listening skills and your glorious fur.

Thanks to Aaron and Hank for understanding, for waiting, for encouraging, and for holding everything together, including me. This is my kind of sandwich. The best part is, as always, the jelly.

Index

Note: Page references in *italics* refer to photographs.

A

Aligot (Stretchy Mashed Potatoes with Cheese), 156–57, *157*

almonds

Bok Choy Salad with Ramen-Almond Brittle, *52*, 53

Coffee with Chartreuse and Smoked Almond Praline, 99–100

Rhubarb-Almond Envelope Tart, 199–200, *201*

Single-Origin Chocolate Cake, 279–80

anchovies

Bundt Pan Chicken with Bagna Cauda Butter, 105–7

Grilled Leek Salad with Hard-Boiled Eggs and Smoky Anchovy Dressing, 311–13, *312*

Smoked Prime Rib with Celery-Leaf Salsa Verde, 154–55

aniseeds

Lacquered Walnuts, *137*, 145–46

appetizers and starters

Baked Spiced Quince with Soft Cheese, 164

Cast-Iron Garlic Shrimp with Chorizo and Green Olives, 152, *153*

Chipotle-Cashew Salsa with Bacon Fat, 250

Crab Legs with Spicy Black Vinegar Dipping Sauce, 119–20, *120*

Deer Liver Mousse with Pickled Grapes on the Vine, 253–55

Deviled Egg Dip, 102–5, *104*

Deviled Eggs with Roman Jewish Fried Artichokes, 190–92, *192*

easy, ideas for, 80–81

Grilled Garlic Bread with Bacon Fat and Smeared Tomato, 239

Grilled Pickled Half-Hots, 26, *33*

Homemade Boursin with Grilled Bread, 38–39

Pâté Grandmère, 149–51

Raw Oyster Bar, 270

Reformed Dill Dip with Iced Garden Vegetables, 204–5

Sardines with Lardo and Parmesan on Bran Crispbread, *93*, 93–95

Steamed Eggplant with Chile Oil, Lemon, and 'Nduja, *58*, 59–60

Sylta, 165–66, *167*

apples

Apple Fritto Misto with Peels, Lemons, and Sage, *68*, 68–69

Pastis du Quercy, 75–78, *79*

Apricot Snickerdoodles, *251*, 251–52

Artichokes, Roman Jewish Fried, Deviled Eggs with, 190–92, *192*

Arugula and Mustard-Miso Sauce, Smoked Sausages with, 242, *243*

Asian condiments, 332

Asparagus, Wok-Fried Black Pepper, 195

B

Backstrap (Venison Loin) Bordelaise, *256*, 256–58

bacon

Braised Collards with Smoky Tomato, 229–30, *230*

buying, 334

Feijoada for a Crowd, *307*, 309–10

Grilled Pickled Half-Hots, 26, *33*

bacon fat

Bacon Fat–Roasted Cauliflower with Herb Salad, 74

Chipotle-Cashew Salsa with Bacon Fat, 250

Grilled Garlic Bread with Bacon Fat and Smeared Tomato, 239

ideas for, 334

saving, 334

Bagna Cauda Butter, Bundt Pan Chicken with, 105–7

baking sheets, 323

Baklava, Mincemeat, *137*, 140–41

Barbecue, Open-Air, with Salmuera and Chimichurri, *285*, 294–97, *295*

basil

Basil Oil, 227

Boiled Zucchini with Herb Oil, 31, *32*

Chitarra Pasta with Roasted Cherry Tomatoes, 61–64, *62*

Coconut Creamed Corn with Basil Oil, 227, *230*

Iceberg Plate Salad with Green Chile Dressing, 86, *87*

Muskmelon Caprese, 244, *245*

Orange Julius with Basil, *237*, 238

Tomato-on-Tomato Salad, *212*, 213

bay leaves, 332

beans

dried, buying, 330

Fava Bean Butter, 29, *33*

Feijoada for a Crowd, *307*, 309–10

beans (*continued*)

Green and Yellow Beans with Garlic, *223*, 231

Marinated Chickpea Salad with Lemon and Swiss Chard, 298–300, *299*

Reformed Dill Dip with Iced Garden Vegetables, 204–5

Three-Bean Salad with Salumi, Celery Hearts, and Smoked Provolone, 208–10

beef

Feijoada for a Crowd, *307*, 309–10

Homeground Burgers with Hot-and-Sauer Pub Cheese, *206*, 207–8

Open-Air Barbecue with Salmuera and Chimichurri, *285*, 294–97, *295*

Quick Steamed Pastrami, 182–83

Slow-Smoked Brisket Pastrami with Creamy Zhug, 179–81, *180*

Smoked Prime Rib with Celery-Leaf Salsa Verde, 154–55

Spiced Meatballs with Cream Gravy, 168

Wood-Fired Rib Eye Steaks with Fava Butter, 27–29, *33*

Beets, Marinated Roasted, and Grapes with Radicchio and Hazelnuts, 184–86

Bitter Lettuces with Warm Brown Butter Vinaigrette, Fried Shallots, and Duck Gizzards Confit, 263–66, *264*

black currants

Black Currant Finger Jell-O, 44, *44*

Black Currant Juice, 45

black pepper

Addie's Pepper Cukes, 229

Wok-Fried Black Pepper Asparagus, 195

Black Vinegar Dipping Sauce, Spicy, Crab Legs with, 119–20, *120*

Bok Choy Salad with Ramen-Almond Brittle, *52*, 53

bourbon

Buttercup Bourbon Pie, 133–34, *135*

Cilantro Lime Juleps, 202–4, *203*

Bran Crispbread, *93*, 94–95

breads

Bran Crispbread, *93*, 94–95

Classic Buttery Dressing, *123*, 126

Grilled Garlic Bread with Bacon Fat and Smeared Tomato, 239

Homemade Boursin with Grilled Bread, 38–39

Hot Water Rolls, 197–99

Burgers, Homeground, with Hot-and-Sauer Pub Cheese, *206*, 207–8

butter

Bundt Pan Chicken with Bagna Cauda Butter, 105–7

buying, 335

Fava Bean Butter, 29, *33*

C

cabbage

Cider-Braised Red Cabbage Wedges, 260

Citrusy Braised Red Cabbage, 170, *171*

Green Cabbage Sipping Soup, 177–78, *178*

Matafans: Raised Potato and Cabbage Pancake, 72–74, *73*

Reformed Dill Dip with Iced Garden Vegetables, 204–5

cakes

Bohemian Poppy Seed Coffee Cake, *138*, 138–40

Lemon Nemesis, *232*, 233–34

Pastis du Quercy, 75–78, *79*

Single-Origin Chocolate Cake, 279–80

Sticky Date Olive Oil Cake, 188–89, *189*

capers

Green Salad with Invisible Vinaigrette, 187

Grilled Leek Salad with Hard-Boiled Eggs and Smoky Anchovy Dressing, 311–13, *312*

Smoked Prime Rib with Celery-Leaf Salsa Verde, 154–55

carbon-steel pans, 323

Carpaccio, Zucchini, 300–301

carrots

Caramelized Carrots, 159

Creamed Carrot Coins, 184

Reformed Dill Dip with Iced Garden Vegetables, 204–5

Cashew-Chipotle Salsa with Bacon Fat, 250

cast-iron pans, 322

cauliflower

Bacon Fat–Roasted Cauliflower with Herb Salad, 74

Crispy Curried Cauliflower with Mustard Seeds, 173

Reformed Dill Dip with Iced Garden Vegetables, 204–5

celery

Green Salad with Invisible Vinaigrette, 187

Smoked Prime Rib with Celery-Leaf Salsa Verde, 154–55

Three-Bean Salad with Salumi, Celery Hearts, and Smoked Provolone, 208–10

Winter White Salad, 64–65

Celery Root, Caramelized, and Crispy Shiitakes, Warm Wilted Spinach with, *97*, 97–98

Chartreuse and Smoked Almond Praline, Coffee with, 99–100

cheese

Aligot (Stretchy Mashed Potatoes with Cheese), 156–57, *157*

Baby Greens with Glassy Pecans and Pecorino, 131–32

Baked Spiced Quince with Soft Cheese, 164

Chitarra Pasta with Roasted Cherry Tomatoes, 61–64, *62*

Fava Bean Butter, 29, *33*

Grilled Pickled Half-Hots, 26, *33*

Homeground Burgers with Hot-and-Sauer Pub Cheese, *206*, 207–8

Homemade Boursin with Grilled Bread, 38–39

Mascarpone Whipped Potatoes, 169

Muskmelon Caprese, 244, *245*

Reformed Dill Dip with Iced Garden Vegetables, 204–5

Sardines with Lardo and Parmesan on Bran Crispbread, *93*, 93–95

Smoky Tomato Terrine, 34–36, *35*

Squash Bake with Goat Cheese Custard, 262–63

Three-Bean Salad with Salumi, Celery Hearts, and Smoked Provolone, 208–10

Watercress and Bibb with Smoky Blue Cheese Dressing, 161

Zucchini Carpaccio, 300–301

Cherries, Potted Sour, 249

chicken

Bundt Pan Chicken with Bagna Cauda Butter, 105–7

Chicken Stock, 259

Crispy Smashed Chicken Breasts with Gin-and-Sage Jus, 70–72, *71*

Double-Dipped Fried Chicken, 222–24, *225*

Gizzards Confit, 266

Open-Air Barbecue with Salmuera and Chimichurri, *285*, 294–97, *295*

Pork-Stuffed Barbecued Chicken Thighs, 273–75, *274*

whole, cutting into pieces, 226

chickpeas

dried, buying and cooking, 330

Marinated Chickpea Salad with Lemon and Swiss Chard, 298–300, *299*

chile oil

Homemade Chile Oil, 60

Steamed Eggplant with Chile Oil, Lemon, and 'Nduja, *58*, 59–60

chiles

Chipotle-Cashew Salsa with Bacon Fat, 250

Creamy Zhug, *180*, 181

dried red Chinese, 332

Homemade Chile Oil, 60

Honeydew and Cucumber Salad with Cilantro-Lime Dressing, 278–79

Iceberg Plate Salad with Green Chile Dressing, 86, *87*

Chimichurri, 296

Chipotle-Cashew Salsa with Bacon Fat, 250

chives

Bacon Fat–Roasted Cauliflower with Herb Salad, 74

Chive Oil, 178

Reformed Dill Dip with Iced Garden Vegetables, 204–5

chocolate

Chocolate Syrup, 99

Coffee with Chartreuse and Smoked Almond Praline, 99–100

Single-Origin Chocolate Cake, 279–80

Cider-Braised Red Cabbage Wedges, 260

cilantro

Chimichurri, 296

Chipotle-Cashew Salsa with Bacon Fat, 250

Cilantro Lime Juleps, 202–4, *203*

Creamy Zhug, *180*, 181

Honeydew and Cucumber Salad with Cilantro-Lime Dressing, 278–79

Iceberg Plate Salad with Green Chile Dressing, 86, *87*

cinnamon

Apricot Snickerdoodles, *251*, 251–52

Spicy Cinnamon Flan, *302*, 303–4

citric acid, 331

Clams, Littleneck, and Coconut, Corn Soup with, *271*, 271–72

cleaning up, note on, 316–17

coconut milk

Coconut Creamed Corn with Basil Oil, 227, *230*

Corn Soup with Coconut and Littleneck Clams, *271*, 271–72

Garlic and Coconut–Scented Rice, 89

Coffee Cake, Bohemian Poppy Seed, *138*, 138–40

Coffee with Chartreuse and Smoked Almond Praline, 99–100

colanders, 324

collard greens

Braised Collards with Smoky Tomato, 229–30, *230*

Sopped Greens with Butter-Roasted Walnuts, 43

confit

Gizzards Confit, 266

Nightshade Confit, 39–41, *40*

cookies

Apricot Snickerdoodles, *251*, 251–52

Olive Oil Thumbprints with Lemon Curd, *137*, 144–45

Sesame Pralines, *137*, 143

corn

Coconut Creamed Corn with Basil Oil, 227, *230*

Corn Soup with Coconut and Littleneck Clams, *271*, 271–72

Milk Corn, 210, *211*

Crab Legs with Spicy Black Vinegar Dipping Sauce, 119–20, *120*

cranberries

Cranberry Cookie Tart, 174, *175*

Sour Orange Cranberry Jelly, *123*, 127

cream
  buying, 334
  Coconut Creamed Corn with
    Basil Oil, 227, *230*
  Creamed Carrot Coins, 184
  Sour Cream Whip, 189
  Spiced Meatballs with Cream
    Gravy, 168
  Whipped Cream, 281
Crispbread, Bran, *93*, 94–95
cucumbers
  Addie's Pepper Cukes, 229
  Honeydew and Cucumber
    Salad with Cilantro-Lime
    Dressing, 278–79
  Smashed Garlic Cucumbers,
    49
Curried Cauliflower, Crispy, with
  Mustard Seeds, 173
custards
  Spicy Cinnamon Flan, *302*,
    303–4
  Squash Bake with Goat Cheese
    Custard, 262–63
cutting boards, 325

D

dates
  Sticky Date Olive Oil Cake,
    188–89, *189*
  Turnip-Date Gratin, 130–31
Deer Liver Mousse with Pickled
  Grapes on the Vine, 253–55
desserts
  Apple Fritto Misto with Peels,
    Lemons, and Sage, *68*, 68–69
  Apricot Snickerdoodles, *251*,
    251–52
  Black Currant Finger Jell-O,
    44, *44*
  Bohemian Poppy Seed Coffee
    Cake, *138*, 138–40
  Buttercup Bourbon Pie,
    133–34, *135*
  Cranberry Cookie Tart, 174,
    175
  Lacquered Walnuts, *137*,
    145–46

Lemon Nemesis, *232*, 233–34
Mincemeat Baklava, *137*,
  140–41
Olive Oil Thumbprints with
  Lemon Curd, *137*, 144–45
Pastis du Quercy, 75–78, *79*
Pavlova with Winter Citrus,
  Good Olive Oil, and Salt,
  90–91
Rhubarb-Almond Envelope
  Tart, 199–200, *201*
Rhubarb-Raspberry Pie,
  214–15
Sesame Pralines, *137*, 143
Single-Origin Chocolate Cake,
  279–80
Spicy Cinnamon Flan, *302*,
  303–4
Sticky Date Olive Oil Cake,
  188–89, *189*
Deviled Egg Dip, 102–5, *104*
Deviled Eggs with Roman Jewish
  Fried Artichokes, 190–92,
  192
diffuser, 326
dill
  Creamy Baby Turnip Salad
    with Dill, 196–97
  Green Salad with Invisible
    Vinaigrette, 187
  Reformed Dill Dip with Iced
    Garden Vegetables, 204–5
dips
  Deviled Egg Dip, 102–5, *104*
  Reformed Dill Dip with Iced
    Garden Vegetables, 204–5
Dressing, Classic Buttery, *123*,
  126
drinks
  Black Currant Juice, 45
  Cilantro Lime Juleps, 202–4,
    203
  Coffee with Chartreuse and
    Smoked Almond Praline,
    99–100
  note on, 17–18
  Orange Julius with Basil, *237*,
    238

Rhubarb Lemonade, 308–9
  Whiskey-Sour Gelatin Shots
    with Potted Sour Cherries,
    247, 248–49
duck
  Bitter Lettuces with Warm
    Brown Butter Vinaigrette,
    Fried Shallots, and Duck
    Gizzards Confit, 263–66, *264*
  Gizzards Confit, 266

E

eggplant
  Nightshade Confit, 39–41, *40*
  Steamed Eggplant with Chile
    Oil, Lemon, and 'Nduja, *58*,
    59–60
eggs
  buying, 335
  Deviled Egg Dip, 102–5, *104*
  Deviled Eggs with Roman Jew-
    ish Fried Artichokes, 190–92,
    192
  Grilled Leek Salad with Hard-
    Boiled Eggs and Smoky
    Anchovy Dressing, 311–13,
    312
  Potato Tortilla, 240–41
equipment and tools, 321–27

F

Feijoada for a Crowd, *307*,
  309–10
fennel
  Lacquered Walnuts, *137*,
    145–46
  Winter White Salad, 64–65
fish. *See also* anchovies
  Deep-Fried Sour Cream Wall-
    eye, *83*, 83–85
  Grilled Leek Salad with Hard-
    Boiled Eggs and Smoky
    Anchovy Dressing, 311–13,
    312
  Sardines with Lardo and Par-
    mesan on Bran Crispbread,
    93, 93–95
fish sauce, 331

Flan, Spicy Cinnamon, *302*, 303–4
flour, 330
food processor, 327
freezer foods, 335
funnels, 326

G

garlic
  Bundt Pan Chicken with Bagna
    Cauda Butter, 105–7
  buying, 334
  Cast-Iron Garlic Shrimp with
    Chorizo and Green Olives,
    152, *153*
  fresh, about, 334
  Garlic and Coconut–Scented
    Rice, 89
  Green and Yellow Beans with
    Garlic, *223*, 231
  Grilled Garlic Bread with
    Bacon Fat and Smeared
    Tomato, 239
  Smashed Garlic Cucumbers,
    49
  Smoked Prime Rib with Celery-
    Leaf Salsa Verde, 154–55
gelatin
  Black Currant Finger Jell-O,
    44, *44*
  Whiskey-Sour Gelatin Shots
    with Potted Sour Cherries,
    247, 248–49
Gin-and-Sage Jus, Crispy
  Smashed Chicken Breasts
  with, 70–72, *71*
Ginger-Glazed Baby Back Ribs,
  Mei's, 46–48, *47*
gizzards
  Bitter Lettuces with Warm
    Brown Butter Vinaigrette,
    Fried Shallots, and Duck
    Gizzards Confit, 263–66,
    264
  Gizzards Confit, 266
grapes
  Marinated Roasted Beets and
    Grapes with Radicchio and
    Hazelnuts, 184–86

Pickled Grapes on the Vine,
  254–55
graters, 324
green beans
  Green and Yellow Beans with
    Garlic, *223*, 231
  Three-Bean Salad with Salumi,
    Celery Hearts, and Smoked
    Provolone, 208–10
greens. *See also specific greens*
  Baby Greens with Glassy
    Pecans and Pecorino,
    131–32
  Green Salad with Invisible
    Vinaigrette, 187
  Sopped Greens with Butter-
    Roasted Walnuts, 43
  Stir-Fried Greens and Leeks,
    276–78
  Stir-Fried Peas and Their
    Greens, 54
ground cherries
  Muskmelon Caprese, 244,
    245

H

ham
  Feijoada for a Crowd, *307*,
    309–10
  Ham Cooked in Milk, Honey,
    and Sage, 193–95, *194*
Hazelnuts and Radicchio, Mar-
  inated Roasted Beets and
  Grapes with, 184–86
herbs. *See also specific herbs*
  Bacon Fat–Roasted Cauliflower
    with Herb Salad, 74
  Boiled Zucchini with Herb Oil,
    31, *32*
  Honeydew and Cucumber
    Salad with Cilantro-Lime
    Dressing, 278–79
  types of, 333
Honey, Milk, and Sage, Ham
  Cooked in, 193–95, *194*
Honeydew and Cucumber Salad
  with Cilantro-Lime Dressing,
  278–79

hot pads, 324–25
Hot Water Rolls, 197–99

I

ingredients, 329–35

J

Jell-O, Black Currant Finger, 44,
  44
Jelly, Sour Orange Cranberry,
  123, 127
Juleps, Cilantro Lime, 202–4,
  203

K

knives, 327
kohlrabi
  Iceberg Plate Salad with Green
    Chile Dressing, 86, *87*
  Reformed Dill Dip with Iced
    Garden Vegetables, 204–5
  Winter White Salad, 64–65

L

lamb
  Open-Air Barbecue with Sal-
    muera and Chimichurri, *285*,
    294–97, *295*
lardo
  Lardo-Crisped Roasted Turkey
    with Mushroom Gravy, *123*,
    123–25
  Sardines with Lardo and Par-
    mesan on Bran Crispbread,
    93, 93–95
leeks
  Grilled Leek Salad with Hard-
    Boiled Eggs and Smoky
    Anchovy Dressing, 311–13,
    312
  Stir-Fried Greens and Leeks,
    276–78
lemons
  Apple Fritto Misto with Peels,
    Lemons, and Sage, *68*,
    68–69
  Lemon Nemesis, *232*, 233–34
  Meyer, about, 333

lemons (continued)
  Olive Oil Thumbprints with
    Lemon Curd, *137*, 144–45
  Rhubarb Lemonade, 308–9
lentils
  buying, 330
  Three-Bean Salad with Salumi,
    Celery Hearts, and Smoked
    Provolone, 208–10
lettuce
  Baby Greens with Glassy
    Pecans and Pecorino, 131–32
  Bitter Lettuces with Warm
    Brown Butter Vinaigrette,
    Fried Shallots, and Duck
    Gizzards Confit, 263–66,
    264
  Green Salad with Invisible
    Vinaigrette, 187
  Iceberg Plate Salad with Green
    Chile Dressing, 86, *87*
  Watercress and Bibb with
    Smoky Blue Cheese Dress-
    ing, 161
lime
  Cilantro Lime Juleps, 202–4,
    203
  Honeydew and Cucumber
    Salad with Cilantro-Lime
    Dressing, 278–79
liver
  Deer Liver Mousse with
    Pickled Grapes on the Vine,
    253–55
  Pâté Grandmère, 149–51

M

mandoline, 325
maple syrup, 332
Matafans: Raised Potato and
  Cabbage Pancake, 72–74, *73*
meat. *See also* beef; pork; venison
  Open-Air Barbecue with Sal-
    muera and Chimichurri, *285*,
    294–97, *295*
  Three-Bean Salad with Salumi,
    Celery Hearts, and Smoked
    Provolone, 208–10

Meatballs, Spiced, with Cream
  Gravy, 168
menus
  affordable drinks, 17–18
  composing, 337
  cooking recipes ahead, 14
  notes on, 12–13
  planning with frugality, 15
menus (casual walkabouts)
  Argentinian-Style Asado, 287–93
  Secretly Thrifty Brazilian-
    Inspired Buffet, 306
menus (holiday)
  Easter Feast, 190
  Fourth of July, 202
  Holiday Baking, 136
  Spangler Family Christmas
    Eve, 162–63
  St. Patrick's Day, 176
  Thanksgiving, 118–19
  Thielen Family Christmas, 148
menus (perennial parties)
  Annual Birthday Blowout for
    My Brother, 268
  Deer Camp Feast, 246–47
  Family Brunch Around the Fire
    Pit, 236
  An Outdoor Fried Chicken
    Party, 222
menus (Saturday night)
  All-You-Can-Eat Fish Fry, 82
  A Creative More-Time-Than-
    Money Sort of Menu, 70
  Homemade Chitarra Pasta
    Work Party, 56
  A Lazy Day's Summer Lunch,
    38
  New York City Chinese Barbe-
    cue at Home, 46
  A Nordic Backcountry Ski
    Supper, 92
  Pent-Up Winter Grilling, 102
  Supper Club Night: Steak and
    Sides, 25
meringue. *See* Pavlova
milk
  Ham Cooked in Milk, Honey,
    and Sage, 193–95, *194*

Milk Corn, 210, *211*
Mincemeat Baklava, *137*,
  140–41
mint
  Boiled Zucchini with Herb Oil,
    31, *32*
  Miso-Mustard Sauce and Aru-
    gula, Smoked Sausages with,
    242, *243*
mixing bowls, 326
mortar and pestle, 327
Mousse, Deer Liver, with Pickled
  Grapes on the Vine, 253–55
mushrooms
  Lardo-Crisped Roasted Turkey
    with Mushroom Gravy, *123*,
    123–25
  Warm Wilted Spinach with
    Caramelized Celery Root and
    Crispy Shiitakes, *97*, 97–98
Muskmelon Caprese, 244, *245*
Mustard-Miso Sauce and Aru-
  gula, Smoked Sausages with,
  242, *243*
Mustard Seeds, Crispy Curried
  Cauliflower with, 173

O

offset spatulas, 325
oils
  Basil Oil, 227
  Chive Oil, 178
  Homemade Chile Oil, 60
  types of, 330
Olive Oil Thumbprints with
  Lemon Curd, *137*, 144–45
olives
  Cast-Iron Garlic Shrimp with
    Chorizo and Green Olives,
    152, *153*
  Steamed Eggplant with Chile
    Oil, Lemon, and 'Nduja, *58*,
    59–60
onions
  Citrusy Braised Red Cabbage,
    170, *171*
  Fun House Baked Potatoes,
    108, 109

Potato Tortilla, 240–41
types of, 333
oranges
    Citrusy Braised Red Cabbage,
        170, *171*
    Orange Julius with Basil, *237*,
        238
    Pavlova with Winter Citrus,
        Good Olive Oil, and Salt,
        90–91
    Sour Orange Cranberry Jelly,
        123, 127
    Sour Orange Platter Salad with
        Parsley and Pistachios, 314,
        315
oregano
    Chimichurri, 296
Oyster Bar, Raw, 270

P

Pancake, Raised Potato and Cab-
    bage, 72–74, *73*
parsley
    Bacon Fat–Roasted Cauliflower
        with Herb Salad, 74
    Chimichurri, 296
    Creamy Zhug, *180*, 181
    Green Salad with Invisible
        Vinaigrette, 187
    Grilled Leek Salad with Hard-
        Boiled Eggs and Smoky
        Anchovy Dressing, 311–13,
        312
    Smoked Prime Rib with Celery-
        Leaf Salsa Verde, 154–55
    Sour Orange Platter Salad with
        Parsley and Pistachios, 314,
        315
    Yuca Fries Persillade, *182*, 183
Pasta, Chitarra, with Roasted
    Cherry Tomatoes, 61–64, *62*
Pastis du Quercy, 75–78, *79*
Pâté Grandmère, 149–51
pâté/terrine mold, 324
Pavlova with Winter Citrus, Good
    Olive Oil, and Salt, 90–91
peanut butter
    Sesame Pralines, *137*, 143

peas
    butter variation made with, 29
    Reformed Dill Dip with Iced
        Garden Vegetables, 204–5
    Stir-Fried Peas and Their
        Greens, 54
    Yellow Split Pea Soup with
        Spareribs, 96
Pecans, Glassy, and Pecorino,
    Baby Greens with, 131–32
peppers. *See also* chiles
    Braised Collards with Smoky
        Tomato, 229–30, *230*
    Creamed Poblano Spinach, 158
    Grilled Pickled Half-Hots, 26,
        33
    Nightshade Confit, 39–41, *40*
    Sweet-and-Sour Marinated
        Peppers with Swiss Chard,
        110, *111*
phyllo dough
    Mincemeat Baklava, *137*,
        140–41
pickles
    Pickled Grapes on the Vine,
        254–55
    Potted Sour Cherries, 249
pies
    Buttercup Bourbon Pie,
        133–34, *135*
    Rhubarb-Raspberry Pie,
        214–15
pink salt, about, 166
pistachios
    Pâté Grandmère, 149–51
    Sour Orange Platter Salad with
        Parsley and Pistachios, 314,
        315
    Tomato-on-Tomato Salad, *212*,
        213
plastic wrap, 326
poppy seeds
    Bitter Lettuces with Warm
        Brown Butter Vinaigrette,
        Fried Shallots, and Duck
        Gizzards Confit, 263–66, *264*
    Bohemian Poppy Seed Coffee
        Cake, *138*, 138–40

Rhubarb-Almond Envelope
    Tart, 199–200, *201*
pork. *See also* bacon; ham; lardo;
    sausages
    Feijoada for a Crowd, *307*,
        309–10
    Mei's Ginger-Glazed Baby
        Back Ribs, 46–48, *47*
    Open-Air Barbecue with Sal-
        muera and Chimichurri, *285*,
        294–97, *295*
    Pâté Grandmère, 149–51
    Pork-Stuffed Barbecued
        Chicken Thighs, 273–75, *274*
    Spiced Meatballs with Cream
        Gravy, 168
    Sylta, 165–66, *167*
    Yellow Split Pea Soup with
        Spareribs, 96
potatoes
    Aligot (Stretchy Mashed Pota-
        toes with Cheese), 156–57,
        157
    buying and storing, 334
    Fun House Baked Potatoes,
        108, 109
    Mascarpone Whipped Potatoes,
        169
    Matafans: Raised Potato and
        Cabbage Pancake, 72–74,
        73
    Potato Tortilla, 240–41
    Salt Potatoes, 30, *33*
    Spiralized Roast Potatoes, *128*,
        129
    Steamed and Glazed White
        Sweet Potatoes, 88
pot holders (aka hot pads), 324
pots and pans
    carbon-steel pans, 323
    cast-iron pans, 322
    stainless steel pots and pans,
        322
    woks, 323
Praline, Smoked Almond, 100
Pralines, Sesame, *137*, 143
prep bowls, 326
Puff Pastry, Quick, 199–200

Q

Quince, Baked Spiced, with Soft Cheese, 164

R

Radicchio and Hazelnuts, Marinated Roasted Beets and Grapes with, 184–86
radishes
 Iceberg Plate Salad with Green Chile Dressing, 86, *87*
 Reformed Dill Dip with Iced Garden Vegetables, 204–5
 Winter White Salad, 64–65
Ramen-Almond Brittle, Bok Choy Salad with, *52*, 53
Raspberry-Rhubarb Pie, 214–15
recipes, make-ahead, 337–40
red currants
 Citrusy Braised Red Cabbage, 170, *171*
 tart variation made with, 174
rhubarb
 Rhubarb-Almond Envelope Tart, 199–200, *201*
 Rhubarb Lemonade, 308–9
 Rhubarb-Raspberry Pie, 214–15
rice
 Garlic and Coconut–Scented Rice, 89
 Jasmine Rice, 50–51
 Sticky Rice, 275–76
 types of, 331
Rolls, Hot Water, 197–99
rubber spatulas, 324

S

sage
 Apple Fritto Misto with Peels, Lemons, and Sage, *68*, 68–69
 Crispy Smashed Chicken Breasts with Gin-and-Sage Jus, 70–72, *71*
 Ham Cooked in Milk, Honey, and Sage, 193–95, *194*
salads
 Baby Greens with Glassy Pecans and Pecorino, 131–32
 Bitter Lettuces with Warm Brown Butter Vinaigrette, Fried Shallots, and Duck Gizzards Confit, 263–66, *264*
 Bok Choy Salad with Ramen-Almond Brittle, *52*, 53
 Creamy Baby Turnip Salad with Dill, 196–97
 Green Salad with Invisible Vinaigrette, 187
 Grilled Leek Salad with Hard-Boiled Eggs and Smoky Anchovy Dressing, 311–13, *312*
 Honeydew and Cucumber Salad with Cilantro-Lime Dressing, 278–79
 Iceberg Plate Salad with Green Chile Dressing, 86, *87*
 Marinated Chickpea Salad with Lemon and Swiss Chard, 298–300, *299*
 Marinated Roasted Beets and Grapes with Radicchio and Hazelnuts, 184–86
 Muskmelon Caprese, 244, *245*
 Smashed Garlic Cucumbers, 49
 Smoky Tomato Terrine, 34–36, *35*
 Sour Orange Cranberry Jelly, *123*, 127
 Sour Orange Platter Salad with Parsley and Pistachios, 314, *315*
 Three-Bean Salad with Salumi, Celery Hearts, and Smoked Provolone, 208–10
 Tomato-on-Tomato Salad, *212*, 213
 Watercress and Bibb with Smoky Blue Cheese Dressing, 161
 Winter White Salad, 64–65
 Zucchini Carpaccio, 300–301
salsa
 Chipotle-Cashew Salsa with Bacon Fat, 250
 Smoked Prime Rib with Celery-Leaf Salsa Verde, 154–55
salt, pink, 166
salt, seasoning with, 16–17
Salumi, Celery Hearts, and Smoked Provolone, Three-Bean Salad with, 208–10
Sardines with Lardo and Parmesan on Bran Crispbread, *93*, 93–95
sauces
 Chimichurri, 296
 Creamy Zhug, *180*, 181
sausages
 Cast-Iron Garlic Shrimp with Chorizo and Green Olives, 152, *153*
 Classic Buttery Dressing, *123*, 126
 Feijoada for a Crowd, *307*, 309–10
 Open-Air Barbecue with Salmuera and Chimichurri, *285*, 294–97, *295*
 Smoked Sausages with Mustard-Miso Sauce and Arugula, 242, *243*
 Steamed Eggplant with Chile Oil, Lemon, and 'Nduja, *58*, 59–60
scales, 325
Sesame Pralines, *137*, 143
shallots
 Bitter Lettuces with Warm Brown Butter Vinaigrette, Fried Shallots, and Duck Gizzards Confit, 263–66, *264*
 buying, 333
shellfish
 buying and thawing shrimp, 151
 Cast-Iron Garlic Shrimp with Chorizo and Green Olives, 152, *153*
 Corn Soup with Coconut and Littleneck Clams, *271*, 271–72

Crab Legs with Spicy Black
Vinegar Dipping Sauce,
119–20, *120*
Raw Oyster Bar, 270
shrimp
buying and thawing, 151
Cast-Iron Garlic Shrimp with
Chorizo and Green Olives,
152, *153*
sieves, 324
Simple Syrup, 204
Snickerdoodles, Apricot, *251*,
251–52
sodium nitrite, 151, 166
soups
Corn Soup with Coconut
and Littleneck Clams, *271*,
271–72
Green Cabbage Sipping Soup,
177–78, *178*
Yellow Split Pea Soup with
Spareribs, 96
sour cream
Creamy Baby Turnip Salad
with Dill, 196–97
Creamy Zhug, *180*, 181
Deep-Fried Sour Cream Walleye, *83*, 83–85
Reformed Dill Dip with Iced
Garden Vegetables, 204–5
Sour Cream Whip, 189
soy sauce, 332
spider, 327
spinach
Creamed Poblano Spinach,
158
Warm Wilted Spinach with
Caramelized Celery Root
and Crispy Shiitakes, *97*,
97–98
Split Pea, Yellow, Soup with
Spareribs, 96
squash
Boiled Zucchini with Herb Oil,
31, *32*
Buttercup Bourbon Pie,
133–34, *135*
Nightshade Confit, 39–41, *40*

Squash Bake with Goat Cheese
Custard, 262–63
Zucchini Carpaccio,
300–301
stainless steel pots and pans, 322
Sticky Date Olive Oil Cake,
188–89, *189*
stocks
Chicken Stock, 259
Turkey Stock, 259
stovetop heat diffuser, 326
Sweet Potatoes, White, Steamed
and Glazed, 88
Swiss chard
Marinated Chickpea Salad with
Lemon and Swiss Chard,
298–300, *299*
Stir-Fried Greens and Leeks,
276–78
Sweet-and-Sour Marinated
Peppers with Swiss Chard,
110, *111*
Sylta, 165–66, *167*
syrups
Chocolate Syrup, 99
Simple Syrup, 204

T

tahini
Sesame Pralines, *137*, 143
tamari, 332
tarts
Cranberry Cookie Tart, 174,
175
Rhubarb-Almond Envelope
Tart, 199–200, *201*
terrine mold, 324
terrines
Smoky Tomato Terrine, 34–36,
35
Sylta, 165–66, *167*
toban djan (doubanjiang)
about, 331–32
Mei's Ginger-Glazed Baby
Back Ribs, 46–48, *47*
tomatoes
Braised Collards with Smoky
Tomato, 229–30, *230*

Chipotle-Cashew Salsa with
Bacon Fat, 250
Chitarra Pasta with Roasted
Cherry Tomatoes, 61–64,
62
Grilled Garlic Bread with
Bacon Fat and Smeared
Tomato, 239
Muskmelon Caprese, 244,
245
Nightshade Confit, 39–41, *40*
Reformed Dill Dip with Iced
Garden Vegetables, 204–5
Smoky Tomato Terrine, 34–36,
35
tools and equipment, 321–27
Tortilla, Potato, 240–41
turkey
fresh, buying, 122
frozen, buying, 122
Lardo-Crisped Roasted Turkey
with Mushroom Gravy, *123*,
123–25
serving sizes and yields, 122
thawed, buying, 122
thawing, 122
timeline, 121
Turkey Stock, 259
turnips
Creamy Baby Turnip Salad
with Dill, 196–97
Reformed Dill Dip with Iced
Garden Vegetables, 204–5
Turnip-Date Gratin, 130–31
Winter White Salad, 64–65

V

vanilla, 331
vegetables. *See also specific vegetables*
Reformed Dill Dip with Iced
Garden Vegetables, 204–5
venison
Backstrap (Venison Loin)
Bordelaise, *256*, 256–58
sourcing, 258
wet-aging, 258
vinegar, types of, 331

W

Walleye, Deep-Fried Sour
Cream, *83*, 83–85
walnuts
Lacquered Walnuts, *137*,
145–46
Mincemeat Baklava, *137*,
140–41
Sopped Greens with Butter-
Roasted Walnuts, 43
Watercress and Bibb with
Smoky Blue Cheese Dress-
ing, 161

whipped cream
Sour Cream Whip, 189
Whipped Cream, 281
whiskey
Single-Origin Chocolate Cake,
279–80
Whiskey-Sour Gelatin Shots
with Potted Sour Cherries,
247, 248–49
whisks, 324
wine, affordable, 17–18
woks, 323
wooden spoons, 324

Y

Yellow Split Pea Soup with
Spareribs, 96
Yuca Fries Persillade, *182*, 183

Z

Zhug, Creamy, *180*, 181
zucchini
Boiled Zucchini with Herb Oil,
31, *32*
Nightshade Confit, 39–41, *40*
Zucchini Carpaccio,
300–301